The Moral Stake in Education

Contested Premises and Practices

Joan F. Goodman
Professor of Education
University of Pennsylvania

Howard Lesnick
Jefferson B. Fordham Professor of Law
University of Pennsylvania

For permission to use copyrighted material, grateful acknowledgment is made to the copyright holders on p. 297, which are hereby made part of this copyright page.

Library of Congress Cataloging-in-Publication Data

Goodman, Joan F.
   The moral stake in education : contested premises and practices / by Joan F. Goodman and Howard Lesnick.
      p. cm.
   Includes bibliographical references and index.
   ISBN 1-4392-2878-7
   1. Moral education. I. Lesnick, Howard, 1931– II. Title.
LC268.G59 2000
370.11'4—dc21   00-057527

Booksurge Publishing
Please visit our website at http://www.booksurge.com

ISBN 1-4392-2878-7

2 3 4 5 6 7 8 9 10—03 02 01

*W*e dedicate this book
to the teachers
in our country's
elementary and
secondary schools,
to whom we owe so much
and give so little

Brief Contents

Contents

Foreword

A great deal of attention is now being paid to the moral dimensions of education. Hardly a day goes by without some public pronouncement by policy makers and political figures about "character education." Kevin Ryan, long a champion of character education, refers to this new attention and excitement as the *character education bandwagon.* The problem with any such bandwagon, and there are all too many of them in American education, is that all of the hoopla and excitement tends to obscure the differences among substantive approaches and to confuse substantive programs with the oftentimes slickly promoted products that play off public intuitions and biases about how to educate children.

In this book, Joan F. Goodman and Howard Lesnick provide educators a way through the sticky morass of the "flavor of the month" character education fad to an informed approach to the moral education of children. They illuminate the important sources of controversy about how best to engage in moral education, and do so in a way that takes the classroom teacher seriously as a colleague and fellow scholar. This is an extremely accessible book that connects the real concerns and experiences of teachers with the wealth of scholarship and research that exists on the topic. Goodman and Lesnick provide entry into the debates that roil the field, and give teachers the tools to generate informed classroom practices. This is not a cookbook; there are no recipes between these covers. Instead, this book is better thought of as a road map that the teacher can use to chart a course toward the moral education of students.

At the heart of the controversy is whether moral education should be about inculcating the existing norms of society into children, or enabling students to critically evaluate themselves and society from a moral point of view. Goodman and Lesnick recognize that these are not simply differences in educational theory, but reflect broader philosophical disagreements between liberal and conservative political stands. The authors have a point of view, but their overarching goal is to provide teachers with a way to transcend these differences and bridge the liberal, social-critical/conservative, tradition-supporting divide.

They do so through an ingenious and engaging device reminiscent of the dialogues of Greek philosophers. Instead of Socrates and Meno, the authors employ classroom teachers as characters in an ongoing discussion about how to resolve practical classroom scenarios. One of these teachers, a novice, generally assumes the liberal stance, while another, slightly more experienced colleague and friend generally takes the conservative position. Following each scenario, the authors examine the premises that guide the teachers' responses in a scholarly analysis, which is in turn supported by a segment at the end of each chapter providing relevant excerpts from leading authors, contemporary and classical. The reader is left well informed, and armed to draw his or her own conclusions about best practices.

Through this imaginative and engaging process, the authors convey a number of critical ideas about moral education. For one thing, they successfully demonstrate how inescapable issues of morality are in the everyday lives of classrooms. No teacher reading this book will be able to claim that he or she does not have a role in children's moral education. From the structure of a classroom seating arrangement to the nature of academic assignments and grading practices, the classroom is shown to be rife with moral content and meaning. The authors, however, do not succumb to the temptation to reduce morality to the conventions and norms of classrooms or the society at large. Conventions, such as hand raising, for example, are recognized as an agreed-upon method of signaling when a student wishes to talk, and are differentiated from moral issues of fairness and harm to others. At the same time, the authors guide the reader to struggle with the space between morality and convention, such as when a student's failure to raise his hand before speaking unfairly steps on the ability of other students to speak. Such rather mundane examples allow the authors to enjoin educators to avoid the error of skewing the goals of moral education around the preservation of existing social convention, while also enabling teachers to understand, as Durkheim argued, that the classroom with all of its norms constitutes a moral community analogous to society as a whole.

The authors forthrightly confront the limitations of what they refer to as "laundry lists" of virtues being promulgated by some who have taken front row seats on the new bandwagon. Goodman and Lesnick point out that such lists all too often leech conventions into the realm of morality and skew the educational agenda. Such lists politicize the notion of virtue, and thereby alienate or suppress those teachers, parents, and students whose notions of virtue may differ from the "official" criteria for being a good person. Goodman and Lesnick provide an insightful review of existing commercial character education programs. Their discussion recognizes the problems teachers face in attempting to sort through the glossy and slick products emerging from the new moral and character education industry. Teachers and administrators will find this section of the book to be a valuable asset in their efforts to assess such programs.

In sum, this is a most unusual book that is at once practical and reflective, accessible and scholarly. Educators reading this book will come away with a deeper understanding of the moral stake in education, and with the tools to approach moral education.

REFERENCES

Durkheim, E. (1925/1961). *Moral education*. Glencoe, IL: The Free Press.
Ryan, K. (1996). Character education in the United States: A status report. *Journal for a Just and Caring Education*, 2, 75–84.

Larry Nucci
University of Illinois at Chicago
October, 2000

Acknowledgments

We appreciate the opportunity that many teachers, administrators, and parents in the school systems of Philadelphia and Lower Merion, Pennsylvania, Cherry Hill, New Jersey, and Baltimore, Maryland, gave us to meet with them, observe their school operations, and hear and discuss their ideas and experience.

We benefitted greatly from the conscientious and skillful research assistance of Debby Coppola, Class of 1999 in the Master's Program at the Graduate School of Education, and Elizabeth Carrott and Dorothy Alicia Hickok, Class of 2001 at the Law School, University of Pennsylvania; from the engagement with the manuscript by Education School students in a course on Values and Education; and from the unfailingly expert and responsive assistance of the Law School's reference, information technology, and secretarial staff.

We are grateful to the many members of our families who, over several years, offered us helpful reactions to our drafts and our thoughts on a wide range of matters great and small; and to our Law School colleague Professor Stephen J. Morse for his careful and informed reading.

On behalf of the publisher, we thank the following reviewers for their comments: Dr. Kevin Ryan, Boston University; Natasha Levinson, Kent State University; Dr. Samuel M. Craver, Virginia Commonwealth University; Dr. David Strom, San Diego State University; Michael K. Altekruse, University of North Texas; and Walter Feinberg, New University of Illinois.

Finally, we thank one another for a remarkable collaboration. In the process of planning and writing together—and each of us is quite literally responsible for every word in this book—we came to take to heart the message we preach: Not only can one *talk* and *work* effectively across differing world-views, anchored in two long-lived lives, but one can also surmount the limitations of very different professional and academic disciplines, and be better off for having done so.

Joan F. Goodman
Howard Lesnick

xiii

Meno: Can you tell me, Socrates: Is virtue something that can be taught? Or does it come by practice? Or is it neither teaching nor practice that gives it to a man but natural aptitude or something else?

Socrates: You must think I am singularly fortunate, to know whether virtue can be taught or how it is acquired. The fact is that far from knowing whether it can be taught, I have no idea what virtue itself is. . . .

Meno: . . . is this true about yourself, Socrates, that you don't even know what virtue is? Is this the report that we are to take home about you?

Socrates: Not only that, you may say also that, to the best of my belief, I have never yet met anyone who did know. . . . What do you yourself say virtue is? I do ask you in all earnestness not to refuse me, but to speak out. . . .

Meno: But there is no difficulty about it. First of all, if it is manly virtue you are after, it is easy to see that virtue of a man consists in managing the city's affairs capably, and so that he will help his friends and injure his foes while taking care to come to no harm himself. Or if you want a woman's virtue, that is easily described. She must be a good housewife, careful with her stores and obedient to her husband. Then there is another virtue for a child, male or female, and another for an old man, free or slave as you like, and a great many more kinds of virtue, so that no one need be at a loss to say what it is. . . .

Socrates: I seem to be in luck. I wanted one virtue and I find that you have a whole swarm of virtues to offer. . . . Even if they are many and various, yet at least they all have some common character which makes them virtues. That is what ought to be kept in view by anyone who answers the question, What is virtue? Do you follow me?

Plato, *Meno*

Part 1

Introduction

Chapter 1

Overview of the Book

Our questions are Socrates' and Meno's—What is virtue? How can it be taught?—and our book a broad inquiry into them. Like Socrates, we think it essential to begin by asking what virtue is. Unlike him, however, we do not think that consideration of the second question must await an answer to the first. Indeed, it cannot. As we will suggest, moral education takes place, willed or not, planned or not.

Yet how does one plan the means in the absence of knowing fully the ends? This dilemma is at the core of our book and a genesis of it. For although we see schools as "moral thickets," inevitably addressing moral issues, yet we see the educational solutions as complex, elusive, and inherently contestable. There is today a widely perceived sense of moral crisis, which has aroused a "hue and cry" for moral education, as well as an undercurrent of deep skepticism. The natural tendency in these circumstances is to move immediately to answers, and to focus on techniques. Appreciating both the urgency and the skepticism, our consideration of answers and techniques follows a sustained exploration of the sources of the controversies that beset the field.

We believe it critical to proceed in this way, for if the existence of important and legitimate differences are not acknowledged and taken seriously, positions on moral education degenerate into posturing, and the possibilities for rational accommodation are lessened. In our view, the field is excessively characterized by highly polarized thinking, caricaturing, even demonizing, the "other side." We have taken as our task the effort to recognize, to understand sympathetically, and (to the extent possible) to transcend the battle lines.

We question two differing sets of beliefs, each widely held: One is that education at school is solely a matter of academic knowledge and pedagogic techniques, while moral education is the responsibility of children's families

3

or faith communities. The second is that, although moral education belongs in school, and is much needed, it is a simple, relatively uncontroversial matter of telling students what is right and wrong and maintaining incentives for right conduct. While we agree that teaching is saturated with moral questions, we believe that complexity and controversy are inherent in moral education, embedded as it is in disagreements on the nature of morality, the processes of moral development in children, and larger issues of justice and morality in social life. It is only by respecting, articulating, and engaging with these differences that we can hope to get beyond talking past or against one another.

Far from being a product of recent changes in American society, these differences have long been with us. We are gravely concerned by the moral anesthesia that besets contemporary culture. All too often, the choice between doing what is right but costly and what is advantageous but morally flawed is viewed as just that, a choice, with the moral option accorded no obligatory weight. Yet the task of moral education calls for more by way of response than moral outrage and a passionate call for a return to the "eternal verities" or an (imagined) idyllic past; more also than desperately trying to keep the peace by splitting (or ignoring) the differences, or despairingly wringing one's hands in futility.

We think it important to acknowledge at the outset that the words we use carry a lot of baggage. To many, the terms "virtue" and "morality" have connotations that at best are out-of-date—typically focused narrowly on sex—and too often conjure up a smug piety. In the education world, the term "character education" has come into wide use as a way of avoiding this baggage; yet, it has become associated with a particular approach to moral education, which many challenge as excessively narrow and simplistic. The term "values education" is perhaps no better: To some it seems to assume implicitly that "we" share the same values; to others it is too broad a concept, ranging beyond matters with moral valence to include anything (such as exercise) thought worthwhile. In retaining the traditional words, we ask the reader to bear in mind that we mean them simply as pointing to that which is good, without begging the question of their meaning.

The book is intended to assist those concerned with the relation between education and moral action in understanding and appreciating the many dimensions of the moral issues confronted by teachers, students, parents, administrators, and the wider community. We address three groups of potential readers: students in university-level courses, such as applied ethics, education and values, and educational methods, foundations, or theory; teachers and educational administrators seeking guidance in thinking through an emergent and controversial field and coming to grips, perhaps through inservice work, with pressing everyday problems; and citizens concerned about the health of our educational system, especially in public schools.

The structure of the book is designed to raise and grapple with the intricacies of the field in a style that is accessible yet intellectually honest and rigorous. Each chapter uses a three-part structure: It begins with a set of incidents in the classroom, entitled "At School," that portray scenes involving teachers and students, administrators and parents, dealing with, disagreeing over, and thinking critically about true-to-life moral scenarios. The next section, "At the University," moves from—underneath, we might say—the participants' responses to the incidents to unpack the underlying assumptions, perceptions, and priorities that prompt them. A final section, "At the Library," presents a relatively brief, focused sampling of classical and contemporary writing on the subject of the chapter.

This tripartite scheme is designed to bring the reader immediately into provocative and realistic situations that call out for a reaction, but then to go beyond them. The progression from concrete classroom incidents, to analysis, to readings enables the reader to appreciate the relevance of philosophical, political, educational, and psychological theory to a teacher's ordinary classroom practices. The use of dialogue and narrative preceding reflections and writings is intended to serve as a stimulating trigger for class discussions. In our own teaching, we have found that moral education is inevitably exciting when it starts with daily practice, turgid and dull when it starts with theory. If the latter is to be of interest, the link to practice must be manifest.

The dialogue format of the initial sections of each chapter allows us to capture the splits of opinion fairly and clearly, and encourages the reader to take a nonpolarized approach to controversial questions. Our hope is that the scenarios, discussion, and readings will nudge individuals to look around the bend of their personal worldviews.

The book, while ambitious in its breadth, is not all-encompassing. The reader should bear the particularity of our subject and method in mind. Our major effort is to discern and give voice to underlying, usually implicit, premises—about morality, about education, about the world—that influence one's views concerning moral education, then to suggest how moral education programs tend to be shaped in response to those premises. Although we recognize the strength of the view that moral education cannot realistically be segmented off as a separate "subject," we have not undertaken to write comprehensively about morality and the curriculum. We do not present an analysis of the many critiques of education in the literature (and the lay press), nor an empirical evaluation of outcomes associated with differing approaches. In our treatment of competing approaches, we have tried to avoid labeling them (as traditionalist, critical, feminist, etc.), conscious of the way in which labels tend to energize people to line up, prematurely and combatively, on one side or the other according to their response to the label. We share the "growing dislike" to which John Stuart Mill referred, for "anything resembling a badge or watchword of sectarian distinction" (Mill 1861/1979, 7, n.1).

In addition, we have not attempted to represent the various stakeholders within our culture. Recognizing the impossibility of capturing the diversity of economic, racial, ethnic, or religious settings in which schooling is carried on, we have resisted the temptation to place each scenario in a recognizably different school setting. Such a technique not only claims a deceptively oversimplified representativeness; it leads too easily to thinking that a person's demographic characteristics provide most of what one needs to learn to understand his or her worldview. We have instead used a single cast of characters, whose identities are minimally displayed, but whose interactions over the course of a single year address fundamental questions about the nature of morality and moral development.

We recognize that some aspects of our approach do not take account of a more radical critique of education, including moral education. The premises of such a critique are that: (1) serious structural inequalities of race, gender, and class pervasively affect our response to questions of moral education; and (2) unless one engages at the outset with the role of such inequalities, the attempt to describe and evaluate differing perspectives must simply replicate them. Even if we fully shared that view, which we do not, we could adopt it as a point of departure only at the cost of our attempt to integrate differing, even warring, ways of looking at the world.

We have also avoided the sort of hot-button issues—sex, drugs, religion, censorship—that dominate newspaper accounts of the moral climate of schools. The problems confronted in the scenarios, while simple and even prosaic, were chosen for their capacity to trigger complex questions, without prompting a fully mobilized "preset" body of responses. We have located the scenarios in an elementary school, where we can focus on the fundamentals of moral education—basic premises of moral and pedagogic theory—without the hot-button issues so fully claiming foreground attention.

Finally, this is not a how-to-do-it book, to be consulted hurriedly as a classroom threatens to descend into (momentary) chaos. We believe that the book gives practical assistance to teachers in dealing with the actual problems (and opportunities) they face, but it seeks to do that by enhancing their awareness of the complex embeddedness of those problems in the theoretical issues we address. We believe that greater understanding will tend to bring about wiser interventions. Rather than offering a catalogue of sage advice, however, we suggest parameters for a moral education program, parameters that remain ever alive to, and often inclusive of, divided opinions.

Following two introductory chapters, Part Two (Chapters 3 and 4) examines "the moral" as a concept. Chapter Three asks: With what is morality concerned, and how do moral values differ from other values? What follows from classifying a value as moral? Is morality a matter of conduct, motivation, or character, or is it concerned rather with the decision-making process that precedes an act? What is the place of consequences in judging an act?

Chapter 4 engages the question of ethical relativism, the claim that moral standards are necessarily conventions of culture, lacking inherent validity, and clarifies the distinction between relativism and pluralism, examining the case for (and the limits of) a pluralist response to moral diversity. It asks, how do we know what is right? Where do moral judgments come from? What gives them normative justification? It considers society, tradition, authority, reason, emotions, and religion as sources of legitimacy.

Part Three (Chapters 5, 6, and 7) begins by engaging Socrates' question: Is there such a quality as "virtue" (that which is good), or is there only an aggregation, a "swarm" or "bag," of many virtues? Chapter 5 recounts the ways in which American attitudes toward moral education have changed since the rise of the "common school" in the nineteenth century, and examines the current revival of the concept of virtue ethics and the hazards and potential of attempts to generate a catalogue of virtues. Chapters 6 and 7 grapple with the moral environment of the school, school system, and community, considering how the values of integrity, accountability, and professionalism play out in contexts where teachers, administrators, and parents confront value conflicts.

Part Four (Chapters 8 and 9) moves to Meno's question, what we term the pedagogy of moral education. In Chapter 8, we examine differing premises about fundamental psychological and philosophical positions—the processes of child development, the roles of cognition and emotion, theories of teaching and learning, the setting of moral priorities—and how these premises cause educators to lean pedagogically in one direction or another. We make a case for the primacy of moral identity as the overarching goal of moral education and a major determinant in the construction and application of a pedagogy. Against this framework, we consider the appropriateness and efficacy of various teaching methods designed to develop good moral character: discipline and compassion, precept and example, democratic self-governance, pro-social action projects, and sustained and honest reflective engagement with moral questions. We further emphasize the critical importance to a moral education program (as to an academic program) of a developmentally staged approach. Finally, we stress the centrality of the individual classroom teacher in shaping and implementing any program, and the need for a school system to facilitate teachers' motivation and capacity to play that role.

Chapter 9 gets down (as much as it usefully can) to brass tacks, presenting an actual moral education program developed by the protagonists of the scenarios. The program offers benchmarks rather than details, attempting to avoid both excessive abstractness and excessive specificity. It seeks to find common ground within, while allowing sufficient scope for, significant disagreements. It emphasizes—along with the critical role of teachers in planning and executing moral education, and the need to stage the effort—the necessary commitment of the school and broader community, the articulation of core values to be protected, and the joint responsibilities of students and teachers.

The foregoing paragraphs have expressed some of our own assumptions: the complexity and controversy inherent in moral education; the critical need to articulate and understand underlying premises, rather than immediately begin debating specific proposals; the importance of developing an integrative, nonpolarized approach. A few additional ingredients of our point of view bear acknowledgment here: First is the importance of learning to listen across differences, not as a matter of giving in to demands for "equal time" but because our differing views are typically honest responses to problems that we all should recognize call for amelioration. If we think that a proposed response is wrong-headed, it is a serious error to think that the problem will disappear by "trashing" the response. The problem in all likelihood is a real one, and persists.

Second, as we develop fully in Part Four, there has been an excessive focus on figuring out the proper content of moral codes, whether of character or behavior. Concluding that the need is rather to emphasize ways to foster the development of moral identity, we advocate the creation and mainte-nance of schools and classrooms that are what we term "open moral commu-nities." Process is here both a means and an end.

Finally, our work is frankly aspirational. We believe it essential not to sur-render so fully to the call to be "practical" that we embrace simplistic or overly modest "solutions" that have the very *impracticality* of being unable to make any real difference. Thinking seriously about morality, about what it means to be human, about what kind of life one wants to lead, is more practi-cal than might first appear; it is inspiring and motivational, engaging the will to do better in ways that can make a difference. We see this book as a study in possibilities.

Chapter 2

School
A Moral Thicket

✳ At School

It's Friday before Labor Day. Maria Laszlo, her lesson plans for the initial days created, reviewed, and revised, had been at school most of the week preparing her fourth-grade classroom for next Tuesday, her first day as a fully credentialed teacher. Busy arranging books on the shelves and creating attractive and useful material for the walls, she had, at least temporarily, lost the sense of dread and agitation, her steady companions during the summer months. Yet she could not throw off an acute uncertainty about herself: Will the children like her? Will they be turned on to learning, have ideas they want to pursue, move beyond the prescribed skill-based instruction? Will she be able to mold them into a cooperative, mutually supportive group of friends and learners?

As Maria unpacked the last box, out spilled a book she borrowed from one of her education professors—was it only last spring? She thought appreciatively of the encouragement Professor Bonham gave during those trying student teaching days. Warmed by the recollection, and in need of a little up-to-date reassurance, she decided to return the book in person.

When Maria arrived at Jan Bonham's office, the door was open as usual, but the desk and chairs were strewn with books and papers. Maria, realizing that a substantial writing project was in process, resolved to drop the book off and leave quickly, but Bonham, welcoming this surprise visit, interrupted her thoughts: "So, if it isn't Maria Laszlo! I'm so glad to see you. How are you? I hear you landed a great job. What have you got there?"

Maria, buoyed by the effusive welcome, relaxed. "Dr. Bonham, I want to return your copy of Lickona.[1] It was a good summer read, but I don't think I'll have much use for it on this job."

---

[1] Thomas Lickona, *Educating for Character: How Our Schools Can Teach Respect and Responsibility* (NY: Bantam Books, 1991).

"But Maria," her teacher remonstrated, "It's just now, as you get started with a new group, that the book will be most helpful."

Maria knew that her former teacher enjoyed a good argument, and had no difficulty disagreeing. "Dr. Bonham, I understand you are into this moral stuff, I've even heard you are writing a book on moral education but, no offense, while it should be useful for one of those 'foundation' courses education students have to take, I don't see how it helps day-to-day in my classroom."

"I guess I'd better find out what you mean," Jan responded. "I'd hate to write a book of such trivial utility."

"Well," Maria continued, "it's not that I don't believe children should learn right and wrong; obviously they should. My own parents, very religious people, pushed moral lessons all the time. But that just isn't my job as a teacher."

"What *is* your job, Maria?" Jan Bonham asked.

"My job is to teach academics, especially reading and math. That's what the principal wants, that's what the parents want, that's what the kids expect, and that's what I've been trained to do. I know way back schools thought moral education should happen in the classroom; maybe it was that way when you went to school. But that's not how it was when I went to school and, with all we've got to do nowadays, it's not a burden I want to add on. Morality is one topic we must leave for the home, or the church."

Jan let pass Maria's evident bracketing her in antiquity with Abe Lincoln and the McGuffey readers. "And how will you teach the children their reading and math, Maria? What will you do when one child shouts out an arithmetic answer, while a quieter kid has shyly begun to raise her hand?—or when another pupil never volunteers? What will you do when one child copies the answers on a quiz from the back of the book? Even the books you choose and your reasons for the choice will have moral significance."

"Professor," Maria persisted, "I know you see these as grave matters. Perhaps they are. But the way I look at it, I'm going to use books I think are exciting and absorbing to children. I'm going to have a few classroom rules, the same ones that everyone else has. I'm going to be kind and caring towards the children, provide a good model, and expect them, with occasional reminders from me, to be kind to one another. I don't need moral philosophers for that."

"Perhaps not," Jan replied. "In any case, Maria, even if you cause me to consign my book ideas to a shredder, I nonetheless have great confidence that you are going to be a much beloved, effective teacher. Be sure to keep in touch. I want to know how it goes during your first months of teaching."

Two weeks later Maria called Jan, and asked if she could come by her office. They met the next day. Maria's face had that same look of earnest concern, but Jan readily observed that her usual high spirits seemed dampened.

"Hi, Maria, it's good to see you again so soon, but you look troubled. Something wrong?"

"Yes. Lots of things are wrong, everything is wrong. I'm turning into one of those 'don't-smile-until-Christmas' monsters. I'm yelling at the kids. I'm totally confused about how to handle them. I can't figure out why they aren't responding. All my planning was useless. Do you know that, from the photos in the folders that the school gave us, I had memorized the name of each child before school started? On the first day I greeted them at the door by name. I was so proud, but they couldn't have cared less. Many kids didn't even look me in the face, never mind shake my hand or talk to me."

"OK, Maria," Jan Bonham responded. "Remember, the faculty here always warns new teachers that the start of school is likely to be tough. It is often so even for experienced teachers. Now why don't you tell me just what's happened."

Maria allowed herself a sigh, then began. "My fantasies died that first Tuesday as the kids walked through the door. The ones who had been together last year separated themselves into a few small, *noisy* groups. They didn't even acknowledge the newcomers in the class. When I asked the class to sit down so we could get started, a bunch of them immediately complained about the chair arrangements—three children around each small table. Four girls insisted they could not be separated. I suggested (on that first day I was still suggesting) that they accept this arrangement until we had an opportunity to discuss the matter as a group. Well, that was mistake number two. Wait? Not these kids. They wanted to discuss it right then. So I backed down and started a class meeting on the spot. (In our Methods class, you told us that a class meeting is a good way to resolve problems.) I presented my views to the children: Today they should take any available seat; in a few days we'd organize work groups that would change from time to time, and we'd plan future seating around the work groups. 'No, no, no,' the four insisted. They'd have none of it. Last year they were allowed to sit together, and they wanted the same treatment this year. Forget all the other stuff—what was fair to the class as a whole, getting to know the new children, thinking about who was being hurt by being left out."

"How did you handle all of that?" Dr. Bonham asked.

"Next day, you better believe it was assigned seats for everyone! The kids grumbled and grumbled. I was stern and unyielding. But it didn't accomplish much. Now everyone reluctantly sits where he or she is assigned; however, they make constant eye contact, mouth words, whisper, and sometimes just plain talk. At first it was just the 'gang of four,' but after a few days other kids, especially the ones who had been together last year, began picking it up too. So, defying everything I believe, I've started a disciplinary system: One point each time they stare, whisper, or talk to each other out of turn. Five points and they miss recess. Ten points, they go to the principal. Would you believe that's already happened. I've already sent a child to the principal! Now, even when they're quiet, I feel their resentment. So much for my wanting to be liked!

"If it were just the seating arrangements and my yelling at the children I wouldn't be in such a dismal mood. At least when assigning seats and insisting on quiet so as to conduct a lesson, I had a sense of my own righteousness. But I've got another problem that has cost me even that.

"It has to do with this kid, Tony. He and his family, though middle class, dress and behave unconventionally—the kids say 'weird.' They live in an old house on a big lot near the edge of town, raise a lot of their own food, and don't use a car at all. He always wears a cap, and when I asked an older teacher if that was against school rules she said, 'Sure. We don't allow that sort of thing in the classroom.' Also Tony comes to school with his clothes showing signs of having just come from work in the family's vegetable garden, mud on his shoes and streaks of I'm not sure what across his shirt and pants, and sometimes on his face. The other kids tease him. They complain that he 'stinks.' He doesn't really, though. I think he changes his clothes as often as anyone, but he does look more like a farmer than a suburban student. The others don't want him in their games."

"What did you do?" Jan Bonham inquired.

"I thought of calling his parents, but his last year's teacher told me not to do it. 'They'll just defend him,' she said. 'They don't believe the school has any business telling them how their kid should dress and act.' I've gently invited Tony at least to wash his face and take off his hat, but it was useless. He spends a lot of his day alone reading books; incidentally, he's very bright. Sometimes he wants to join the others on the playground, but when they reject him he doesn't act as if he's bothered much. He's your classic loner, maybe by nature, maybe because of his parents. Who knows?"

Maria drew a breath, got up from her chair, and crossed the room. She went on: "So what do I do about Tony, Dr. Bonham? Is it our business whether he wears a hat or not? I know it goes against school policy, although I don't know whether there is any formal 'rule,' but anyway, does such a policy or rule make sense? I don't question that enforcing rules is part of my job, but I confess to some trouble doing it unless the rule makes sense to me, and I'm not sure this one does."

"Maria," Dr. Bonham interjected, "are you asking whether you should think a student wrong to violate a school rule, such as one against wearing hats in class, unless you believe that the rule is a good one?"

"Well, sort of; at least, it's a question," Maria answered. "In general, I've got no problem with this rule. But if a child wore a hat for religious reasons, we'd feel we had to let that pass, wouldn't we? And suppose Tony were African American? We read a lot in our classes about how symbolic actions like keeping a hat on might be a cultural thing, and refusing to take it off might be what the authors called a 'counter-hegemonic' act, expressing opposition to assimilation."

"Is Tony black?" Jan Bonham asked. "I know several African-American teachers who are quite firmly *against* the kind of response you are talking about . . . "

Maria interrupted, "Yes, I know, and anyway, Tony is white. But is his resistance to me any less an aspect of his identity—just as entitled to be respected by a school—as it would be if triggered by his being part of a group? And what about Tony and his clothes not being tip-top clean? As long as he is disease-free (the nurse checked him along with all the others when school began, and she told me he is fine), who gets hurt but himself? Can we even say that he's hurting himself? Einstein had pretty wild hair; I bet no one bothered him about it, at least outside of school. Don't Tony's parents have a point? I guess they're indifferent to the fact that his appearance keeps other kids away from him. Should I care? Or is the problem that the other children are being intolerant and unfriendly toward him? Should I be after *them*? Tony persists in doing things that annoy his classmates. His habits aren't really any of their business, but is it right for me to expect much tolerance and sympathy from nine-year-olds, who are at an age where they are intensely focused on friendships, 'best friends,' and all that?

"I know I'm reeling off questions, but while I'm at it, I have some more. I guess I'm also stuck on the matter of the children's seating. How much decision-making authority should they have, how much should I preserve? How flexible should I be, and how do I decide that? Once a decision is made, either by me or by the class, and some balk, what should be the consequences and who determines them? Is it asking too much to expect nine-year-olds to accept my authority without a protest, to be sensitive to the feelings of others, to show kindness towards new or 'weird' children?

"I went to talk to my friend, Hardie, about these doubts of mine—you remember Hardie Knox, don't you, from your Foundations class a few years ago? He's teaching too now—and he kind of lit into me for being so 'wimpy.' That's how he put it. 'Your job is to teach more than math and language arts,' he claimed. 'It's to make them decent human beings. And that means first and foremost that they have to learn to do what they're told by the teacher, and not pick an argument over every little thing. What difference does it make *why* you want them to take off their caps, sit in groups of three instead of four, or dress the way everyone else does? The point is, once you tell them what you want, you have to stand behind it. Otherwise, you're teaching them that they can whine or cajole their way out of anything that their little minds tell them is not fun or fair. That's a prescription for turning them into willful, self-indulgent brats, first little brats and then grown-up brats.'

"I didn't appreciate Hardie's tough talk, and I accused him—a bit too strongly, I admit—of wanting to turn out a bunch of mindless automatons. 'I'm not saying,' he responded, 'that no crazy idea of a teacher can ever be questioned by a kid, but what you are asking of the class is perfectly usual and reasonable. If children—and, remember, you are dealing with fourth-graders; they're not yet budding philosophers—if children get their way over something like not wanting to take off their cap, how are they going to learn to deny themselves things that really matter to them later on, like getting an "A" by cribbing a friend's paper even though they didn't do any work, or cutting school when a "real important" ball game is coming up?'

"Well, Dr. Bonham," Maria continued, "you may recall that Hardie sounds off a little more assertively than one might want, but maybe he does have a point. Am I just 'giving in?' Am I doing them harm by listening to their complaints, by taking their concerns seriously? Of course kids need the structure and boundaries—two important words in this business, right?—they get from learning to respect authority. But they also need the chance for choices, don't they? From choice comes responsible decision making. We give even two-year-olds opportunities for choice."

Dr. Bonham put down her coffee mug. "Maria," she began, "You're into a pack of problems that are or should be critical concerns of teachers, and of folks like me, who try to teach people to be teachers. First, there's no denying that you're confronting some real tough, real important, but also real ordinary questions. These problems, and the broader issues from which they surface, are the problems and issues every teacher in every school has always confronted, though I suspect challenges are greater now than in prior decades as we increasingly question and discard traditional practices. Second, the domain of morality and moral education, which as I remember you told me a few weeks ago you didn't need to think about, includes everything you bring up. What you are questioning involves the obligations of children to one another; the obligations of children to conform to group mores versus their right to depart at times from those mores; the role of a teacher in 'socializing' children despite resistance from families; the warrant of teachers for determining and enforcing consequences; and the choice of appropriate ways of doing that—moral questions all.

"Third, Maria, I cannot (nor can anyone else) provide you with fully satisfying answers to these problems. They do not have the clarity of arithmetic questions; they are decisions about the sort of human community we care to establish given our educational responsibilities, the kinds of students we have (their families, their histories, their development), our personal morality, and our own limits. What we can do, and all we can do, together is craft ways of thinking about these problems by a close examination of your struggles: What behaviors do you care about and why? How much control should you exercise over children, and in what areas? What are your—yes—*moral* objectives for children? How do you determine them? How do you prioritize them? What happens when objectives conflict? How do you encourage children to reach the objectives you've set? Again, how do you make choices among alternatives?"

Jan Bonham stops, noticing Maria's frown at her use of the word "moral." She decides to confront her resistance directly. "Maria, you, and many others, resist the language of morality, yet you converse comfortably about classroom management techniques and classroom rules. I ask you, what are these techniques and rules if not inducements for children to accept your notions of good behavior? When you set up codes of conduct for the class, expectations for their behavior towards you and each other, aren't you establishing standards of right and wrong?

"I don't mean to suggest that everything you ask of a child is a matter of morality. What I am saying, Maria, is that teaching is saturated with morality. You are a moral instructor, like it or not. And whether your friend Hardie is right or wrong about what he said so firmly to you, the things he was saying are answers to moral questions. Since you can't avoid your moral role, can I persuade you to give it some careful consideration?"

Maria listened attentively. Although still skeptical and uncomfortable with the image of herself as moral educator—she did not sign on to becoming a pastor—the incidents were sufficiently troubling and confusing that she could not refuse Jan Bonham's request. "OK, Dr. Bonham, what do you think I should have done?"

"Maria, asking questions and carefully considering options are the best ways to make wise choices. You didn't sit in my course for a semester and come away thinking I would tell you what you should have done, even if I could. I know you want a quick fix—we'd all like that. But don't minimize the benefit of careful probing. Since the days of ancient Athens the discomfort of probing has paid off handsomely, in more considered, wiser, more self-assured—in short, more professional—choices.

"We need to work together to identify and address some basic questions, and see where that points us. I'll need your help and you'll need mine. I have the advantage of being detached from the hurly-burly of a roomful of kids, not to mention colleagues, supervisors, and parents, throwing problems and conflicting solutions at you. I've also been able to read widely and mull over what a lot of folks over the years have said about the issues. You have what I don't, the experience of a classroom of fourth-graders. You can share with me the real problems that arise daily, the lessons learned from students' responses to your initiatives, and the guidance provided by discussions with your colleagues.

"As I said to you before, there is no teacher on earth who has not faced your problems—perhaps we can think of them as opportunities—in one form or another. You are unusual only in the sensitivity and care you bring to them. I will try to use your quandaries as the really good examples they are, to tell you a little about this book on moral education that a colleague and I are writing."

❖❖ At the University

We believe strongly that the kinds of problems that Maria Laszlo raised deserve the most careful attention, from teachers (including prospective teachers and teachers of teachers) and educational professionals to be sure, but also from parents, school board members, and concerned citizens. Our aim in this book is to give all of those groups some of what they need in order to come to grips with such problems in an informed and constructive way.

The sophistication of educators in dealing with the challenge of teaching academic subjects is not matched by a parallel depth in addressing the question of moral education. This is so in part because, like Maria, many educators reject moral language as impositional, and so dismiss the need for teachers to become more sophisticated in moral decision making. Others, while not dismissive of moral language, make light of the dilemmas. To them, moral questions have obvious answers, and excessive scrutiny and reflection only immobilize instructional efforts. These folks believe teachers should learn the "how to" of moral instruction but not get bogged down in analysis; contemplation, they contend, is best left to philosophers.

We disagree with both of these positions. We see classroom rules as grounded in moral questions, however much they may be treated as merely technical (as by the term "classroom management"). Educators Theodore and Nancy Sizer have put the point well:

> Morality is embedded in all formal education. The experience of schooling changes all children, some for the better, some unhappily. Often the changes are hardly the ones planned by the teacher or even apparent to him. Nonetheless, teachers must carry a major burden, along with the family, in helping children to meet and deal justly with moral problems.
> . . . There is no "morality-free" school, no valueless teaching. Any interpersonal experience contains a moral element, virtually by definition, and a classroom is no exception.
> *(Sizer and Sizer 1970, 3–4)*

We believe further that the "how to" of moral instruction is itself a complex set of choices, and depends upon a careful unraveling of the standards we hold, their origins and justifications. Again, Sizer's and Sizer's words are helpful:

> There was a time when "moral problems" were recognized as the core of formal schooling. These problems were cast in sectarian religious molds, and youngsters were "taught" moral conduct. Oliver Twist got his moral lessons from Mr. Bumble, as did the boys at Rugby from Thomas Arnold and Williams men from Mark Hopkins. There was an appealing simplicity to their task: "right" and "wrong" were clear and undisputed and were to be learned directly. If one could recite righteous precepts, one would practice them—or so the crude pedagogy of the day implied. The nineteenth-century teacher sermonized, and his charges listened (sometimes) and learned (some things). Crude and philosophically simpleminded though the sermonizing tradition may be, it had its effect. [T]he moralisms of the prairie have a strong hold on the large remnant of Middle America. . . . For a class of people it worked; it took hold. *But was it moral?*
> The answer is a qualified no. . . . While abstract morality is surely no more or less complex than it has always been (God knows that Dickens' slums were no better than ours), teaching toward it in any profound way is far more complicated than earlier schoolmasters may have believed. . . .

> While . . . the attempt to teach morality *must* be made by teachers, . . .
> they must approach their task vigorously and yet carefully, aware of all its
> intricacies and dangers. . . . The "morality" to be taught is more than a
> litany from McGuffey and infinitely more subtle and complex.
> *(Ibid.) (emphasis in original)*

One purpose of our book is to help educators recognize the many dimensions of the moral issues they confront, and to become more limber in their reflections upon them. So armed, we believe, they will make considered choices among options, both about the values they choose to teach and the pedagogy they use. To think that moral education is a simple matter is not merely a harmless failure of perception, for it opens the door to practices that (as we shall illustrate below) are actually immoral in intention or effect. A certain perplexity in one's response to moral questions is itself an ingredient of moral judgment. Recall Socrates saying to Meno that the slave boy would never have inquired into an idea until he had "fallen into perplexity" about it (Plato 1961, 368).

THE ROLE OF CONTENDING WORLDVIEWS

Consider the basic questions about morality that incidents like Maria's raise. She asked whether she should care, whether it matters, that Tony wears a hat, has a streaked face, muddy shoes, or a "farmer's" clothes. Does it matter where children sit, whether they return a teacher's greeting, whether they reject another child? Dress conventions are after all just that, conventions. So, too, seating arrangements. Does the breach of a convention take on a moral dimension under certain circumstances, or is it significant only as a matter of convenience, involving Maria's desire to create or preserve an environment that best enables her to follow her lesson plan?

Certainly the behaviors described cannot be termed clearly and seriously wrong. If, for example, Tony repeatedly beat another child in the bathroom, or was stealing from his locker, we would have little trouble making a judgment both about the moral aspect of the problem and the need to intervene. In the incidents that arose in Maria's classroom, however, we must begin by asking whether, and why, they touch fundamental moral values at all.

Maria's perplexity is hardly surprising, for the pundits are as divided on identifying the boundaries of morality as they are on defining its content or the proper school responses. One reason for this division is that the issue, although having a technical dimension, is not wholly so; rather, it is bound up with one's basic worldview. Consider, for example, Tony's refusal to doff his cap or change out of his "farming" clothes before going to school. Plainly, the norm that leads most of us to think it inappropriate or disrespectful to wear a hat indoors is a social convention. Wearing or removing a hat has no intrinsic moral valence. What would Tony learn by being told to remove his hat in class? First, he might learn that in our society wearing a hat in class is *taken* as a signal of lack of seriousness or respect, and that he should avoid giving people that signal. Second, he might learn that he should set aside his own impulses, his own desires, and his own views about the meaning of wearing or removing a hat, and defer to the judgments, and follow the behaviors, of teachers, peers, and "society." He would learn this cognitively, as a norm ("Remove your hat in class," or "Do as your teacher says"), but also as a habit, not requiring conscious thought.

The division is over the question whether this "learning" is a good thing, or perhaps more precisely whether it is so clearly a good thing. People of a generally conservative stance would tend to answer, yes: The school policy against hats is not merely an arbitrary convention. The removed hat (like the act of standing for the national anthem) has symbolic significance, expressing respect for a teacher and a school, and for learning. Respect for proper authority is a major social good, indeed, a necessity for social harmony. Tony's individuality is not at risk here in any serious way, and he will be a better person as an adult if he learns, through the inculcation of habit, to take his private preferences less seriously, to take more seriously the adverse reactions of his peers. It is in his own interest to be socialized to act as his fellows do in matters like dress. In this way he will grow up able to exercise the self-control and deference to the collective interest that is both the requisite of moral conduct and a principal ingredient of it. (The excerpt from Emile Durkheim, p. 23, in the following section of this chapter, is a classic expression of this view.)

By the same token, it does not matter that Maria prefers a particular seating arrangement only as a convenience for her walking around the room, or even just as a reflection of her aesthetic preference. It is reasonable for a teacher to require obedience for its own sake, and she need not justify every rule or practice as enhancing the learning environment. Teaching respect itself enhances the learning environment.

From within a liberal stance, the matter is far more ambiguous. First, the instruction, "Take off your hat," may be intended to convey a message about disrespect—although in some social groups it is *wearing* a hat, rather than removing it, that signals respect—but it may be questioned whether the message conveyed is as much about respect as about authority: "Do what teacher says." That latter message is morally equivocal to a liberal, for along with the obvious need to respect authority is the contending value of challenging the misuse of authority. To one with a liberal mindset, such misuse is neither rare nor trivial, and it is as important to moral development to teach children to question as to follow the demands of those in power. More broadly, according to a liberal worldview, the idea that moral action is aided by encouraging unreflective habitual decision making seems questionable. What children need to learn is how to think about difficult moral questions: to subordinate their self-regarding impulses, to be sure, but then to *reflect* on the process of moral decision making, to learn to think for themselves, and to exercise moral judgment.

Underlying these differences about authority and habit are deeper divisions regarding the nature of morality, the objectives of moral instruction, and the nature of the child. Conservatives put greater weight on obedience to authority and habit formation because they perceive morality as composed largely of certain "right" responses. Although there are gray areas, for the most part the moral good is clear, absolute, transcendent, universal. As William J. Bennett, Secretary of Education in the Reagan administration and a leading conservative proponent of the "character education" movement, has said: "You won't find many people who are going to argue: 'No, honesty is not a part of good character,' or, 'No, courage isn't really admirable'" (Bennett 1991, 131). Virtuous people are those with the strength—a strength that takes prolonged cultivation—to follow moral rules automatically, even against their self-interest: tell the truth, don't cheat, respect the laws.

From these premises, it follows that to a conservative the primary objective of moral education is to inculcate character in children through insistent and directive teaching, especially around the "hard" virtues such as courage, temperance, honor, fortitude, and self-discipline. Conservatives are more concerned with the child's actions than with his or her reasoning, which, they suspect, easily falls prey to rationalization. Although wanting the child to develop personal conviction and commitment, and not simply to obey mindlessly, they believe that steady adherence and devotion to morality develop through the constant practice of performing moral duties. Children by nature are not disposed to morality; without the strong hand of adults, ministers of the culture, children are likely to become unruly and lawless. Again, in Bennett's words: "If we want our children to possess the traits of character we most admire, we need to teach them what those traits are. . . . They must achieve at least a minimal level of moral literacy that will enable them to make sense of what they will see in life and, we may hope, will help them live it well" (id., 133). Certainly, they cannot be expected to subjugate self-interest to a consideration of others.

Liberals begin with a more suspicious stance toward authority, and toward the fundamental justice of the prevailing social order. (For an eloquent example, see Purpel 1999, especially Part One.) Therefore, seeing significant *immorality* in unquestioning adherence to conventional norms, and perceiving morality as proceeding largely from critical inquiry, they are less committed to habit building. The moral good is not clear but contingent and variable, reached by the exercise of skilled impartial judgment, taking into account the complex set of competing interests in each morally relevant situation. Virtuous people, according to their lights, take fundamental principles, such as equity and fairness, and determine the appropriate action by carefully reflecting on particular circumstances and choices. American philosopher John Dewey (1859–1952), a pre-eminent exemplar of this viewpoint, held that morality is not adherence to authoritative traditions but the resolution of conflicts between personal rights and social obligations, approached through a "reflective morality" rather than a "customary morality." Moral truth, to Dewey, is in constant flux, "not merely because all truth has not yet been appropriated by the mind of man, but because life is a moving affair in which old moral truth ceases to apply" (Dewey 1994, 144).

It follows then that the liberal's primary educational objective is enabling children to think about their actions, especially to reflect on how they impinge on the interests of others. While liberals tend to emphasize the "soft" virtues—tolerance, sympathy, benevolence, reciprocity—they are less concerned with the action of the child than with the care taken in deciding on it. Powerful commitments to the moral life, they believe, depend on this practice of vigorous reflection and will emerge from it. Children have built-in propensities for moral living. They are by nature sympathetically attuned to others. This propensity requires nurturing, but that nurturing should be subtle and, to the extent possible, indirect rather than didactic. So, for example, from a Deweyan perspective Maria should neither automatically condemn Tony's cap wearing as an affront to her or the school's authority, nor automatically allow it as an expression of individual autonomy. Rather she should subject his action to the deliberation of all concerned, considering whose interests (individual and community) are affected, and in what ways, by the presence or absence of a rule against wearing hats in class.

ENGAGING THE DIVIDE

These divergences in underlying premises about the nature of morality and the nature of the child trigger sharp disagreement about the educational needs of children, and generate much of the heat in the debates over moral education. E. F. Schumacher has expressed this divergence in words that bear recalling here:

> [L]ife presents us with a very big problem—how to educate our children. We cannot escape it; we have to face it, and we ask a number of equally intelligent people to advise us. Some of them, on the basis of a clear intuition, tell us: "Education is the process by which existing culture is passed on from one generation to the next. . . . For this process to be effective, authority and discipline must be set up." Nothing could be simpler, truer, more logical and straightforward. Education calls for the establishment of authority for the teachers and discipline and obedience on the part of the pupils.
>
> Now, another group of our advisers, having gone into the problem with the utmost care, says this: "Education is nothing more nor less than the provision of a facility. The educator is like a good gardener, whose function is to make available healthy, fertile soil in which a young plant can grow strong roots; through these it will extract the nutrients it requires. The young plant will develop in accordance with its own laws of being, which are far more subtle than any human can fathom, and will develop best when it has the greatest possible freedom to choose exactly the nutrients it needs." In other words, education as seen by this second group calls for the establishment, not of discipline and obedience, but of freedom. . . .
> (Schumacher 1977, 122–123) (emphasis omitted)

Stated as polarities, each stance seems to include some basic truths and ignore others. For example, a conservative should acknowledge, we believe, that the value of inculcating the habit of "respect" by enforcing the hat rule is undermined by enforcing it *solely* as a matter of the teacher's authority. For then all that Tony learns is that he had better not cross his teacher in whatever foolish whims she might invoke against his preferences. The liberal, by turn, needs to acknowledge that the capacity for moral reflection is a factor of the child's maturation, and that it is good for children to learn to inhibit impulses, postpone gratification, follow an etiquette, and show respect to others, including those in authority. Only through such training will they cultivate strong habits of self-discipline that later on can be put to moral purposes. One doesn't have to be a Spartan to believe that enduring some discomfort, submitting to some authority, builds character. The courage and steadfastness often demanded of morality are not options for those without self-control.

We agree then with William Bennett that courage and honesty are virtues to be taught, but they must be conceptualized and situated if they are not to become mere slogans. It takes courage, after all, to rob a bank, and the kindness that leads one to withhold an honest comment is sometimes morally preferable to blunt outspokenness. We agree too with John Dewey that deliberation over options is morally preferable to mindless obedience, but such a preference does not deny that long-standing traditions should not be lightly discarded. We recognize the value, depending on a child's age and circumstances, of cultivating a certain amount of rule-ordered behavior.

In subsequent chapters we elaborate further on the various facets of this debate. For the moment, two thoughts—divergent though they are—need to be borne in mind. First, it seems apparent that, however one might try to integrate both poles, agreement on priorities is not easily achieved, and perhaps should not be expected. Second, we should not lose sight of their considerable common ground. Most fundamentally, for both sides the moral dimension of life is critical, and its diminished presence in contemporary society is profoundly disturbing. For both, morality provides a framework for human aspirations, without which life dissolves into the pursuit of pleasures that inevitably fail to satisfy while seriously marring the fabric of social life.

We have begun with the problems raised by Maria Laszlo's story of her first few weeks teaching fourth grade because they draw us into the question whether moral education is a worthwhile subject of serious thought, because they pose the question whether there is a useful distinction between matters of moral (or immoral) action and those that are merely conventional, and because they uncover fundamental disagreements about the nature of morality and moral education. More specifically, Maria's story raises the question whether practices that may be thought to be only conventional nonetheless serve as moral guides, especially for younger children, because they help them to develop habits of self-discipline, habits which foster self-denial when morality so demands. This demand can involve regard for the interests and needs of others as well as oneself, respect for rightful authority, and critical reflection to check the tendency toward rationalization.

It is clear, we think, that the issues are not of recent vintage, a product of the contemporary "culture wars." The excerpts that follow in this chapter—from two leading educational theorists of earlier times and an American observer of Japanese elementary education—illustrate enduring differences in theoretical and experiential approaches to these questions.

*** At the Library

The eighteenth century philosopher, Jean Jacques Rousseau, and the nineteenth-century sociologist, Emile Durkheim, have left their imprint on contemporary education—Rousseau on progressive education, Durkheim on the communitarian movement. Divergent in their insights and prescriptions, they nicely "book-end" Maria's perplexity about moral education.

Rousseau only partially fits the popular impression of him as an advocate of permissiveness and indulgence in the education of children. He was surely an apostle of liberty:

> [T]he greatest of all blessings is not authority but liberty. The man who is really free only desires what he can perform; he can then perform all that he desires. This is my fundamental maxim. It needs only to be applied to children and all the rules of education will flow from it. *(Rousseau 1964, 91)*

He advocated a hands-off-children policy, leaving them unbridled to learn freely from their encounters with nature, for, in the famous words of the opening passage of *Emile*: "Everything is good as it leaves the Author of things; everything degenerates in the hands of man" (Rousseau 1979, 37). Adults should, therefore, remain backstage except to control the level of environmental exposure.

However, while opposed to discipline imposed by adults, he believed strongly in the discipline of the natural consequences resulting from a child's actions. The "yoke of discipline" is to be replaced by the "yoke of necessity."

Jean-Jacques Rousseau, *Emile*
(1979, Book II, 92, 93, 100)

Let us set down as an incontestable maxim that the first movements of nature are always right. There is no original perversity in the human heart. . . . Therefore, up to the time when the guide of *amour-propre*, which is reason, can be born, it is important for a child to . . . respond only to what nature asks of him, and then he will do nothing but good.

I do not mean that he will never do damage, that he will not hurt himself, that he will not perhaps break a valuable piece of furniture if he finds it in his reach. He could do a considerable amount of wrong without wrongdoing, because the bad action depends on the intention of doing harm, and he will never have this intention. If he had it one single time, all would be lost already; he would be wicked almost beyond recall.

Do not give your pupil any kind of verbal lessons; he ought to receive them only from experience. Inflict no punishment on him, for he does not know what it is to be at fault. Never make him beg pardon, he could not know how to offend you. Devoid of all morality in his actions, he can do nothing which is morally bad and which merits either punishment or reprimand.

[For example, the child] breaks the windows of his room; let the wind blow on him night and day without worrying about colds, for it is better that he should have a cold than that he be crazy. Never complain about the inconveniences he causes you, but make him be the one to feel those inconveniences first.

While discipline (instilling the habit of adherence to rules through adult authority) was anathema to Rousseau, it was *the* essential element of morality to Durkheim. He found no freedom in a state of nature. Left unbridled, children become overwhelmed by their passions and social life disintegrates; inclinations fully liberated are tyrannical, and enslave rather than free us. Discipline, therefore, is a corrective against our "infinite aspirations." Constraints and rules are good apart from the behaviors they proscribe, for prohibitions, by reining in the appetites, provide a wall against the insatiability of one's passions and ambitions. Thus, to Durkheim, it is the obligation of teachers to establish rules, and to enforce them authoritatively through proper sanctions.

▾▾

Emile Durkheim, *Moral Education*
(1925/1961, 46, 48–49, 146–151)

We come to this important conclusion. Moral discipline not only buttresses the moral life, properly speaking; its influence extends further. . . . [I]t performs an important function in forming character—and personality in general. In fact, the most essential element of character is this capacity for restraint or—as they say—of inhibition, which allows us to contain our passions, our desires, our habits, and subject them to law.

[I]nsofar as our inclinations, instincts, and desires lack any counterbalance, insofar as our conduct hangs on the relative intensity of uncontrolled dispositions, these dispositions are gusts of wind, erratic stop-start affairs characteristic of children and primitives, which as they endlessly split the will against itself, dissipate it on the winds of caprice. . . . It is precisely in this development of self-mastery that we build up moral discipline. It teaches us not to act in response to those transient whims, bringing our behavior willy-nilly to the level of its natural inclinations. It teaches us that conduct involves effort; that it is moral action only when we restrict some inclination, suppress some appetite, moderate some tendency. At the same time, just as any rule about anything that is relatively fixed or invariable stands above all individual caprice, and as moral rules are still more invariable than all the others, to learn to act morally is also to learn conduct that is orderly, conduct that follows enduring principles and transcends the fortuitous impulse and suggestion. Thus, will is generally formed in the school of duty.

▼▼▼▼▼

Discipline is thus useful, not only in the interests of society and as the indispensable means without which means regular cooperation would be impossible, but for the welfare of the individual himself. By means of discipline we learn the control of desire without which man could not achieve happiness. Hence, it even contributes in large measure to the development to that which is of fundamental importance for each of us: our personality. The capacity for containing our inclinations, for restraining ourselves—the ability that we acquire in the school of moral discipline—is the indispensable condition for the emergence of reflective, individual will. The rule, because it teaches us to restrain and master ourselves, is a means of emancipation and of freedom. Above all, in democratic societies like ours is it essential to teach the child this wholesome self-control. For, since in some measure the conventional restraints are no longer effective—barriers which in societies differently organized rigorously restrict people's desires and ambitions—there remains only moral discipline to provide the necessary regulatory influence. Because, in principle, all vocations are available to everybody, the drive to get ahead is more readily stimulated and inflamed beyond all measure to the point of knowing almost no limits.

. . . [W]e do not mean to suggest that the child receives genetically certain predetermined moral predispositions. The weapons that nature puts at our disposal cut two ways; everything depends on how they are used. Hence, the futility of those recurrent discussions as to whether the child is born moral or immoral, or whether he has in him more or less of the positive elements of morality or immorality. So put, the problem is not amenable to any clean-cut solution. To act morally is to conform to the rules of morality. Now, the moral law is outside the consciousness of the child; it is elaborated independent of him; he begins to have contact with it only after a given point in his life. . . . All that he has at birth are some very general dispositions, which are crystallized in one way or another according to how the educator exerts his influence, that is, according to the manner in which this potential is put to work.

But meanwhile the child must learn respect for the rule; he must learn to do his duty because it is his duty, because he feels obliged to do so even though the task may not seem an easy one. Such an apprenticeship, which can only be quite incomplete in the family, must devolve upon the school. In fact, there is a whole system of rules in the school that predetermine the child's conduct. He must come to class regularly, he must arrive at a specified time and with an appropriate bearing and attitude. He must not disrupt things in class. He must have learned his lessons, done his homework, and have done so reasonably well, etc. There are, therefore, a host of obligations that the child is required to shoulder. Together they constitute the discipline of the school. It is through the practice of school discipline that we can inculcate the spirit of discipline in the child.

▼▼▼▼▼

This, then, is the true function of discipline. . . . It is essentially an instrument—difficult to duplicate—of moral education. . . . When children no longer feel restrained, they are in a state of ferment that makes them impatient of all curbs, and their behavior shows it—even outside the classroom. . . .

. . . Doubtless when one examines the rules of conduct that the teacher must enforce, in themselves and in detail, one is inclined to judge them as useless vexations; and the benevolent feelings, which childhood quite naturally inspires in us, prompt us to feel that they are excessively demanding. Is it not possible for a child to be good and yet fail to be punctual, to be unprepared at the specified time for his lesson or other responsibilities, etc.? If, however, instead of examining these school rules in detail, we consider them as a whole, as the student's code of duty, the matter takes on a different aspect. Then conscientiousness in fulfilling all these petty obligations appears as a virtue.

In reading the following description of a Japanese first-grade classroom, note how it combines a whole-hearted commitment to creating an explicit moral environment, where rules, habits, and self-discipline pervade, with an equally pervasive child-centeredness.

Catherine C. Lewis, *Educating Hearts and Minds: Reflections on Japanese Preschool and Elementary Education*
(1997, 36–46, 52–53)

Westerners hear a great deal about the high academic achievement of Japanese children. But . . . Japanese educators are concerned with many aspects of children's development. Children's intellectual development is taken seriously—but so is their need for friendship, for connection to a caring classroom community, for whole-hearted involvement in sports, music, and art. [A] day with a first-grade class [will allow us] to see the ways that concern for children's social, academic, and civic development is interwoven throughout the lessons and activities of the school day. . . .

It's almost 9 a.m. The large banner over the blackboard in Ms. Ishii's first-grade classroom says, *"Tomodachi ni naro. Saigo made gambaro"* ("Let's be friends. Let's persist until the end"). The blackboard shows the agenda for the morning meeting and the subjects to be studied that day. Students play and talk noisily until the two student monitors for the day come to the front of the classroom and ask their thirty-four classmates to be seated. Most students take their seats and quiet down quickly, but the monitors must quiet several children by calling their names. All students are seated and quiet when, a few moments later, Ms. Ishii enters the room. On a cue from the monitors, all students rise, bow, and chorus, "Teacher, good morning." Ms. Ishii bows and greets them in return. Students take their seats, except for the monitors, who announce, in unison, the beginning of morning meeting and the first item on the agenda: attendance. Ms. Ishii calls the roll. Children shout,

"Present" when their names are called, trying to outdo one another with the loudness of their shouts. "Great—you've got lots of *genki* (energy) today," responds Ms. Ishii to the loud shouts.

The two monitors announce, from the board, the next item for the morning meeting: "Things to tell the class." A child raises his hand and one student monitor calls on him. "My tooth fell out last night," the boy volunteers. At that, a number of children begin shouting out how many teeth they've lost. The monitors ask children to raise their hands if they want to talk. It takes two minutes for the monitors to quiet the class, and Ms. Ishii sits silent during this time. Finally, the class settles down and the monitors call on several more students. . . . The monitors then announce the next item: news from the teacher. Ms. Ishii speaks: "I want to praise something today. Every morning you pass by the 'aunties' who work in the kitchen and I know you say good morning in your hearts. But today you said, 'Good morning' with your voices. I was very happy and I know they were very happy." Ms. Ishii nods to the monitors, who announce, "Morning meeting is over. Take out your notebooks for social studies." Checking to see that all children have accomplished this, the monitors then announce, "Social studies will begin. Let's greet the teacher." Once again led by the monitors, the children stand, chorus, "Teacher, please (teach us)," and bow.

Social studies begins. As homework, children have visited local parks and copied in their notebooks the rules posted at the parks. Ms. Ishii asks students to report the rules they found and explain the reasons for them. One student reports, "I found the rule 'Don't play with balls here.' I think it's because balls might hit people." This student calls on another student, who adds, "Especially, balls might hit mothers with babies." This student, in turn, calls on another child whose hand is raised. For about twenty minutes, discussion continues in this manner, with each child calling on another child.

The students' comments build on one another remarkably well, with many students making reference to their classmates' comments: "This is similar to the rule found by Ishikawa-san . . ." or "In addition to the reason Kojima-kun mentioned, another reason might be . . ." Sometimes a number of children want to comment, and they wave their hands furiously at the child who is speaking. Ms. Ishii writes each new rule on the board. Occasionally Ms. Ishii too raises her hand and is called on by a student. Usually she plays devil's advocate: "Why shouldn't we take leaves off a tree? That doesn't hurt anyone," or "It's OK to play in phone booths, isn't it?"

. . . The ten- or twenty-minute breaks between classes are bedlam, as students noisily visit, play tag, and even mount each other's shoulders for "chicken fights" in the classroom. Ms. Ishii leaves the classroom during some of these breaks; even when she's present, though, she makes no move to stop the shouting and games.

Second period is Japanese composition. Children spend the first fifteen minutes recalling their recent class trip to dig sweet potatoes. "What was most fun?" begins Ms. Ishii. "Pulling hard," "Finding that my potato was huge," "Having my potato slip right out of the ground when I pulled it," come the enthusiastic responses. Hearing the last response, Ms. Ishii asks: "Did anyone have a different experience?" and several children shout out that their potatoes wouldn't come out even when they tugged and tugged. "Why?" asks Ms. Ishii, and several children volunteer their ideas: that the potato had deep roots, that several potatoes attached to the stem all pointed in different directions. Ms. Ishii illustrates these ideas on the board and asks children to think about whether their potatoes looked like her sketches or looked different.

The remaining thirty minutes are devoted to writing. Ms. Ishii circles the room looking at what children are writing. She occasionally addresses questions or comments to the class: "What was the place like where we dug the potatoes?"; "What was the day like?"; "What were you thinking as you were digging, and how did you feel?"; "Write what you felt when the potato came out"; "Write so that someone who's never been to dig potatoes will know just what it's like." Interspersed are occasional practical instructions, such as "Don't mix up the two ways of writing *o.*" Ms. Ishii concludes the lesson: "Some children were able to write many lines, some just one or two. If you couldn't write much, practice at home tomorrow so everyone can write many lines on Monday."

Today's third-period lesson, mathematics, is canceled in order to devote a double period to physical education; the class needs to practice the lively jazz dance routine that will be performed the next day as part of Sports Day. . . . Ms. Ishii is pleased with the dancing except for the timing of one step in which children are supposed to jump backward to the center of their small circles, bump backsides, and jump up in mock surprise. Ms. Ishii explains that the step's humor depends upon good timing—that the jump in mock surprise must appear to be the result of the backside bump. As she has the class practice this sequence for the third time, Ms. Ishii says, "Watch yourself and others and see if everyone's starting at the right time. We'll have *hansei* (reflection) on this point later." Twenty minutes before the end of the double period, the students return to the classroom and assemble in their small groups. Each small group talks about whether it has the correct timing for the backside bump and devises strategies for helping children who are off (such as signaling them when it's time to start jumping).

The monitors announce the end of physical education and the beginning of lunch. Without a word of instruction from the teacher, children suddenly move in many directions. Some push desks together into dining areas for each group; others don hairnets and white aprons and fetch carts of food from the kitchen; others pass out straws and milk and set places for the classmates who are serving food. Children eat lunch with their fixed groups. On the wall, a richly decorated poster made by sixth-graders says, "Let's enjoy school lunch"; under it, a handmade sign lists this month's goal for school lunch: "To learn to eat a variety of foods without leaving any." A few minutes into lunch, the vice-principal's voice comes over the public address system: "Are you enjoying your lunch?" He goes on to give a brief talk, thanking by name several children who, on their own initiative after school, picked up litter on the school grounds and in a local park.

The fifth and final period of the day is devoted to the once-weekly class meeting. Sometimes class meeting features a class skit, a splashfest in the pool, or some similarly playful activity selected by the students. But sometimes, like today, students discuss an issue facing the class. . . . Ms. Ishii begins the meeting. "What does *saiko* [utmost] mean when we're talking about Sports Day?" Children raise their hands and volunteer various responses: "Running your hardest"; "Pulling your hardest in tug-of-war"; "Doing your best.". . . Ms. Ishii goes on through each event of Sports Day and asks students to talk about what "doing your utmost" means. She then asks them to think about one way they're going to do their utmost the next day and calls on several children to share their ideas with the class. Most of the children volunteer that they want to run fast or dance beautifully, but one child says, "I want to sit still when the important people give their speeches. I want to sit so still that even my mother will think I did a good job." Ms. Ishii singles this student out for praise: "Ms. Takeda is so praiseworthy. She's chosen her most difficult thing to try hard at. We all know she's often cautioned for fidgeting when we're supposed to sit still. Tomorrow, when everyone's watching her, she wants to do her best to sit still. I hope you'll all think, like Ms. Takeda, about what is most difficult for you and vow to try hard at it tomorrow."

Ms. Ishii nods to the monitors, who come to the front of the class and announce, "Class meeting is over. End-of-day meeting will begin." The monitors ask each group to report on its goal for the week and whether the group accomplished it. Several of the groups chose "No forgotten things" as a goal. Others chose "Being ready at the start of every lesson" or "Not fighting." After several minutes of discussion within the groups, each group reports to the class briefly: "The members of our group remembered all their belongings this week"; "We were ready most of the time, but on Tuesday we had a hard time settling down for lessons."

The students then talk within their groups once again, to choose group goals for the following week. A few minutes later, a representative from each group announces its goal; about half the groups have chosen new goals, and the other half have decided to try again at the preceding week's goal. The monitors then call on chore groups to make any needed announcements. Only the Flower group has an announcement today: They thank children for bringing in flowers and ask them to bring flowers next week so they can again have flowers for each group's dining area. The monitors choose a song—a rousing song that will be sung at the athletics festival the next day—and lead the class in singing it. Finally, they ask the class to stand and to bow and thank the teacher. In turn, Ms. Ishii asks the class to bow to the monitors and to thank them for their service to the class that day. "Enjoy tomorrow! Goodbye!" says Ms. Ishii, and school is over.

[The author notes that schools generally post lists of school, classroom, or group goals. Nearly half of the goals focus on friendship, cooperation, and other aspects of social and emotional development; academic goals comprise fewer than 10 percent of the stated goals. The following table is one example.]

Content of Moral Education for Grades 1 and 2

1. *Things Primarily Related to Oneself*
   (1) Leading an ordered life by being attentive to health and safety, treating objects and money carefully, keeping the area around oneself organized, and avoiding thinking only of oneself
   (2) Fully carrying out the study and work that are one's own responsibility
   (3) Taking the initiative in doing things one thinks to be good
   (4) Leading a life that is relaxed and ingenuous, not dishonest or deceptive

2. *Things Primarily Related to Relationships with Others*
   (1) Being cheerful with others by endeavoring to use greetings, language, and actions that are pleasant
   (2) Being warmhearted in contacts with younger children and older persons near oneself and showing them kindness
   (3) Getting along with friends and helping them
   (4) Thanking the people in daily life who care for one

3. *Things Primarily Related to Relationships with Nature and the Sublime*
   (1) Feeling intimate with the nature that's near oneself; being kindhearted in treatment of plants and animals
   (2) Having a heart that values life
   (3) Having contact with beautiful things and feeling ennobled by them

4. *Things Primarily Related to Relationships with Groups and Society*
   (1) Treating carefully things that are used by everyone and upholding promises and rules
   (2) Feeling love and respect for one's parents and grandparents and actively helping at home
   (3) Feeling love and respect for one's teachers, feeling intimate with the people at school, and enjoying classroom life

❦❦❦❦❦

The goals found their way not only into class meetings but also into academic lessons. Under a banner that read, "Let's become children who put their strength together," Ms. Ueda introduced a first-grade social studies lesson by talking about her own brother and two sisters. [H]er brother was an accountant who could cook well but could not get up in the morning. The teacher noted that she herself could not draw well and had a hard time remembering Japanese ideographs but could sing well. She ended by explaining how they put their strength together to make a happy family: "My sister corrects my writing, my brother cooks gourmet meals, I help everyone sing. . . . We are lucky to have each other, but in this class, we're even luckier because we have the strengths of thirty-six people that we can put together.". . . Students then met in their small groups to brainstorm ways that family members helped one another and ways that class members helped one another.

Social and ethical goals consistently shaped class meetings and lessons in social studies and moral education, and they often found their way into other subject areas as well. Goals of "Helping one another" and "Pooling strength" were fundamental to many lessons in science, mathematics, music, art, and physical education. Children reflected on helpfulness at the same time as they investigated water volume . . . ; they pursued a social studies project with the twin goals of "Building a three-dimensional model of the neighborhood and making sure all children in the group get a chance to say their ideas"; they played music together and then discussed both their musical performance and the strengths and weaknesses of the cooperation that shaped it. [S]ometimes the social and academic goals of a lesson were so intertwined that I couldn't distinguish them.

PART 2

The Moral as a Concept

Chapter 3

The Grammar of Morality

Once Maria Laszlo had secured a fragile truce over seating arrangements, she was able to go back to "just teaching." It wasn't long, however, until she found herself drawn into thinking again about the place of morality and moral education in her classroom. It all began when Peter, possessed of a big brother and a large weekly allowance, came to class with a batch of baseball cards. Within days the children were pulling cards from tote bags and lunch boxes, and spending every spare moment (outside of class time) trading. The activity uncorked a torrent of competition among the students; for a fourth-grade class a great deal of money was being brought to school and spent. Maria noticed that some children were getting $25.00 for a card, others no more than a few dollars. The rich were getting richer, and Maria strongly suspected that the successful traders, some of whose bargaining practices verged on bullying, were taking advantage of the more gullible boys. Worse, more than once cards apparently disappeared from students' desks; enraged children were accusing others of stealing. Finally, Maria began to overhear a fair amount of pretty crude language, usually directed at a fellow student and muttered in low voices.

Maria was troubled by the childrens' emotional and social blindness, their greed and materialism, their discord and bad language, the possible stealing. But she questioned whether to act on her impulse and simply forbid baseball cards in class. Although she despised the acquisitiveness, the jockeying for position, the showing-off associated with the trading, she realized that her reaction was probably personal, reflecting her identification with the excluded, exploited, weaker kids. She realized that baseball card–trading was a time-honored pastime—her cousin had a much treasured collection—and

33

that it might be a natural and relatively harmless way to learn "social skills." So the kids were thoughtless and insensitive to each other: Was that so terrible, especially when limited to this one activity? Was this particular insensitivity any worse than teasing or gossiping? Stealing was another matter, but it had not been proven; she resolved to keep a sharper eye on that aspect of the problem.

The bad language, much as it could really get to her, was part of many people's everyday vocabulary. Maria was certainly aware how unlikely it was that she could prohibit at school what goes on continuously, and is widely accepted, outside. The same was true, actually, about buying and selling baseball cards. The children weren't the only ones Maria knew with a craving for money, nor the only consumers of expensive items. Money is one of our society's highest values, and so long as the card-trading did not interfere with academic instruction, even if it had some troubling fallout, maybe she should let it go, see this as a craze that would dissipate with time, and not the affair of a teacher or the school.

So Maria kept her own counsel—which was not difficult for her, thinking as she did that "moral matters" were part of her job only when they kept her from doing her "real" job. But the sudden eruption of a large and loud fight among her students in the cafeteria lunch line brought the question to a head. While the class was waiting its turn for food service, Peter, still king of the cards, negotiated a trade with his classmate Mark, giving a Brady Anderson card in an even exchange for a Ken Griffey, Jr. Alfred, a friend of Mark, observed the transaction, and vigorously took umbrage: "You can't do that, Peter; you know that's no-fair. Mark, don't be a damn fool. Don't give that cheating asshole your Griffey."

Peter's anger flared up, and his voice rose. "Fuck off, Alfred. Get out of his face. It's none of your damned business. Where were you, Mister goody-goody, yesterday when someone stole my Greg Maddux card?"

Alfred moved menacingly towards Peter. "You stupid idiot, why don't you go straight to hell! You're just a big, fat bully. Leave Mark alone or I'll beat the shit out of you."

Maria was mortified. Children and teachers were watching the scene intently. Her heart racing, she moved rapidly, grabbed the cards and the boys, took them to the end of the line, and sternly commanded them to see her immediately after lunch. Peter, inflamed over the incident, muttered another "fuck" as he released his cards.

When it was time for the talk, Maria, still smarting with anger and humiliation, decided that she should not then try to sort out her responses to the incident and the broader problem it had so dramatically returned to center stage. So she simply asked the boys to think over the event and come to school the next day prepared to talk about it. She realized that she needed to do the same.

Maria left the school building, trying to identify the aspects of the trading-card experience that might call for a response. Although knowing that most of her colleagues would have no difficulty condemning all the elements of the incident, she still wondered: What exactly was the offense? Was the swearing wrong in itself? Was it wrong when directed to, or at, a fellow student?—or at her?—in front of her colleagues? What about Peter swindling Mark?—and Peter's accusation regarding the theft of his Greg Maddux card? Was card-trading itself the villain?—or the association of trading and money?—or the easy resort to manipulative, aggressive bargaining methods with classmates? The answers to these questions would help her decide whether to confine a discussion to the three children involved, open up the subject with all the students who traded, or even engage the entire class in discussing how the trading excluded and hurt people, led to unacceptable speech, manipulation of one another, maybe even outright theft; also, how it was degrading the general moral climate of the class. Until she knew what judgments to make, she couldn't even begin to think about how to intervene.

"When a teacher gets cursed out by her student in the cafeteria . . . ," Hardie Knox's voice spun Maria around, "she's entitled to have a colleague buy her a cup of coffee."

"That sounds like a great idea, Hardie," Maria responded sincerely, "but you may be buying yourself an earful along with the coffee."

"I don't doubt it. That little scene in the caf didn't look as if it came from nowhere."

Maria quickly realized that thinking and talking were a lot better than just thinking—and that thinking, talking, and listening might be better yet! She and Hardie had different approaches to their job. He seemed to agree with Jan Bonham that the classroom was full of moral questions, central to their work, while Maria still thought of them as difficulties to be dealt with when they came up, more as diversions from teaching than as part of it. At the same time, Hardie seemed to agonize so much less about how to respond to moral questions, while she found real dilemmas everywhere she looked. Truth to tell, she also found his classroom atmosphere a bit too strict and stuffy for her taste. But he was a friend, a good teacher, and a pretty good listener, even if he did tend to see solutions where she saw questions.

Maria told Hardie the story of what preceded the blow-up in the cafeteria. "Hardie," she went on, "part of me has wanted to put card-trading totally off-limits since day one. Of course, I don't allow it during class time, but now I need to decide whether it's time to put a stop to it altogether, limit it further in some way, or talk with the class about the problems it seems to have created. I could use some help getting clear on which are real problems, and which are minor and best ignored.

"Take swearing. No one likes to be cussed out in public. But should we try to stop all use of foul language? I don't like to hear it, to me swear words degrade the language, and the speaker too, when they become habitual. Yet it's just ingrained in the talk of so many people nowadays. Is it really anything worse than saying 'like' all the time, or wearing revealing clothes? I guess students should realize that things like that will hurt them when they get out of school and into the workplace (or higher education), but maybe the words aren't really wrongful unless they are being used to attack another person. There's a difference between swearing that is mean, directed *against* someone, or really defiant, and the talk we hear from children every day, the 'what the fuck, who the fuck, this fuckin' thing.'"

Hardie was shaking his head more and more vigorously. "So what if people are offended only because swearing is a social no-no?—or if in a particular case it doesn't seem directed at anyone? Suppose there are times where it's just a tough-guy way of talking, meant to impress and not to hurt? Sure, kids and a lot of adults are desensitized to swearing, but the fact remains that there's nothing good to be said for it. It does degrade the classroom environment, and just ruling it out of bounds is a lot simpler than trying to explain a bunch of fine distinctions."

"Hardie, the truth is that I'm much more bothered by the callous manipulations in some of the kids' card-trading. To them, their classmates are just things to be pushed around for their own self-aggrandizement. Talk about behaviors that have moral implications for later life! I saw some embryonic corporate raiders at work in my class, and that's where some moral education would make a lot more sense than imposing our cultural speech patterns on them."

"Maria, some of those corporate raiders are their parents, or they would be if they could pull it off. And, as I recall, one of the buildings at the University where we met is named for a particularly successful—and, from what I've heard about him, particularly nasty—one. You'd be raising a hornet's nest complaining about good old American initiative."

"But everyone says moral education starts with simple things like respect for others and their feelings. How do I let the card-trading pass when, in its own way, it's just as unfeeling and vicious as a hearty 'fuck you' can ever be?"

"I would get at that in a little less challenging way. I teach students respect for one another with positive routines—call them rules if you want. We've been talking today more about inhibiting the immoral than fostering the moral. The point of my 'rules' is less to forbid than to cultivate what I call 'character.' I insist on a lot of behaviors that I see as character-building. Every morning, for instance, the kids stand up and greet me, and I them. They tutor younger children, say the Pledge, clean up the pets' cages, write notes to anyone who is sick, water the plants, straighten the room before lunch, and so forth."

"Just when I thought we were on the same train," said Maria sadly, "I see our cars separating. What has a mindless ritual like 'Good morning, Mr. Knox,' got to do with developing character, and what has what you call character, which seems like mere obedience, got to do with kindness and caring?"

"Nothing and everything," Hardie came back. "Standing and saying 'Good morning, Mr. Knox,' is not directly character-promoting. Pick your own routines. In Montessori schools, children carry tubs of water about to learn not to spill. You might prefer a more socialized routine like having one child tutor another. Believe me, I'm not saying the choice is unimportant. I'm not saying routines are interchangeable, that they can't be abused. There is a danger. They can become petty acts imposed just to get submission. But that's something to keep in mind in deciding what routines to select and how many to have.

"The point is that routines exert what our old school friend Durkheim called 'the spirit of discipline,' and that spirit is a precondition for accepting moral authority. Without discipline and self-control one is unlikely to be a person of character—considerate, benevolent, honest, courageous, respectful, responsible, steadfast, loyal—because all those traits require the capacity to restrain our 'me first' impulses. If the Peters of the world have strong self-discipline and the character it promotes, I'd bank on it, they will be less likely to swear at me or each other and, yes, less likely to exploit an innocent kid, more likely to be kind and fair.

"Let me see if I've got what you're saying straight, Hardie," Maria began. "Your routines are supposed to make the kids self-disciplined. The particular routines you pick don't matter much. They can come from old-fashioned codes or modern educational ideas. You suggested tutoring; I assume it could also be visiting a nursing home, or collecting food for a hunger drive. The point, or one point, of the discipline is that, beyond the goodness of the act itself, the discipline promotes character because character depends upon self-control. And strong character is necessary if children—if any of us, I suppose—are to be both reflective and morally responsible actors. Is that it?"

"Sounds OK so far, Maria. I'd go after the swearing—we're not talking yet about how I'd stop it—and let the card-trading go, although if you wanted to say, no cards in class at any time because they tend to cause a lot of disruption, I'd back you 100 percent. I'd let the lecture on the ethics of capitalism go, too. Instead, pick something simple and nonthreatening that will teach them to spend a little time thinking about someone other than Number One. OK with you?"

"Well, maybe . . . "

"I hear a pretty important 'but' just around the bend," Hardie smiled.

"It's funny," Maria replied, "to me you're making the problem more complicated than I would with all of my theorizing, but you also seem so much more sure of your impulses. I really don't want to make my kids do or not do something just because of my own personal reaction to it. I'm not as comfortable with your assurance that it's good for them, anyway, to learn to do what they're told. I find the whole thing a lot more perplexing and ambiguous than you do, but the last thing I want to do is to turn class into a philosophy lab.

"Anyway, I can't keep picking at this now. Our talk has really been helpful. Don't mistake my crabbiness about not knowing where it leads me, but there is life after 3:00. I wish we could put this on the agenda for tomorrow's faculty meeting, instead of the bureaucratic trivia we usually talk about. Anyway, thanks, for the conversation—and the coffee, too."

"Mutual, Maria. Don't let my 'Here's the answer' style fool you. I also got a lot out of our talk."

"So, Lady," Agatha Cerine, a fellow fourth-grade teacher, fell in alongside Maria as she walked toward the school building the next morning, "you and Hardie tête-à-tête in the coffee shop for an hour or so after school! Something I should know about?"

"No, Aggie, at least not what you have in mind. And anyway he's not my type—nor, I suspect, would I be his, even if he weren't spoken for. But for sure you must know what we were talking about. You probably saw—and heard!—what happened with my students in the caf yesterday."

"Not really, I wasn't that close. You shouldn't feel the whole school was listening in, Maria."

"Yeah, I guess I do think everyone, not excluding Fred Helter [the principal], got an earful of how I can't control my class! We're a little early for the meeting, so let me tell you the quick version of what I've been wrestling with. Your mind runs more toward ed theory than mine, so maybe you could put the thing in a context that I could sit still for."

Maria gave Aggie a brief account of her conversation with Hardie, and their differing reactions to what she'd been troubled about.

"Hard stuff," Aggie began. "I know Hardie's way of thinking a little bit, and you're both onto some pretty basic questions."

"But, Aggie," Maria interjected, "I'm not in school anymore. I have work to do and chopped-up pieces of time to do it in. When one of my students is yelling, 'Fuck you!' at another one, or muttering it at *me*—and Peter did exactly that yesterday—I can't reread Kant or Dewey, or even my old notes from Jan Bonham's class. I can't even call a halt and go look for you or Hardie. I need to have it all clear in my mind beforehand. So maybe Hardie's right; I shouldn't agonize so much. But—oh, I don't know! You see what a bind I'm in!"

"You're doing a lot better than most of us, just by caring about the questions," Aggie responded. "And, sure, you can't figure things out on the spur of the moment, but now you can look back on what happened, not to beat up on yourself because of what you did or didn't do yesterday, but for what it helps you to understand. It helps us, I should say; it's not as if Hardie and I, or Helter either, have it all worked out.

"You and Hardie lean in opposite ways on two or three pretty basic questions. For one, I think you see being reflective about questions of right and wrong as a big part of being a good person."

"Right!" Maria animatedly responds. "I want children to inspect their actions and come to their own decisions. That's why I don't like a whole lot of rules. That's why, despite my fury at the boys, I'm not inclined to punish them. Even if Peter intentionally injured Mark, because it was pay-back time or just because he wanted to take advantage of him, if Peter didn't, couldn't, consider any other options, maybe we shouldn't be so tough on him."

"And I'd say one reason you lean that way is that moral questions aren't always easy to spot, or to answer when you know you've got one. And so you don't want your students just to jump to your tune, at least unless you're pretty sure it's the only way to sing on key."

"Right again!" Maria interjected, "Hardie just doesn't seem to care about the students' learning to *understand* what's right and wrong."

"Maybe, although I think it's more that Hardie sees reflection as just one piece of morality, and not as valuable a piece as you see it. But mostly, he'd say that reflection requires self-control if it is to be honest, dispassionate, and disinterested. So first the critters need to learn to control their impulses. Without that, they haven't much of a chance of becoming the reflective person you want them to be, or the kind, generous people you both want them to become."

"If you're taking my name in vain, at least I get to listen in!" The two women had not noticed Hardie coming into the room for the meeting.

"I'm sorry, Hardie. I really wasn't complaining about your nutty ideas to Aggie."

"No problem. I heard you say something about critters needing to learn to control their impulses, Aggie. If that's what Maria told you, I think I'll plead guilty right away, and be proud of it."

"And doesn't that," Aggie went on, "have something to do, but not everything to do, with the disagreement the two of you have over what to do about swearing in school?"

"What do you mean?" It was Maria who said it first, but Hardie was about to as well.

"Hardie, would you have a 'no swearing' rule just for the sake of teaching your kids to follow a rule, and not worry as much as Maria whether swearing is really wrong?"

"In a way, maybe, but . . . "

"It's the 'but' that is what I mean," Aggie went on. "It does matter to you that swearing, even if it isn't 'really' wrong, is still something that bothers a lot of people and is going to get in the way of your students' making their way in the world."

"Right," Hardie responded, lapsing into thought before going on. "Maria is bothered by card-trading in itself, not just the abuses she's mentioned, but I think that's just a personal thing with her."

"Yes," Aggie replied, "But suppose Maria thought that card-trading *was* 'really wrong'?"

"Well, if it were, that'd be different," Hardie smiled, "but I'd try to persuade her that she would be wrong to think that. If she saw card-trading going on that amounted to one kid's deliberately swindling another, she should stop that because swindling is plain immoral; it unjustifiably takes advantage of another person. She could also stop card-trading in class if she thought it interfered with the academic work, or if the kids just kept letting it get out of hand, because, even though it's not morally wrong in itself, the boys doing it had shown themselves unable to keep their actions within tolerable boundaries."

"OK," Aggie went on, "so one question is what makes some things 'really wrong,' others something that 'bothers a lot of people,' and still others 'just a personal thing'? We can say that we do and should want to put a stop to things in the first category, if we can; that we shouldn't try to be boss on things in the third; and that we should follow our impulses without a lot of agonizing in the middle group. I think, Hardie, that's pretty much where you come out."

"Maybe so," Hardie mused. "I do agree that moral values have a commanding quality, which trump other values. You certainly wouldn't say to a child, 'Stealing is wrong, but if you really like those sneakers take them,' but you might say, 'Baked potatoes are better for you than French fries, but eat whichever you want.' So if you believe, like me, that the moral education of school children is important, then you'd forbid swearing that was deprecating kids."

Once again, Maria felt frustrated by these hair-splitting distinctions. "Hardie, I thought I was the one who agonized too long. You're supposed to be making distinctions that will give us guidance. You sound like a chapter from one of Bonham's books."

Aggie intervened. "Sorry, Maria, but the fact is that this stuff is not simple. In fact, what Hardie has said so far is the easy part. The harder question is how we know into which box a specific act goes—whether it's swearing, or that kid you once mentioned to me, who wore his hat in class. When, and why, is swearing just wrong, and its prohibition therefore obligatory; when is it just something that we can choose to use to teach self-control; and when is it something that is just a convention, which we should be wary about imposing on everyone?"

"Well, I do think that's a harder question," Maria spoke up firmly, "but I'm not sure that Hardie cares much."

"Now, I *am* glad I got here in time. Of course I care, although perhaps not as much as Maria. If you'll both hold still for three seconds of theory, I still like what Durkheim said: We enter the domain of the moral when we enter the domain of the social, when we rub up against the interests of others. That means that swearing is in the moral sphere, and is wrong, when it hurts another person."

Aggie jumped in eagerly at this point. "But this is where it gets really hard. How literally should we take you, Hardie? 'When it hurts another person': That means that what makes an act immoral, or not, is its *consequences*. There's surely something to that. Consequences matter to our moral judgments. Suppose Peter meant to swindle Mark, but Mark actually knew the value of his Ken Griffey card. If he wasn't misled at all, but didn't care because he's crazy about Brady Anderson, then perhaps Peter did no harm.

"But it gets harder still," Aggie continued. "Morality is a lot more than the consequences that follow an act. For myself, I look more at the morality of the person than of the act the person committed. So, if Maria's student purposely misled a classmate into paying too much for a card—assume he was as naive as Mark appeared to be and the guy didn't know he was getting a bad deal—I'd say we should judge him harshly. He has a bad *motive*. It's like the classic case of the person who caps off a lifelong career of white-collar crime with a gift to a university, to get his name on a building and some respectability for himself and his family. I'm not for awarding him any medals for finding a new way of feathering his nest."

"But, Aggie," Maria replied, "maybe bad motives and bad consequences both matter. Hardie's right, isn't he, that it does seem to matter whether you swear into the air, so to speak, or swear *at* someone else? And yet, you're right, too, Aggie—I guess all of this *is* more complicated than I would like—we usually do consider more than the act itself. We haven't mentioned a person's *knowledge*. For instance, when a three-year-old takes money from her parent's dresser, we don't call it stealing. She doesn't know better. We excuse her and maybe tell her not to do it, or make sure we don't leave our money around so she can reach it.

"When condemning someone, we also presume—I'm on a roll now—that he or she had a *choice* about the act. If a kid is literally forced to do something wrong by a parent's or older brother's threats of harm, we would excuse him or her. And we judge differently the kid who swears because he is surrounded by such language, and no one has told him not to use it, from the kid who has been taught they are forbidden.

"You're right, Aggie, about motive. I heard Peter talk about payback for Mark's theft of his Greg Maddux card. If true, that has to be factored in too, doesn't it? And what if Peter had been bribed to do the trade? When I break up fights between kids, I always ask who started it and why."

Aggie looked around at the room starting to fill up. "Let me throw a little more oil on this fire, before the meeting starts and we're knee-deep in announcements. I spoke a minute ago about caring about the goodness of the person, not the act. Isn't there something to be said for *character*, not only as a condition of morality, as Hardie thinks self-control is a value, but as part of morality itself? Aren't character traits such as courage and generosity themselves moral virtues?"

"Yes and no," Hardie responded, expecting the exasperated smirk that he gets from Maria. "To me, character traits are connected to moral activity, but not the same as it. To use an overworked analogy, character traits—well-established, permanent, structural capacities—are like the computer's hard drive, whereas moral acts—diversified, contextually complex, requiring flexibility—are its programs. Character is often morally neutral. I mean we say benevolence and respect are good, but as you obviously know benevolence can become infantilization, respect can become blind submission, and courage can be used to ignoble ends. Character traits for me are dispositions. Let's say one is disposed, primed, to be respectful. Character traits are the slow-grown capacities that stand in readiness to be summoned when moral action is required. My classroom routines and discipline help grow those capacities; reflection, so dear to you, Maria, is critical when action decisions are called for. It's not an either-or business."

"Well," Aggie chimed in, "either we stop talking or we'll become the first item on the agenda for this meeting. Thanks, guys, for letting me in on the conversation. I wish we could have more like it around here."

✱✱ At the University

The questions that these three elementary-school teachers are exploring are as fundamental as they are knotty. We think of them as concerning the "grammar" of morality.

First, what distinguishes moral questions from other questions of values? This is the issue of the scope of the "moral domain," including the moral stake in convention-respecting behavior.

Second, what follows from the decision to characterize an act as having moral significance? We will examine the meaning of two qualities said to characterize a matter having moral valence, *obligatoriness* and *universalizability*.

A third set of questions asks, what is the focus of moral questions? Do they look mostly to what one *does*, doing (or avoiding) certain acts? If so, should acts be judged immoral because they are thought to have harmful consequences, or on account of some inherent quality? Alternatively, is morality more a question of the sort of person one *is*, as is suggested by the concept of "good moral character?" Or, should the focus be on neither an act itself nor on character, but on the actor's motivation or decision-making process?

These questions make up a complex agenda, with a bewilderingly abstract sound. It may seem a far cry from the very concrete issues with which Maria, Hardie, and Agatha were grappling. Yet, unlike Moliere's bourgeois gentleman unknowingly speaking prose, these teachers are aware that their practical, down-to-earth responses to specific, pressing questions thrust upon them in their day-to-day work are embedded in philosophical and psychological premises. Maria is reluctant to acknowledge the significance of that awareness, but we believe that systematic exposure and consideration of these premises is essential if we are to understand our own and others' reactions to contested issues of educational policy and practice.

Every school puts forth a variety of values. Foremost perhaps are academic and pedagogic ones, but schools also promote values regarding such diverse concerns as recreational activities, artistic sensibilities, vocational choices, and personal health. Many such values may be thought to take on a moral dimension; the study of literature, for example, may enhance students' ethical sensibilities. What, however, of eating too much rich food, or failing to prepare conscientiously for a tennis game? Are there circumstances in which such actions take on moral significance? More generally, by what criteria are we to decide that a matter has moral significance?

One might come at the question from the other direction, asking what difference it makes whether a matter has moral significance: What characteristics do such matters tend to have? How, for example, would Maria or Hardie (or you) think differently about swearing were it viewed as an infraction of a moral, or a conventional, norm? Some will think that this latter question is the prior, others would begin (as we do) with the former. Obviously, both need to be addressed and considered.

We look first at a response that seeks to ground the scope of the moral domain in the idea that the rightful province of the moral is the regulation of those of our actions that affect others; in Emile Durkheim's famous dictum: "[T]he domain of the moral begins where the domain of the social begins" (Durkheim 1925/1961, xi).

THE MORAL DOMAIN: SOCIAL VERSUS INDIVIDUAL

Durkheim asserts: "To act morally is to act in terms of collective interest" (ibid.). John Dewey, though often at odds with Durkheim, agrees. Morality, to Dewey, "is as much a matter of interaction of a person with his social environment as walking is an interaction of legs with a physical environment" (Dewey 1922, 318). Similarly, the contemporary moral educator Roger Straughan identifies morality as referring "to those situations, dilemmas, problems, decisions and choices which require the consideration of other people's welfare, interests and rights; and 'non-moral' to everything that lies outside that boundary" (Straughan 1982, 5). Isolated on a desert island, a self-indulgent person might pursue his or her desires without objection; there is no one to hurt. Insofar as his actions do or do not contribute to his welfare we might judge them wise or foolish, but not morally good or bad. But when another person arrives, he must curb his appetites and consider the other as also deserving. As ethicist Sidney Callahan, writing from a Christian feminist perspective, puts it: "Since no one lives alone in the world, . . . moral questions concern actions involving other human beings and their welfare" (Callahan 1994, 62).

Although the equation of the moral with the social seems intuitively sound as a generalization, taken literally it may be both too narrow and overbroad. There may be a moral element in what appears as wholly personal self-improvement, and in our response to such questions as the treatment of animals and the natural world. At the same time, there may be some social settings that generate expectations that make no moral claims. We will address each of these possibilities in turn.

First, is it true that monitoring one's personal life—control over appetites, fitness regimes—serves a moral purpose only as it affects others? The idea that attending to one's own interests is not only morally permissible but morally desirable, that there is such a domain as *personal* morality, is not just a trendy product of our current narcissism. It finds powerful expression in philosophical and religious traditions. From a religious outlook one's primary fealty and duties are to God. That relationship, while obligating our treatment of others, may well demand a personal purity of thought, deed, and prayer that has nothing to do with "society," yet powerfully shapes the meaning of a person's "interests."

It was the very personal nature of such demands that elicited the scornful disapproval of the socially oriented moralist, David Hume (1711–1776), who referred deprecatingly to the "monkish" virtues of "celibacy, fasting, penance, mortification, self-denial, humility, silence, solitude." Sensible men, he observed, will see the pointlessness of such "superstitions":

> [They] neither advance a man's fortune in the world, nor render him a more valuable member of society; neither qualify him for the entertainment of company, nor increase his power of self-enjoyment. . . .We observe, on the contrary, that they cross all these desirable ends; stupify [*sic*] the understanding and harden the heart, obscure the fancy and sour the temper. We justly, therefore, transfer them to the opposite column, and place them in the catalogue of vices. . . .
> *(Hume 1983, 73–74)*

Although also writing from a secular stance, philosopher Jeremy Bentham (1748–1832)[1] included the pursuit of one's own interest as a primary moral value. A self-regarding virtue—an example is eating disagreeable food because it is good for you—is no less important than an other-regarding virtue—eating less so that another might have food—for both serve to maximize the overall state of human pleasure (Bentham 1970/1996).

By equating to this extent morality and pleasure, Bentham appears to erase the line between social and individual concerns, including both self- and other-regarding acts within the moral realm. Yet, he calls the former "prudence," the latter "beneficence." Thus, even as he extends the moral canopy, he keeps alive the distinction between values that serve the self and others (id., 284). Translated into our school setting, it may be that promoting self-development (say, through nutrition and calisthenics) is prudent, but it does not rise to the same level as promoting social responsiveness.

It may be, then, that the moral extends beyond the social. The issue has real salience in the school setting. Beyond any moral significance of personal self-definition, society has a stake in enabling children to reach their potential, for the person is emergent and what is not undertaken in childhood may be beyond reach as an adult. The loss is to the community of which the student is and will be a part, not merely to the individual.

---

[1] Jeremy Bentham is regarded as the founder of utilitarianism, which measures the morality of actions according to their contribution to overall happiness, specifically, the greatest happiness to the greatest number of people.

Another aspect of the "moral domain" question, you will recall, is whether morality encompasses *all* aspects of our social lives. In what sense should we think of such social behavior as dress codes, recreational or food choices, orderliness, promptness, or courtesy as matters of morality, not because of their impact on the actor alone, or their long-term effect on the larger society, but because they offend norms that are merely conventional?

THE MORAL DOMAIN: CONVENTIONAL VERSUS MORAL

Maria is inclined to distinguish fairly sharply between moral and conventional norms. Tending to regard disapproval of swearing and perhaps of card-trading as in the latter category, she is reluctant to impose her norms on her students. Hardie, while also distinguishing convention from morality, sees an important moral lesson to be learned by children in being required to follow conventions. He sees moral significance in codes of behavior, even though harm to others is involved only in the special sense that they may be offended or otherwise put off by the very unconventional quality of nonconforming actions.

In the preceding chapter, Tony's objection to removing his hat, although interpreted by some as signaling disrespect was, in itself, the violation of a mere convention. Though adherence to some conventions—e.g., driving (in this country) on the right rather than left side of the road—may be critical, because breaking them threatens palpable harm to others, that is not normally the case. Even Durkheim, with his highly inclusive view of morality, exempted a portion of the school's discipline:

> It is not necessary that children's attitudes, their bearing, the way they walk or recite their lessons, the way they word their written work or keep their notebooks, etc., be predetermined with great precision. For a discipline so extended is as contrary to the interests of real discipline as superstition is contrary to the interests of true religion.
> *(Durkheim 1925/1961, 153)*

The question is whether a line can be drawn in the sand separating the customary and the moral. It has been suggested that such a line exists. Consider, for example, the distinction propounded by the following statements:

> Conventions are the agreed-upon uniformities in social behavior determined by the social system in which they are formed. . . . Conventions are arbitrary because there is nothing inherently right or wrong about the actions they define. . . .
>
> [M]oral considerations are not arbitrary but stem from factors intrinsic to actions: consequences such as harm to others. Although moral prescriptions (i.e., "It is wrong to hurt others") are an aspect of social organization, they are determined by factors inherent in social relationships as opposed to a particular form of social, cultural, or religious structure.
> *(Nucci 1991, 22)*

Supporting this approach are the findings of some authorities that the moral and conventional are so universally perceived as separate realms that even three-year-olds grasp the distinction. Children, it is asserted, draw the same distinctions as adults; moral rules refer to acts, such as hurting or stealing, that seriously affect others, while conventions are supported by a group but understood as inconsequential social practices, not plainly binding. Violations of conventions, even if thought wrongful, are seen as less serious and deserving of milder punishment than moral infractions.

Nucci's study of students attending a Roman Catholic high school and college bears out this bifurcated thinking. Students were asked through a questionnaire whether it would be permissible for the Church to remove various rules that the authors classified as either moral or amoral. The rules were divided into two sets, one including acts (stealing, killing, rape, slander) widely considered to be harmful or unjust, and the other acts (failing to fast before communion, using contraceptives, masturbation, premarital sex, divorce) that the authors considered simply to violate convention. Nearly all respondents believed that the Church would be wrong to remove the rules prohibiting moral transgressions, while more than half thought that, so long as the Church decided to allow the act, it would not be wrong to breach an existing convention.[2] The students responded similarly when asked whether members of other religions could (again, assuming their religious authorities gave permission) rightfully engage in conduct transgressing existing norms. Even without a religious prohibition, the respondents believed that some conduct, such as slander and stealing, was just plain wrong (Nucci 1989, 183–203).

These empirical findings are reminiscent of normative ideas familiar in Western secular and religious law. Anglo-American law distinguishes between actions that are *malum in se* and those that are *malum prohibitum*, wrongs "in themselves" and wrongs prohibited by an enacted law. Murder, for example, is thought to be inherently wrongful, indeed, declared unlawful *because* it is so plainly wrong; driving a truck carrying weight in excess of a legal limit is wrong only because it is contrary to an enacted law. The moral principle, if any, is to obey a proper law, and if the legal weight limit is raised, driving the same load becomes perfectly proper.

The Roman Catholic distinction between natural law and positive law is to like effect. Eating meat on Friday was deemed wrongful for Catholics over many centuries, but only because the Church prohibited it. Since that ban was lifted, it has become permissible. Adultery, however, or murder, could not be rendered licit by Church decree; they are contrary to natural law.

It would be helpful if we could separate out behaviors that really matter from those that are mere conveniences, required through a temporary, and

---

[2] We will consider in Chapter 4 the significance of the fact that the respondents apparently did not believe that individuals could properly act in violation of conventions so long as they continued to be upheld by the Church itself.

perhaps arbitrary, consensus. It would allow experimenting with rules and foster tolerance of deviations and discontinuities in traditions, while holding fast to the "fundamental." The rational distinctions that have been drawn, and the empirical findings suggesting that the children in Nucci's study intuitively grasp them, add a measure of confidence to this possibility. However, we must pause (always) over claims of rationality and innateness.

The first critique of this bifurcation goes to what is termed "domain overlap." Many of our moral rules seem to fit both the conventional and moral domains. A recently recognized example is smoking by students or their parents. For many years, it was noncontroversial to assume that smoking, however improvident, was a personal not a moral matter. One could imagine a teacher saying, "I can expect parents not to 'beat up' their children but I can't expect them not to smoke in front of their children. That is their right. And, while I can prohibit smoking in school, it is another matter to tell students that they cannot carry cigarettes (putting aside the effect of a law forbidding their possession by minors) for use when they leave the school grounds." But today there is substantial disagreement. Given that smoking is a documented health hazard, that parental smoking is known to influence children's decisions, and indeed that exposure to secondhand smoke is itself hazardous to children, is a teacher obligated to take less of a laissez-faire position?

Another controversial category is illustrated by rules of etiquette—how we address and greet people, how we serve and eat, and the like. These are conventional, but some may be taken as, and are not infrequently meant as, expressions of respect. Where one can fairly say that disrespect is intended, the grounds for categorizing the action as wrongful seem strong. But what is the significance of the fact that, irrespective of the actor's intention, an act is *taken* as a sign of disrespect? May individuals or society move an action (such as calling adults by their first names or holding a door for a woman) from the conventional/optional to the moral/mandatory category simply by reason of *their* taking offense?

Hardie Knox asks his students to stand up when he enters the room to signal their respect not just to him but to teachers more generally and to the learning process, although he knows there is nothing inherently important about standing. To that extent he is willing to impose social understandings of the meaning of a student's actions on those who might not share them, indeed, might not even have known of them until the matter came up in the classroom. Apart from its value in developing self-control, the convention of standing for teachers fosters concern for the reaction of others, which to Hardie has plain moral salience. Conventions thus can have derivative moral value. Maria Laszlo is dubious about the legitimacy of this line of thought.

A more troubling problem arises when a societal convention may not only fail to embody a moral imperative, but may actually be morally problematic. If so, it is not merely morally *allowable* to violate it; it may be affirmatively *immoral* for society to enforce it. Traditional assignment of the obligations and privileges associated with sex roles provides an important example.

Using gender to decide who does the shopping, handles the finances, prepares the meals, and cares for the children is not self-evidently an innocuous, if somewhat arbitrary, convention. To many people today, it rather implicates vital issues of fairness and justice.

A third critique questions whether the line between the domains is not largely the product of a child's nurturance. Twentieth-century psychologist Jerome Kagan, following David Hume, suggests (1984) that all moral concepts originate in sentiment (as opposed to reason). The good is what makes us feel good, the bad is what makes us feel guilty, and sentiments are conditioned by social upbringing. Thus, five-year-olds understand that it may be acceptable to wear the "wrong" clothes but unacceptable to steal a child's toy. Why? Because improper dressing typically receives less familial disapproval—as simple as that. If distinctions between convention- and morality-grounded standards rest on emotional reactions then, as Kagan recognizes, when sentiments shift so do moral judgments. What offends us greatly, moderately, or not at all has less to do with rational distinctions between the consequential and inconsequential, the permanent and changeable, than with the emotional reactions of significant adults in a child's life.

The question appears more complex when we consider that the moral/conventional division may express not merely the attitudes of individual parents, but deeper cultural norms. In recent years, our society has tended to regard social practices as contracts entered into voluntarily by autonomous individuals, and as such as independent of the moral order. The conviction that people are entitled to choose many aspects of their lives predisposes one to collapse the moral domain into the conventional. The extent to which this has happened and should happen—as in the example of consensual sex between unmarried adults—is a source of great disagreement among us. More traditional societies view social arrangements, including those embodying serious status inequalities, as fundamental and permanent, thereby collapsing the conventional into the moral. In such communities, people are morally obligated to fulfill their predestined social duties and are so judged; what many of us see as conventions they see as emanating from natural law.

In orthodox Hinduism, for example, customs such as arranged marriages, food taboos, sleeping arrangements, menstrual seclusion, and cremation are seen as part of the given moral order.

> What is natural or moral has not been narrowed down to the idea of an individual, empowered and free to create relationships at will through contract. Forms of human association are thought to be found (natural law), not founded (conventionism). In those parts of the world, the idea that social practices are conventions plays a minimal role in the child's developing understanding of the source of obligations.
> *(Shweder, Mahapotro, and Miller 1987, 4)*

In a comparative study of children and adults in America and among Brahman Hindus in India, Shweder and his associates illustrate these profound cultural differences. While both Indians and Americans, they point out, might consider it wrong for a doctor to refuse medical treatment because a patient cannot pay the fee, for Indians that wrong is less serious than for a widow to eat fish, or for a menstruating woman to cook for or sleep in the same bed as her husband. Indeed, these authors contend, for Brahman Indians hardly any rules are perceived as conventional. The designation of social rules as merely conventional, and thus not inherently important, is entirely culturally determined (ibid.).

These cross-cultural data remind us that the Brahman outlook found a significant counterpart in our society until some decades ago, and it still has strong support. In Victorian England, according to philosopher Alasdair MacIntyre:

> [S]trong notions of impropriety attached to violations of the compartmentalizing boundaries of social life. To know what conversation, what manners, what clothing was appropriate and proper to whom, where, and when was indispensable social and moral knowledge. . . . And impropriety was itself understood to be a species of immorality. *(MacIntyre 1990, 26)*

The idea that moral norms are culturally determined is itself contested precisely because it tends to undermine the importance of maintaining a robust domain of the moral. The belief that there is a moral valence to convention-respecting behavior (even if culture-dependent) tends to make respect for convention a matter of obligation for individuals, especially children, so long as social institutions like schools choose to require adherence to the specific convention in question.[3] This point of view received its classic expression by Emile Durkheim (quoted in Chapter 2, p. 24):

> [T]he child must learn respect for the rule; he must learn to do his duty because it is his duty, because he feels obliged to do so even though the task may not seem an easy one. Such an apprenticeship, which can only be quite incomplete in the family, must devolve upon the school. In fact, there is a whole system of rules in the school that predetermine the child's conduct. He must come to class regularly, he must arrive at a specified time and with an appropriate bearing and attitude. He must not disrupt things in class. He must have learned his lessons, done his homework, and have done so reasonably well, etc. There are, therefore a host of obligations that the child is required to shoulder. Together they constitute the discipline of the school.
>
> ❦❦❦❦❦
>
> This, then, is the true function of discipline. It is not a simple procedure aimed at making the child work, stimulating his desire for instruc-

---

[3] Recall that the Catholic students studied by Nucci premised their response on the assumption that the Church had decided to withdraw its former prohibition.

tion, or husbanding the energies of the teacher. It is essentially an instrument—difficult to duplicate—of moral education.
(Durkheim 1925/1961, 147–149)

Maria believes that the imposition of obligations on students requires a
stronger ground of justification than convention. She would be especially re-
pelled by the rigor of Durkheim's position, but draws back from a milder version as well. A person's view on these questions implicates the issue of the validity of authority and tradition as sources of moral guidance (an issue we
consider in Chapter 4).

The distinction between morality and convention may therefore be questioned on polar grounds: either that it is all morality or that it is all convention. The former view is comfortable with the imposition of traditional
conventions on nonconformists. Its adherents would admonish teachers,
schools, and school systems to uphold the moral importance of insisting on
convention-respecting behavior, and not readily to find traditional conventions (such as those reflecting gender roles) morally objectionable. The other
view does not look to customary practices for moral precepts. It rather sees
moral value in fostering a critical attitude toward traditional norms and developing reflective, independent thinking about matters of moral choice. It
views traditional conventions not only as often lacking affirmative moral
value, but as at times possessing a *negative* moral valence, as morally objectionable. It seems evident to us that the degree of attraction to (and repulsion
from) each of these poles powerfully influences the way one applies the
moral/conventional dichotomy.

Perhaps we can usefully consider the question of the moral domain by
turning from attempts to define its scope to examining its effects. We will consider some characteristics that are associated with matters thought to have
moral significance, specifically the hypothesis that moral principles are both
obligatory and *universal*.

THE MORAL DOMAIN: OBLIGATORY

Morality is, above all, typically regarded as prescriptive. It does not describe
behavior, it evaluates it. Morality tells us what we ought to do and not do.
Obligation carries the meaning of its Latin root, *ligare*, to bind. In the words
of the twentieth-century British philosopher, R.M. Hare: "[A] moral judgement has to be such that if a person assents to it, he must assent to some imperative sentence derivable from it" (Hare 1952, 171–172).

Yet, may one reason in a converse direction, asserting that obligation is
not merely a characteristic of a moral norm, but a basis for terming a norm
moral rather than conventional? The question is as to the source of obligation, specifically, whether the empirical fact that a norm is widely perceived as
obligatory warrants our assigning it moral force. Certainly, the *absence* of such
a consensus implies that we are outside the moral domain. Imagine a teacher

who is offended by a student's illness, a teacher who believes that being sick is a purposeful evasion of responsibility and an assault on the well-being of the group. Presumably we would have no sympathy for such a person's indignation. We would in fact suggest she seek help for her distorted thinking. Samuel Butler's satirical fantasy, *Erewhon*, portrayed an entire society that believed illness was an intentional avoidance of responsibility. It had laws against illness, putting sick people in prison while treating with sympathy and solicitude those who forged checks and robbed banks. The sick were held in contempt, made to feel guilty, and sent to "straighteners." Vandalizing a widow's home, by contrast, merited only a simple apology for the inconvenience it caused.

The more challenging question is whether, to establish that a traditional norm is a moral matter, it suffices that there is widespread support for its obligatory character, notwithstanding a widespread challenge to it. So, Maria does not like crude language but recognizes that, although some doubtless feel as she does, swearing has become quite common and many no longer object to it in most forms. It is for that reason that she is inclined to view it more as a matter of taste than morality. Although she, or others, might ask (or tell) students not to swear in front of her as a matter of courtesy, she is reluctant simply to forbid it outright. Maria is more inclined to move against the exploitative, manipulative qualities expressed in card-trading, which she tends to feel are antisocial qualities even though not generally condemned in our culture. She holds back from acting on that belief, however, recognizing the widespread acceptability of those qualities, even though she doesn't personally accept the moral judgment implicit in that acceptance.

Over the past decades many practices thought a matter of obligation— avoiding "illegitimate" births or personal debt are negative examples, caring for the poor and visiting the sick are positive ones—seem to have lost their moral valence and entered the domain of taste and preference. Although changes in moral thinking may have played a causal role in changes in social practices, anyone familiar with twentieth-century social history will probably not need convincing that moral judgments tend to follow, more than lead, changes brought on by nonmoral forces (such as credit cards and birth control measures). One of the enduring "fault lines" in current cultural controversies is between those who strongly regret the decline of the scope of obligation and those who tend to welcome it. Maria's reluctance to judge swearing as wrongful is in significant part a reflection of her attraction to the "welcoming" end of that spectrum. One who is more respectful of tradition as a moral litmus test would more readily respond to the call to take a stand against the further "erosion" of moral standards, and would find less reason to perceive as personal his or her moral stance.

If it is moral judgments that tend to have an obligatory component, what of judgments that are not morally grounded? The words "good" and "ought" have both moral and nonmoral meanings. "Good weather is not morally good; the wrong way to sew on a button is not morally wrong; commendation of your style as a golfer, or of you for your style as a golfer, would not be moral commendation" (Warnock 1971, 12). These judgments carry no imperative; one "ought" to sew and golf well only if one *chooses* those goals. So, we say, "If you want to get good grades, you ought to do your homework"; "If you want to be a good swimmer, you ought to practice"; "If you want a good education, you ought to go to the University of Pennsylvania." These if-then type of statements were called hypothetical imperatives by the German Enlightenment philosopher Immanuel Kant (1724–1804); they are conditional oughts only. Goodness in a moral sense, however, is obligatory in itself, and it is viewed as appropriate to insist that a child do what he or she must do in order to be good.

THE MORAL DOMAIN: UNIVERSALIZABLE

Maria struggles over the permissibility of swearing because, in part, she is uncertain as to the universality[4] of its wrongness. To say lying and cheating are wrong suggests that they are wrong in all, or virtually all, circumstances and wrong for all, or virtually all, people. It is to say that it is no more right to lie on a rainy than on a sunny day, to lie to the weak than to the strong, to lie for a good outcome than for a bad one, or for Mark than for Peter to lie.

One meaning of universal, then, is our willingness to generalize the rightness or wrongness of the act (or belief) across almost all circumstances and people. You may prefer to lie, choose to lie, or seek to justify a lie, but that does not destroy the proposition that, presumptively at least, it is a wrongful act. The principle of universality as essential to morality goes deep in our moral tradition. Core to the ethical philosophy of Immanuel Kant is his famous categorical imperative, "I should never act except in such a way that I can also will that my maxim should become a universal law" (Kant 1785/1993, 14). This axiom is analogous to the religious precept to do unto others only what you would have others do unto you. The test of any moral principle is its susceptibility to being universalized, being applied to all those in similar situations.

The principle of universality asks of a moral actor that he or she accept a *disinterested* point of view. In ethicist Sidney Callahan's words:

> The central insight and personal commitment undergirding the moral life is that other persons and their interests are as valuable as ones own. While ones private interests are vividly experienced and of immediate concern, moral persons accept the reality that certain basic interests of others have claims equal to one's own. . . . Duties are the names given to those responses that one feels bound or pulled or obligated to do.
> *(Callahan 1994, 62)*

---

[4] In using this simpler term hereafter, we will mean it in the special sense of universalizable, rather than as indicating that the practice in question is universally *regarded* as wrong.

This focus on disinterestedness leads some to a vigorous identification of moral norms with a system of rules thought to express their implications in various situations. According to Emile Durkheim, moral behavior "conforms to pre-established rules":

> To conduct one's self morally is a matter of abiding by a norm. . . . This domain of morality is the domain of duty; duty is prescribed behavior. . . . Thus, we can say that morality consists of a system of rules of action that predetermine conduct. They state how one must act in given situations; and to behave properly is to obey conscientiously.
> (*Durkheim 1925/1961, 23–24*)

The apparent consensus supporting the principle of universality masks, however, significant differences in the rigor of the concept, by reason of the inherent ambiguity in the notion of similar situations. The debate is over what we will term "strong" versus "open" universality—the reluctance or readiness to allow aspects of particular contexts to rebut the presumption or narrow its scope. To some, moral principles apply with a minimum of conditions; qualifications are seen as "exceptions," undermining the moral imperative of the norm. To others, however, it is only with perceptive attention to the nuances of moral contexts that one can judge the rightness or wrongness of actions or intentions. In its polar form, this latter view comes close to denying the idea of universalizability altogether.

The following story, told by the anti-Nazi martyr, Lutheran pastor Dietrich Bonhoeffer, poses the question:

> [A] teacher asks a child in front of the class whether it is true that his father often comes home drunk. It is true, but the child denies it. The teacher's question has placed him in a situation for which he is not yet prepared. He feels only that what is taking place is an unjustified interference in the order of the family and that he must oppose it. What goes on in the family is not for the ears of the class in school. The family has its own secret and must preserve it. The teacher has failed to respect the reality of this institution. . . . As a simple no to the teacher's question the child's answer is certainly untrue; yet at the same time it nevertheless gives expression to the truth that the family is an institution *sui generis* and that the teacher had no right to interfere in it.
> (*Bonhoeffer 1955, 330*)

To Kant, the belief that one had "no right" to ask a question does not justify lying as a response. (See the excerpt at p. 61 in the following section of this chapter.) Bonhoeffer's position appears to rest on the (unspoken) judgment that the teacher's question put the child in an untenable bind. Even if, despite the power dynamic between teacher and child, he had been able to reply by challenging the propriety of the question, such a challenge would probably have been taken as admitting the truth of the teacher's assertion; though framed as a question, it implied that the child's father *was* a drunkard.

To Kant, these fact-specific details are not so much untrue as they are irrelevant; he is reluctant to admit them into the moral calculus.

Legal philosopher Michael Moore has questioned the Kantian view, introducing the concept of "moral plausibility" in support of what we have termed open, rather than strong, universality:

> There are very few (if any) plausible candidates for the kind of short and snappy injunctions that can be fitted on one stone tablet. . . . What would we think of a person who could save his family from wrongful killing by another but refused to do so because the only means available involved: killing the aggressor, telling a lie to the aggressor, or not keeping a promise to the aggressor? Despite Kant's famous views to the contrary, I would think that such a person not only lacks virtue, but that he is derelict in his moral duties.
>
> The point is that moral norms must have exceptions implicit in them to have any moral plausibility. To be morally plausible, "thou shalt not kill" must be taken to be an elliptical reference to a much more complicated norm: "Don't kill, unless in self-defense, to protect your family, to aid in a just war lawfully declared, to execute those deserving of the death penalty such as Adolph Eichmann . . . ," etc. [T]here is no reason to suppose that moral truths are simple. Indeed, as science shows us about the world of fact, there is every reason to think that moral laws are quite complex—as complex as the scientific laws that govern the behavior of physical objects. No one expects all of science to be statable in ten rules of very short compass. *(Moore 1989, 315)*

The "grammar of morality" implicates more than the scope and characteristics of the moral domain. It includes the further question, what is the *focus* of moral judgments? An act does not occur in a vacuum. We need to consider whether, in evaluating an act, one should look to its likely (or actual) consequences or to some inherent quality that determines its goodness. Moreover, beyond attending to the morality of the act itself, most of us believe (particularly with developing children, though to some extent with everyone) that our judgment should also reflect the child's "character," those abiding dispositions that are the wellsprings of action. Finally, we tend naturally to look at the more immediate precipitant of action, the child's present state of mind—his or her knowledge, intentions, motives, capacity to choose another course, and deliberative processes. In the event, it may be these more particular aspects of the moral situation that are most pertinent to our judging. We take up each in turn.

THE MORAL SITUATION: THE SALIENCE OF CONSEQUENCES

According to utilitarian philosopher John Stuart Mill (1806–1873) our moral sightings should fix not on the nature of the act or actor but on the consequences that follow in its wake. "[N]o known ethical standard decides an action to be good or bad because it is done by a good or a bad man, still less because done by an amiable, a brave, or a benevolent man, or the contrary" (Mill 1861/1979, 21). Utilitarian thinking judges the morality of an act by its contribution to overall happiness. It is a form of the broader concept, consequentialism, which describes all approaches that judge the morality of an act by its consequences, whether the salient consequence is overall utility or some other value. Our public life tends to regard consequentialist thinking as self-evidently correct; its wide acceptance fits the pragmatism that has long characterized the American spirit, and is attested by the ready resort to cost-benefit analysis in judging competing policy initiatives.

Its chief competitor in moral thinking takes a rights or duty-based approach to moral questions. Under it, certain actions are wrong because they violate some obligation that we owe to others (or even to ourselves). Lying, for example, is condemned, not because without a certain measure of trust in another's word interpersonal transactions become difficult, but because people are entitled not to be lied to. Why? One answer, derived from Kant, is that to lie to another is to treat him or her as a means to one's own ends, as a thing rather than a person. This second view—which bears the odd term, deontological (from a Greek word meaning that which is binding)—finds support in concern about two ethical failings of consequentialism.

First, in application consequentialism cannot respond adequately to the recognition that judging consequences is a slippery affair at best, seriously complicated by the problems of taking full account of less immediately visible costs and benefits and of assigning quantifiable weights to them. The tendency is to accept rather casual assumptions as to the probable results of differing courses of action—in particular, those pitting long-term against short-term consequences—and to overlook consequences not readily expressed in terms of dollar value. Too casual a calculus of consequences reduces itself to an easy justification for unexpressed political and moral preferences, which should instead be the focus of avowed attention. Examples from personal and public life abound: Consider the question of the harm and the good thought to be done by corporal punishment of children, or by the taxation of capital gains at a preferential rate.

Critics of consequentialism presumably believe (as some assert) that it is especially susceptible to this self-justifying tendency. John Stuart Mill challenges the easy acceptance of such an assertion, asking: "[I]s utility the only creed which is able to furnish us with excuses for evil-doing and means of cheating our own conscience?" His impassioned negative answer is worth recalling:

> They [excuses] are afforded in abundance by all doctrines which recognize as a fact in morals the existence of conflicting considerations, which all doctrines do that have been believed by sane persons. . . . There is no ethical creed which does not temper the rigidity of its laws by giving a certain latitude, under the moral responsibility of the agent, for accommodation to peculiarities of circumstances; and under every creed, at the

opening thus made, self-deception and dishonest casuistry get in. . . . , with greater or with less success, according to the intellect and virtue of the individual. . . .
(Mill 1861/1979, 25)

A second ethical failing seems inherent in consequentialism. It is willing simply to aggregate harms and benefits, regardless of the justification for inflicting or tolerating harms to those who do not deserve them. It is illustrated by the classic hypothetical situation of the five dying people, each of whom needs a different organ to survive. By killing one person, and "harvesting" his or her organs, five lives can be saved, and only one lost, a net gain of four lives. Yet nearly all would condemn the act as obviously immoral. The prospective victim is readily thought to be "entitled" to live, notwithstanding the greater good that assertedly would follow his being sacrificed. That moral intuition, it is posited, is the root of deontological thinking about ethics.

The problem with this hypothetical story is that one would be hard-pressed to find a consequentialist who actually believes that the organ harvest *would* be morally justified. One can find more realistic analogues in much contemporary policy analysis. One example is the practice of group punishment, imposing a sanction on a school class when a single but unknown student has done something wrong, as a means either of forcing the guilty party to come forward or of conscripting his or her classmates in efforts to discourage repetition. Consequentialist justifications for this act would focus on weighing the harm to the innocent students against the good attributed to the act not being repeated or the group coming to take responsibility for (some of) the actions of its members.

A deontological approach would simply say that it is wrong to impose a sanction on an innocent person for the sake of some greater overall good, but a consequentialist would readily come up with situations in which our moral intuition is to the contrary. One example is compulsory vaccination against smallpox.[5] Some suffered, even died, from allergic reactions to the vaccine. These harms were of course not intended, but in other cases some had their personal (at times even religiously based), scruples intentionally overridden. Yet few would question the moral standing of the compulsion involved, in light of the enormous benefit to life and health in the virtual extinction of the disease.

The debate over deontology and consequentialism is an enduring one, with far more complexity than we address here. The excerpt from Strike and Soltis, p. 63 in the next section, is an introduction to the question.

THE MORAL SITUATION: CHARACTER

To some, morality is largely a matter of being a certain sort of person. What sort? One of good character. A person of good character has those reliable

---

[5] We owe this helpful example to Dr. Samuel M. Craver of Virginia Commonwealth University.

characteristics, those habitual ways of reacting, that are virtuous. The term character can, of course, include a fuller constellation of traits (humorous, serious, introverted, extroverted), but here we limit it to traits of moral significance, such as benevolence, bravery, tolerance, steadfastness, persistence, self-restraint, temperance, loyalty, and generosity. (We consider in Chapter 5 the questions whether and how one may generate a "catalogue" of virtues). There is a revival of philosophical interest in character (schools have always considered it central); its origins, however, are ancient, going back to Aristotle, who saw virtue (*arete*) as the greatest good, the goal (*telos*) of all human striving. His major work, *Nichomachean Ethics* (1987), is devoted primarily to explicating the relationship between virtue (that which we desire for its own sake) and other goods productive of happiness (*eudaimonia*). We desire health and money, for example, not in and of themselves, but only insofar as they make possible the pursuit of virtue.

Virtue ethicists prioritize the actor (or agent, as philosophers like to call us) over the act on several grounds: First, they claim, our conduct is in fact derivative of who we are; who we are does not derive from our conduct. Second, it is intuitively obvious that, for the most part, when judging people we appraise their character, their abiding dispositions, goals and overall life patterns; we tend to excuse the moral error made by the well intended and are suspicious of the good deed displayed by the badly intended. Third, the commingling of feelings and thoughts—moral will, moral sensitivity, and moral analysis—that compose any virtue reflects the real-life psychological messiness of moral behavior. (For one articulation of the virtue-ethics approach, see the excerpt by James Griffin at p. 67 in the next section of this chapter, and for a thoroughly worked-out application of the concept of virtue ethics, and its difference from an act-oriented morality, see the excerpt by Rosalind Hursthouse at p. 69 in that section).

The virtue ethicists come in two variants, which compete vigorously with each other in today's marketplace of ideas. To many character-oriented thinkers, moral virtues (such as those mentioned above) have in common their demand for mastery over what used to be termed our "appetites." Contemporary philosopher Philippa Foot refers to virtues as "correctives," because they stand "at a point at which there is some temptation to be resisted or deficiency of motivation to be made good. As Aristotle put it, virtues are about what is difficult . . . " (Foot 1978, 8).

So, Hardie Knox has a number of routines—daily greetings, rituals, chores—in his classroom. The point of them, to Hardie and his like-minded colleagues, is that, while not of intrinsic importance, they "build character." Good character is linked to habit formation: Character refers to personal traits of moral significance, habits to patterns of action. Aristotle (1987, Bk. 2, Chs. 3, 4), for example, who stressed the centrality of character and virtue, asserted that, just as one becomes a builder by building, a harpist by playing the harp, and brave by doing brave acts, one becomes virtuous by acting virtuously.

To Hardie, morality is primarily about developing self-restraint regarding self-serving impulses. It is about becoming able and willing to regard the interests of other people with something other than indifference or competitive hostility. That is why he requires children to perform routines, even though the specific routine may have no independent moral valence. The children's growing self-control, he maintains, will benefit others and add value to the community's well-being. Thus, for Hardie, following reasonable rules is itself a moral matter, and it is a teacher's option to select the (reasonable) rules that he or she will prescribe. For the teacher, deciding whether to prescribe any particular rule is optional; for students, following a rule that the teacher has chosen is obligatory.

Hardie might cite William James in support:

> No matter how full a reservoir of *maxims* one may possess, and no matter how good one's *sentiments* may be, if one have not taken advantage of every concrete opportunity to *act*, one's character may remain entirely unaffected for the better. With mere good intentions hell is proverbially paved. . . . A tendency to act only becomes effectively ingrained in us in proportion to the uninterrupted frequency with which the actions actually occur, and the brain "grows" to their use. *Keep the faculty of effort alive in you by a little gratuitous exercise every day.* That is, be systematically ascetic or heroic in little unnecessary points, do every day or two something for no other reason than that you would rather not do it, so that when the hour of dire need draws nigh, it may find you not unnerved and untrained to stand the test.
>
> *(James 1890/1950, 1: 125–126) (emphasis in original)*

Both Aristotle's and James' thoughts suggest that character-orientation is not so much a description of the nature of morality as it is a pedagogical approach, one grounded in the view that people may be brought to act morally by coming to rely on established qualities ("virtues") cultivated through training. A dominant focus on character and habit may proceed from the implicit belief that there is no great need to dwell on the problem of distinguishing good from bad, that one with a "built" character will act rightly, and that training one to act rightly does not entail a difficult problem of saying what that means.

Maria Laszlo views Hardie's "routines" as needlessly burdensome, even dangerous, exactly because she regards the making of morally sound decisions as more contextual, more nuanced, more difficult than Hardie acknowledges. Excessive emphasis on habit, in this view, may actually make children less likely to do the right thing, for it neglects what they most need to develop, their powers of reflection.

The other variant of virtue ethics owes its current visibility to feminist thinkers such as Nel Noddings and Carol Gilligan who have advocated what is often termed an "ethic of care"(or an ethic of relation). These writers find moral salience in the stance with which an actor views another person, and a surer guide to action in the realm of affect than of habit. They de-emphasize a morality of rules, which would attempt to imprint maxims of behaviors onto children (or adults); such an approach is seen as both excessively binding and, where no rule is in sight, seriously deficient in its ethical strength. According to the ethic of care, the likelihood of pursuing one path or another has little to do with the dogged inculcation of habitual patterns of behavior through rigorous and lengthy apprenticeships and the "curbing" and "correction" of natural appetites. Rather, an ethic of care views as fundamental our ability to call on our inherent capacity for empathy, a natural affective response to the other, though surely needing to be nourished and cultivated. (For a fuller discussion, see the excerpt by Noddings at p. 72 in the next section of this chapter.)

This insight is brought home in a moving description of "righteous gentiles," those who, in World War II, saved European Jews from extermination by hiding them in their homes (Oliner and Oliner, 1988). When the rescuers were asked why they risked their lives for strangers, most cited affiliations with political, religious, or social groups that supported the rescuing efforts; many others were moved by empathy for the Jews' distress. While thus coming to the decision "built" with virtues, in the moment their decisions were spontaneous. For them, "helping Jews was less a decision made at a critical juncture than a choice prefigured by an established character and way of life" (id., 222). Despite the obvious risks, most of the rescuers reported that they made the decision in "minutes" (id., 169), and only a handful reported having reasoned it out. Indeed, many reported not experiencing a choice; they could not do otherwise.

The ethic of care shares with more traditional character approaches the view that a person faced with a moral decision will come to know the right response more or less immediately. Most of our behavior, after all, is not based on deep reflection. Daily, we have opportunities to do what is right—take time for a friend, help someone in distress, resist self-aggrandizement—and to do what is wrong—fabricate false excuses, ignore a request, keep excessive change.

Both variants of virtue ethics, then, while acknowledging that virtues must be nurtured to flourish, are skeptical about the rational component of moral decision making. With contemporary British philosopher Michael Oakeshott, they are more trusting of a spontaneous response than of one that is the product of rational principled reflection. The latter, claims Oakeshott, "breeds nothing but distraction and moral instability"; fortunately, life's decisions are dominated by "settled habit[s] of behaviour" (id. 1962, 74, 79). They take over "in all the emergencies of life when time and opportunity for reflection are lacking" (id., 62). A similar thought is expressed succinctly in a famous Scripture: "Train up a child in the way he should go: and when he is old, he will not depart from it" (*Proverbs* XXII:6).

Yet, we must pause once again before embracing fully the attractions of these thoughts. Talk of virtuous traits may mean rather less than it appears to. Certainly, bravery, loyalty, persistence, and self-denial can be put to evil uses as readily as good. Character-oriented approaches to morality cannot avoid the importance of action, for action is how we come to know character: To be a courageous person, one must do courageous deeds, the caring person is noted for caring actions. The contemporary British philosopher G.J. Warnock insists that actions are more "fundamental" than character, motives, or feelings:

> A person is morally good or bad primarily at least because of what he does or omits to do. A morally bad character is a disposition to act morally badly, or wrongly. Motives typically, and feelings often, tend to issue in actions. [I]t seems that, when moral issues come up, there is always involved, more or less directly, some question of . . . doings or non-doings. . . .
> (Warnock 1971, 12–13)

A final question for us to address then is whether there is a way of combining character and action through a closer look at a person's state of mind, his or her immediate motive to act (rather than settled disposition), his or her intentions, choices, or decisional processes.

THE MORAL SITUATION: THE SALIENCE OF THE ACTOR'S STATE OF MIND

A different set of approaches finds deontology, consequentialism, and virtue ethics all wanting. One variant would look more to the motivation immediately behind the act, asserting, for example, that an act may appear benevolent (or malevolent)—but take on the opposite quality once its intention or motive is known. A child's offer to remain after class to help clean up looks less worthy once we find out that her plan was to rifle the supply closet. More controversially, we may excuse, or at least condemn less strongly, a student's lie when we learn that he sought to save a fellow from unwarranted harm.

An emphasis on motivation may proceed from skepticism about character-oriented, as well as act-oriented, approaches. Maria does not share Hardie's enthusiasm for character-building, or rather her interpretation of character is less puritanical than Hardie's. She too cares about qualities within the person, but she finds the motive of each particular act more important than general dispositions. Virtues and habits, however punctilious and self-restrained, can be mindless, sometimes injurious. Indeed, she is suspicious of those brave stiff-upper-lip folks who are dutiful, who would never cheat or lie, yet are often intolerant, and who have an almost priggish pride in their own goodness.

Another critique of character-based approaches also regards the habits of self-denial, obedience, and caring as morally ambiguous at best, emphasizing instead informed reflection on alternatives. In this view, one version of which is associated with the work of the psychologist and educational philosopher Lawrence Kohlberg (1927–1987), the moral law does not simply set out specific rules. Maria manifests a skepticism about rule-following similar to her skepticism about act-oriented morality. She wants her children to understand the reasoning behind rules, indeed to do their own reasoning and formulate their own rules fitting their own circumstances. John Dewey noted that rule-based habits may become perfunctory and encrusted. Under changed conditions, where reexamination is required, adherence to habit leads us astray: "The 'good' man who rests on his oars, who permits himself to be propelled simply by the momentum of his attained right habits, loses alertness; he ceases to be on the lookout. With that loss, his goodness drops away from him" (Dewey 1908/1960, 132).

The premise of this approach is that the actor may be said to have had a choice; where the capacity to choose is lacking, blame is ordinarily withheld. The legal defense of duress in its traditionally narrow sense is a manifestation of a widely held moral insight: One who is induced by the threat of serious physical harm to commit a wrongful act is normally exonerated. It is not easy, however, to articulate that "certain capacity of choice" which G.J. Warnock (1971, 144) plausibly describes as the condition of culpability. The exoneration surely should not be limited to threats of physical harm; however, it bears emphasis that loss of expected advantages, however strongly desired, plainly does *not* suffice. There is a critical difference between, "I'll beat you up at recess if you don't steal something out of that girl's book bag," and "I won't be your friend [or let you join our club] unless you steal something." The siren song of peer pressure, or the shame of failure—"I had no choice not to cheat on the examination; I needed to pass the course to graduate, and after my parents had paid all that money for my education I couldn't let them down"—may ring sympathetically in the ears of many people, young and older, today, but if there is any meaning to the idea of moral obligation, it must exclude as a justification or excuse the idea that one would have been better off by doing the wrongful act than refraining from it.

We come to the end of our search for the right part of the moral elephant on which to focus: Is it the person or the act, and if the act, its essential righteousness or its consequences? Or do we abandon these larger perspectives and look more narrowly at the action and actor in their immediate context, much as one might observe (and judge) the act of skiing simultaneously with the mountain slope and weather conditions? We leave these as open questions for the moment and turn in Chapter 4 to a related inquiry: What sort of animal are moral judgments, and what are their sources and the bases of their legitimacy?

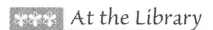 ## At the Library

Immanuel Kant, *On a Supposed Right to Lie Because of Philanthropic Concerns*
(1797/1993, 63–66)

In the periodical *France*, for 1797, . . . in an article bearing the title "On Political Reactions" by Benjamin Constant, there is contained . . . the following passage:

> The moral principle stating that it is a duty to tell the truth would make any society impossible if that principle were taken singly and unconditionally. We have proof of this in the very direct consequences which a German philosopher has drawn from this principle. This philosopher goes so far as to assert that it

would be a crime to lie to a murderer who has asked whether our friend who is being pursued by the murderer had taken refuge in our house.

The French philosopher [Constant] . . . refutes this principle in the following way:

It is a duty to tell the truth. The concept of duty is inseparable from the concept of right. A duty is what in one being corresponds to the right of another. Where there are no rights, there are no duties. To tell the truth is thus a duty, but it is a duty only with regard to one who has a right to the truth. But no one has a right to a truth that harms others.

The [first fallacy] here is in the statement: "To tell the truth is a duty, but it is a duty only with regard to one who has a right to the truth."

▼▼▼▼▼

Truthfulness in statements that cannot be avoided is the formal duty of man to everyone, however great the disadvantage that may arise therefrom for him or for any another. And even though by telling an untruth I do no wrong to him who un-justly compels me to make a statement, yet by this falsification, which as such can be called a lie . . . , I do wrong to duty in general in a most essential point. That is, . . . I bring it about that statements in general find no credence, and hence also that all rights based on contracts become void and lose their force, and this is a wrong done to mankind in general.

Hence a lie defined merely as an intentionally untruthful declaration to another man does not require the additional condition that it must do harm to another. . . . For a lie always harms another; if not some other human being, then it nevertheless does harm to humanity in general, inasmuch as it vitiates the very source of right.

. . . [I]f by telling a lie you have in fact hindered someone who was even now planning a murder, then you are legally responsible for all the consequences that might result therefrom. But if you have adhered strictly to the truth, then public justice cannot lay a hand on you, whatever the unforeseen consequence may be. It is indeed possible that after you have honestly answered Yes to the murderer's question as to whether the intended victim is in the house, the latter went out unobserved and thus eluded the murderer, so that the death would not have come about. However, if you had told a lie and said that the intended victim was not in the house, and he has actu-ally (though unbeknownst to you) gone out, with the result that by doing so he has been met by the murderer and thus the deed has been perpetrated, then in this case you may be justly accused as having caused his death. For if you had told the truth as best as you knew it, then the murderer might perhaps have been caught by neighbors who came running while he was searching the house for his intended victim, and thus the deed might have been prevented. Therefore, whoever tells a lie, regardless of how good his intentions may be, must answer for the consequences resulting there-from . . . , regardless of how unforseen those consequences may be. . . .

▼▼▼▼▼

[Since] it was merely an accident that the truth of the statement did harm to the occupant of the house, . . . [one] does not actually harm the one who suffers be-cause of it; rather, this harm is caused by accident.

───────────

This is the classic statement of the view that duty-based prohibitions—"Do not lie"—admit of no exceptions. Do you find merit in Kant's claim that we are bound to live by those duties that generally benefit humankind, for example, speaking only truth, even when another person may deservedly benefit in a particular instance from our lie? Do you find merit in the idea that, if you have spoken truth, you are not responsible for the consequences, good or bad, but if you have lied, you are responsible, even if you acted in a reasonable attempt to prevent the bad result?

▼▼▼
Kenneth A. Strike and Jonas F. Soltis,
The Ethics of Teaching
(1992, 11–17)

Two Ways to Think about Ethics

[We examine here] the features of two major types of ethical theories—those that decide the rightness or wrongness of an action in terms of its consequences and those that do not. We shall refer to these as consequentialist theories and nonconsequentialist[6] theories, respectively. Let us consider their basic features.

Consequentialist Theories and Benefit Maximization

Consequentialist ethical theories hold that the rightness or wrongness of an action is to be decided in terms of its consequences. One way to understand consequentialist theories is to see them as committed to a principle that we will call the *principle of benefit maximization.* This principle holds that, whenever we are faced with a choice, the best and most just decision is the one that results in the most good or the greatest benefit for the most people. . . . It does not directly tell us what is to count as a benefit or a good. That requires additional reflection. It merely says that once we know what is good, the best decision is the one that maximizes good outcomes. Thus, if Ms. Jones wished to decide on the merits of lying to Mr. Pugnacious [about the behavior of his son, a student in her class, out of fear that he will mistreat the boy] by using consequentialist reasoning, she would have to balance the benefits and harms of lying against the benefits and harms of not lying. . . .

▼▼▼▼▼

Consequentialist theories can differ over what they consider good. The most influential form of consequentialism . . . holds that the good is pleasure or happiness. . . . How do we decide what counts as the greatest good for the greatest number? The starting point in utilitarianism is the assumption that pleasure is good and pain is bad. If we want, therefore, to decide how well off any given individual person is, we must do so by measuring and adding up that person's total of pleasure and pain and by subtracting the total of pain from the total of pleasure. The result gives us a figure that is referred to as that person's utility. Deciding how well off a given society is is a matter of summing the utility of its individual members and dividing by the number of individuals in the population (providing, of course, that such

---

[6] [The authors use the term, nonconsequentialist, to refer to the theory that others (and we in the text) call deontological.]

things can be measured). This figure, known as the average utility, is a measure of general social welfare.

Deciding on the merits of a particular policy is a matter of determining its effects on the average utility. Those policies that produce the highest average utility are the most just. Thinking of moral problems from this perspective has the merit of reminding us that when we are evaluating the morality of an action or policy by judging its consequences, we must consider its consequences for everyone. If Ms. Jones is seriously to decide on the morality of lying to Mr. Pugnacious, she must consider all of the consequences for everyone affected. She must ask not only how her decision will affect her and Johnnie. She must ask such hard questions as whether her reputation as an honest person will be affected and whether any loss of respect for her truthfulness might not make her a poorer teacher. The other children in her class and in the school might also be affected by what she does. Utilitarianism requires that all of the consequences for everyone's well-being be taken into account.

Utilitarians sometimes disagree about whether the principle of benefit maximization should be applied to individual actions or to moral rules. Ms. Jones might reason thus: "The problem with asking me to decide whether it is right in this particular case to lie to Mr. Pugnacious is that I really do not have a very good idea of what the actual consequences will be. Perhaps I will save Johnnie a beating. But it is also possible that Mr. Pugnacious will find out that I lied to him. Johnnie might get an even worse beating then, and Mr. Pugnacious will never trust me again. I do, however, know that in the vast majority of cases the consequences of lying are less desirable than the consequences of truthfulness. Generally, honesty is the best policy. Since I am unsure of what the consequences of lying are in this particular case, I think I should do what I know is best as a general policy."

[Ms. Jones] might also have argued that it is dangerous to have people treat every decision as a case unto itself apart from any general rules of conduct. People are weak. Without the aid of moral rules they will do what is expedient, not what is right. And how can we have laws if we have to decide each and every case apart from the rest? Perhaps, then, it is moral rules or policies, and not actions, that should be evaluated.[7]

Before moving on to consider nonconsequentialist arguments, we should look at two problems with consequentialism. One difficulty is that consequentialism, particularly in its utilitarian form, requires us to have information that is normally difficult or impossible to attain. Consider how difficult it is to compare pleasures or pains. Does good company produce more or less pleasure than good food? Is it worse to sit on a tack or receive a cutting insult? Utilitarianism seems to require us not only to be able to answer such questions, but to quantify them. Next, it requires us not only to know all of the consequences of our actions or policies, but to be able to judge the impact of these actions and policies for the overall distribution of pleasure and pain for everyone affected. It appears that moral behavior requires an omniscience that is unavailable to most of us.

A second difficulty is that utilitarianism can produce results that seem morally abhorrent. Let us imagine that a dozen sadistic people have had the good fortune to have captured a potential victim. They are debating whether or not it would be

---

[7][This is often called rule utilitarianism, as distinguished from act utilitarianism.]

right to spend a pleasant evening torturing their captive. One of the group argues in the following way: "We must admit that by torturing this person we will cause a certain amount of pain. But think how much pleasure we will give ourselves. And there are a dozen of us. While this person's pain may exceed the pleasure of any one of us, it surely cannot exceed the pleasure of all of us. Thus the average utility is enhanced by torturing this person. We ought to do so." Supposing these judgments about the consequences of torture are correct, do the moral conclusions follow? If one accepts utilitarianism, they seem to. Yet we suspect our moral sensitivities would rebel against such an argument. If utilitarianism can justify such actions, perhaps we should be a bit suspicious of it.

NONCONSEQUENTIALIST THEORIES AND RESPECT FOR PERSONS

A second way to think about Ms. Jones's behavior is suggested by another thought. . . . Ms. Jones resents being lied to. Should she not treat Mr. Pugnacious as she expects to be treated by others?

This thought expresses a common moral idea. Its most familiar version is the Golden Rule, "Do unto others as you would have others do unto you." [We can] find out what additional ideas the Golden Rule contains by looking at it in a form offered by the German philosopher Immanuel Kant (1724–1804). Kant's central moral precept is called the categorical imperative. "So act that the maxim of your will could always hold at the same time as a principle establishing universal law." . . .

. . . What does it mean to say that a moral rule should be universal? Kant proposes a test to see if the principle underlying some action can be willed to be a universal law. If you are about to apply some moral principle to someone else, are you willing that it be applied to you in the same way? If you lie, are you willing to be lied to? If you steal, are you willing to be stolen from? . . . Kant has put in a more formal way what was implicit in Ms. Jones's reflection that she should treat Mr. Pugnacious as she would wish to be treated.

According to Kant, the Golden Rule requires that we act in ways that respect the equal worth of moral agents. It requires that we regard human beings as having intrinsic worth and treat them accordingly. [This] principle of equal respect involves three subsidiary ideas.

First, the principle of equal respect requires us to treat people as *ends rather than means.* That is, we . . . cannot treat people as though they were things, mere objects, who are valued only insofar as they contribute to our welfare. . . .

Second, we must regard all people as *free, rational, and responsible moral agents.* This means that we must respect their freedom of choice. And we must respect the choices people make even when we do not agree with them. . . .

Third, no matter how people differ, as moral agents they are of *equal* value. This does not mean that we must see people as equal insofar as their abilities or capacities are concerned. Nor does it mean that relevant differences among people cannot be recognized in deciding how to treat them. It is not, for example, a violation of equal respect to pay one person more than another because that person works harder and contributes more. That people are of equal value as moral agents means that they are entitled to the same basic rights and that their interests, though different, are of equal value. . . . No one is entitled to act as though his or her happiness counts more than the happiness of others. As persons, everyone has equal worth.

. . . Kant would wish to argue that all consequentialist positions will end up treating some persons as though they are means to the ends of others. When we seek to maximize the average happiness, are we not saying that we may trade the happiness of some for the happiness of others so long as the average happiness increases? When we do this are we not treating the happiness of those who are made less happy as a means to the happiness of others?

Thus Ms. Jones has another way to view her decision to lie to Mr. Pugnacious. She does not have to decide what action has the best consequences. She only has to decide whether her conduct conforms to the moral law—whether it can be consistently willed to be a universal rule of human conduct. She must treat Mr. Pugnacious as an end, not a means to someone else's well-being. Then she must do her duty. Ms. Jones, therefore, has a nonconsequentialist way of thinking about her behavior.

Let us consider two difficulties with this way of thinking. First, how can someone decide whether or not they are willing to have lying become a universal rule of conduct? Why is Ms. Jones unwilling to be lied to? What would we say to someone who argues that they are perfectly happy to have lying be a universal rule of conduct, that they do not care if they are lied to? Answers to such questions are soon likely to get us around to considering the undesirable consequences of lying. Lying cannot be accepted as a universal rule precisely because it has undesirable consequences. We cannot live with one another in peace if we are not usually honest. Such a turn of events poses a dilemma for nonconsequentialist theories. If they are unwilling altogether to consider the consequences of actions as relevant to their moral appraisal, it becomes hard to see how we could ever decide whether or not some moral principle could be universally willed. If, however, they are willing to talk about consequences, they will have to explain how they are different from any other consequentialist theory.

The second difficulty concerns how generally or specifically we should express the moral principle that underlies some action. Perhaps it is clear that we could not will lying to be a universal rule of conduct, but is it equally clear that we could not will lying in order to prevent the suffering of a child as a universal rule of conduct? How specific can we make our rules? If we must express them very generally, will our behavior not seem unresponsive to what may be very real and important differences in the circumstances under which we must act? If we can express them with considerable attention to circumstances, we reintroduce all of the vagueness into our choices that the categorical imperative seemed to offer hope of avoiding. . . .

. . . Ms. Jones's assessment of her actions seems to rely on two quite different ways of thinking about ethical matters. Both seem plausible. Neither seems fully adequate. Can these views be integrated in some reasonable fashion?

Virtue theory, as noted in the previous section of this chapter, seeks to avoid the perennial debate between consequentialism and deontology by focusing more on the actor than the act. The first excerpt that follows is a description and defense of a virtue-ethic approach. The next illustrates (rather than describes or defends) such an approach. It uses the specific context of a woman's decision whether to have an abortion. Recognizing the powerful feelings and judgments prompted by almost any discussion of abortion, we encourage you to read it less for whether the author "comes out" where you would than for your reaction to her discussion as a *way of thinking* about morality.

▼▼▼

James Griffin, "Virtue Ethics and Environs"
(1998, 58–62)

There are several lines of thought that seem to me to move us in the general direction of virtue ethics. I shall give the gist of just two of them.

One line of thought focuses on the nature of agents.[8] There is something deeply flawed about the spare, abstract picture of the agent at the heart of most modern moral philosophy. Both Kant and the classical utilitarians think of the moral agent as having little more than rationality and a psychologically rather simple capacity for happiness and unhappiness — "psychologically simple" because it is seen as rooted in the tastes and inclinations with which nature or nurture has endowed us. But this picture does not begin to do justice to the complexity of what it is to live a good life. A good life will, as the classical utilitarians say, contain enjoyable mental states, but it will also contain accomplishment, deep personal relations, understanding, dignity, and so on. Mental states are short term, but other good things in life require long-term commitments, which fill and give shape to our whole lives. Good lives are, therefore, inevitably lives of . . . deep commitments to particular persons, careers, institutions, and causes. And though a few of our enjoyable mental states are rooted in our tastes, most of the other good things in life are not. Nothing is life-enhancing simply in virtue of being the object of desire. We can want the wrong things, things that, when we get them, make us no better off, or even worse off. Our desires, aims, and goals are subject to rational constraints. Certain things are appropriate objects of desire; and though you and I can, because of our individual differences, vary greatly in the sort of life that would indeed be good for us, there are many things that are good generally, good in any characteristic human life.

A life of deep commitments is one in which feelings and dispositions are central. But, like desires, feelings and dispositions are subject to rational constraints. Hume and the subsequent Humean tradition that has dominated much modern moral philosophy and virtually all of the social sciences were wrong to separate reason and sentiment as sharply as they did. Reason is not inert; sentiment is not blind. Emotions have appropriate objects, and they fail as the emotions they are if they are directed at the wrong object. . . . And what motivates us in our search for a good life for ourselves must be compatible with what motivates us in our decent behavior toward others; there is only one person, and one personality, to fill both the self-interested and the other respecting roles.

Our commitments raise problems for direct forms of utilitarianism. We cannot simply abandon deep commitments whenever impartial utility calculation demands

---

[8] [Like most philosophers, the author uses the word agent to mean one who is responsible for his or her actions.]

it. Some of our commitments leave us free enough to do that, but many do not. The sort of persons that we want there to be—and, indeed, that utilitarians themselves should want there to be—cannot be impartial utility-maximizers act by act. Even allowing for all the ways in which the human will can be stretched, there are limits to it: complete impartiality is beyond the capacity of normal human agents.

▼▼▼▼▼

The second line of thought leading in the general direction of virtue ethics . . . centers on moral principles. The typical sort of general principles making up a moral code—say, "Don't deliberately kill the innocent against their will"—may have an important role to play in moral life, but that life cannot satisfactorily be conducted just by learning and applying such principles. The help that general principles give sooner or later runs out. The principle "Don't deliberately kill the innocent" runs out when . . . only by smothering a baby can one stop its cries from giving away the hiding place of the whole group to the Gestapo. Moral life can never be fully reduced to a code—that is, to a set of fairly brief, fairly general rules. Moral judgment may always have to be expressible without reference to particular persons, places, and times, but it may often have to deal with the rare, the unusual, the highly specific. The uncodifiability of ethics creates problems for many deontologists. Deontologists posit certain nonconsequentialist duties. But then they face the problem of identifying these duties. Some try to identify acts that are universally prohibited in virtue of their kind—say, deliberately killing the innocent—but it proves extremely hard to find satisfactory descriptions. This should not surprise us. We do not think that we can satisfactorily reduce a good doctor's behavior toward a patient, or a good teacher's toward a pupil, to a code. We should expect any such codes to be jejune. One learns best how to be a good doctor or a good teacher—perhaps one can only adequately learn—by watching closely someone who does the job especially well.

These two lines of thought—the one about agents and the other about principles—merge into a single line about how human beings can plausibly expect to live their lives well. They cannot plausibly expect to live by appeal to a single background principle, the principle of utility, and enormously complex cost-benefit calculations. Nor can they live by appeal to a code of general principles. They will live largely as prompted by their feelings and dispositions. That is why moral education, largely ignored in modern moral philosophy, is so important. Good behavior largely depends upon good feelings and dispositions, and they require training. . . .

▼▼▼▼▼

What ground does virtue ethics cover? It says, or so I am assuming to start with, that judgments about right and wrong are based on judgments about the virtues. For example, you must not kill the innocent *because* that would be contrary to the virtue of justice. But citing justice as one's reason is merely the shortest of first steps in ethics. Would it be unjust deliberately to kill the innocent in a case of euthanasia? In which cases? What is the content of justice? How, for instance, do we balance the claims of justice against those of beneficence? And clearly not every act of helping someone in need will be an example of the virtue of beneficence. Our feelings, even our kindly feelings, often lead us astray; we can help someone when it would have been better to let the person cope alone. Virtues are the *right* dispositions, and part of what goes into making them right is that they are in the right balance with one another. The proper domain of one virtue limits the proper domain of another. But what is central to any virtue ethics, then, is the deliberation that identifies the *right* dispositions. One can scarcely regard oneself as having given an account of what virtue ethics is unless one has supplied a fairly full account of what this deliberation is like. What sorts of considerations are central to *it*? And may they not turn out to be both independent of, and more basic than, the virtues?

An obvious reply on the part of virtue ethics is that all we need in order to identify the virtues is supplied by a relatively small cluster of ideas, centering on a conception of human flourishing. The virtues, one could then say, are what a member of a kind—a plant, an animal—needs for the kind to be successful. Now, it is true that from this consideration of what a species needs in order to flourish, one can derive at least a few moral conclusions. For the human species to flourish, its members clearly need some sort of respect for one another's lives, and they need a certain amount of benevolence. But the few conclusions that we can draw are too indeterminate to get us far. They leave virtually all the work of giving content to the notions of, say, justice and benevolence still to be done.

▼▼▼▼▼

Rosalind Hursthouse, "Virtue Theory and Abortion"
(1991, 226, 234–240)

The sort of ethical theory derived from Aristotle, variously described as virtue ethics, virtue-based ethics, or neo-Aristotelianism, is becoming better known, and is now quite widely recognized as at least a possible rival to deontological and utilitarian theories. . . . In this article I aim to deepen that understanding . . . by illustrating what the theory looks like when it is applied to a particular issue; in this case, abortion.

As everyone knows, the morality of abortion is commonly discussed in relation to just two considerations: first, and predominantly, the status of the fetus and whether or not it is the sort of thing that may or may not be innocuously or justifiably killed; and second, . . . women's rights. . . . Virtue theory quite transforms the discussion of abortion by dismissing the two familiar dominating considerations as, in a way, fundamentally irrelevant. In what way or ways, I hope to make both clear and plausible.

Let us first consider women's rights. Let me emphasize . . . that we are discussing the morality of abortion, not the rights and wrongs of laws prohibiting or permitting it. If we suppose that women do have a moral right to do as they choose with their own bodies, or, more particularly, to terminate their pregnancies, then it may well follow that a law forbidding abortion would be unjust; on this issue I have nothing to say in this article. But, putting all questions about the justice or injustice of laws to one side, and supposing only that women have such a moral right, *nothing follows* from this supposition about the morality of abortion, according to virtue theory, once it is noted (quite generally, not with particular reference to abortion) that in exercising a moral right I can do something cruel, or callous, or selfish, lightminded, self-righteous, stupid, inconsiderate, disloyal, dishonest—that is, act viciously. Love and friendship do not survive their parties' constantly insisting on their rights, nor do people live well, when they think that getting what they have a right to is of preeminent importance; they harm others, and they harm themselves. So whether women have a moral right to terminate their pregnancies is irrelevant within virtue theory, for it is irrelevant to the question, "In having an abortion in these circumstances, would the agent be acting virtuously or viciously or neither?"

What about the consideration of the status of the fetus . . .?

Now if we're using virtue theory, our first question is not "What do the familiar biological facts show—what can be derived from them about the status of the fetus?" but "How do these facts figure in the practical reasoning, actions and passions, thoughts and reactions, of the virtuous and the nonvirtuous? What is the mark of having the right attitude to these facts and what manifests having the wrong attitude to them?" This immediately makes essentially relevant such facts as that human parents, both male and female, tend to care passionately about their offspring, and that family relationships are among the deepest and strongest in our lives—and, significantly, among the longest-lasting.

These facts make it obvious that pregnancy is not just one among many other physical conditions; and hence that anyone who genuinely believes that an abortion is comparable to a haircut or an appendectomy is mistaken. The fact that the premature termination of a pregnancy is, in some sense, the cutting off of a new human life, and thereby . . . connects with all our thoughts about human life and death, parenthood, and family relationships, must make it a serious matter. To disregard this fact about it, to think of abortion as nothing but the killing of something that does not matter, or as nothing but the exercise of some right or rights one has, or as the incidental means to some desirable state of affairs, is to do something callous and light-minded, the sort of thing that no virtuous and wise person would do. It is to have the wrong attitude not only to fetuses, but more generally to human life and death, parenthood, and family relationships.

. . . I know that this is one of my tendentious points. In partial support of it I note that even the most dedicated proponents of the view that deliberate abortion is just like an appendectomy or haircut rarely hold the same view of spontaneous abortion, that is, miscarriage. It is not so tendentious of me to claim that to react to people's grief over miscarriage by saying . . . "What a fuss about nothing!" would be callous and light-minded, whereas to try to laugh someone out of grief over an appendectomy scar or a botched haircut would not be. It is hard to give this point due prominence within act-centered theories, for the inconsistency is an inconsistency in attitude about the seriousness of loss of life, not in beliefs about which acts are right or wrong. . . .

To say that the cutting off of a human life is always a matter of some seriousness, at any stage, is not to deny the relevance of gradual fetal development. Notwithstanding the well-worn point that clear boundary lines cannot be drawn, our emotions and attitudes regarding the fetus do change as it develops, and again when it is born, and indeed further as the baby grows. [D]eep grief over miscarriage in the later stages is more appropriate than it is over miscarriage in the earlier stages (when, that is, the grief is solely about the loss of *this* child, not about, as might be the case, the loss of one's only hope of having a child or of having one's husband's child). Imagine (or recall) a woman who already has children; she had not intended to have more, but finds herself unexpectedly pregnant. Though contrary to her plans, the pregnancy, once established as a fact, is welcomed and then she loses the embryo almost immediately. If this were bemoaned as a tragedy, it would, I think, be a misapplication of the concept of what is tragic. But it may still properly be mourned as a loss. . . . It would, I take it, be callous and light-minded to say, or think, "Well, she has already got four children; what's the problem?"; it would be neither, nor arrogantly intrusive in the case of a close friend, to try to correct prolonged mourning by saying, "I know it's sad, but it's not a tragedy; rejoice in the ones you have." The application of tragic becomes more appropriate as the fetus grows, for the mere fact that one has lived with it for longer, conscious of its existence, makes a difference. . . .

The fact that pregnancy is not just one among many physical conditions does not mean that one can never regard it in that light without manifesting a vice. When women are in very poor physical health, or worn out from child rearing, or forced to do very physically demanding jobs, then they cannot be described as self-indulgent, callous, irresponsible, or light-minded if they seek abortions mainly with a view to avoiding pregnancy as the physical condition that it is. . . . That they can view the pregnancy only as eight months of misery, followed by hours if not days of agony and exhaustion, and abortion only as the blessed escape from this prospect, is entirely understandable and does not manifest any lack of serious respect for human life or a shallow attitude to motherhood. What it does show is that something is terribly amiss in the conditions of their lives, which make it so hard to recognize pregnancy and childbearing as the good that they can be.

. . . Speaking in terms of women's rights, people sometimes say things like, "Well, it's her life you're talking about too, you know; she's got a right to her own life, her own happiness." And the discussion stops there. But in the context of virtue theory, given that we are particularly concerned with what constitutes a good human life, . . . this is no place to stop. We go on to ask, "And is this life of hers a good one? Is she living well?"

If we are to go on to talk about good human lives, in the context of abortion, we have to bring in our thoughts about the value of love and family life, and our proper emotional development through the natural life cycle. The familiar facts support the view that parenthood in general, and motherhood and childbearing in particular, are intrinsically worthwhile, are among the things that can be correctly thought to be partially constitutive of a flourishing human life. If this is right, then a woman who opts for not being a mother (at all, or again, or now) by opting for abortion may thereby be manifesting a flawed grasp of what her life should be, a grasp that is childish, or grossly materialistic, or shortsighted, or shallow.

I said "may thereby": this *need* not be so. Consider, for instance, a woman who has already had several children and fears that to have another will seriously affect her capacity to be a good mother to the ones she has—she does not show a lack of appreciation of the intrinsic value of being a parent by opting for abortion. Nor does a woman who has been a good mother and is approaching the age at which she may be looking forward to being a good grandmother. Nor does a woman who discovers that her pregnancy may well kill her, and opts for abortion and adoption. Nor, necessarily, does a woman who has decided to lead a life centered around some other worthwhile activity or activities with which motherhood would compete.

People who are childless by choice are sometimes described as "irresponsible," or "selfish," or "refusing to grow up," or "not knowing what life is about." But one can hold that having children is intrinsically worthwhile without endorsing this, for we are, after all, in the happy position of there being more worthwhile things to do than can be fitted into one lifetime. Parenthood, and motherhood in particular, even if granted to be intrinsically worthwhile, undoubtedly take up a lot of one's adult life, leaving no room for some other worthwhile pursuits. But some women who choose abortion rather than have their first child, and some men who encourage their partners to choose abortion, are not avoiding parenthood for the sake of other worthwhile pursuits, but for the worthless one of "having a good time," or for the pursuit of some false vision of the ideals of freedom or self-realization. And some others who say "I am not ready for parenthood yet" are making some sort of mistake about the extent to which one can manipulate the circumstances of one's life so as to make it fulfill some dream that one has. . . .

Once again, this is not to deny that girls may quite properly say "I am not ready for motherhood yet," especially in our society, and, far from manifesting irresponsibility or light-mindedness, show an appropriate modesty or humility, or a fearfulness that does not amount to cowardice.

Following is an excerpt from a leading proponent of what has been called "an ethic of care" or an ethic of "relation." Consider whether and to what extent this approach is similar to virtue ethics.

Nel Noddings, *The Challenge to Care in Schools: An Alternative Approach to Education*
(1992, 15–16, 21–22)

The German philosopher Martin Heidegger described care as the very Being of human life. His use of the term is very broad, covering an attitude of solicitousness toward other living beings, a concern to do things meticulously, the deepest existential longings, fleeting moments of concern, and all the burdens and woes that belong to human life. From his perspective, we are immersed in care; it is the ultimate reality of life.

Heidegger's full range of meanings will be of interest as this exploration continues, but the meaning that will be primary here is relational. A *caring relation* is, in its most basic form, a connection or encounter between two human beings—a carer and a recipient of care, or cared-for. In order for the relation to be properly called caring, both parties must contribute to it in characteristic ways. . . .

In *Caring*,[9] I described the state of consciousness of the carer (or "one-caring") as characterized by engrossment and motivational displacement. By engrossment I mean an open, nonselective receptivity to the cared-for. Other writers have used the word "attention" to describe this characteristic. Iris Murdoch, for example, discussed attention as essential in moral life, and she traced the concept to Simone Weil. Weil placed attention at the center of love for our neighbors. It is what characterizes our consciousness when we ask another (explicitly or implicitly), "What are you going through?" . . .

[B]y engrossment, I do not mean infatuation, enchantment, or obsession but a full receptivity. When I care, I really hear, see, or feel what the other tries to convey.

---

[9] [*Caring: A Feminine Approach to Ethics and Moral Education*. Berkeley: University of California Press, 1984.]

The engrossment or attention may last only a few moments and it may or may not be repeated in future encounters, but it is full and essential in any caring encounter. For example, if a stranger stops me to ask directions, the encounter may produce a caring relation, albeit a brief one. I listen attentively to his need, and I respond in a way that he receives and recognizes. The caring relation is completed when he receives my efforts at caring.

As carer in the brief encounter just described, I was attentive, but I also felt the desire to help the stranger in his need. My consciousness was characterized by motivational displacement. Where a moment earlier I had my own projects in mind, I was now concerned with his project—finding his way on campus. . . . This is motivational displacement, the sense that our motive energy is flowing toward others and their projects. I receive what the other conveys, and I want to respond in a way that furthers the other's purpose or project.

Experiencing motivational displacement, one begins to think. Just as we consider, plan, and reflect on our own projects, we now think what we can do to help another. Engrossment and motivational displacement do not tell us what to do; they merely characterize our consciousness when we care. But the thinking that we do will now be as careful as it is in our own service. We are seized by the needs of another.

What characterizes the consciousness of one who is cared for? Reception, recognition, and response seem to be primary. The cared for receives the caring and shows that it has been received. This recognition now becomes part of what the carer receives in his or her engrossment, and the caring is completed. . . .

*****

Those of us who write about an ethic of care have emphasized affective factors, but this is not to say that caring is irrational or even nonrational. It has its own rationality or reasonableness, and in appropriate situations carers draw freely on standard linear rationality as well. But its emphasis is on living together, on creating, maintaining, and enhancing positive relations—not on decision making in moments of high moral conflict, nor on justification.

An ethic of care—a needs- and response-based ethic—challenges many premises of traditional ethics and moral education. First, there is the difference of focus already mentioned. There is also a rejection of universalizability, the notion that anything that is morally justifiable is necessarily something that anyone else in a similar situation is obligated to do. Universalizability suggests that who we are, to whom we are related, and how we are situated should have nothing to do with our moral decision making. An ethic of caring rejects this. Next, although an ethic of care puts great emphasis on consequences in the sense that it always asks what happens to the relation, it is not a form of utilitarianism; it does not posit one greatest good to be optimized, nor does it separate means and ends. Finally, it is not properly labeled an ethic of virtue. Although it calls on people to be carers and to develop the virtues and capacities to care, it does not regard caring solely as an individual attribute. It recognizes the part played by the cared-for. It is an ethic of relation.

In moral education an ethic of care's great emphasis on motivation challenges the primacy of moral reasoning. We concentrate on developing the attitudes and skills required to sustain caring relations and the desire to do so, not nearly so much on the reasoning used to arrive at a decision.

Chapter 4

The Nature and Sources of Moral Judgments

 ## At School

Maria was slightly delayed the following morning, having stopped briefly at the front office to consult with Fred Helter, the principal. He advised Maria to stand firm: listen to the boys' stories, but briefly, and give them a three-day detention. If she wanted to let them have more say, as he suspected she did, there could be some negotiation around the specifics of the detention—what they would do, where they would do it, what would be said to their parents. Maria was not thrilled with the advice. The quick resolution, the standard punishment, seemed canned.

Entering the fourth-grade classroom Maria's now-attentive ears picked up a familiar covert buzzing, always a tip-off that there was big news. When she spied the poorly concealed gash on Peter's arm and Alfred's purple and puffy eye, she guessed the news. Attempting to sound casual, Maria leaned against her desk and observed, "So, there's been a fight. How about telling me about it now before the bell rings?" Silence. "Look, I'm not asking you to tattle on each other, you don't even have to use names, just let me know if it's over, or if you guys are still angry." More silence.

With exasperation, she tried again. "Boys, please tell me, I can't teach until I know we've got some peace around here." A deepening silence. "I thought we were building a community in this room. How can that work if we don't trust one another enough to talk over what is obviously a big deal? Peter, will you start us off?"

"No, I don't want to talk. It wasn't anything."

Maria saw that she must bide her time. At recess, she put three chairs by her desk and asked Peter, Mark, and Alfred to stay in. Sulkily they slouched into the chairs, Peter shoving his a distance from the others.

She began, "OK, you don't want to talk. Maybe it would help if I get us started and you chime in. What I figure happened is that after school you were still mad at each other over the card-trading that turned sour." She stole a glance at Peter. "One of you started taunting and teasing. That provoked another one, and soon fists were flying. The scuffle got serious and probably others piled on. Right so far?"

"Sort of," Mark grudgingly responded. The others bored holes in the floor with their fixed stares. Maria suspected her approach was not going to yield the whole story, but she sallied forth again.

"I'm not interested in the details of who did what to whom or why, but I am interested in why you think the solution to a dispute is fighting. You know this school has a no-fight policy; you know that. We have a committee on dispute resolution that is supposed to hear from you when there's a problem. How come you didn't go to them? How come you *never* go to them?"

Peter finally broke the silence. Raising his shoulders and moving forward in his chair, he began in a taut voice: "Look, Ms. Laszlo, going to committees and having meetings is not the way we handle stuff. My dad says that when someone says something insulting to me, I should stand up to him. You heard Alfred yesterday, and you should have heard him with my brother. We're supposed to take care of ourselves. Only a sissy walks from a fight."

Peter's word brought Alfred in, taking the baton as Mark's champion. "I'm not sorry for what I said after what he did to Mark. If Peter and his brother want to fight it out, fine with me."

"But what's the point?" Maria protested. "You hit him, he hits you, more people get involved, they get hurt, it escalates, it all gets repeated again and again."

"Ms. Laszlo," Alfred responded, "we just don't see it your way. You talk about respect and all that stuff. Well, we keep our respect by not letting no one take advantage of us. I help Mark out because he's not that strong yet. He helps me plenty with school work. We help each other; we stand up for each other. That's respect for us."

"But don't you see how much better it would be if we all take care of each other and work out our problems as a community?"

Suddenly unable to hold back his anger, Alfred jumped up: "If you don't want us to fight, why didn't you do something to stop Peter in the first place? He started the whole thing. Everyone could see he was abusing Mark."

"I don't see Peter as a bad kid."

"Come on, Ms. Laszlo, take another look. Peter is just a bully. He wants the best set of cards in the school. OK, he's a bully; that's how he is, lots of kids are like that. But if you want to stop the fighting, you gotta stop the bullying; otherwise we'll take care of it ourselves. And talking it out, and going to that dispute resolution place—that's just not our way."

With this final shot, Alfred pushed his chair back and returned his eyes to the floor. Peter kept silent.

Maria realized with a start that she had become the enemy, the boys united against her. "OK, boys, I get where you're coming from. I don't agree, but for now we'll leave it at that. Around school, however, you must understand there's to be no fighting, and no cursing either. I'm going to speak with Connie Comfort, the guidance counselor, before taking further action about what you all did in the cafeteria yesterday."

Connie Comfort was an experienced teacher before she returned to school for graduate work in school counseling. She enjoyed a reputation as understanding but tough. As Maria walked up to the guidance office, she saw Connie doing paperwork. The office door was open and Maria walked right in. Skipping the usual formalities, she blurted out the highlights of yesterday's cafeteria scene and last night's fight.

Connie was sympathetic. "Virtually every teacher has had problems with swearing and fighting, Maria. A lot of what children learn in their outside lives is at odds with the behavior we push at school. What we need to do, what you need to do, is to hold your ground. You need to make it clear that there'll be no fighting in school and get to the parents right away about the problem of their kids squaring off as soon as they leave school property. I'd like you to join me in making sure the school has a clearly spelled-out policy on fighting that is enforced by the faculty."

Maria found little solace in a response that moved so quickly to policy. Like the principal, Connie seemed to Maria to look right past the merits of the two positions. "Connie," she opened, "you're moving too fast for me. I too have been certain that the mediate-your-differences approach was right for school, even right outside of school, although maybe I wouldn't have thought we could enforce it there. But now I've been thinking that the kids may have a point.

"There are strong friendships and strong rivalries among them, and they watch each other's backs. It works. Alfred emboldens Mark; without Alfred, Mark would be easy prey. He could never go up against Peter alone, never mind taking on that tight Peter-and-his-brother combination. But these coalitions are cemented by confrontation and payback. They are part of the kids' world, part of their friendships. It all makes sense to them. Are you really so certain we should be interfering?"

"But Maria," protested Connie, "you can't be suggesting that we just let kids fight it out, that might makes right around here."

"Everyone has told me all my life, Connie, that I've got my head in the clouds. Well, maybe they're right. Anyway, my peace-making way isn't working; the kids don't respect me. What they are saying is that life is about competition, about winning and staying on top until you're toppled. They jostle for position and power. A certain amount of aggression is part of their system.

"The truth is that's how it is with humans and animals everywhere, right? We're not talking about killing, or knives or guns, just a limited 'fair fight.' You know, when the Bible said, 'Eye for eye, tooth for tooth, hand for hand, foot for foot, burn for burn, wound for wound, stripe for stripe,' it was out-lawing excessively violent retribution, but not proportionate violence."

"Oh great, Maria, you *are* suggesting we let kids slug it out in school!"

"No, we can't allow it in the classroom, that's clear. But," Maria persisted, "outside the classroom? Should we be down on them for it? The angrier they get, the more we crack down, the less they respect us. Now we don't even allow children to play dodge ball at recess; soon we won't give them recess al-together. Should we be so-o-o disapproving? What I'm trying to say, Connie, is that though it's not my way, not your way, it's not so clearly a horrible way; there is something very natural and normal and eternal about getting even. Who am I to say it should be repressed entirely (as if it could be repressed), when that's the way they and their families—and the world for that matter—live?"

"Maria, don't give me all that relativistic who-can-judge crap. If . . . "

"Just let me finish, Connie. I'm also wondering about the price we pay in working so hard to kill their way of 'dispute resolution.' There was an energy in the kids' talking about fair/unfair, getting even, that I sure hadn't seen in the negotiation meetings we drag them to. Good, thick friendships always have their share of indignation. Maybe our way isn't just a hopelessly naive idea; maybe it's got a real downside. It flattens and weakens relationships."

Connie rose from her chair, amazed. "Maria, what world, or at least what school, allows *any* fighting?"

"For one, I've read that in Japan teachers of young kids do permit fight-ing," Maria rejoined. "And it certainly is true that many of the parents ap-prove of it, at least off the school grounds. They don't want their children—especially their sons—growing up as weaklings. We don't prepare them for the world by insisting that everything goes to dispute-resolution committees."

"For sure," Connie tried again, "it's human nature to have in-groups and out-groups, and group loyalty, too, but there's a lot in 'human nature' that's just wrong. Fighting it out is one example. I agree that the kids' attachments to each other are strengthened when they face a common enemy. But surely it's a mistake to have them see each other, fellow classmates, as enemies, in school or out of school. We need to stop that and help them to form bonds that don't depend on anger toward others."

Maria drew a breath. "Maybe," she went on more quietly, "what you're saying, Connie, is that it's not my job to jump all over them about fighting; I should let that one go, and help them enlarge their circle of loyalty."

"I don't recall saying or even thinking that, Maria, and I'm not ready to buy in, especially not the 'letting it go' part. However, it's an intriguing idea. That way you're not confronting them with their wrongness, more with their definition of the foe. Let's talk some more and maybe get Fred Helter to join us."

Maria departed in considerable doubt about her own "intriguing idea." Not to tell kids to stop fighting; not to tell them something as obvious as,

"You shouldn't be hurting one another." That was a lot to swallow. Wasn't it wrong? And what would be the point of enlarging the in-group, assuming she could (which was a huge assumption), if it just focused the aggression on another set of kids who then became the out-group. Support firmer, larger coalitions and pretty soon she'd be hearing about gangs.

Yet, Maria could not rest easy with the question. The students and their parents believed in the rightness of fighting; to defend yourself and others you cared for seemed to be a genuine moral principle, and even though she and the school didn't share it, she wasn't ready to dismiss the parents' approach. After all, it wasn't as if they were celebrating a life of violence, wanting their kids prepared for a militia or a vigilante group. Their ambitions for children were the same as those of the school. They saw in the willingness to fight—"taking care of yourself," as the kids put it—a tool for character-building. Without a certain toughness, grittiness, and moral fiber, the virtues of courage and loyalty, they believed, were pretty hollow hopes.

Restless with her thoughts, Maria went to Connie's office at lunchtime the next day to continue their conversation. She found her munching on a sandwich. Connie waved her to a chair, and asked: "So Maria, did a night's sleep clear your head?"

"Afraid not, Connie, I've come back for another round."

"You mean you still want to defend our little warriors?"

"No, or maybe; mostly I need to think through their position, much as I wish I could just reject it flat out."

"I don't get it, Maria. Aren't you bending over backward to justify something that is completely contrary to your own standards? You know that at school we teach children—as we must—to resist turning to their fists each time someone gets in their way. Unless they can subdue their anger by rational thinking, in school and out, they can't possibly grow to be decent, fair-minded people."

"I'm not suggesting we give them a free pass on violence and abandon reason," said Maria, frustrated at Connie's complacent self-assuredness. "I'm suggesting that maybe limited acts of violence have a justified place in their relationships. They and their parents certainly think so, all of them, including Peter, who was the target of the fight."

"Maria, beyond letting nature, tooth and claw, 'express' itself, what good can come of aggression? Even if a little fighting is not so terrible in fourth grade, we happen to live in a viciously violent society where the fists of today become the knives of tomorrow and the guns of the day after—not to mention the wars."

"Maybe, Connie, we shouldn't be so quick to sneer at human nature," Maria shot back. "We're sure ready to call on it when we're boosting empathy and altruism. Isn't it possible that if you want the empathy and altruism you'd better allow for the anger? I was always taught God made us the way we are for a reason; perhaps we don't like or understand why we are aggressive, but we better respect it. I translate that as meaning maybe we can't be so cavalier in assuming the hostile part of human nature must be entirely suppressed and replaced with the kindly part. You try to tamp down aggression at one spot, out it bulges at another, maybe in a worse form."

"Maria, are you playing devil's advocate with me?" asked a sobered Connie.

"I suppose so, given my basically pacifist leanings, but hear me out. To fight is not just a natural function like breathing that we've got to put up with. It's an expression of feeling and, I don't need to tell you, feelings are valuable; they're believable, they're real. I'm not so sure there isn't more honesty, more truth, more dependability in emotions, even hostile ones, than in reason. The indignation and loyalty that was behind the boys' fighting—that was good stuff. The purpose of their fighting was to right an injustice, not to celebrate the glory of battle.

"At least in fourth grade, the kids are as much physical as rational beings. Of course we have to curb their physicality; the question is how much, in what circumstances, and in what way. It's one thing to say there have to be rules to protect people from really getting injured, or to say fighting is not appropriate at school. It's another to say it's just flat-out 'wrong.' My brothers fought; they're decent people. Now that I look back I believe their fights also were usually a means to an end, and the end was often a matter of fairness, of principle."

"Maria, I appreciate what you've 'shared,' as they say in my field. I mean that. Much of it sounds plausible, especially the thought that we'll never eliminate aggression. But I still think we all should do our best to stop the fighting. It's a good zero-tolerance prohibition, a good limit. And, not to be smug or anything, my guess is that after you're done with your fair-minded considerations, you'll see it my way."

Maria recognized that Connie might be right in her prediction. She was nonetheless a bit ticked off by the patronizing note in Connie's "wrap-up." It was with a slightly abrupt edge therefore that she allowed the ringing of Connie's telephone to give her the opportunity to rise quickly and toss off a breezy, "Thanks for your time, Connie," as she returned to her classroom.

✸✸ At the University

Maria and her students have incompatible positions on a genuine moral issue: She, like many teachers and school systems, is committed to a rejection of violence as a proper response to injury, while Alfred, Mark, and Peter regard limited violent retribution an appropriate response to verbally aggressive acts showing disrespect. It is important to understand initially that each side in this disagreement makes a *moral* claim; that is, whether right or wrong, the boys are not simply rationalizing wilful behavior. Nor do they seem to be making the *relativist* claim that Maria should not seek to judge the rightness of their actions because neither side is right or wrong, that the matter is simply one of the norms of a subculture. Both sides seem to agree that there is a right and a wrong response to what went on the preceding day. Recall Alfred's impassioned words:

> We just don't see it your way. You talk about respect and all that stuff. Well, we keep our respect by not letting no one take advantage of us. I help Mark out because he's not that strong yet. He helps me plenty with school work. We help each other; we stand up for each other. That's respect for us.

Moral Claims

While a relativist position may be thought to support the boys, it does so only in the sense that it challenges the right of Maria, or anyone else, to say that they are wrong. More fundamentally, it undermines the moral premises of *both* points of view, for it asserts also that one cannot say either one is right. Consider, for example, a statement that Maria might avow: "It is wrong to respond to provocation or a slight with even a moderate act of violence." Relativism does not disagree with this statement in the sense that it regards it as false. Rather, it denies that the statement has what philosophers call "truth value" at all. That is, it cannot be thought either true or false, in the sense that the statements, $2 + 2 = 4$, and $2 + 2 = 5$, both have truth value, one being true (has truth), the other false (lacks truth). According to a relativist, one who says "fighting is wrong" can be saying nothing more than "I don't like it." The disagreement is simply a matter of "taste." Political philosopher Isaiah Berlin (1909–1997) described relativism in these words:

> [T]he judgement of a man or a group, since it is the expression or statement of a taste, or emotional attitude or outlook, is simply what it is, with no objective correlate which determines its truth or falsehood. I like mountains, you do not; I love history, he thinks it is bunkum: it all depends on one's point of view. It follows that to speak of truth or falsehood on these assumptions is literally meaningless.
> *(Berlin 1959/1992, 80)*

A significant corollary of this analysis is that, were one to reject relativism, one would only have *exposed*, but would not have *answered*, the question whether it is the boys or Maria who are right. It is a mistake to believe that one can establish the correctness of his or her moral judgments simply by attacking relativism. One claiming moral validity for a particular point of view must rebut any claim of relativism *and* must establish that he or she has correctly discerned the morality of the matter.

Alfred might have presented his claim as a *pluralist* one. Pluralism differs from relativism in that it does not contend that the moral issue has no right answer. Assuming or believing that there is such a thing as right and wrong, it nonetheless takes seriously the questions: How do we know what is right?

How certain must we be of our belief before we are warranted in acting on it as if it were undeniably true? It notes the empirical fact that people—sincere, well-meaning, honest in their outlook—differ on the answer, and asserts that, although each of us may feel justified in believing that he or she knows the truth of the matter, a specific view should not too readily be imposed on those who do not share it. Rather, an appropriate degree of humility in a teacher counsels against concluding with certainty that he or she has the right answer to a moral question. Accordingly, institutions like schools should narrow the range of issues on which those who speak for the institution enforce their moral judgments on students.

It should be noted that the question of pluralism arises in contexts involving the setting of public policy, the stance of an institution, such as a school, or the raising of children within a family. In this instance, the source of the issue of pluralism is the fact that Maria and the school have a certain authority over Alfred and his friends; they have the power (and the responsibility) to decide whether to allow, or to seek to discourage, the boys from settling some disputes with their fists. When Maria expresses concern about "imposing" her view on students, she is examining the strength of a pluralist claim.

We will examine the question of pluralism more fully at the end of this section. For the present, we note that pluralism should not be invoked as a response to questions regarding one's own moral outlook. Many people, when asked whether they approve or disapprove of certain conduct, will give a pluralist response: "In a democracy, we are each free to decide." Yes, but the question was, what is *your* decision? To be opposed to the coercion of those who disagree is not to say that one has no values or opinions on matters of morality. To find in a commitment to pluralism a basis for having or expressing no opinions whatever is, in our judgment, a serious evasion of moral responsibility. We believe that each of us is morally obliged to attempt, as best he or she can, to discern the truth of the matter. (See the excerpt, p. 105 in the next section of this chapter, by the contemporary philosopher Christina Hoff Sommers, who trenchantly questions the tendency to emphasize questions of social policy at the expense of questions of individual moral decision making.)

Let us consider further the content of the contending views of morality presented in Maria's classroom. Most teachers, as we have noted, would (and do) advocate resolution of conflict through verbal rather than physical means.[1] For Maria, violent retribution is a highly destructive ethic, one that separates children from each other, that works against community-building,

---

[1] Many would not characterize the typical measured punishments of a school's disciplinary system—for example, mandatory detention or school service—as "physical" (although others would). Some would regard as legitimate certain forms of corporal punishment, undeniably physical though they are, although those opposing all corporal punishment do so precisely because of its physical quality.

that promotes aggression and enmity. She cannot countenance it in her class-room, and wants to help her students learn to avoid it outside as well.

Yet, it is not obvious that the opposing ethic is wrong. Alfred's assertion has some intuitive moral integrity to it, does it not? Violence in the service of self-respect, along with codes that specify the occasions for and appropriate measure of it, has not only been an observable aspect of many cultures; it has often been regarded as appropriate.

In a fascinating study, Richard E. Nisbett and Dov Cohen describe the "Culture of Honor" as it is played out in the descendants of Scotch-Irish herdsmen now living in the rural south (Nisbett and Cohen 1996). For them, violence is seen as a "legitimate response to insult, as an appropriate means of self-protection, and as a justifiable tool for restoring order" (id., 32). From such a premise, violence is a relatively unproblematic method of disciplining children, at home and at school. The Southern code is similar to the urban "code of the streets," where an excessively long stare is widely interpreted as a manifestation of disrespect, and (like being on the wrong "turf") is viewed as warranting or even provoking a violent response. "Each neighborhood," observes sociologist Elijah Anderson, "is considered responsible for public behavior within its boundaries." He goes on: "It is not uncommon for a young man to walk up to a complete stranger, particularly a young male, and demand to know his business or ask who gave him permission to use 'these streets.' If the stranger gives no acceptable answer, there may be a fight" (Anderson 1990, 39; see also Anderson 1999).

Literature is rife with characters insistent on revenge as a matter of justice and psychic relief. In *Orley Farm* (Trollope 1861/1985), Joseph Mason claims family property inherited years before by his half-brother, Lucius. After successfully defending his right to the property against Joseph, Lucius learns that his mother (Joseph's stepmother) had forged the will that gave him the land; he thereupon disclaims his interest, ceding victory to Joseph. Joseph, advised by his lawyers to accept the land and be done with the matter, responds: "No, by heaven. What I have first to look to is her punishment. . . . Nothing shall make me tamper with justice." Trollope observes: "The property was sweet, but that sweetness was tasteless compared to the sweetness of revenge" (id., 390–391).

Peter's stance is a mild form of this ethic. He does not buy into the morality of turning the other cheek. Perhaps he will forgive after an apology, or after he has gotten his "licks" in, but his morality is to hang tough, to stand up for himself. Maria's appeal to him—what if everyone resorted to violence to get even?—convinces him not at all, for Peter truly believes that "getting even" is *right* as well as realistic. The general welfare, as it were, is strengthened when everyone appreciates, "You mess with me and you'll be sorry." For Peter, this is the essence of "respect" and the best method for keeping peace. Moreover, it is supported by the widespread (although contested) belief that wrongful conduct can only be set right by appropriate retribution. Current trends in pedagogy, as well as the prevailing ethic in foreign relations here and abroad, illustrate this belief.

This difference of view implicates the central problems of morality. Some educators (like some others) will greet such questions with disdain: "Everyone knows what is right and wrong, what is good and bad behavior. Don't waste my time with those stuffy academic games." At the other pole are strong advocates for a "nobody knows" or a relativist stance.[2] Witness the question, "Whose values get taught?" which has so inhibited moral education. As questions, both of these positions deserve serious exploration; as conversation-stoppers, seeking to shut off the inquiry at the outset, we reject them. The "everyone knows" response seeks merely to silence those who do not share prevailing moral views on some matters, by suggesting that their views are hopelessly deviant; the "no one knows" position confuses a critique (which may in specific cases be warranted) of the unacknowledged bias that infects many moral evaluations with the counterintuitive position that there is no such thing as a correct moral judgment.

THE QUESTION OF AN OBJECTIVE GOOD

Many philosophers have maintained that goodness is not an objective set of facts but a judgment we impose upon the world. To say that X (something or someone) is good is to say nothing more than, "I approve of X." Goodness is not a tangible physical object, not a physical law (gravity), not an analytic fact (2 + 2 must equal 4 because of the meanings of "4," "2," and "+"). It is not the sort of thing that can be studied by the natural or social sciences.

In this view, the answer to the fundamental question of ethics, "How shall I live?" can only be, "It's your choice" (although also your responsibility). We grope in the dark; as the existentialist philosopher Jean-Paul Sartre asserted starkly, "We are alone, with no excuses" (Sartre 1973, 86). As a means of granting morals the necessary authority to control our social dealings, we may choose to see them as objective facts, rather than as subjective preferences, but this is self-deception. Values are not part of the world, but merely a reflection of an attitude toward the world. Morality is necessarily something we invent, unanalyzable and lacking any external or rational authority. In the words of David Hume, morality "is more properly felt than judg'd of. . . . " (Hume 1896, bk. III, part I, sec. I, 470). In taking a position similar in some ways, British philosopher G. E. Moore (1873–1958) denied that one can derive an "ought" from an "is." To attempt that is to commit what he famously termed the "naturalistic fallacy," to confuse the desired with the desirable (G. E. Moore 1993, esp. 92–95).

---

[2] As a philosophical matter, although both a "nobody knows" and a relativist position embody a skeptical stance, they differ in that the latter is ontological, dealing with the nature of reality—e.g., "there is no such thing as moral truth"—while the former is epistemological—"whatever the truth may be, there is no way to know it for sure." For most purposes, including ours, this difference may be elided.

Yet, we resist the extreme skepticism that is sometimes grounded in such insights.[3] If morality is nothing more than an individual's or group's subjective choice, the projection of personal preferences upon the world, then neither Maria nor the boys can make a claim of rightness for their view. Their school, of course, can establish a policy, asserting its rightness and enforcing submission to it; however, when Peter enters another subculture devoted to a different set of rights and wrongs, he may be obliged to govern himself by *its* norms. But this is problematic: Rule by a transient, local authority lacks a credible moral foundation, lacks any grandeur or sense of its "overridingness," and makes one's willingness to submit less a matter of conscience than of coercion. Indeed, history supports the fear that to believe that the good (which ought to be enforced upon everyone) is solely the making of one's state, one's tribe, or one's leaders, is to take a fateful step along the path toward totalitarianism. Only an external standard of morality, by which the actions of the powerful may be called to account, can protect us from despotism.

More personally, one's beliefs as to the right and wrong of a matter tend to be bound up in an underlying conviction that those beliefs are actually true. A person asserting that a certain act is right (or wrong) does not ordinarily *appear* simply to be telling us something about himself. "[T]he person is attempting simultaneously to affirm something about his own approvals, and also to claim that if the person addressed knew of certain factors or if he underwent certain experiences, he would agree with him in attitude" (Morgenbesser 1973, 77). As the twentieth-century philosopher J. L. Mackie has observed, "the denial of objective values can carry with it an extreme emotional reaction, a feeling that nothing matters at all, that life has lost its purpose." He goes on:

> Of course this does not follow; the lack of objective values is not a good reason for abandoning subjective concern or for ceasing to want anything. But the abandonment of a belief in objective values can cause, at least temporarily, a decay of subjective concern and sense of purpose. (*Mackie 1990, 34*)

Philosopher-classicist Martha Nussbaum has eloquently described the cost of a systematic refusal to view ethical judgments as anything but the expression of wholly personal preferences:

> [Such a refusal] omit[s] something very fundamental to human life, namely the disposition to make ethical commitments and to get upset

---

[3] To thinkers such as Hume and Moore, moral sentiments or intuitions originate within the human person, and not in the external world. They do not, however, infer that as a result a person's sentiments or intuitions are idiosyncratic, varying widely from one to another. Rather, they reflect commonalities arising from our common humanity. See the further discussion of Hume in the next segment of this section, p. 86.

about them. . . . Natural human practices are full of moral argument and moral stand-taking. . . .

It seems, furthermore, that we might not want to live in the world these skeptics would give us. In that world . . . there would . . . be no commitment to fight for justice against a tyrant's pressure, no commitment to engage in any sort of unpopular or radical reform, no commitment to help a friend in trouble when help would impose difficulty, and no commitment to help [another] in her struggle for survival.
(Nussbaum 1994, 208–209)

(See also the descriptions of the corrosive effect of extreme moral skepticism by students in the excerpts by two contemporary teachers, Kay Haugaard and Robert Simon, at pp. 107 and 109 in the next section of this chapter.)

We therefore search for genuine justifiable bases of moral authority. Such bases have been perceived in human nature, human aspirations, reason, human limitations, shared foundational principles, and authority. Each of these justifications we find both powerful and incomplete.

GROUNDING THE GOOD: HUMAN NATURE

To Isaiah Berlin, morality is "constitutive of human beings as such," part of our essential nature. Knowledge of the good and the desire to be good are as intrinsic to human nature as the ability and desire to love or communicate. Human beings commit to a common morality "as part of what in their moments of self-awareness constitutes for them the essential nature of man" (Berlin 1959/1992, 202–203). His reasoning warrants quotation:

[T]here are . . . certain moral properties which enter equally deeply into what we conceive of as human nature. [I]f we meet someone who cannot see why (to take a famous example) he should not destroy the world in order to relieve a pain in his little finger, or someone who genuinely sees no harm in condemning innocent men, or betraying friends, or torturing children, then we find that we cannot argue with such people, not so much because we are horrified as because we think them in some way inhuman—we call them "moral idiots."

▼▼▼▼▼

[T]o speak of our values as objective and universal . . . is to say that we cannot help accepting these basic principles because we are human, as we cannot help (if we are normal) seeking warmth rather than cold, truth rather than falsehood, to be recognized by others for what we are rather than to be ignored or misunderstood.
(Id., 203–204)

Berlin goes on to contend, not only that "human nature" contains these objective criteria of morality, but that we can discover them through noticing what moral principles in fact have been "long and widely recognised" as "basic." These, he asserts, are "universal ethical laws." He continues:

> When such canons seem less universal, less profound, less crucial, we call them, in descending order of importance, customs, conventions, manners, taste, etiquette, and concerning these we not only permit but actively expect wide differences.
>
> ❧❧❧❧❧
>
> When we resist aggression, or the destruction of liberty under despotic regimes, it is to these [universal] values that we appeal. And we appeal to them without the slightest doubt that those to whom we speak, no matter under what regime they live, do in fact understand our language; for it is clear, from all evidence, whether they pretend otherwise or not, that in fact they do. . . .
> (Id., 204–206).

Two centuries earlier, Hume asserted that morality is embedded in our basic emotional responses, which enable us both to identify the good and desire the doing of it. We experience "warm feelings" of approval when we engage in virtuous acts, and "disgust" when we engage in vice. The good, happiness, is promoted by our natural "tender sympathies"; the evil, human misery, meets with natural disapproval. "It appears that a tendency to public good, and to the promoting of peace, harmony, and order in society, does always, by affecting the benevolent principles of our frame, engage us on the side of the social virtues" (Hume 1983, 50).

A related view looks not so much to one's emotional capacities as to (what is closely related) human intuition. "Intuitionism" is the claim, as described by contemporary American philosopher John Rawls, that "moral principles when suitably formulated express self-evident propositions about legitimate moral claims. . . ." (Rawls 1971, 35). Abjuring the attempt to ground morality in the objective world, the intuitionist would find a reliable guide in the intuitive faculty.

Hume's view that we are "biologically prepared" to develop moral standards finds an echo among contemporary theorists. Child psychologist Jerome Kagan notes that "the capacity to evaluate the actions of self and others as good or bad is one of the psychological qualities that most distinguishes *Homo sapiens* from the higher apes" (Kagan 1984, 112). And philosopher-mathematician Bertrand Russell has expressed a similar thought, with an appropriate tone of wonder:

> A strange mystery it is that nature, omnipotent but blind, in the revolutions of her secular hurryings through the abysses of space, has brought forth at last a child, subject still to her power, but gifted with sight, with knowledge of good and evil, with the capacity of judging all the works of his unthinking mother.
> (Russell 1903/1957, 107)

Newborns, without enough ability to know where they end and the next infant begins, nonetheless will cry when they hear others crying, in what psychologist Martin Hoffman has labeled "global empathy." At eleven months seeing another child fall and cry, the infant sucks her own thumb and buries her head in her own mother's lap. By the second year the child is aware of herself and others as physically, but not emotionally, distinct. In this "egocentric" stage, for example, a thirteen-month-old gets his own mother to comfort a crying friend or offers his much-loved doll to a sad-looking adult (Hoffman 1982, 281–313).

By age two children are aware of standards of right and wrong. Like laughter or fear of strangers, the competence to code acts into moral categories, Kagan suggests, is innately wired. These moral prohibitions are stoked by their emotional sources: The temptation to violate a societal standard produces in children unpleasant feelings—distress, anxiety, and shame. Such feelings are the origins of conscience; once removed by a society, so too is the moral sting. Hence, when an act carries no distress or shame—as has happened in recent decades with respect to some sexual practices—it moves from being a moral to a conventional violation, or no violation at all. Categories of good and bad, claims Kagan, are universal, but "surface ethics" and the associated anxiety, shame, and guilt will shift among communities depending on specific political and social conditions (Kagan 1984, 112–153).

Because our survival as social animals requires cooperation, evolutionary biologists believe that natural selection has fostered not only an ethical code in "lower" animals, but the specific virtue of altruism.[4] Animals protect their young even at the risk of their own lives; they share food, give warnings, help the injured. This makes evolutionary sense. Reciprocal altruism, it turns out, serves the self-interest, as it were, of the species.

Even if these thinkers seem right in grounding a moral code in human nature, the question remains how one establishes its specific content. Maria's preference for negotiation and nonviolence over retaliation and aggression cannot be derived from either Hume's equation of morality with sentiments of approbation or a utilitarian justification. Peter, Alfred, and their families approve of their particular behaviors, and believe that they promote overall happiness, while Maria's way would generate both disapproval and unhappiness among them.

Maria's line of thinking may claim Kant as an ally. He argues against resort to happiness, or any consequence, as the criterion for morality (recall the discussion in Chapter 3, pp. 55), and while he grants that happiness is universally desired (although not necessarily desirable) Kant, unlike Bentham and Mill, denies the existence of a consensus on its cause or nature. It is a useless, as well as an infirm, criterion for judging an act, because no one knows what makes for general happiness, nor even what an individual really wants for oneself.

---

[4] See, e.g., Peter Singer 1981; Robert Wright 1994; Richard Dawkins 1976; James Q. Wilson 1993.

Does he want riches? How much anxiety, envy, and intrigue might he not thereby bring down upon his own head! Or knowledge and insight? Perhaps these might only give him an eye that much sharper for revealing that much more dreadfully [those] evils which are at present hidden but are yet unavoidable. . . . Or long life? Who guarantees that it would not be a long misery? Or health at least? How often has infirmity of the body kept one from excesses into which perfect health would have allowed him to fall, and so on? . . . The problem of determining certainly and universally what action will promote the happiness of a rational being is completely insoluble.
(Kant 1785/1993, 27–28)

Nor can Maria readily turn to the moral innateness of empathy, altruism, and reciprocity. First, the solution offered by Alfred and Peter makes an appeal to empathy, fairness, and reciprocity. More importantly, intuition and emotion do not provide good moral benchmarks. Hume is naive in believing warm feelings of self-approval are reliably associated with prosocial behavior and disapproval with antisocial actions. According to contemporary psychological research, our emotions have survived evolutionary extinction not because they promote morality, but because they function as an early alert system that promotes self-preservation: Under threat one feels fear and flees; under attack, or when a desired goal is unattainable, one feels anger and fights. "To present all aggression as undesirable, even evil, is like calling all wild plants weeds: it is the perspective of the gardener, not the botanist or ecologist" (de Waal 1996, 183). (For an analysis finding some positive value in aggression, see the excerpt by the contemporary British philosopher Mary Midgley, at p. 106 in the next section of this chapter). We post-Darwinians grant to human nature both hostile and benevolent emotions; we can understand the boys' fight as a normal emotional response. Feelings of empathy and altruism share the table with timidity and aggression, and approval can be apportioned to any or all of them.

To some, goodness may be grounded in our aspirations, for part of being human is a longing for self-improvement, a desire within human nature to bootstrap the limitations of human nature.

GROUNDING THE GOOD: HUMAN ASPIRATIONS

The claim that the good is grounded not exactly in what we are but in what we yearn to be is not subject to proof. It does however find support in the lives of many: Foremost are those who seek moral truth (and often believe they have found it) whether through religion or otherwise. It also is supported by an assortment of psychologists who believe the search for moral purpose is a primary motivational force, comparable to Freud's "will to pleasure" or Alfred Adler's "will to power." The goal of our lives, says Victor Frankl, is not "self-actualization" but "self-transcendence" (Frankl 1962,

112). Without moral meaning we are at best bored, with little interest in life, and material goods alone will not save us from indifference or even despair. By contrast, legal philosopher Edmund Cahn asserted:

> [A] magnanimous deed . . . inspires a pervasive euphoria. One feels, as it were, literally buoyant. [It] proclaim[s] in the teeth of prescribed, accepted, and usual consequences that these need not occur. [A] magnanimous impulse rips a hole through the seemingly ineluctable net of cause and effect. It is like working a miracle.
> *(Cahn 1955, 209)*

What is not obvious is how to translate human aspirations to a concrete set of virtues. Alasdair MacIntyre (1990) argues that virtues are defined by established roles within the social structure. Homer saw virtue personified in the courageous warrior admired for his strength as well as his fidelity. To Aristotle, law-abidingness was a primary virtue, for the political community (the *polis*) mirrored individual morality. Aristotle also found moral virtue in honor (the mean between vanity and pusillanimity) and courage (the mean between rashness and cowardice). By contrast, MacIntyre points out, the early Christians believed the rich were destined for hell while virtue lay in humility (probably a vice to Aristotle), faith, hope, and love. In the Philadelphia of Benjamin Franklin, virtue was expressed by cleanliness and industry.

It is both the strength and weakness of aspirations that they are vague and various. In a "teaching moment," for example, is it more caring to assist or refrain from assisting? The most we can hope for is that the aspiration for virtue will nag at us with steady insistence, and that we develop the "right" sort of filter to perceive the morally significant in any given situation. But this is a lot to expect, most especially of children whose purposefulness does not generally extend beyond the day or week. Virtue aspirations, along with our innate emotions, may provide a certain level of preparedness, but they do not clarify the nature of moral decisions, just as physical fitness prepares us to compete but does not give us the skills to succeed in an athletic contest.

If elemental emotions and human aspirations fail to produce moral standards, do other parts of our nature house a basic morality? Kant tells us that the source of goodness lies not in our feelings, which can be cold and indifferent, at best unreliable, but in our reason. Although in a sense another aspect of "human nature," its tendency to turn our attention toward supposedly objective and inexorable principles of thought leads many to treat it as separate from what we have just examined.

GROUNDING THE GOOD: REASON

To Kant, what we do out of sympathetic inclinations—care for the sick, undercharge a needy customer, go to unusual trouble to keep our word to a friend—though deserving of praise and encouragement, has no moral content. Contrary to Hume, that which makes us feel good, even that which makes others feel good, is for Kant too temporal, variable, and potentially self-serving to be canonized into a universal ethic. Only that which is done from duty rises to a moral good for Kant. If, for example, we take care of ourselves because we judge our lives pleasurable or even useful, our behavior may be wise but not moral.

> On the other hand, if adversity and hopeless sorrow have completely taken away the taste for life, if an unfortunate man, strong in soul and more indignant at his fate than despondent or dejected, wishes for death and yet preserves his life without loving it—not from inclination or fear, but from duty—then his maxim indeed has a moral content.
> *(Kant 1785/1993, 10)*

Our moral obligations, asserts Kant, consist of duties grounded in the categorical imperative, which emanates from "pure" reason, that is, reason untarnished by any experiential considerations of personal intentions or actual consequences. Self-preservation, for example, is a duty because if suicide were universalized there would be no humanity left, no self to preserve, thus making suicide contradictory to reason. Not stealing is a duty because there is no stealing without property; if everyone were to steal, then there would no longer be any such thing as property and the word would lose all meaning, again a self-contradiction. Keeping a promise is a duty: Although there may be prudential reasons for breaking a promise—for example, to protect another from harm—to do so is a breach of one's moral duty because promise-breaking destroys the concept of a promise. (We encountered a classic illustration of Kant's position in Chapter 3, p. 61.)

Kant's approach has generated strong criticism, on several grounds. First, it has been read, although perhaps erroneously, as preferring duty over love as a moral reason for action, and as deeming duty-based action morally sufficient, even when not accompanied by caring feelings. Consider this response:

> Eliminating sentiment from duty-based ethics does more to undermine the credibility of Kantian deontology than any problem arising from the universalizability requirement. It is counter-intuitive to suppose that my trustworthiness and reliability are devoid of normative value just because *I want* to keep my promises. . . . Parents who take care of their children's needs from a sense of duty alone are morally superior, in Kantian evaluative terms, to those parents who care for their children because they love them. However, no amount of dutifulness can compensate for the emotional deprivation caused by parents who have merely done their duty.
> *(Roberts 1994, 111) (emphasis in original)*

A second critique of Kant's reasoning focuses on his understanding of the idea of universalizability, discussed in the preceding chapter. Maria can invoke his categorical imperative intuitively to justify a peaceful approach to dispute resolution. In arguing that one fight will escalate into another and another, she is saying that, if everyone acted violently there would be no end to the escalation of violence, discord, and ill-will. (This is the lesson learned by the patriarchs of the Houses of Montague and Capulet in Shakespeare's *Romeo and Juliet*.) One can agree, however, that as a general matter nonviolent negotiation is obviously preferable to mutual injury, but does that mean there are no circumstances where retaliation is morally permissible? Acts are embedded, the product of personal and group histories. The question is not whether Alfred, in taking on Peter, committed an abstract wrong, but whether he did so given the circumstances—defending a perceived wrong done to Mark.

Universalizing an imperative means treating *similarly situated* people alike. But the judgment of rightness or wrongness is directed not to the disembodied act but to the act-in-context. One way to justify the boys' behavior, without dismissing Kant's injunction, is to interpret "similarly situated" more narrowly: The aggression would not be wrong under parallel conditions, here including the swindling of a naive by a sophisticated boy, the perceived failure of adult authority, established loyalty patterns, and modest retribution acceptable to all concerned.

Of course, to allow the introduction of context threatens to dissolve the supposed objectivity of the categorical imperative. However, since the concept of "similarly situated" can rationally be expanded or shrunk, reason alone cannot generate directives that will single out one from among a range of apparently justifiable practices. While wariness about allowing context to distinguish situations is therefore wise, it should not harden into an absolute refusal to consider context. Would the prohibition of promise-breaking, for example, apply to the abandonment of a promise to one's family to take an expensive vacation because an aging parent suddenly needed help with a hospital bill? Intuitively, context at times makes a compelling moral claim, and reason does not tell us to what extent we should take account of, or ignore, context and consequences.

A final problem in applying Kantian ethics to real life is that, although moral law is purportedly the product of pure reason, in fact it explicitly includes a consideration of outcomes. Before acting one is to ask what would be the *consequence* if everyone always did what one now wants to do. A moral obligation is not independent of all interests, merely independent of the agent's personal interests. This stress on impartiality is critical to our notions of equality, a bulwark against arbitrary favoritism and arbitrary discrimination. But in this context, Alfred would assuredly make the claim, in opposition to Maria, that for *all* kids in his situation to act as he did would do social good, not harm. Kant's universality and impartiality maxims do not obviate the need to consider whether that judgment is true or false.

Kant and Hume sought to ground morality within the human psyche— Hume in our innate sentiments of approval and disapproval, Kant in deductions from pure reason. Others have suggested that morality originates neither in our natural approbation for that which is good and disapprobation for the bad, nor from our *positive* human sympathies. Rather, it is grounded in our *limited* human sympathies.

GROUNDING THE GOOD: HUMAN LIMITATIONS

Assume that we possess benevolent natures, enjoy the happiness of others, and feel the pang of conscience when we commit wrongful actions. Yet, this view begins, fundamentally we are concentrated on our own happiness, even at the expense of others. The approach has been expressed powerfully by G. J. Warnock:

> [M]ost human beings have some natural tendency to be more con-cerned about the satisfaction of their own wants, etc., than those of oth-ers. A man who does not like being hungry, and who is naturally inclined to take such steps as he can to satisfy his hunger, may very well care less, even not at all, about the hunger of others, and may not care at all whether anything is done to satisfy them. Even if he does care to some extent about others, it is quite likely to be only about *some* others—family, friends, class, tribe, country, or "race."
>
> ▼▼▼▼▼
>
> Resources are limited; knowledge, skills, information, and intelli-gence are limited; people are often not rational, either in the manage-ment of their own affairs or in the adjustment of their own affairs in rela-tion to others. Then, finally, they are vulnerable to others, and dependent on others, and yet inevitably often in competition with others; and, human sympathies being limited, they may often neither get nor give help that is needed.
>
> ▼▼▼▼▼
>
> Now, the general suggestion that (guardedly) I wish to put up for consideration is this: that the "general object" of morality, appreciation of which may enable us to *understand* the basis of moral evaluation, is . . . to countervail "limited sympathies" and their potentially most damaging effects.
>
> *(Warnock 1971, 21, 23, 26) (emphasis in original)*

To like effect is J. L. Mackie: "[A] morality is a system of a particular sort of constraints on conduct—ones whose central task is to protect the interests of persons other than the agent and which present themselves to an agent as checks on his natural inclinations or spontaneous tendencies to act" (Mackie 1990, 106).

Even Hume recognized that natural benevolence goes only so far. We "naturally" prefer our children to our nephews and them to the children of strangers; we "naturally" have a greater desire to protect our own property than that of others. However, to secure our interests requires broad social co-operation, and the establishment of fair rules that remedy our "unequal affections." Justice, or the protection of the common interest, originates in this social predicament and is therefore an "artificial" rather than "natural" virtue. It is a means of moderating our limited generosity that surfaces when we compete for limited resources. In conditions of extraordinary plenitude, then, there may be no need for morality, in conditions of extreme impoverishment no possibility of it (Hume 1983, 20–24).

History has tragically documented the truth of Hume's observations. Reflecting on survival in Auschwitz, Primo Levi writes of the shame he felt when liberated, because of his awareness of how his moral sense, like that of others, had been diminished:

> Not by our will, cowardice, or fault, yet nevertheless we had lived for months and years at an animal level: our days had been encumbered from dawn to dusk by hunger, fatigue, cold, and fear, and any space for reflections, reasoning, experiencing emotions was wiped out. We endured filth, promiscuity, and destitution, suffering much less than we would have suffered from such things in normal life, because our moral yardstick had changed. Furthermore, all of us had stolen: in the kitchen, the factory, the camp, in short, "from the others," from the opposing side, but it was theft nevertheless. Some (few) had fallen so low as to steal bread from their own companions.
>
> ▼▼▼▼▼
>
> I felt innocent, yes, but enrolled among the saved and therefore in permanent search of a justification in my own eyes and those of others. The worse survived, that is, the fittest; the best all died.
> *(Levi 1988, 75, 82)*

Morality, according to these thinkers, although not strictly an outcrop of human nature, grows from a recognition that limited human sympathies, in combination with limited resources, require a system of regulation if we wish to promote the general well-being. In most situations, we welcome rules of justice that will control our partialities (to ourselves, family, and friends) and restricted compassion.

Nonetheless, to agree that morality originates in our limited sympathies is to acknowledge that the content of morality is a human artifice; we have fallen back on our own invention, and its objectivity seems doubtful. The corrosive effect of our recognition that many of our preferences are cultivated, and culture-bound, remains unchallenged.

In addition, a morality based on "limited sympathies" cannot resolve the controversies that surround the content of morality and the justification of utilitarianism. The boys in Maria's class, for example, thought the pleasure of card-trading a good end, notwithstanding (perhaps because of) the competition and struggle that attend it. They were aware of the possible swindling, and took care of it as they thought fair. To Maria, the boys' means of punishing improper acts were themselves wrongful. A Kantian would presumably agree, but a utilitarian might defend not only the propriety of the boys' fighting but even the moral basis of a "laissez-faire" approach to their trading practices.

The boys might argue that the fight had a good outcome because, despite the minor injuries, it strengthened social bonds and left them feeling that they had solved their own problem in their own, mutually acceptable, way. The "swindling" might be deemed justified, or at least not a proper subject of deterrence, on the ground that Mark's experience of being "swindled," while temporarily upsetting, will teach him wariness, to his greater long-term benefit. Even Peter is more likely to acquire better business practices from learning over time that sharp practices may prove costly to him than from having his teacher lecture him about fairness.

Attempts, therefore, to universalize morality at the level of rules are clearly problematic. In response, some philosophers have sought to ground objective moral demands in principles rather than rules. A principle does not specify behavior but embodies broad criteria, which guide rather than prescribe decisions. Can individuals seeking moral guidance, recognizing that in any particular situation principles will not yield specific moral answers, nonetheless discern basic principles that are widely accepted and serviceable as signposts?

GROUNDING THE GOOD: SHARED PRINCIPLES

The principles suggested by philosophers as fundamental and universal, though they are abstract and imprecise, may help to test and validate or invalidate our moral choices. Mill, whose influence so permeates modern liberal democracies, suggested two basic premises from which we can deduce right and wrong. The first, which grounds what Kant and others call "perfect duties," is framed as a negative injunction: Do not do that which interferes with the rights of others. *Do no harm.* The most fundamental human right, to Mill, is the freedom to pursue one's own interests, to express one's own conscience, as long as the liberty of others is not threatened; the most fundamental wrong is the abridgment of that freedom. "[T]he only purpose for which power can be rightfully exercised over any member of a civilised community, against his will, is to prevent harm to others" (Mill 1859/1993, 78). Individuals have the perfect right to pursue their own interests, but that right is limited by the equal right of every other person. If we interfere with a person's interests we must do so impartially; any selective distinctions in assigning rights, privileges, and punishments must be justified as relevant. To be fair is to avoid arbitrary decisions, to give those whom we do not know or actively dislike the same treatment as those we favor.

The second premise, generating "imperfect duties," is a positive injunction: Be helpful and charitable. *Be beneficent.* While Mill regarded it as important, he saw only the first duty as morally obligatory.

Justice implies something which it is not only right to do, and wrong not to do, but which some individual person can claim from us as his moral right. No one has a moral right to our generosity or beneficence because we are not morally bound to practice those virtues towards any given individual.
(Mill 1861/1979, 49)

Mill privileged not-harming over helping because "a person may possibly not need the benefits of others, but he always needs that they should not do him hurt" (id., 62).

David Hume found in the principle of utility itself a basis for emphasizing the moral stature of the positive, "imperfect" duties: "[N]o qualities are more [e]ntitled to the general good-will and approbation of mankind than benevolence and humanity, friendship and gratitude, natural affection and public spirit, or whatever proceeds from a tender sympathy with others, and a generous concern for our kind and species" (Hume 1983, 18). The utility "resulting from the social virtues forms, at least, a *part* of their merit," Hume insisted, "and is one source of that approbation and regard so universally paid to them" (ibid.) (emphasis in original). Again, we see how malleable utilitarian principles are.

To contemporary philosopher John Rawls, whose principles of justice have been extremely influential, Mill's position on equality is insufficient because it permits great substantive inequalities. Whereas Mill, the utilitarian, would justify substantive inequality with a claim that overall social satisfaction is enhanced when there is minimum interference in the pursuit of happiness, Rawls, drawn to Kantian notions of human inviolability, does not believe such minimal restrictions on freedom make for a just society.

Rawls, therefore, proposes two principles of justice. The first, "each person is to have an equal right to the most extensive basic liberty compatible with a similar liberty for others" (Rawls 1971, 60), resembles Mills "perfect duties." But the second principle, justice as fairness, imposes further obligations. It demands substantive equality, not merely respecting political goods but all the major goods a society values: "liberty and opportunity, income and wealth, and the bases of self-respect" (id., 62). In the service of this equality, "social and economic inequalities are to be arranged so that they are both (a) to the greatest benefit of the least advantaged and (b) attached to offices and positions open to all under conditions of fair equality of opportunity" (id., 83). It is unjust, Rawls maintains, for social institutions to cause those advantaged by virtue of their greater talent, wealth, or power to accumulate more of the socially desired goods, unless the least advantaged benefits most as well.

The three principles—doing no harm, beneficence, and justice as fairness—are not only widely endorsed in our tradition and consonant with our intuitive moral sensibilities, they are widely espoused by other cultures as well. The contemporary moral philosopher, Sissela Bok, asserts: "All human groups, first of all, and all religious, moral, and legal traditions stress some form of positive duties regarding mutual support, loyalty, and reciprocity. Children have to be reared and the wounded, weak, and sick tended" (Bok 1995, 13). She goes on:

> All societies have stressed certain basic injunctions against at least a few forms of wronging other people—chief among these "force and fraud," or violence and deceit.
>
> [All societies have] norms for at least rudimentary fairness and procedural justice in cases of conflict regarding both positive and negative injunctions. . . .
> *(Id., 15–16)*[5]

(A fuller statement of Bok's views is found in the next section of this chapter, p. 111).

While such generic principles have considerable appeal and support, and the reader too may find an appreciable comfort level in them, critics point out that, as a way-station between ultimate moral sources and applicable codes, principles either overly or insufficiently constrain one's choices. The source of the problem is that the human situation said to give rise to moral systems— our "limited sympathies," in tension with our social interdependence—does not obviously or inevitably imply any particular set of principles, and the casting of principles in very general terms seems to gain less in breadth of support than it loses in useful substance.

Principles may be criticized for excessive vagueness. Absent an existing tradition that guides and limits the *interpretation* of principles, the values of no harm, beneficence, and fairness can justify widely incompatible norms. To be helpful, principles must be embedded in the purposes (*telos*) of a society and the social structures that support those purposes. According to contemporary philosopher Alasdair MacIntyre (1984), the practices and customs of a community—the "ways" in which we live—generate a hierarchy of virtues, which gives meaning to its underlying principles. One society values courage over compassion, another the reverse; even the identical virtue finds various expressions. In an individualistic society, for example, a mistreated child may be applauded for speaking out on his own or an injured friend's behalf; this prepares him well for taking large economic risks as an adult. In a more collectivist society, the same child might win praise for accepting his loss without complaint; this prepares him for being cautious before risking the collective interest. In both cases the virtue is labeled courage.

Criticizing principles for undue specificity (rather than excessive vagueness) are those who are skeptical when they are premised on individual rights and liberal democratic systems. They would not overlook or too broadly condemn societies that emphasize hierarchically organized social relations, such

---

[5] To similar effect are the conclusions of British philosophers Mary Warnock (1996, 49) and R. S. Peters (1974, 286).

as the New England Puritans or traditional Brahmin Indians. In those communities individual interests are subordinated to, or subsumed by, the interests of group harmony. The Brahmin who feels justified in beating his errant wife might assert that, in doing so, he is protecting the social order, and that his behavior is, indeed, morally indicated (obligatory and universalizable). His first responsibility and primary obligation is to a social structure that rests on the obedience of wives to husbands. Autonomous decision making would threaten that social structure. Interests and morals are not to be constructed by individuals, but accepted as part of the established traditions; one inherits them as a consequence of one's role and place in society.

This attitude, manifested today in tradition-oriented segments of contemporary society, has an egalitarian version as well. Mill's liberalism, such a critic would contend, fails to recognize its legitimation of societal indifference to the substantive welfare of others. Freedom to pursue one's own interests can mean enormous accumulation of power, privilege, and cultural control in the hands of a very few. Maria, like many teachers, seeks a fairness that is more than procedural; she wants substantive fairness, fairness that protects and ensures the welfare of everyone. She finds it unjust that, in the card-trading incident, a clever few accumulate money because they know how to take advantage of the naive. She wants to restrict Peter from "having it all."

Principles, then, either lack the actual neutrality that might entitle them to near-universal approval or are sufficiently open-textured that they simply defer the question of choice among plausible subjectivities. They are either grounded in customary practices, serving to rationalize the status quo, or, if kept at arms length from custom, offer scant guidance. The source and nature of moral authority remain elusive.

Contemporary social critic James Davison Hunter has soberly observed: "Intending to deepen innate moral sympathies and even build character, moral education takes shape in ways that make that impossible" (Hunter 2000, 225). "Every generation has sought to make moral education inclusive and universal. Yet without fail, any consensus that is achieved is soon attacked (and legitimately) as narrow, sectarian, not inclusive. In turn, a more inclusive solution is then offered, and the process repeats itself" (id., 77). "The quest for inclusiveness," he suggests, "can be pursued only by emptying lived morality of its particularity" (id., 210).

There are, however, many today who would find the ground of morality where society fairly confidently found it in years past, in traditional authority itself—whether the authority of culture, the family, or religion. To the role of contending attitudes toward the legitimacy of these sources of moral guidance, we now turn.

GROUNDING THE GOOD: AUTHORITY

"[T]he powers that be," in the classic words of St. Paul, "are ordained of God. Whosoever therefore resisteth the power, resisteth the ordinance of God" (*Ro-*

mans 13:1–2) (King James version). This famous thought captures several aspects of the belief that the search for an objective grounding of moral truth is not difficult, for the search for truth is primarily an exercise not in self-discovery, but in achieving conformance of one's self with the moral principles laid down by legitimate authority.

Chief among these, of course, is the authority of religion, which posits the Divine Will as the source of moral guidance, and the community of faith as its primary expositor. In the pre-modern world, the governmental structure set up under the monarchy drew its legitimacy from religion itself; the wearer of the English crown was (as his title pronounced) "King, by the grace of God." In later times, "the powers that be" meant in effect the prevalent norms of the democratic society in which we grew up. More specifically, and especially salient with respect to children and their upbringing, it meant one's parents and teachers.

On this view, moral education is the systematic reinforcement of the moral values that these sources espouse, and most especially the reinforcement of their legitimacy. It is *not* the development of the capacity to grapple with moral dilemmas, to reflect on complex moral questions; nor is it the validation of whatever actions flow from a conscientious process of decision making.

In premodern society, all of this was taken as self-evidently true. Modernism questioned the legitimacy, first, of monarchy, and of a hereditary aristocracy; then of a status-based world, in which one's calling and one's village were derived from one's parents; then of a state religion, as the rise of Protestantism, and its fragmentation, presented us with the choice between "toleration" and endless warfare. Today, the moral justification of all inherited values has been powerfully challenged. All authority is thought by many to be legitimate only if voluntarily assented to. That I view the Scriptures as the word of God is no reason why you should pay it attention; that you believe parents should be encouraged or allowed to determine their children's actions and life-choices is no reason why other people's children should be subjected to your regime; that you want to protect yourself, your children, and everyone else, from the rampant sexualization of children (and adults), whether in the name of self-actualization or of a higher gross national product, is no reason why society should come to your aid; if you believe that the "discovery" of America by Columbus was an event in human history to be celebrated, rather than primarily to be atoned for, you should make equal space for those who would teach that it set in motion a human disaster, the effects of which are still being reinforced. The bumper sticker, "If you don't believe in abortion, don't have one," expresses the point succinctly—and those who do not share that view as to the particular example might applaud it in other contexts.

The evolution of attitudes toward the authority of the teacher has illustrated this broader social phenomenon: originally, an axiomatic acceptance of the teacher's status as a widely respected source of moral guidance and discipline, then a more cautious insistence on considering the justification for the exercise of authority, more recently a tendency to "debunk" any attempted justification as a rationalization for power. To those who regard traditional sources of authority as for the most part legitimate, or at least believe that the delegitimation of authority has gone far beyond what is proper, moral education is essentially the restoration of respect for those sources of authority. To those who find significant *immorality* in all of the traditional holders of authority—religion, culture, and the family—it is essentially achieving liberation from those strictures.

It is, in our view, one's beliefs in this area, perhaps more than any other factor, that account for one's response to the many specific issues with which this book is concerned. However, we do not think it possible to arbitrate between these contending worldviews. Pronouncing one or the other position correct would simply establish membership in one of the contending camps. We two (the authors of this book) find ourselves at some significant distance from one another on the question (even though neither of us is wholly at one pole), and extended joint exploration of the question has not bridged that gap.

What is possible, and in our view essential, is to seek to find a way to understand, if not to decide between, the conflicting views. Those who continue to support the moral world of our forebears need to understand what is the basis of its fervent rejection, *in the name of morality*, by many of their fellow citizens. Those who share that fervor need, in our judgment, to leaven it with a sincere appreciation of what is being *lost* as well as gained in the wholesale rejection in our culture of the normative force of tradition, and the special pain that such rejection occasions for those who have remained content with the morality they were taught, and find our society systematically weaning their own children away from it.

GROUNDING THE GOOD: PLURALISM

Like our nineteenth-century forebears, we live in an age of declining moral certitudes. A number of major changes in our world have contributed to this decline, each of great moment and great complexity, and each warranting extended attention. However, we are not writing a history of our times, but only seeking to emphasize the fact that the issue of moral education is embedded in that history. Accordingly, we simply catalogue here some of the factors we have in mind:

- philosophically, the failed quest for universally acknowledged Truth;
- technologically, the rising influence of science, the rapidity of technological change, and the rise of instantaneous global communications;
- politically, the end of colonialism and the delegitimation of racially and religiously based notions of fitness to rule;
- sociologically, the continuing secularization of American life, the accelerating presence of multiple cultures within a single society, and the challenge of postmodernist thinking;

- psychologically, widened acceptance of the belief that an individual's instinctual nature and personal history ought to be regarded more hospitably in judging the morality of his or her actions.

These forces have had two polar effects: They have greatly strengthened the idea that moral relativism is self-evidently sensible, while at the same time fostering a resurgence of commitment to orthodoxy in morals, politics, religion—and education. This polarization of thought has made the search for common ground more important as well as more elusive.

Two conclusions are suggested (although not compelled) by the preceding portions of this section: First, thoroughgoing moral relativism just does not fit our intuition that moral good, and evil, *do* exist; second, none of the attempts to ground moral reality succeed in reducing moral questions to matters that one conscientious decision maker can resolve in a manner that is entitled to persuade or silence another.

Although individually plausible, together these conclusions give rise to a conundrum, out of which the case for value *pluralism* takes on strength. Pluralism asserts that, although each of us may strongly believe that objective criteria support at least certain of our value choices—that values are not just a matter of taste—one person's or group's beliefs do not justify insisting that others, who believe the contrary, nonetheless live by them. Some regard this pluralism of civil society as a regrettable necessity, perhaps hopefully a temporary necessity, until enough of their fellow citizens come to see the rightness of their views and the political will emerges to act on them. Pluralism as a philosophical stance, however, is rooted in a celebration, rather than a grim and grudging acceptance, of diversity of moral insight. Contemporary philosopher Lawrence Hinman looks for a "middle ground between relativism and absolutism [that] incorporates insights from both." He goes on:

> From relativism, it retains the sensitivity to the contextuality of our moral beliefs and the recognition that moral disagreement and conflict are permanent features of the moral landscape. From absolutism, it retains the commitment to the relevance of reasoned discourse in the moral life and the belief that some moral positions are better than others.
> *(Hinman 1994, 48)*

As humans—and this idea can be expressed in religious as well as secular terms—we are created with the capacity and the desire to seek, to know, and to follow the good, but since in all of those capacities and desires we are limited, none of us can claim or be claimed to have authoritatively found the Truth. Pluralism is therefore the *only* political or philosophical stance compatible with the hope that a society will remain committed to the continuing search for moral understanding, for the good.

Recall our contention, earlier in this section, that pluralism is not a responsible approach to arriving at an *individual's* understanding of morality. Pluralism addresses the *social* context. To the extent that it speaks to our moral decision making as individuals, it affects not the content of our opinions and beliefs but the intensity and fervor with which they are held, the attitude that we take toward those whose moral sense differs from our own. Pluralism, we believe, is an approach to the question how a society (or social institution such as a school) should respond to the fact that there is a great, although not limitless, diversity of values among people of good will. This diversity takes several related, but distinguishable, forms: (1) values that appear to be shared at some fundamental level but are applied in inconsistent ways because of differing premises about human psychology; (2) values that are shared but accorded differing priorities and that therefore cannot be ordered in an agreed-upon hierarchy; and (3) values that squarely conflict and are therefore incompatible. We will examine aspects of each of these variants.

(1) Diversity of ethical norms may largely reflect differing understandings of human nature or psychology, or of other empirical premises embedded in historical circumstances. The underlying ethical values may differ far less than first appears.

Consider, for example the Puritans of colonial New England. Without doubt their child-rearing objectives and practices, strict beyond strict, would be judged immoral, even criminal, today. Puritan parents swaddled their infants the first four months after birth to prevent movement of limbs and head; babies were hung on hooks while parents carried out daily chores; children were flogged with bundles of birch until blood flowed, and threatened with witches and ghosts, the torments of Hell, death, and damnation. Parents demanded extreme deference: When they entered a room the children rose and were not permitted to sit until their parents did so; when parents spoke children desisted even if they were in the middle of a conversation (Stone 1977).

Can we see such practices, so at variance with ours today, as other than vicious, cruel, profoundly immoral? Is there a way to "enter" this society, grasp their situatedness, and judge their values as, if not acceptable, at least not wholly evil?

Much of the Puritan approach to child-rearing was embedded in their understanding of the idea of original sin. The goal of life was to achieve salvation; to be saved, the taint of sin that is ours at birth must be eliminated. Parents prepared children for salvation by breaking their evil wills. This effort required full submission and obedience. "My word must be their law," was the code of the famous preacher, Cotton Mather. If that could be accomplished through affection, fine; if it required fear, fine too, for "[b]etter whipt than Damn'd" (see Morgan 1966, 103). If parents instilled in children habits of righteousness that became customary to them, the children would be the beneficiaries. "[I]f we accustom our selves to bear the Yoke in our Youth, it will afterwards fit more easy on our necks, it will not gall and fret us: The Commands will not be grievous unto us. Custom will lighten the Burden and endear the Yoke" (Thomas Foxcroft, as quoted, id., 94) (emphasis omitted).

A tight line of command was accepted by the society. Reverence and submission were due from children to mothers, mothers to fathers, fathers to the church and God. Salvation was not merely otherworldly. Puritans were required to establish a "visible" kingdom of God, "a society where outward conduct would be according to God's laws, a society where a smooth, honest, civil life would prevail. . . ." (id., 3).

Puritan parents believed tenderness and kindness produced waywardness; today, many believe the opposite: *punitiveness* produces waywardness. They "read" their children as naturally impulsive, disorderly, and hedonistic; today, many read their children as naturally loving and empathic. Puritan society had no ambivalence over right and wrong or the obligation of parents to bring children into conformity. The view that parents should support autonomy over obedience, should help children pursue autonomous interests and proclivities, would have struck them as negligent, probably sinful. So they advocated the birch, while we more willingly urge the embrace. Yet the premise of their approach, the belief that the child-rearing practices of parents were a major influence on the growth of children into law-abiding citizens, is widely shared today.

We have chosen a rather extreme example, although the consciousness of the Puritans is not wholly absent from contemporary America. We (some of us) may think the Puritans to have been grievously wrong, and their contemporary analogues even more so, with less understandable bases for their error. But the teaching of pluralism is not to demonize those who thought as they did and, today, not to move too quickly to call for the larger society to put the matter beyond individual family choice. Indeed, the example of child-rearing practice illustrates the point. Within limits that do not reach very far into family life, we as a society tend to think that the truth of these matters should be left for individual parents, and subcultures to discern, free of a national moral plebescite. Yet, this quickly becomes problematic for a school, which reflects in many ways majoritarian views on critical aspects of child-rearing and moral development. (We will examine in Chapter 7 some of the genuine difficulties presented by the desire of parents whose ways differ from most to have their values incorporated into the life of the school, or into the school life of their children.)

(2) When there is apparent agreement on certain moral values, the more difficult task is to rank or choose among them. For there are multiple goods. Self-control, respect, reverence, simplicity are one set of goods; spontaneity, expressiveness, affection, doubt, and beauty are another. The Puritans leaned toward the former, perhaps we (some of us) favor the latter. Even within a culture that has established fundamental principles, there is moral disagreement over time and within any historical time period.

One need not look far for examples. The United States, committed to an ethic of equality and liberty, supports an economy in which the daily earnings of some are more than the yearly earnings of others, and in which substantially more is spent on a suburban child's public education than that of his urban peer. The moral justification of these conditions is publicly contested because it puts at issue multiple goods, which different citizens (like different societies) rank differently. Freedom is often pitted against equality—"total liberty for wolves is death to the lambs" (Berlin 1959/1992, 12)—just as justice is pitted against mercy, tolerance against conviction, and individual loyalty against group harmony. Each of us may be quite convinced that equality is more, or less, important than freedom. Pluralism counsels against moving too easily from an individual judgment on that question to a societal one.

(3) At times, the diversity of values may be not merely a difference in apparent values or the ranking of goods, but reflect profound disagreement on the nature of a moral community. The morality of Indian Brahmans, for example, may be irreducibly at variance with that of the Western democracies. Individual autonomy, individual rights, and equality before the law are simply not the primary goods of Brahmin culture. (See the discussion of the Schweder study, p. 48, in Chapter 3). Some applications of this ethic strike many Americans as quite shocking. While it may be justifiable to decide as a polity that pluralism should not go so far as to permit members of that culture to continue to live by their cultural norms when they reside here, pluralism does suggest remaining aware of the ways (limited, perhaps) in which such a culture has its own integrity.

As this example reveals, pluralism, if it is to remain distinct from relativism, must police its boundaries. Some moral choices, even if sincerely made, are not to be accepted in the name of pluralism. There are actions—for example, the wanton killing of innocent people—that, across cultures and centuries, we all agree are immoral. G. J. Warnock puts the point this way:

> [I]t is *not* true that every moral question is "a matter of opinion," still less a matter of taste or personal preference, or choice. That lying, murder, and violence for the sake of my private pleasures is morally wrong is a proposition that I may, of course, view with complete indifference. I may even think it right to do what is morally wrong. I can of course deny that proposition, refuse to admit it, as I can, if sufficiently brazen, deny anything at all. However, the proposition is true, and not disputably so. (*Warnock 1971, 124–125*)

How does this pluralist approach apply to Alfred's initial justification of fighting?[6] The answer would be easy if his notion of respect, and standing up for yourself, was invoked to justify a fight with knives. But a limited use of fists, in a constrained encounter to which all of the participants apparently

---

[6] "We just don't see it your way. You talk about respect and all that stuff. Well, we keep our respect by not letting no one take advantage of us. I help Mark out because he's not that strong yet. He helps me plenty with school work. We help each other; we stand up for each other. That's respect for us."

consented and in which the two sides were of approximately equal strength and size, is another matter. Like the other means of "grounding the good" that we have examined, no answer is logically enshrined by pluralism. What to one is "indisputably" wrong, to another is arguably but not indisputably so. Pluralism finds it easier to assert that a boundary exists than to suggest in any very helpful way its contours.

One who believes, for example, with Connie Comfort that it is extremely important to "hold the line" against all violent forms of disputing will think it plain that the boys should be told that what they did was wrong. (Recall that the fight occurred after school and off its property; no one is suggesting that the boys be punished by the school for what they did.) Others might prefer a more "understanding" response, acknowledging the plausibility of Alfred's claim but emphasizing the danger that resort to violence may overstep acceptable limits. These contrasting priorities will reflect in part teachers' differing levels of confidence in vigorously condemning the specific conduct in question. They will, however, also reflect differing attitudes to questions examined in the preceding chapter regarding the relative value of habituating children to rules, as against encouraging them to become reflective and responsible for the consequences of their actions.

More specifically, support for a limit on a pluralist response might be found in the idea that a school may properly seek to socialize students to attitudes and behavior that are morally worthy, even if not obligatory, but are systematically discouraged in our culture. Again, the resort to nonviolent, mutually respectful modes of settling disputes and redressing grievances provides an example. A quick outburst of violence finds daily reinforcement in the world that children observe and participate in; "talking it out," giving and receiving feedback, peer mediation, and such responses hardly have equal time in students' consciousness as they develop their own moral sense. One might justify Maria's intervention on the ground that, just as students must be required to read good literature if they are to be able to exercise an informed choice in later life, a truly pluralist intervention, one that enables her students to learn about and experience *both* approaches to conflict, requires her to present the nonviolent option as one with which her students must engage while they are in her classes.

When the matter in question concerns the actions of students while *at school*, the case for pluralism is often overcome by the felt needs of the institution. Many would say that a school, or teacher, should not be expected to tolerate, indeed, should not tolerate, even a moderate and understandable use of retaliatory violence by a student. Others will question whether our delegitimation of nearly all manifestations of aggression in children does not go too far, whether judged in terms of the reasonableness of teachers' expectations of consistently pacific conduct in school or in terms of the consequences to children of pervasive repression of aggressive tendencies.

More broadly, schools will often respond inhospitably to parental concerns that some aspects of the program affront the parents' moral or educational priorities. Examples of such concern are the presence (or absence) of certain units of study, exposure (or lack of exposure) to certain career options, emphasis (or de-emphasis) on successful participation in competitive sports, or on community service as part of the educational program. Many of these issues are seen as implicating important moral values, and parents will invoke (perhaps without naming it as such) the pluralist value of allowing *them* to determine the moral influences on their child. At times, however, schools will override parental objections on the basis of inconsistency with the majority moral judgment or of the simple administrative need for uniformity. We consider aspects of this difficult and important problem in Chapter 7.

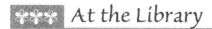 At the Library

Christina Hoff Sommers, "Ethics Without Virtue: Moral Education in America"

(1984, 387–389)

The new interest in applied ethics is . . . a phenomenon to be welcomed. Public discussions of controversial issues will surely benefit from the contributions of philosophers, and the literature of applied ethics should be read by anyone who seeks a responsible understanding of topical issues. In reading the anthologies of applied ethics, a student encounters arguments of philosophers who take strong stands on important social questions. These arguments often shake a student's confidence in moral relativism.

Nevertheless, the literature of applied ethics . . . has little or nothing to say about matters of individual virtue. The resurgence of moral education in the college thus reinforces the shift away from personal morals to an almost exclusive preoccupation with the morality of institutional policies. After all, most students are not likely to be involved personally in administering the death penalty or selecting candidates for kidney dialysis; and, since most will never do recombinant DNA research, or even have abortions, the purpose of the courses in applied ethics is to teach students how to form responsible opinions on questions of social policy. A strong ethical curriculum is a good thing, but a curriculum of ethics without virtue is a cause for concern.

The applied ethics movement in the universities started in the late nineteen sixties when philosophers became interested once again in normative ethics. The new university moralists [however, are] addressing themselves, not to the vices and virtues of individuals, but to the moral character of our nation's institutions. Take a look at almost any text used today in college ethics courses . . . and you will find that almost all of the articles consist of philosophical evaluations of the conduct and policies of schools, hospitals, courts, corporations, and the United States government.

Inevitably the student forms the idea that applying ethics to modern life is mainly a question of learning how to be for or against social and institutional policies.

Appropriately enough, many of the articles sound like briefs written for a judge or legislator. In that sort of ethical climate, a student soon loses sight of himself as a moral agent and begins to see himself as a moral spectator.... This is not to deny that many of the issues have an immediate personal dimension. They do, but the primary emphasis is not on what one is to do as a person but on what one is to believe as a member of society—in other words, on ideology and doctrine rather than on personal responsibility and practical decency.

... Today the student is learning that normative ethics is primarily social policy. This being so, ... the individual's task is to bring the right civic institutions (the true moral agents) into place. The student tacitly assumes that ethics is not a daily affair, that it is a matter for specialists, and that its practical benefits are deferred until the time of institutional reform.

The result of identifying normative ethics with public policy is justification for and reinforcement of moral passivity in the student. Even problems that call for large-scale political solutions have their immediate private dimension, but a student trained in a practical ethics that has avoided or de-emphasized individual responsibility is simply unprepared for any demand that is not politically or ideologically formulated. The student is placed in the undemanding role of the indignant moral spectator who needs not face the comparatively minor corruptions in his own life.

We share Professor Sommers' concern over the pervasive tendency to prefer to debate ethical aspects of public policy rather than to grapple with the choices that we face in our individual, family, school, and work lives. As we said in the Introduction, we seek in this book to acknowledge and honor the complexity and subjectivity of our daily moral judgments by probing their nuances and the premises that guide our responses to them, in contexts that call upon the individual teachers, administrators, and students in the scenarios to make morally significant choices.

The following reading supplies a philosopher's reasoning in support of the specific challenge posed by Maria's students: whether (putting aside cases of self-defense) it is always wrong for people to respond to grievances through physical means.

Mary Midgley, *Wickedness: A Philosophical Essay*
(1984, 88–90)

THE FUNCTIONS OF AGGRESSION

Undoubtedly, we need to understand the dangers of our innate aggressive tendencies, just as we do those of our motives. But we can scarcely do this unless we also understand their positive functions. If we think of aggression as Freud did, as a pure wish for destruction, it is hard to see any positive function for it.... But is anger like this? Is it something which it would be a good thing to get rid of entirely?

Ought we to proclaim "freedom from anger" as a fifth freedom, and aim to eliminate all conflict from human life? . . .

To decide about this, we have to consider realistically the part which mild, controlled aggression actually plays in human social life. As with fear, it is probably best to start here by looking at the behavior of small children. At this simple, primitive end of the spectrum, simulated attack is a marked and essential part of play. This is not because children are full of hatred and destruction. It is because the sense of otherness, the contact with genuinely distinct personalities around them, fascinates them, and it is best conveyed by mild collision. Laughter and other distancing devices safeguard the proceedings — but the wish to collide, to invade another's world, is a real one. Without that contact, each child would be isolated. Each needs the direct physical clash, the practical conviction that others as well as himself are capable both of feeling pain and of returning it. Surprising though it may be, that interaction lies at the root of sympathy. The young of other social animals play in the same mildly aggressive way, and derive the same sort of bond-forming effects from it.

Besides play, however, children also need at times more serious clashes. Real disputes, properly expressed and resolved, seem essential for their emotional unfolding. In this way they begin to get a fuller sense of the independent reality of others. They find that there is somebody at the other end. They learn to control their own anger, to understand it and to reason themselves out of it. A quarrel which is worked through and made up can be profoundly bond-forming. But they need to feel anger before they can control it and to learn that it can sometimes be justified. They learn the difference between justified and unjustified anger, and come to accept that justified anger in others can be the consequence of one's own bad conduct. What they learn is thus not to eliminate anger and attack from their lives, but to use these things rightly. And in adults, right up to the level of saints and heroes, this is an essential skill. Mild, occasional anger is a necessary part of all social relations and serious anger gives us, as I have suggested, a necessary range of responses to evil. Our linked capacities for fear and anger — for fight and flight — form a positive organ to be used, not a malfunction. This no more commits us to misusing it than our having feet commits us to kicking people.

The readings that follow present, first, two teachers' emotional and analytic responses to the claim that one cannot judge any act as moral or immoral, then a portion of Sissela Bok's attempt to avoid the polar positions of relativism and dogmatism.

▼▼

Kay Haugaard, "The Lottery Revisited"
(1997, B4)

Once again I was going to teach Shirley Jackson's short story "The Lottery." . . .

The story opens with a depiction of the residents of an American country village. It is a brilliant summer morning, and people are gathering for some kind of annual ritual. The people are portrayed as warm, loving, hard-working, and earnest; they pique our curiosity by mentioning, but not describing, a lottery that is important to the crops. Mr. Adams starts to say that some villages have stopped the lotteries, but Old Man Warner cuts off all further discussion by declaring those people a "pack of young fools."

We get to know one family—the Hutchinsons. Tess Hutchinson, the mother, arrives late for the public drawing, explaining that she had to do the dishes. Her twelve-year-old daughter talks with friends; her little son, Dave, gathers a pile of stones—the sort of thing little boys play at. According to the custom, Tess's husband draws a ticket for the whole family from a black box. Nothing prepares the first-time reader for what happens next: Everyone, including four-year-old Dave, sets on Tess Hutchinson and stones her to death. This is a lottery for human sacrifice.

The story always impressed the class with the insight that I felt the author had intended: the danger of just "going along" with something habitually, without examining its rationale and value. The power of public pressure was illustrated chillingly, in the ease with which the conversation about other villages' dropping the practice had been squelched.

In spite of the changes that I had witnessed over the years in anthologies and in students' writing, Jackson's message about blind conformity always spoke to my students' sense of right and wrong. Jackson had made an important and powerful point, which I hoped my students would take to heart, becoming more analytical about why things are done as they are.

"So, what did you think of 'The Lottery'?" I asked as soon as I sat down in front of the class. Beth, a slender, stylish woman in her mid-40s, pushed up the sleeves of her enormously baggy sweater as she spoke: "I was rather surprised that this seemed to be taking place in the United States and like it was right now."

"Yes, it does make it more shocking when the characters seem like people we might know, or even be, doesn't it?" I said. . . .

. . . I turned to Edward . . . "What was your response to the story, Edward?" He bounced the foot of his crossed leg and looked up with a kind of bored expression. "It was all right. It wasn't that great." But, I pressed, "[h]ow about that ending, where the whole village turns on one of their neighbors and kills her with stones? Had you read it before?" Edward furrowed his brow but refused to be impressed. "No, I hadn't read it before. It was all right."

I could not believe these responses. Everyone seemed so blase. Giving up on Edward, who was never very vocal in discussions, I turned to Richard, a slightly graying elementary-school teacher. "Why do these people perform this ritual, Richard, this human sacrifice?" He took a deep breath. "Well, I agree with Beth that it was pretty surprising to have it take place right today, as it were." "But why do they do it?" I persisted. "Uh, well, it isn't too clear."

Someone else spoke up. "For the crops. They do it so the crops will grow well." "That's one of the reasons they give," I responded, pleased that someone had found a clue in the text. "Is that a sufficient justification? Any other reason?"

▼▼▼▼▼

"I was wondering if there was anything religious about it," said Beth. "If this were part of something of long standing. It doesn't seem to be religious." "Would that make a difference, if it were part of a religious ritual?" Beth furrowed her brows and gazed toward the ceiling.

"There isn't anything mentioned in the story about religion, but it does seem related to religious traditions of human sacrifice intended to make the crops grow better," I said.

"Oh, well, if it was something like that . . . ," Beth responded. "How do you mean? That would make it all right?" "Are you asking me if I believe in human sacrifice?" Beth responded thoughtfully, as though seriously considering all aspects of the question. "Well, yes," I managed to say. "Do you think that the author approved or disapproved of this ritual?" I was stunned: This was the woman who wrote so passionately of saving the whales, of concern for the rain forests, of her rescue and tender care of a stray dog. "I really don't know. If it was a religion of long standing."

For a moment I couldn't even respond. This woman actually couldn't seem to bring herself to say plainly that she was against human sacrifice. . . .

"There have been studies," said Richard, "about certain cultures, and they show that, when there aren't any killings for a long time, the people seem to . . . require it to satisfy this. . . ." I listened in a state of shock as Richard went on to describe a psychological theory he had read that seemed to espouse the social function of a certain amount of bloodshed. "It almost seems a need," he concluded in cool, reasonable tones.

It was too much. I had always tried to keep my personal feelings out of class discussion and allow the students to discover a story's theme and significance as much as possible. But I had reached my limit. "There certainly are precedents for it," I said, "but does a precedent necessarily make something right? I think the author strongly disapproves of this ritual and is attempting to shock us into re-examining our activities every now and then to see if they still seem justified and functional."

I went on, probably longer than I should have. "The Aztecs believed that the sun would not rise if they did not feed the hummingbird god Huichtlipochtli with human blood. This was their rationale for human sacrifice. But we know that the sun will rise on its own. Are these things justified on the basis of precedent?"

I turned to Patricia, a 50-something, redheaded nurse. She had always seemed an intelligent person of moderate views. "Well, I teach a course for our hospital personnel in multicultural understanding, and if it is part of a person's culture, we are taught not to judge, and if it has worked for them. . . ."

At this point I gave up. No one in the whole class of more than twenty ostensibly intelligent individuals would go out on a limb and take a stand against human sacrifice. I wound up the discussion. "Frankly, I feel it's clear that the author was pointing out the dangers of being totally accepting followers, too cowardly to rebel against obvious cruelties and injustices." I was shaken, and I thought that the author, whose story had shocked so many, would have been shaken as well.

The class finally ended. It was a warm night when I walked out to my car after class that evening, but I felt shivery, chilled to the bone.

Robert L. Simon, "Suspending Moral Judgment: The Paralysis of 'Absolutophobia'"
(1997, B5)

"Of course I dislike the Nazis," one of my students commented, "but who is to say they are morally wrong?" Other students in my classes on moral and political philosophy have made similar remarks about apartheid, slavery, and ethnic cleansing. They make the assertion as though it were self-evident; no one, they say, has the right even to criticize the moral views of another group or culture.

. . . I have recently seen an increasing number of students who . . . accept the reality of the Holocaust, but they believe themselves unable morally to condemn it, or indeed to make any moral judgments whatsoever. Such students typically comment that they themselves deplore the Holocaust and other great evils, but then they wind up by suspending moral judgment.

In an increasingly multicultural society, it is not surprising that many students believe that criticizing the codes of conduct of other groups and cultures is either unwise or prohibited. They equate such criticism with intolerance and the coercive imposition of a powerful culture's norms on the less powerful.

Does a decent respect for other cultures and practices really require us to refrain from condemning even the worst crimes in human history? Does it make moral judgment impossible?

I maintain that it does not. The growing moral paralysis of some of our best students arises because they have become entangled in abstract premises that, however fashionable they may be, are grounded in confusion and misunderstanding.

To begin with, note that students—and others—who feel that a respect for other cultures requires them not to criticize practices different from their own already are making moral judgments. . . . They believe, for example, that we ought to respect other cultures, that we ought to be tolerant of practices different from our own, and that we ought to welcome diversity rather than fear it. In fact, not only are they making moral judgments, they are making precisely the ones that should lead to condemnation of the Nazis.

How, then, can we explain this unwillingness to condemn great evils? Although there probably is no simple explanation, several assumptions by students play a role.

The first is that . . . those who make moral judgments are felt to be "absolutists," and, of course, we all know there are no absolutes. The idea seems to be that those who assert absolutes are dogmatic and intolerant, and that they advance simple, inflexible general principles that allow no exceptions. Students, therefore, believe that making moral judgments means that they are closed to further discussion—that they would be taking an inflexible stand that they must maintain, come what may. Perhaps the inflexibility and closed-mindedness of much of what passes for political debate in our society reinforces this image.

But although there may be some absolutists among us, and perhaps even some "absolutes," there is nothing about moral judgment that requires inflexibility, intolerance, fanaticism, unwillingness to argue and debate, or an inability to recognize that many issues exist on which reasonable people of good will may disagree. In fact, as I've noted, the claim that we ought to be tolerant and willing to consider the viewpoints and arguments of others is itself a moral judgment, one that many of our skeptical students make, however unwilling they may be to acknowledge it.

An antidote to this reluctance to make moral judgments, then, is to replace "absolutophobia" with an appreciation of the richness, diversity, and openness that make up moral discourse and moral judgment. Discussion of moral issues need not consist of two fanatics asserting conflicting principles they regard as self-evident; it can involve dialogue, the consideration of the points raised by others, and an admission of fallibility on all sides.

The second assumption that students should examine is that we are so inextricably embedded in our own individual perspectives—or those of our social or ethnic group, race, or gender—that the kind of impartiality or detachment from our own viewpoint that moral judgment requires is impossible. One of my students summed up this view on a recent examination paper, arguing that the social constructions of race, gender, and class make impartial assessment of a moral issue impossible.

What this student failed to consider is that . . . , although we certainly do need to be aware of biases that may taint our evaluations, asserting that such biases are so pervasive and inescapable that they make objectivity impossible undercuts the very possibility of having reasons for our opinions at all—including reasons for thinking that we are all biased.

Crude forms of relativism, then, are open to strong logical objection. What then, makes these views, which are so vulnerable to reasoned criticism, so pervasive? What gives them so strong a hold on so many students? Part of the answer probably lies in students' interpretations (or misinterpretations) of multiculturalism and postmodernism. As understood by the relativist student, these views suggest that any criticism of another culture's practices is a kind of cultural imperialism. Second, the postmodern rejection of many of the ideals of the Enlightenment is taken to imply that, because we all speak from some particular perspective, truly objective moral knowledge is impossible to attain.

Sophisticated multiculturalists surely do not want to assert that all views are equally justified, for on many issues they claim that multicultural approaches are more justified than traditional ones. Similarly, sophisticated postmodernists surely want to claim that their own critique of many ideals of the Enlightenment is itself well-founded. So if multicultural and postmodernist approaches are to avoid intellectual incoherence, they cannot support the crude relativism that we are hearing from some of our students.

Sissela Bok, *Common Values*
(1995, 10–11, 13–18)

CULTURAL DIVERSITY AND COMMON VALUES

Does it make sense to envisage a morality shared across cultural, linguistic, and other barriers? In what sense can we still speak . . . of "morals for mankind?" Or even of . . . "consensus morality" within a society? And how, in speaking thus, can we also grant the fullest respect for cultural and other diversity? It is not possible, many argue, to insist on respecting both difference and sameness when it comes to moral values: on honoring individual and cultural diversity while also holding that certain moral values go to the heart of what it means to be human. . . .

Such doubts are understandable. Too often in the past, those who have spoken of universal values have intended to impose their own religious and political value systems coercively as a pattern for all to adopt. And even in the absence of aims to dominate and conquer, we have to ask whether it is not simply naive to invoke common values or consensus morality. . . .

Not all societies have developed ideals such as those of liberty, equality, or the sanctity of life, much less identical ones. The same is true of views regarding religious faiths or political systems, not to mention the rules regarding diet, clothing, and sexuality that differ so greatly among societies. What values, then, can lay claim to being more universally present in spite of the differences on so many other scores? I suggest that there are three categories of values so fundamental to group survival that they have had to be worked out in even the smallest community.

*****

A.   . . . [A]ll religious, moral, and legal traditions stress some form of positive duties regarding mutual support, loyalty, and reciprocity. Children have to be reared and the wounded, weak, and sick tended. As the Roman thinker Cicero puts it, nature brings human beings together for purposes of survival and implants in them "a strangely tender love" for their offspring.

Many traditions—Judeo-Christian, Muslim, Confucian, Buddhist, and Hindu among them—also expressly enjoin children to obey and honor their parents. . . .

The injunctions to honor and obey parents and to offer other forms of family and group support differ greatly in scope; even the most limited ones are too often outrageously violated in practice. Otherwise they would not need to be stated as injunctions and commandments. But any community in which they were altogether lacking would be short-lived.

*****

B.   The second category of fundamental values consists of negative duties to refrain from harmful action. All societies have stressed certain basic injunctions against at least a few forms of wronging other people—chief among these "force and fraud," or violence and deceit. From the Ten Commandments to Buddhist, Jain, Confucian, Hindu, and many other texts, violence and deceit are most consistently rejected, as are the kinds of harm they make possible, such as torture and theft. . . . They have been [condemned] in works as different as the Egyptian Book of the Dead, the Icelandic Edda, and the Bhagavad-Gita.

*****

C.   A third category of basic values worked out in all societies consists of norms for at least rudimentary fairness and procedural justice in cases of conflict regarding both positive and negative injunctions. . . . Views regarding the modalities of justice differ, as do legal systems; but all societies share certain fundamental procedures for listening to both sides and determining who is right and who is wrong in disputes. Thus, in working out the basics of fairness, every known society with rules for trials has rejected the bearing of false witness—something that vitiates a fair trial from the outset. Likewise, all societies have some rule of "treating as equal what is equal under the accepted system," just as it is everywhere perceived as unfair, from childhood on, to punish one person for what someone else has done.

*****

The fact that certain values are so widely recognized does not mean that people automatically acknowledge them as held in common, least of all among enemy groups. . . . And the three categories of value are limited in scope even within communities. Violence, for example, against women, or children, or slaves and servants has been common from biblical times on.

In setting forth the three categories of values, therefore, my intention is not to suggest that they can somehow serve right away as cross-cultural standards of conduct. . . . Rather, I suggest viewing them in a minimalist perspective. The term *minimalist* . . . characterize[s] a limited set of fundamental values, helpful in specifying the characteristics and possible functions of values recognizable across cultural and other boundaries.

Part 3

The Content of Morality

Chapter 5

The Good at School

A "Swarm of Virtues"?

 ## At School

Leaving school one wintry afternoon, Maria was startled to hear the principal's voice on the intercom announcing a forthcoming in-service presentation on character education by Jan Bonham, her old "Educational Foundations" teacher. This had not been listed on the school calendar and, struggling not to be paranoid about it, she wondered what precipitated the invitation.

Spying Connie Comfort coming from the rest room, she asked, "Connie, do you know anything about this Bonham business?"

"Me? She was *your* teacher!"

"Connie, cut it out! That little talk we had makes me wonder whether you put Helter up to this."

"Come on, Maria, you don't really think that everything happening around here is about you! Yes, Helter was there in the cafeteria, but believe me he's been getting complaints about the kids from staff, teachers, and just last week from a bunch of parents. One of them might have been the mother of that kid, Mark, in your class."

"What about, exactly?" Maria asked.

"Nothing we don't already know: That the cafeteria is bedlam, with kids talking rudely to food servers, saving seats for friends, discarding wrappers, and sometimes even food, on the floor; that the school property is a mess, with littered hallways, dirty bathrooms, and some graffiti on the walls; that the children curse, shove, fight, interrupt teachers and each other, talk during class, chew gum; that they look awful, with some of the older boys sporting weird hair cuts and a few of the older girls wearing eye makeup, nose rings, and some very tight skirts."

"So, is Jan Bonham supposed to descend from the ivory tower to tell us how to deal with this stuff?" Maria asked with irritation. "Why in the world didn't you talk Helter out of that idea?"

"Because," Connie responded, "I thought bringing Bonham here was better than Helter's alternative."

"Which was . . . ?"

"'Cracking down,' I think it's called. Assigning a fleet of monitors—you can guess who the monitors would have been—to the hallways, lunchrooms, bathrooms, and the grounds outside school."

"Well, thanks, I guess, for heading that off, but now we'll have a lesson on Aristotle's virtues and the kids will stop chewing gum, right?"

"Maria, let's give her a chance. I share your doubts. I told Helter we needed something practical; none of the airy-fairy stuff of the college classroom. But look, sometimes 'practical' doesn't cut it either. What Helter described was plenty practical but neither you nor I could stomach it. Some of those parents didn't want him to stop at monitors, either; they suggested bathroom passes, silence in the hallways, assigned seats in the cafeteria, parental sign-offs on every piece of homework, more detentions, and. . . . "

"OK, Connie, I get the picture. Listen, I've nothing against Bonham; in fact I like her. It's just that turning every trouble into an issue of morality still bugs me, not to mention that the finger seems to be pointing especially at me, on account of that blow-up in the caf. But I'll come with an open mind. See you there."

Maria arrived early for the in-service to greet her former teacher. Jan Bonham seemed pleased, although a bit embarrassed, to see her.

"Maria Laszlo, hello! Good to see you again. I knew you were teaching here but, remembering our last conversation, I'm afraid you're here today under compulsion. You haven't become a convert to moral education, have you? Should I have brought along those summer books to lend back to you?"

Put at ease by Bonham's lighthearted manner, Maria replied, "Well, I've got to admit I may be a little ways closer to retrieving them than I was in August, but you don't quite yet have a convinced disciple on your hands."

"Maybe today will turn the tide," Jan smiled. "Meanwhile, how about giving me a hand with these displays. I'd like to lay the booklets out on the table and tack the charts to the wall."

Maria began rummaging through the large well-stocked bags, pulling out posters, spiral notebooks, videos, handouts, articles. She vaguely recognized the materials. They came from the better known moral education programs—Character Counts Coalition, Character Education Curriculum, Child Development Project, Community of Caring, Heartwood Curriculum, Jefferson Center for Character Education, Just Schools. Maria was glad to realize—what she shouldn't have doubted—that this in-service would not be focused on *her*, her students, her problems, or her competence. She was also happy that it apparently wasn't going to be a heavy theory trip, either, but whatever relief that awareness gave her was overcome by her immediate discomfort with the materials she was looking at. Was morality these days taught in glossy spirals and laminated posters, with a lot of superficial catch-words? So much stuff! Lots of people and lots of money must have been harnessed to their production. A whole new industry was blooming.

She thought back to her parochial school days. The nuns would have been appalled by this; her parents, too. It felt crude (even though it was slick), blatant, excessive, yet also insufficient—something like shopping for food in a huge, oversupplied supermarket, with rows of products all overwrapped, overdecorated, and overpromising. These moral instructions, she feared, would be as thin, fragile, and overmarketed as the colorful cellophane wrappers that contained them.

She also realized that the packaged, 1-2-3-step approach reminded her of reading workshops she had attended. Given the various and complex ways children come to read, those ordered prescriptive curricula were troubling enough, but helping children become decent human beings through a laminated-poster approach?

Decency, she mused, is a subtle accomplishment. You pick it up, mostly at home, in little ways: You notice how family members treat one another, how they express their care and expectations for you and others. Learning to be decent is more like learning to love than learning to read. It's about cultivating a generous spirit, aspiring to be better, do more, embrace worthy challenges. She was beginning to get a handle on her nagging misgivings: Morality was too precious, she revered it *too* much, to see it turned into concrete step-by-step lesson plans. Maybe that was why she was wary of bringing it into the school curriculum in the first place.

Jan broke in on her reverie: "How's it going, Maria? What do you think of this stuff?"

Maria chose to respond only to the first question. "Sorry, Dr. Bonham, I got distracted by the materials. I'll get the job done quickly so you can start on schedule."

After briefly introducing the topic and its importance, Bonham spent the first hour of the in-service explaining the gist of each moral education program. There was considerable variety among them in both content and method of delivery, and each was more complex than she had first noted. Maria's rush to judgment was, once again, too precipitous.

Take the Character Education Curriculum (Character Education Institute, 1994). True, she was turned off by the glossy prepackaged items, their "pricey-ness," and most especially the word lists. She recalled the endless vocabulary lessons from her own schooling: how she would memorize, and then promptly forget, the definitions. For starters, the Character Education Curriculum upholds the basic universal values of *"honesty, truthfulness, generosity, kindness, helpfulness, justice, tolerance, honor, courage, convictions, equality, freedom."* In addition it emphasizes, *"good self-esteem, responsibility, drug prevention education, self-discipline for setting and achieving goals, critical thinking, decision-making skills, resisting negative peer pressure, respect for rules, laws, and authority, accepting individual differences, cooperative learning, economic security"* (id., 3).

No doubt the words have a ringing cadence (also a preachy one), but where do they get you? What's the difference between honesty and truthfulness, between generosity and helpfulness? Aren't there times when honesty is unkind, when generosity is unhelpful? And how did self-esteem get on the list of moral traits? Do we check out a person's self-esteem when judging her character? It struck her as sloganeering and, once again, as trivializing the preciousness of morality, even granting a sincere effort by the curriculum designers to deliver it.

On the other hand, the sample dilemmas used by the Character Education Curriculum pose genuine tough quandaries—Should, and when should, one turtle give up his swing for another? What's the difference between tattling and honesty? Is it fair for children to exclude others from play groups? Perhaps these issues did need to be brought up deliberately through lesson plans, and not just when a "problem" arose, which was her bent.

Character Counts (of the Character Counts Coalition, 1995) struck Maria as fairly similar. It has audio and video tapes, books, posters and kits, and a list of virtues called the Six Pillars: *Trustworthiness* (including Honesty, Integrity, Promise-Keeping, Loyalty), *Respect for Others, Responsibility* (including Accountability, Excellence, and Self-Restraint), *Fairness, Caring, Citizenship.*

At first glance the Heartwood Curriculum for Elementary School Children also looked like yet another iteration with its list of attributes: *courage, loyalty, justice, respect, hope, honesty,* and *love.* But it attempts, through legends and folk tales from the world's literature, to guide children toward ethical literacy by helping them structure a responsible system of values (An Ethics Curriculum for Children, 1992). Maria's imagination was piqued by the thought that stories, sufficiently complex and relevant, might be a great discussion tool for increasing moral awareness.

The Jefferson Center program (1995) also has a strong process element, with the acronym STAR (stop, think, and review). She found this more behavioral approach stilted and artificial.

The Child Development Project takes a different tack. It stresses "sociomoral development" through cooperation, community-building, and "positive affective relationships" (Battistich et al. 1991). Its word list has two "central components"—*cooperative learning* and *developmental discipline* (self-control and "internalization of prosocial values")—along with three "supportive components"—*promoting social understanding, helping activities,* and *highlighting prosocial values.* Fairness, responsibility, honesty, tolerance, and courage are subsidiary to, or incorporated into, the other components. To Maria, the Child Development Project seemed less packaged and more process-oriented than the others. The authors apparently expect that morality will emerge from children if adults encourage their understanding of, and feelings for, one another. The tone seemed softer, gentler. Maria was drawn to the "constructivist," "collaborative," "caring" emphasis, and she appreciated the absence of posters, videos, and kits. Still she squirmed. "Cooperative learning" sounded good but she now knew how easily it gets undermined. In her class, cooperation often deteriorated into the dominant kids lording it over submissive ones and children complaining about one another. And she thought it might be very Pollyannish to bank on the emergence of goodness from a group of children. Peter and company had certainly taught her that.

While Maria was alternately struggling against her judgmental crabbiness and succumbing to it, Hardie, seated a few rows away, was beaming with enthusiasm. At the break, as Maria headed for the Child Development Project, he beckoned her to the Character Counts Coalition table.

"Get a look at this great stuff, Maria. These folks really have their act together. The Six Pillars provide a terrific structure for what we should all be doing. And what an impressive membership they've got: it runs the gamut from William Bennett to Marian Wright Edelman.[1] I'd like to order copies of the Pillars and have them displayed prominently in my room. Wouldn't you? Sure beats the maps and planets now up on the walls. I wonder if we can get Helter to pony-up funds."

Noting Maria's quizzical look, Hardie pushed ahead. "For God's sake, don't tell me Maria Laszlo disapproves of *Trustworthiness, Respect, Responsibility, Fairness, Caring,* and *Citizenship?*"

"Disapprove? No, Hardie, it's not disapproval. Just something in me says 'not so fast.' These lists of virtues; I think they're heavy-handed, blunt, old-fashioned, and unlike you, pretty vacuous when it gets down to day-to-day coping."

"Heavy-handed, Maria?"

"Yeah, heavy-handed. Values need to be experienced, claimed by, not forced on, children. Attaching words to bulletin boards, even pointing them out to kids at opportune moments, will have about as much impact as those posters of the night sky. And vacuous, too, because any demand can be justified as a matter of respect and responsibility. Did you ever read the *Handbook for Schooling Hitler Youth?* [Brennecke 1938]. It talks a lot about promise-keeping, courage, loyalty, responsibility, discipline, unselfishness."

"That's absolute rubbish, Maria," said Hardie, obviously irritated by the Nazi reference. "Of course, any word or concept can be undermined, even 'love' and 'beauty.' I cherish those words, and I can't fathom your distaste for them. Yes, they're old-fashioned, hardly a mark against them. They express who we are, we as a country, we as citizens who believe in playing by rules, in treating one another fairly and generously. They're about taking our responsibilities seriously so we can preserve our freedoms and our way of life. When I hear and read those words I stand a little taller, a little prouder, and I strive a little harder to be worthy of them. Your skepticism diminishes their nobility and, frankly, Maria, it diminishes the capacities of children to participate in their grandeur."

"Hardie, let's not descend into name-calling. I apologize for the crack about the Hitler Youth. I too am a proud American, if also a critical one—and that too is part of our grand tradition. Maybe we can have some reasonable

---

[1] Marian Wright Edelman, a civil-rights lawyer in the Mississippi of the 1960s, is the founder and director of the Children's Defense Fund, a liberal children's advocacy organization. On Bennett, see p. 19, above.

discussion of the moral ed programs in the next hour. I hear Bonham calling us back into session."

Sure enough, Bonham started by asking the teachers for their reactions. There was a good bit of discussion of the various instructional approaches and there were clear faculty preferences, which divided more or less on gender lines. The female teachers, particularly bothered by children's insensitivity and cruelty to each other, warmed to the possibility of promoting caring and cooperation as school-wide objectives. The men, bothered more by students' laziness, sloppy habits, and indifference to learning, wanted to push responsibility and discipline. Only Aggie Cerine raised a question about the very notion of choosing virtues for classroom instruction.

"You know, my mother was an elementary school teacher," Aggie began, "and I remember her showing me stuff from just after the Second World War, which was much like some of these programs—minus the videos and kits. The 'lessons' were infused with patriotism and American pride. That felt good to my Mom, and it didn't take a whole lot of persuasion for me or my folks to think we had important civic responsibilities. When my Dad leafleted the neighborhood on behalf of a good government candidate, I'd go along. But I recall my mother saying that the instructional material didn't work. The kids found it boring, they'd pass notes to friends, and I doubt whether it was effective. True, they didn't shoot one another then, their parents didn't get divorced a lot, and teenagers didn't have babies, but that had nothing to do with teachers promoting virtues.

"I kind of like the newer ideas from the Child Development Project. I like asking children to reflect on what they are doing, not just telling them what to do. There is the premise, of course, that by thinking and talking, then examining options, they will grow into morality. It's a premise I buy. If we teachers keep at it, raise moral consciousness, I bet the kids will get it. They are capable of voluntarily putting aside their own self-interest for the benefit of others. Who needs ten 'universal values,' six 'pillars,' two major and three minor 'components,' or seven 'attributes'?

"I know I'm rattling on a long time, but it seems to me that morality is really very simple. It boils down to one thing—fairness, or (if you like Lawrence Kohlberg) justice. Basically, it's just the Golden Rule. The hard part is making that rule important in your life, really wanting to live by it, and then figuring out just what it means to live it day-by-day."

Now it was Maria's turn to beam, while Hardie, without waiting to be recognized, blurted out as soon as Aggie finished talking: "You're a great woman, Aggie. The Golden Rule alone would be splendid in a world of Aggies, but not in my classroom. In my class it's each kid for himself and no one for learning. Turning the kids into moral creatures is hard work; you've got to be demanding, tough, concrete, and crystal-clear about laudable behavior."

By this point, it was Jan Bonham who was beaming. Turning to Fred Helter, she said, "I can see what a wonderfully thoughtful and engaged group of classroom teachers you have put together here, Dr. Helter. I only wish that my graduate students had had the chance to hear such cogently argued differing positions on this important question of values education. While your responses make me especially sorry that we have run out of time, I am confident that you will continue to talk over what we have started discussing. Many thanks for having me here."

At the University

Athough some of Jan Bonham's materials whetted her appetite and the goals were surely alluring, Maria continues to resist "moral education," even while her awareness and perplexity over moral problems increase. True, she is no longer so adamantly skeptical of the need for schools to tackle morality, but she suspects that all this talk about "character" misses much that is essential—a *virtue-ethic* critique. Her experience with card-trading, swearing, and fighting suggests that situational factors are critical in making and judging moral decisions. Yet most of the moral education programs locate morality within the child, his or her possession of virtues, rather than look to the situated act, e.g., whether it is OK to swear, trade baseball cards, or have a "fair" fight. As we have noted, Maria believes that the qualities of the person are not unimportant. She treasures the friends whose loyalty she can depend upon, but because of what they are loyal *to* and how she predicts they will *act*, not their "loyalty" *per se*.

Furthermore, she is skeptical over the selection, variety, and sheer quantity of the virtues—a *laundry-list* critique. No two programs promulgate the same ones or make clear how they connect. The Character Counts Coalition, for instance, includes trustworthiness, respect for others, fairness, and responsibility (within which it includes accountability, excellence, and self-restraint). But self-restraint could sensibly stand alone, or be absorbed by fairness, while fairness could be absorbed by respect. Moreover, she could imagine adding virtues such as nonviolence, generosity, and forgiveness—or are they to be included in caring and citizenship?

More disturbing, the "leeching" of conventional values into the moral domain and the preoccupation with a subset of virtues seem to Maria to skew the agenda of "character education" in ways that need to be acknowledged and explicitly justified—a *skewing* critique. Too often, the case for the entire effort is made by reference to plainly wrongful conduct—stealing, exploitative sexual activity, violence. Then a program is presented as responsive to such conduct, without making the case for the far broader reach that it inevitably has.

Although she understands Hardie's attraction to virtue words, there is a gnawing concern that the terms are at once overly amorphous and connote a "political" spin that, again, is not acknowledged and can be dangerous. The most popular ones, respect and responsibility, are abstractions, but with harmful (as well as beneficial) potential. Responsible to whom? For what? Do the demands of every teacher become the responsibilities of every student? Even when a demand conflicts with other obligations? Even when it is a meaningless chore? Are teachers expected to be responsible toward, and to respect, students? Do powerful people and institutions (teachers and schools) have the "responsibility" to act so as to *deserve* respect?

Remembering her own student days, she realizes the coercion latent in the idea of respect; she has seen how it can blunt rather than enlarge the conscience. Respect is easily transformed into subservience (child to adult, woman to man, follower to leader). So the issue remains, respectful of whom and for what? The question, who gets to establish the meaning of "respect"? need not be considered as a conversation-stopper, but it does call for serious engagement. Peter and friends have their brand of respect; she has hers.

Maria suspects that lists of moral virtues give too much authority to mere conventions. The virtue of excellence, for example, has often been taken to legitimize making moral judgments about academic and athletic performances, perhaps even penmanship and push-ups. That may have been OK for Aristotle, but it is worrisome to Maria, who wants to restrict, not enlarge, acts of moral judgment. And where do the lists end? Why not add table manners and diet, dress and entertainment preferences? In short, all the virtues may accomplish is to reinforce a middle-class respectability. Despite her resistance to theory, Maria recognizes that without some underlying idea that justifies a specification of virtues the leeching is all but inevitable. Distinctions between the moral and conventional domains, between self- and other-serving values, between enduring fundamental principles and changing social practices, get blurred in the virtues approach. Composing the lists strikes her as carelessly ad hoc.

Maria was delighted when Aggie reduced morality to the Golden Rule. The Golden Rule, unlike the virtue lists, is ennobling; it *summons* her. Like Aggie, she believes morality is straightforward and agreed-upon. But the devil is in the details, in how to interpret the Golden Rule and how to make it a constant in one's life. That's why Maria intuitively is less resistant to programs like the Child Development Project, Heartwood, or Just Schools. They seem to be aimed at sensitizing the conscience, at evoking moral desires through stories or group experiences, and providing opportunities for children to think about their reactions. She realizes, though, that such an approach presupposes a responsiveness in children to evocative stories and morally challenging situations. It relies heavily on students' persistent goodwill and self-monitoring skills— quite a lot to expect, more than she does expect, of nine- and ten-year-olds (not to mention most adults). Yet Maria has to admit that, putting aside her gut reactions to his reasoning and looking just at how children conduct themselves, Hardie's class, with its highly directive air, is more of a moral community than her own. His kids are quite simply kinder to one another than hers.

Maria's uncertainty is not only pedagogic: How can a teacher best affect children's moral development? It also reflects the elusiveness of the more theoretical question, how we specify the content of moral goodness. Is it the accumulation of named virtues that we each do and do not possess? That seems to be the Aristotelian approach behind such programs as the Six Pillars. Or is it more how we accommodate conflicting interests as they arise in order to maximize fairness? That would fit the more Deweyan Child Development Project approach. Oversimplified, her questions raise once more the issues we posed in Chapter 3: Is morality centrally situated in the person, or in the act and its context? Is it heteronomous (located in community traditions) or autonomous (located in individual decision making)?

These crucial questions have generated a vigorous contemporary debate. Participants within each "camp" tend to be aligned with broader political positions. Proponents of character education often attract those with generally conservative political positions, to whom education is to a substantial extent a relatively directive matter, transmitting traditional values. In educational philosophy, they draw from Aristotle and Durkheim. Critics often prefer a focus on learning as a process, designed more to evoke a student's own moral sensibilities; they lean toward the liberal, drawing support from Kant, Dewey, and Kohlberg. But the alignment between political and moral stances may be a historical accident. A virtue-oriented approach that prized caring and tolerance could be liberal. For example, Ted Sizer, the liberal educational reformer, wants schools to cultivate decency: And what, for Sizer, is decency?

> Decency in the American tradition . . . comprises fairness, generosity, and tolerance. Everyone should get a fair shake. People who are in trouble or who for whatever reason are weak deserve a special hand; the big guys should not force their way on the little guys.
> *(Sizer 1992, 121)*

One proposing a "character education" approach, of whatever content, has perforce to provide responses to two questions, the questions with which this book began: first, in Socrates' terms, What is "virtue?" What qualities (or conduct) are described as "good?" and, second, the pedagogical question, How can schools best teach children to be good? We deal primarily with the first of these questions here, largely deferring the pedagogical issue to Chapter 8.

Maria's qualms and questions, and the political priorities that lurk about virtues, are best understood against an examination of the historical antecedents of character education: how schools came to focus on virtues and to make the selections they did.

A HISTORICAL PERSPECTIVE: THE MORAL MANDATE[2]

Doubting the value of moral education is a very modern concern. At least until the mid–twentieth century "moral education" would have been as redundant

---

[2] The material in this section on the history of character education draws predominantly on the following sources: Elson 1964; Johnson 1995; Kaestle 1983; McClellan 1992; Tyack and Hansot 1982; Yulish 1980.

a statement as "old grandfather." It went without saying that grandfathers were old and American schools taught morality. In the early public schools and continuing into the twentieth century nothing, including the 3Rs, competed in significance with character training. Refracted through today's prisms, that training has much more of a long-ago-and-far-away strangeness than other educational changes. Three distinguishing features, we believe, account for this remoteness:

(1) Character training, though presumptively secular, was infused with a strong Protestant religiosity;
(2) Character training, designed to counter free-for-all American commercialism, became the most valued and pervasive goal of education;
(3) Character training was heavily focused on self-restraint and obedience.

We consider briefly each of these features.

(1) Moral instruction prepared children to be "Americans," to partake of the country's sacred mission—democratic republicanism as an expression of Christian faith. Puritanism, as much political theory as religious doctrine, blended its democratic creed with a secular but religiously toned moral creed. And truly blended it was. "America" was God's handiwork. Americans were the Chosen People making their home (the City upon a Hill) in the Promised Land under a Moses-like leader, George Washington. Their Constitution, like the Ten Commandments, was divinely inspired:

> [T]hough the Constitution and the Bill of Rights made no provision for a state church—quite the contrary—there was an implied and unchallenged understanding that America was a religious country, that the republic was religious not necessarily in its forms but in its bones, that it was inconceivable that it could have come into existence, or could continue and flourish, without an overriding religious sentiment pervading every nook and cranny of its society.
> *(Johnson 1995, 31)*

The unity of religion and politics continued even after Puritan dominance declined. Americans in the nineteenth century cherished the faith that "their nation was destined to reach the peak of human civilization and, with God's help, to overcome all obstacles to material preeminence and spiritual elevation" (Kaestle 1983, 94). To disbelieve in the providence of America was "to resist the will of God" (de Toqueville 1835/1994, 7).

Leaders of the common (public) school movement, though propelled by a passionate religious faith, were restrained by an equally passionate commitment to religious tolerance. They therefore sought a curriculum that was nonsectarian but not nonreligious, a pan-Protestantism that could be accepted by all. Despite the official church and state separation, the church, through a powerful clergy exercising control over community customs and domestic life, taught a civically infused religion, while the state, through its growing public education system, taught children religiously saturated morality.

The great apostle of public schooling, Horace Mann, for example, advocated religious instruction only to the point that it conflicted with a child's religious conscience (Mann 1957). That freedom of conscience was, however, narrowly construed, as attested by the schools' adoption of the King James Bible as a text. The proviso that teachers resist commentary was thought sufficient to preserve its nonsectarian quality. The National Teachers Association (forerunner of the National Education Association), while acknowledging (in 1869) that "the teaching of partisan or sectarian principles in our public schools, or the appropriation of public funds for the support of sectarian schools is a violation of the fundamental principles of our American system of education," nonetheless asserted that "the Bible should not only be studied, venerated, and honored as a classic for all ages, people, and languages . . . but devotionally read, and its precepts inculcated in all the common schools of the land" (Tyack and Hansot 1982, 74–75).

(2) Protestant and republican ideologies had much in common: they were antidoctrinal, antihierarchical, and individualistic in spiritual and political expression. Nevertheless, there was tension between the two ideologies: Democracy's expansive notions of freedom—personal, political, and economic—uncorked indulgent impulses and legitimated greed in ways that, if not inhibited, promoted social disruption and vice. For a democratic and limited government to flourish, citizens had to exercise vigilant self-governance.

During the colonial period, self-governance had been grounded in the moral and literacy training found in the home, where severe Puritan discipline was firmly rooted. Families were the central authority of cultural control, relied upon by the state to do the required social policing, but lest they slacken, public officials were given oversight responsibilities to inspect homes and check up on parenting. If fault was found, children were removed from their parents' custody. Schools, sparse in number, were merely an extended arm of powerfully controlling families, churches, and local authorities.

As the country became more populous and mobile in the nineteenth century; as freedom, prosperity, and security increased; as cities were built and immigration increased; as the rational and secular ideas of the Enlightenment took hold, the religious and other traditional restraints of colonial society diminished. To counter such centrifugal forces, to preserve individual commitments to high standards of moral conduct, leaders of nineteenth-century society made their mission the inculcation of self-discipline and upright behavior.

> Even as nineteenth-century Americans worked to clear away the institutional restraints of colonial society, they moved in precisely the opposite direction in the realm of morals and personal behavior, abandoning the relaxed style of the eighteenth century in favor of an insistence on rigid self-restraint. . . . The combination of impulses toward freedom and

moral rigidity was less a cultural contradiction than a reflection of the belief that the growing absence of external, institutional restraints required the development of strong internal controls. In the minds of nineteenth-century Americans, the price of liberty was rigorous self-discipline and upright personal conduct.
(McClellan 1992, 17–18)

Horace Mann, highly respected and influential, spoke urgently against unrestrained freedom:

> If republican institutions do wake up unexampled energies in the whole mass of a people, and give them implements of unexampled power wherewith to work out their will, then these same institutions ought also to confer upon that people unexampled wisdom and rectitude. . . . If they multiply temptations, they must fortify against them. If they quicken the activity and enlarge the sphere of the appetites and passions, they must, at least in an equal ratio, establish the authority and extend the jurisdiction of reason and conscience. In a word, we must not add to the impulsive, without also adding to the regulating forces.
> *(Mann 1964, 101)*

Not surprisingly primary schools, which by the mid-nineteenth century were expected to educate most children, took on moral education as their chief mission. "The survival of the American republic depended upon the morality of its people—not in armies or constitutions or inspired leadership—but in the virtue of the propertied, industrious, and intelligent American yeoman" (Kaestle 1983, 79). Morality displaced all other educational priorities; it was included in every subject, accompanied by a strong anti-intellectualism.

> That virtue is superior to knowledge or even wisdom is continually stressed, as in this admonition by Alice Cary: "Little children, you must seek Rather to be good than wise"; or, on a more advanced level: "Man's intellect is not man's sole nor best adorning." . . . The "useful knowledge" offered in the school was useful to success in the material world, but it was also expected to produce those qualities of character that we associate both with Puritanism and with the self-made man; thrift, hard work, and the rejection of frivolity.
> *(Elson 1964, 226)*

Schoolbook heroes were admired for their morality and patriotism, not their intellectual standing; George Washington was lauded more for his honesty than for his political or military judgment. Moral lessons permeated texts, spellers, and arithmetic books, as well as readers. Art, symbol of an effete and decaying Europe, was discouraged as a worthwhile activity or school subject, except insofar as it lent itself to moral propaganda. Moral lapses rather than ineptitude were the preferred explanation for student failures, no matter the activity. (Thus the remedy for poor spelling was development of a "spelling conscience.")

The burden of transmitting moral training rested, of course, on teachers, mostly single or widowed women. But teachers were not without enforcement authority. They had considerable moral authority in the eyes of parents and, if the need arose, were "empowered" to use the rod in cases of moral infractions, for on their success rested the success of the American political experiment.

(3) The question, "Which values?" that staple of contemporary moral discourse, would have been as odd to a nineteenth-century educator as the question, "Should schools teach morals"? Schools operated under a national moral consensus. Textbook authors "painted good and evil in stark, absolute terms and left no gray areas in their moral education—no room for interpretation, no flexibility to apply values as shifting contingencies might dictate. Only absolute rules rigidly adhered to, they believed, could provide a reliable guide to behavior and protect against the enormous temptations of the day" (McClellan 1992, 26).

Because moral education was the mechanism through which children became good (self-governing) citizens, the morals taught were, to contemporary eyes, harsh. It was required that children show "rigid self-restraint, rigorous moral purity, and a precise cultural conformity" (id., 17). Repeatedly the following qualities were included on lists of character traits: obedience, deference, submission, self-control, discipline, sacrifice, temperance, simplicity, frugality, industry, self-help, reverence, truthfulness, bravery.

Morality was not only tough but pervasive. These educators would not have drawn the distinctions we discussed in Chapter 3 between the moral and conventional domains. Binding rules governed every aspect of life: decorum (appropriate dress, manners, and etiquette), personal habits (frugality, cleanliness, and punctuality), work habits (thrift, persistence, honesty, diligence, perseverance), recreation (health, fair play), and citizenship. The last was particularly stressed until it became what, to a modern sensibility, appears excessively chauvinistic: a good person was a good American, aware of the special privileges of living in this singularly blessed and singularly virtuous country.

A HISTORICAL PERSPECTIVE: THE MORAL MANDATE CHALLENGED

By the turn of the twentieth century, both the extent and nature of moral education came under critical scrutiny. External to education, technological advances, increased prosperity and leisure, attraction to less severe modes of child-rearing, and an increasing demand that schools prepare children for industrial work threatened the Victorian, puritanical, everything-is-moral curriculum. Internal to education, John Dewey advanced a "situation ethic," what he called "reflective morality," over a more traditional "virtue ethic." Although virtues (Dewey tended to call them dispositions) mattered, they were secondary to right action. And right action was fluid, reflecting ever-changing human interests and social conditions, not to be contained in prescriptive codes drawn from static virtues.

> In quality, the good is never twice alike. It never copies itself. It is new every morning, fresh every evening. It is unique in its every presentation. For it marks the resolution of a distinctive complication of competing habits and impulses which can never repeat itself.
> *(Dewey 1922, 211)*

For this reason, wise moral decisions, according to Dewey and his followers, do not emerge from fixed catalogues of virtues. One arrives at the moral act through constant deliberation, guided by generic principles (e.g., human equality and a search for the common good) and aided by virtuous predispositions. "Virtue" is not a set of durable hard-as-rock qualities yielding permanent truths. Such "virtues" will fail either because they have not been (and cannot be) translated into specific appropriate actions—What does frugality mean in affluent times and in times of duress?—or because, if translated, they become spiritless and unexamined legalisms that cut off moral growth.

Notwithstanding growing support for Dewey's approach in the early twentieth century, traditional moral educators moved toward ever more explicit and targeted objectives. Partaking of the nation's enthusiasm for testing, they began measuring children's character and specifying deficits, much as we now measure achievement and intelligence. (The approved answers were determined either by a self-appointed authority or by response frequencies.) The following examples, drawn from Yulish's study (Yulish 1980, 242–243), illustrate the predictable biases of the period:

a. I always play alone,
b. I play with just one playmate,
c. I want many playmates.
   Correct answer, c.

a. I make much noise,
b. I am noisy sometimes,
c. I keep very quiet.
   Correct answer c.

a. I obey but don't like it,
b. I have my own way,
c. I like to obey.
   Correct answer c.

Elaborate codes of character were written and promulgated for use in classrooms and extracurricular clubs (such as the Boston Virtue Clubs, Thrift Clubs, Prompt Clubs, Courtesy Clubs), and by emerging youth groups such as the Boy and Girl Scouts, 4-H clubs, and Campfire Girls (McClellan 1992, 60). According to the twelve points of the Boy Scout Law, a Scout is Trustworthy, Loyal, Helpful, Friendly, Courteous, Kind, Obedient, Cheerful, Thrifty, Brave, Clean, and Reverent.

Another popular codification was *The Children's Code of Morals for Elementary Schools*, written by William J. Hutchins and adopted by many schools (Hutchins 1917). The Code (a version of which may be found at p. 143 in the next section of this chapter), and the character tests, illustrate a number of features common to character education in the early twentieth century.

First, continuing with past traditions, "character" was thought to be inclusive of all manner of activities—e.g., sports, work, health, social behavior (Hutchins 1917)—and of personal qualities—e.g., being cheerful, courteous, friendly, and thrifty (Boy Scouts). Other codes of the time widened the range further, including, for example, a sense of wonder, love of nature, love of the beautiful, worthy use of leisure (Birmingham Board of Education 1936).

Second, the codes extended to the narrowly specific—e.g., children should hold no spite or grudges (Hutchins 1917); they should accept "defeat without a whine or an alibi . . . victory without a boast or brag" (Birmingham Board of Education 1936, 14). The character tests included "opposition to thumb-sucking, boxing as opposed to fighting, studying with lamp behind instead of in front of the person, and the necessity of girls helping their mothers" (Yulish 1980, 241). A test developed for the Detroit public schools declared:

> A good child *never* slammed doors, ate fast, talked too loud, wiggled in his seat, swore, kept a messy desk, ran in the hall, used his hands in talking, played unfair, hurt animals, was noisy at home, whispered in school, had bad habits, lied, or was bad when his parents went away.
> *(Id., 242) (emphasis in original)*

Third, the codes were personally demanding, even repressive—emphasizing duty, reliability, self-control, self-reliance (Hutchins 1917), obedience, reverence, and bravery (the Boy Scouts). A Character Inventory Chart went so far as this:

> The negative qualities to be avoided were delicateness, illness, unfairness, deceitfulness, suspiciousness, sadness, unsociableness, wavering, depression, rudeness, vulgarity, unwillingness, hindering, doubtfulness, cowardliness, hopelessness, laziness, idleness and recklessness . . . A person was of less than perfect character if he were sad, depressed, or felt hopeless or doubtful. Even illness was viewed as a sign of character deficiency.
> *(Yulish 1980, 246)*

Habits of obedience—subjugation of the will, regularity, punctuality, order, silence, and industry—much stressed in the tests and codes, were to be made "semi-mechanical."

Fourth, the codes were grounded in patriotism. Most of the ten rules in the Children's Code begin with the admonition: "Good Americans are _____" ("self reliant," "reliable," "loyal," etc). In the spirit of Durkheim, character tests and codes did not distinguish individual from state morality. The state was the "highest manifestation of the divine spirit in man" (Durkheim 1925/1961, 16). Self-realization came from freely and joyously obeying the laws of the state and the authority of the school, never from conscientious resistance, because the state expressed the highest moral ideals (ibid.). "The morality of the social system as a system was beyond question; the moral quality of the society was therefore to be improved by improving the moral quality of individuals" (Kaestle 1983, 81).

Finally, despite an obvious overlap (self-discipline, courage, cooperation, kindness, responsibility, trustworthiness, citizenship), the contrast between the virtues prized in the early twentieth century and today is notable. In particular, three qualities found in contemporary lists were not featured in traditional ones: autonomous decision making and critical thinking, compassion (although kindness was often mentioned), and self-esteem.

A Historical Perspective: Character Education in Decline at Mid-Century

Traditional character education was badly wounded in 1928–1930 with the publication of what must be ranked one of the most influential social science reports ever issued, the three-volume *Studies in the Nature of Character*, by Hugh Hartshorne and Mark May (1928). This first empirical investigation of children's morality focusing on deception and self-control—primarily the work of a professor of religious education (Hartshorne) and an academic psychologist (May)—was extraordinary in its scope. The study of deception, for example, was based on work with 11,000 children ages eight to sixteen. To measure deceit, the authors offered students multiple opportunities to cheat (in the classroom, athletic competitions, party games, and on homework), to lie (by asking students if they cheated on some of the prior tests), and to steal (by exposing students to money and small items they could steal unnoticed). The findings, that moral behavior was highly affected by context and that there was little cross-situational consistency in children's actions, appeared to undermine a basic tenet of character education by suggesting that honesty was not a fixed feature of the person.

> The results of these studies show that neither deceit or its opposite, "honesty," are unified character traits, but rather specific functions of life situations. Most children will deceive in certain situations and not in others. Lying, cheating, and stealing as measured by the test situations used in these studies are only very loosely related. Even cheating in the classroom is rather highly specific, for a child may cheat on an arithmetic test and not on a spelling test, etc.
> *(Id., vol. 1, 411–412)*

A closer look at the work reveals more complexity. The authors did find that some children were more pervasively inclined to honesty, and that such children tended to have better grades for deportment, to be better adjusted, and to come from more progressive schools and more privileged backgrounds. Deceit was unrelated to sex and increased with age. Still, all children cheated when situational pressures ("incentives to deceive") outweighed personal dispositions. The authors' sophisticated and balanced integration of virtue and situation ethics is worth quoting at length:

> The child brings to school as part of his own inner equipment three sets of interrelated factors bearing on his practice of school honor: first, his ambition for school achievement, no matter how aroused, how large or how small, or how influenced by the school itself; second, his standards, code, or ideals regarding the methods by which he shall get what he wants, whether by genuine achievement or by hook or crook; third, his responsiveness to such standards, including his ability to obey them, to resist temptations to ignore them, to keep them in mind, etc.
>
> In school, the child faces a complex situation many aspects of which are involved in any single act of deception. There are the general school standards, which he becomes aware of through hearsay or direct statement by the authorities; the code of the classroom, which he learns in like manner; the example of the other pupils, to which by nature he may be more or less susceptible; the relation of the teacher to the pupils, whether friendly and cooperative or hostile; the personality, prestige, and statements of the examiner and the extent to which he allows opportunity to use deceptive methods; and the particular stimulus of the test itself [whether the materials make cheating easy or not]. Some children do not take advantage of the opportunity to cheat under ordinary school motives. Presumably these are cases in which the standards brought to school or achieved in school are against dishonest practices and in which also there is the ability to adhere to such standards in the face of temptation. . . .
>
> Those who yield to the opportunity to deceive do not do so in any wholesale way, however, but in a rather specialized way according to the particular situation in which they are placed [that is, a child may regularly cheat if given an answer sheet to grade himself but never cheat if it means hurting a classmate].
>
> (Id., 398–399)

As a consequence of their findings the authors suggest (in the spirit of Dewey) that teachers will not improve children's morality through virtue-inculcation, but by creating school climates that avoid heightening incentives for deception and strengthen the will to resist them.

> [T]he mere urging of honest behavior by teachers or the discussion of standards and ideals of honesty, no matter how much such general ideas may be "emotionalized," has no necessary relation to the control of conduct.
>
> [T]he main attention of educators should be placed not so much on devices for teaching honesty or any other "trait" as on the reconstruction of school practices in such a way as to provide not occasional but

consistent and regular opportunities for the successful use by both teachers and pupils of such forms of conduct as make for the common good.
(Id., 413–414)

This scholarly challenge to the premises of virtue education was reinforced by the changes in the culture that accompanied the middle third of the century. While the school's moral mandate was gradually eclipsed by its academic mission, doctrines of self-restraint and self-discipline were losing ground to those of self-expression and self-fulfillment. Child-rearing norms were in flux: The post-war baby boom (1945–1963) brought with it gentler approaches to child care. It was a time when the richness and creativity of inner experience, and the free expression of natural instincts, came to be trusted—and repression mistrusted—as never before. In addition, rising affluence, the promotion of consumerism, and suburban life styles made a self-denying morality appear quaint, clearly dated, if not worse. Modern problems would yield to science and reason, to the flexible pragmatism of Dewey rather than the rigid virtues of the Victorians.

The times were hospitable to the view that values were home-grown, not eternal, that individuals, even children, should do their own value-making, and that moral education was the enabling of students to do so consciously. In 1966, with the publication of *Values and Teaching*, Louis Raths, Merrill Harmin, and Sidney B. Simon described a new program, termed "Values Clarification." Values, they maintained:

> tend to be a product of our experiences. They are not just a matter of true or false. One cannot go to an encyclopedia or to a textbook for values. . . . This means that we are dealing with an area that isn't a matter of proof or consensus. It is a matter of experience. So, if a child says that he likes something, it does not seem appropriate for an older person to say, "You shouldn't like that." Or, if a child should say, "I am interested in that," it does not seem quite right for an older person to say to him, "You shouldn't be interested in things like that."

> 𝄞𝄞𝄞𝄞𝄞

> As teachers, then, we need to be clear that we cannot dictate to children what their values should be since we cannot also dictate what their environments should be and what experiences they will have.

(Raths, Harmin, and Simon 1976, 84–85)

Although "we may be authoritative in those areas that deal with truth and falsity," the rightness of a value choice was said to be of much less importance than the *process of valuing*. In any case, values imposed are values dismissed:

> We are interested in the processes that are going on. We are not much interested in identifying the values which children hold. We are much more interested in the process because we believe that in a world that is changing as rapidly as ours, each child must develop habits of ex-

amining his purposes, aspirations, attitudes, feelings, etc., if he is to find the most intelligent relationship between his life and the surrounding world, and if he is to make a contribution to the creation of a better world.
(Ibid.)

The process involves choosing freely from alternatives after consideration of the consequences, publicly affirming one's choices (what the authors term "prizing"), and taking specific action, repeatedly, reflecting those choices.

Values clarification then is a near-complete rejection of the virtue ideology dominant from the dawn of public schooling: Where all acts had been a matter of shoulds and should nots, the obligatory now shrank to near invisibility, behavior a matter of individual determination; where goodness had consisted of character traits formed through strenuous habit-training, it now consisted of individual decision making; where goodness had been located in fused religious and civic traditions, it now was located in one's private experience; where goodness had focused on control over our weaker selves, it now focused on expression of our inner selves.

Despite its radical subjectivity, individualism, and relativism, values clarification achieved moderate popularity in the 1970s; then it inevitably met with sharp resistance. The contemporary character education effort is one reaction. However, the case for character education cannot rest solely on the limitations of values clarification, for there plainly are additional choices. Character education not only denies the relativity and subjectivity of values, insisting instead that there are objective qualities of goodness that are independent of particularized experiences; it regards them as readily discernible and not especially controversial. One response, which rejected both values clarification and virtue ideology, was the cognitive-developmental moral theory of Lawrence Kohlberg.

LAWRENCE KOHLBERG AND THE CRITIQUE OF THE "BAG OF VIRTUES"

To Kohlberg, within whose pantheon are Immanuel Kant, John Dewey, Jean Piaget, and John Rawls, a virtues approach is pure cotton candy, signifying nothing. He speaks dismissively of a "bag of virtues," a collection of ill-assorted and trivial terms grouped so arbitrarily and so vaguely that nothing follows from their use:

> Although it is true that people often cannot agree on details of right and wrong or even on fundamental moral principles, we all think such "traits" as honesty and responsibility are good things. By adding enough traits to the virtue bag, we eventually get a list that contains something to suit everyone.
>
> *****
>
> One difficulty with this approach to moral character is that everyone has his own bag. However, the problem runs deeper than the composition

of a given list of virtues and vices. Although it may be true that the notion of teaching virtues, such as honesty or integrity, arouses little controversy, it is also true that a vague consensus on the goodness of these virtues conceals a great deal of actual disagreement over their definitions. What is one person's "integrity" is another person's "stubbornness," what is one person's honesty in "expressing your true feelings" is another person's insensitivity to the feelings of others. This is evident in controversial fields of adult behavior. Student protesters view their behavior as reflecting the virtues of altruism, idealism, awareness, and courage. Those in opposition regard the same behavior as reflecting the vices of irresponsibility and disrespect for "law and order."
(Kohlberg 1981, vol. 1, 9–10)

We see here a critique that Maria's complaints echo. Kohlberg objects to the unlimited stockpiling of virtues and their lack of embeddedness in any transcendent source (Maria's *laundry-list* critique), as well as their sponginess, which insufficiently constrains interpretation and invites resort to unacknowledged biases (Maria's *skewing* critique). Virtues writ large—discipline, courage, altruism—are contestable. Does discipline mean submitting to another's judgment or speaking out? Is discipline clearly good or often at the expense of creative risk-taking? Is the intemperate impulsive act sometimes praiseworthy? Virtues writ small—truth-telling—may be informative but remain of uncertain scope. Does one tell the truth when it seriously hurts another?

Primarily, however, Kohlberg objects to defining morality as a set of personal characteristics (Maria's *virtue-ethic* critique). For Kohlberg, virtuous conduct does not reside in character traits but in the rational process of resolving conflicts. Inspired by Kant, Kohlberg believes that virtue is not many but singular, not pluralistic but universal, and finds its source not in authority or convention but in the child's cognitive (rational) development. Moral education is a matter of teaching children how to *think* morally rather than one of exhortation or prescription. A person is virtuous to the extent that she or he resolves conflicting claims as an autonomous agent guided by prescribed rational principles. "I define morality in terms of the formal character of a moral judgment, method, or point of view, rather than in terms of its content" (id., 170).

In reaching a decision, for example—in Kohlberg's most famous scenario—whether a man should steal drugs from a pharmacist to save the life of his dying wife, one should be guided by Kant's formal procedures (discussed in Chapters 3 and 4) *universalizability* (implying *disinterestedness*) and *obligation*. In approaching each moral issue, according to Kohlberg, we should remove considerations of how our actual personal situatedness might be affected by the decision. This is another way of expressing the Golden Rule: Act so that, on whatever "side" your interests may fall, you will find the results fair. Inevitably, Kohlberg asserts, we will adopt Rawlsian principles of justice:

Maximize the liberty of every individual compatible with the liberty of others, and allow no inequalities unless they benefit the least advantaged. The essence of virtue, then, is *Justice.*

But justice is not like the virtues advanced by proponents of character education. It is not a behavioral disposition or (like virtues such as honesty) attribute of the person (see Kohlberg 1970, p. 69).

Kohlberg's most original contribution is his conception that the moral position of universal and impartial reasoning is, as it were, built into our genes. Cognitive development proceeds through moral stages. Young children inhabit a "preconventional" moral realm (Kohlberg's stages one and two). They obey rules either because punishment follows from disobedience or, later, because it is in their self-interest to respect the interests of others. The egocentricity of this stage is a natural consequence of cognitive limitations. When a child reaches the conventional level (stages three and four), her tit-for-tat philosophy gives way to a broader perspective that considers other people's interests, not only in terms of her own, but with concern, respect, and impartiality. Only at the postconventional level (stages five and six and not reached until late adolescence, if at all) does one understand that rules are relative to a group and must be transcended by the Kantian universal principles. Thus the highest stage of psychological development maps the highest morality. The aim of education is development because the end stage of development is morality.

Kohlberg's grand effort to unite the psychology of cognitive development with the liberal natural-rights tradition of Kant is a great achievement. His application of the rich educational implications of his theory in the "Just Schools" he founded (of this more in Chapter 8) places his contribution near to that of John Dewey. But every aspect of his approach to the definition of virtue remains contested. (We leave aside criticisms of his stage theory.) Two criticisms most relevant to our discussion of virtue have been previously encountered—the preference for highly rarified, abstract reason as a guide to moral truth, and the claim that a reasoned application of the principle of justice generates cross-cultural obligations, overriding any case for moral pluralism. We consider here a third critique, his attempt to identify a *single* value, justice, as the embodiment of virtuous action.

The American philosopher Michael Sandel, in a critique of John Rawls, questions the superiority of justice to such virtues as personal and civic attachments. Where such attachments prevail, he asserts, there is little need for justice.

> Consider for example a more or less ideal family situation, where relations are governed in large part by spontaneous affection and where, in consequence, the circumstances of justice prevail to a relatively small degree. Individual rights and fair decision procedures are seldom invoked, not because injustice is rampant but because their appeal is pre-empted by a spirit of generosity in which I am rarely inclined to claim my fair

share. Nor does this generosity necessarily imply that I receive out of kindness a share that is equal to or greater than the share I would be entitled to under fair principles of justice. I may get less. The point is not that I get what I would otherwise get, only more spontaneously, but simply that the questions of what I get and what I am due do not loom large in the overall context of this way of life.
(Sandel 1982/1998, 33)

Sandel is plainly not convinced that justice is to be preferred to benevolence. Not only may a family (a school too?) be better off when pervaded by a "spirit of generosity," but the arrival of justice can be a positively malevolent influence. Consider what it can do to a relationship:

If, out of a misplaced sense of justice, a close friend of long standing repeatedly insists on calculating and paying his precise share of every common expenditure, or refuses to accept any favor or hospitality except at the greatest protest and embarrassment, not only will I feel compelled to be reciprocally scrupulous but at some point may begin to wonder whether I have not misunderstood our relationship. The circumstances of benevolence will to this extent have diminished, and the circumstances of justice grown.
(Id., 35)

Sandel's point has a broader salience than the need to leaven justice with benevolence: Any attempt to reduce goodness to a single quality seems to us bound to fail. The insistence on a single quality—whether it is a trait of character, a right act, or a well-motivated act—even if valid for what it includes, is dubious for what it rules out. Virtue can inhere in something as abstract as justice or as concrete as giving to charity; can be dispositional, like courage, or behavioral, like keeping appointments; can be a "corrective" against weak impulses, as with temperance, or the expression of our magnanimous impulses, as with benevolence; can be as culturally specific as dietary rules or as transcultural as mercy. If this observation is correct, it not only questions the effort to reduce virtue to a single quality. It suggests also that the search for a logically compelled list is no more likely to succeed.

Yet despite Kohlberg's—and Maria's—objections, there is much to be said for a virtue-ethic approach. Schools deal with a child's emergent nature; unlike courts, they are not in a position to weigh fully the consequences and motives of acts, and to determine degrees of culpability. Readying the child with "built" habits and dispositions rather than imparting codes of action makes sense. Virtues also recognize the centrality of desires and emotions in moral decision making. Alasdair MacIntyre has observed (attributing the view to Aristotle) that to act virtuously is to act "from inclination formed by the cultivation of the virtues" (MacIntyre 1984, 149). To like effect is contemporary American classicist and philosopher Julia Annas: "Virtues . . . are the expression, albeit cultivated, of our desires, our life objectives, our happiness"

(Annas 1993, 55). In this process of "cultivation," adults play a critical role in orienting children's raw feelings (anger, affection, joy) to worthy ends.

We believe that, rather than seeking to specify one optimal enumeration of virtues, effort should be put into identifying the minefields we stumble upon when constructing *any* list of virtues. Chief among these, because it applies so broadly, is the need to avoid *polarization* of alternatives. We will illustrate the importance of that factor in considering the problems of the tendency to *skew* one's proposed designation of virtues, and the related concerns of *contentlessness* and *triviality*.

CONCLUSION: PERTINENT CONSTRAINTS ON A "VIRTUES" APPROACH

In considering the charges of *contentlessness* and *triviality*, it is important to acknowledge that they cannot be wholly refuted. Virtues are not reliably action-directing; indeed, the more so they appear, the less they seem concerned with character rather than act. As a preemptive barrier, however, the allegation of vacuousness is overdrawn. That "respect" does not always prescribe action with clarity does not mean that "disrespect" cannot be identified and deprecated. A nonpolarized approach seeks to enfold the charge of contentlessness into the work of moral education, recognizing it as a hazard to be honored in carrying on that work, a concern that needs to be taken most seriously.

In responding, however, to the legitimate concern about the vagueness inherent in significant moral virtues, it is important not to trigger that of triviality. One form of that failing arises from the temptation to focus excessively on actions that are easily measured and reported, but only bluntly expressive of significant virtues. Requiring uniform dress of students may, for example, serve values like equality and decorum—by discouraging conspicuous displays of wealth and creating a more serious atmosphere—and may encourage some students toward acting morally. It is fatuous to regard it as accomplishing much along those lines, however, and the danger is that its ready quantifiability and reportability will lead school systems to accept it as a significant indicium of moral uplift. The same concern is appropriate with respect to programs of character education that overemphasize activities like posters and awards. The effectiveness of a character education program is not to be gauged by any such highly tangible, readily measurable elements.

Care needs also to be taken, we believe, that, in an eagerness to reinforce traditional norms of decorous behavior, we do not blur the distinction between morality and convention. It trivializes the idea of "virtue" to apply it to such matters as running in the halls, chewing gum, and being late to class. It is perfectly reasonable to have and enforce rules against such actions, but it is another matter to think of them as morally significant matters. Understandably, busy, often harried, teachers will urge the *primary* importance of such rules of order. Although they may thereby be making moral education possible, they should not think that they are also acting on the possibility. (See the excerpt by Joan Goodman at p. 147 in the next section of this chapter.)

The charge of *skewing* also needs to be taken seriously, again not as a "preemptive strike" against the entire idea of character education, but as a concern about much of its articulation. The polarization of the educational scene today has led many to feel that they can uphold the pole about which they care most deeply only by responding suspiciously to the insistent urgings of the partisans of the other pole. Those who place great value on children's being quiet and orderly, for example, need to attend also to the pedagogical value of teaching them to remain curious and inquisitive, just as those emphasizing tolerance and forbearance in judging others—for example, a student whose persistent use of inappropriate language carries over to moments when he is speaking in class—need to take seriously the need to "police the boundaries" of those virtues. In both cases, the challenge is to be watchful lest pursuit of one's favored set of virtues inhibit development of the other.

The program of character education developed by Thomas Lickona seems to us to be one example of a successful grappling with that challenge. (See the excerpt from a leading book of his at p. 149 in the next section of this chapter.) Other approaches, however, plainly succumb (with no great sign of struggle) to the hazard of polarization. Consider the program upheld as exemplary by sociologist Edward A. Wynne. According to Wynne, it has the following characteristics:

> Adults model good moral conduct. They work diligently; are obedient to school rules and policies; . . . and take pride in the school and their community.
>
> Pupils are encouraged and even required to engage in many forms of service. They are teacher's aides, tutors, and crossing guards; deliver presentations at assemblies; and participate in service activities and clubs, student councils, athletic teams, and fund-raising for the school. . . .
>
> Discipline and monitoring are stressed. Typical forms of misconduct are clearly prohibited by well-publicized rules vigorously and fairly enforced. . . .
>
> A relatively uniform sense of purpose exists. Adults and children alike give the same concrete answers when asked about matters of school policy.
>
> Academics are taken seriously. Significant amounts of homework are regularly assigned, collected, graded, and returned. Diverse efforts are made to improve the quality and quantity of instruction provided by teachers. Pupils are grouped to facilitate instruction. Pupils who do not know the required materials are not passed on. Frequent, rigorous exams are administered. Honor rolls, report cards, and recognition assemblies are used to emphasize the value of academic excellence.
>
> There are often occasions for good-spirited fun. . . . Ceremonies are an important means of stressing school values. Assemblies, daily classroom flag salutes, awards assemblies, and occasions for "appreciation" are standard events. . . . School pride is an important theme. . . .
>
> (Wynne 1991, 147–148)

Although many of these practices have considerable merit when embedded in a balanced program, just that quality is absent in this compilation. Note the complete lack of any critical faculties thought indicative of "good moral conduct"; the severely limited activities thought to constitute "service"; the priority given "academic rigor," as compared to the breezy reference to "diverse policies" addressing the question of the quality of instruction; the emphasis on students being given "the same concrete answers" when asked about school policies; and the th nness of "school pride" resting on ceremonies and awards, without any larger purpose informing their content. In discussing the challenge of instituting such a program, Wynne notes that, "where necessary, the principal must confront and subdue dissident pupils, teachers, and parents opposed to the basic aims of the program" (id., 150). Despite the emphasis in the essay on "youth suicide and homicide, out-of-wedlock births, criminal arrest, and drug use" as the problems giving rise to a need for action (id., 139), the "opposition" would surely come, not from those who support such activities, but from those who find the response seriously deficient.

Educational critic Jonathan Kozol's words seem apt as applied to approaches like this: 'You look in vain through this list for anything that has to do with an original child or an independent style." The emphasis is on "obedience characteristics" (Kozol 1967, 175–176). We believe that schools must take seriously Kozol's insight that, "the whole concept of respect for unearned and undeserved authority is bitter . . . to children" (id., 179). The "bitterness" powerfully undermines the very respect that a school is purporting to reinforce. An emphasis on respect for the authority of teacher and school is valid and valuable in itself. However, a nonpolarized approach hospitably accommodates an equal insistence that teachers and school do what they can to *merit* respect. The point of attending to the problem of meriting respect is not that, if a teacher or school *has* fallen seriously short, disrespectful conduct should be allowed, let alone encouraged. It is that those insisting that students be respectful not reflexively or defensively condemn as disrespectful those who call attention to the falling short, that they rather pay serious and sustained attention to the factors that prompt loss of respect—and do so, not as a vague, long-range goal, never to be fulfilled, but as an urgent and serious need, precisely in the name of respect.

More fundamentally, the effort to avoid a polarized approach to character education is grounded in a realization that it is a grievously limited response, not only to the educational needs of schoolchildren as students, but to the complexity of their needs simply as people. The French writer Simone Weil has written profoundly, in our judgment, of the need for "opposites" to "balance and complete one another." Consider how the following nonpolarized articulation of basic human needs could inform an effort to develop a virtue-centered approach to moral education:

The human soul has need of equality and of hierarchy. Equality is the public recognition, effectively expressed in institutions and manners, of the principle that an equal degree of attention is due to the needs of all human beings. Hierarchy is the scale of responsibilities. . . .

The human soul has need of consented obedience and of liberty. Consented obedience is what one concedes to an authority because one judges it to be legitimate. . . . Liberty is the power of choice within the latitude left between the direct constraint of natural forces and the authority accepted as legitimate. . . .

The human soul has need of truth and of freedom of expression. The need for truth requires . . . that in the domain of thought there should never be any physical or moral pressure exerted for any purpose other than an exclusive concern for truth. . . .

The human soul has need of some solitude and privacy and also of some social life.

The human soul has need of both personal property and collective property. Personal property never consists in the possession of a sum of money, but in the ownership of concrete objects like a house, a field, furniture, tools, which seem to the soul to be an extension of itself and of the body. . . . Collective property is not defined by a legal title but by the feeling among members of a human milieu that certain objects are like an extension or development of the milieu.

The human soul has need of punishment and of honour. Whenever a human being, through the commission of a crime, has become exiled from good, he needs to be reintegrated with it through suffering. The suffering should be inflicted with the aim of bringing the soul to recognize freely some day that its infliction was just. This reintegration with the good is what punishment is. Every man who is innocent, or who has finally expiated guilt, needs to be recognized as honourable to the same extent as anyone else.

The human soul has need of disciplined participation in a common task of public value, and it has need of personal initiative within this participation.

The human soul has need of security and also of risk. The fear of violence or of hunger or of any other extreme evil is a sickness of the soul. The boredom produced by a complete absence of risk is also a sickness of the soul.
(Weil 1986, 208–209)

If a virtues approach succeeds in avoiding the hazards of vacuousness, trivialization, and polarization, it can serve as one vehicle for moral education. But we should appreciate the difficulty of sitting simultaneously in multiple seats. To emphasize one virtue while remaining watchful of those that compete and conflict, to select one virtue-derived action while holding onto alternatives as well, to target the single child while staying sensitive to the groups and institutions influencing that child, is a tall order indeed. It demands ongoing reflection within ourselves and with others. Such individual virtuosity would be difficult to maintain in the most supportive setting. Can it reasonably be incorporated into the life of a school, given the demands and limitations of that setting? Much of the remaining chapters of this book are devoted to an engagement with that question.

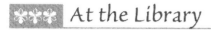 **At the Library**

William J. Hutchins, "The Children's Morality Code"
(1924, 292)

Boys and girls who are good Americans try to become strong and useful, worthy of their nation, that our country may become ever greater and better. Therefore, they obey the laws of right living which the best Americans have always obeyed.

I. THE LAW OF SELF-CONTROL

Good Americans Control Themselves

Those who best control themselves can best serve their country.

1. I will control my tongue, and will not allow it to speak mean, vulgar, or profane words. I will think before I speak. I will tell the truth and nothing but the truth.
2. I will control my temper, and will not get angry when people or things displease me. Even when indignant against wrong and contradicting falsehoods, I will keep my self-control.
3. I will control my thoughts, and will not allow a foolish wish to spoil a wise purpose.
4. I will control my actions. I will be careful and thrifty, and insist on doing right.
5. I will not ridicule nor defile the character of another; I will keep my self-respect, and help others to keep theirs.

II. THE LAW OF GOOD HEALTH

Good Americans Try to Gain and Keep Good Health

The welfare of our country depends upon those who are physically fit for their daily work. Therefore:

1. I will try to take such food, sleep, and exercise as will keep me always in good health.
2. I will keep my clothes, my body, and my mind clean.
3. I will avoid those habits which would harm me, and will make and never break those habits which will help me.
4. I will protect the health of others, and guard their safety as well as my own.
5. I will grow strong and skillful.

III. THE LAW OF KINDNESS

Good Americans Are Kind

In America those who are different must live in the same communities. We are of many different sorts, but we are one great people. Every unkindness hurts the common life, every kindness helps. Therefore:

1. I will be kind in all my thoughts. I will bear no spites or grudges. I will never despise anybody.
2. I will be kind in all my speech. I will never gossip nor will I speak unkindly of anyone. Words may wound or heal.
3. I will be kind in my acts. I will not selfishly insist on having my own way. I will be polite: rude people are not good Americans. I will not make unnecessary trouble for those who work for me, nor forget to be grateful. I will be careful of other people's things. I will do my best to prevent cruelty, and will give help to those who are in need.

IV. THE LAW OF SPORTSMANSHIP

Good Americans Play Fair

Strong play increases and trains one's strength and courage. Sportsmanship helps one to be a gentleman, a lady. Therefore:

1. I will not cheat; I will keep the rules, but I will play the game hard, for the fun of the game, to win by strength and skill. If I should not play fair, the loser would lose the fun of the game, the winner would lose his self-respect, and the game itself would become a mean and often cruel business.
2. I will treat my opponents with courtesy, and trust them if they deserve it. I will be friendly.
3. If I play in a group game, I will play, not for my own glory, but for the success of my team.
4. I will be a good loser or a generous winner.
5. And in my work as well as in my play, I will be sportsmanlike—generous, fair, honorable.

V. THE LAW OF SELF-RELIANCE

Good Americans Are Self-Reliant

Self-conceit is silly, but self-reliance is necessary to boys and girls who would be strong and useful.

1. I will gladly listen to the advice of older and wiser people; I will reverence the wishes of those who love and care for me, and who know life and me better than I. I will develop independence and wisdom to choose for myself, act for myself, according to what seems right and fair and wise.
2. I will not be afraid of being laughed at when I am right. I will not be afraid of doing right when the crowd does wrong.
3. When in danger, trouble, or pain, I will be brave. A coward does not make a good American.

VI. THE LAW OF DUTY

Good Americans Do Their Duty

The shirker and the willing idler live upon others, and burden fellow-citizens with work unfairly. They do not do their share for their country's good.

I will try to find out what my duty is, what I ought to do as a good American, and my duty I will do, whether it is easy or hard. What it is my duty to do I can do.

VII. THE LAW OF RELIABILITY

Good Americans Are Reliable

Our country grows great and good as her citizens are able more fully to trust each other. Therefore:

1. I will be honest in every act, and very careful with money. I will not cheat, nor pretend, nor sneak.
2. I will not do wrong in the hope of not being found out. I cannot hide the truth from myself. Nor will I injure the property of others.
3. I will not take without permission what does not belong to me. A thief is a menace to me and others.
4. I will do promptly what I have promised to do. If I have made a foolish promise, I will at once confess my mistake, and I will try to make good any harm which my mistake may have caused. I will so speak and act that people will find it easier to trust each other.

VIII. THE LAW OF TRUTH

Good Americans Are True

1. I will be slow to believe suspicions lest I do injustice; I will avoid hasty opinions lest I be mistaken as to facts.
2. I will hunt for proof, and be accurate as to what I see and hear. I will learn to think, that I may discover new truth.
3. I will stand by the truth regardless of my likes and dislikes, and scorn the temptation to lie for myself or friends, nor will I keep the truth from those who have a right to it.

IX. THE LAW OF GOOD WORKMANSHIP

Good Americans Try to Do the Right Thing in the Right Way

The welfare of our country depends upon those who have learned to do in the right way the work that makes civilization possible. Therefore:

1. I will get the best possible education, and learn all that I can as a preparation for the time when I am grown up and at my life work. I will invent and make things better if I can.

2. I will take real interest in work, and will not be satisfied to do slipshod, lazy, and merely passable work. I will form the habit of good work and keep alert; mistakes and blunders cause hardships (sometimes disaster) and spoil success.

3. I will make the right thing in the right way to give it value and beauty, even when no one else sees or praises me. But when I have done my best, I will not envy those who have done better, or have received larger reward. Envy spoils the work and the worker.

X. THE LAW OF TEAM-WORK

Good Americans Work in Friendly Co-operation with Fellow-Workers

One alone could not build a city or a great railroad. One alone would find it hard to build a bridge. That I may have bread, people have sowed and reaped, people have made plows and threshers, have built mills and mined coal, made stoves and kept stores. As we learn better how to work together, the welfare of our country is advanced.

1. In whatever work I do with others, I will do my part and encourage others to do their part, promptly, quickly.
2. I will help to keep in order the things which we use in our work. When things are out of place, they are often in the way, and sometimes they are hard to find.
3. In all my work with others, I will be cheerful. Cheerlessness depresses all the workers and injures all the work.
4. When I have received money for my work, I will be neither a miser nor a spend-thrift. I will save or spend as one of the friendly workers of America.

XI. THE LAW OF LOYALTY

Good Americans Are Loyal

If our America is to become ever greater and better, her citizens must be loyal, devotedly faithful, in every relation of life full of courage and regardful of their honor.

1. I will be loyal to my family. In loyalty I will gladly obey my parents or those who are in their place and show them gratitude. I will do my best to help each member of my family to strength and usefulness.
2. I will be loyal to my school. In loyalty I will obey and help other pupils to obey those rules which further the good of all.
3. I will be loyal to my town, my State, my country. In loyalty I will respect and help others to respect their laws and their courts of justice.
4. I will be loyal to humanity. In loyalty I will do my best to help the friendly relations of our country with every other country, and to give to everyone in every land the best possible chance.

If I try simply to be loyal to my family, I may be disloyal to my school. If I try simply to be loyal to my school, I may be disloyal to my town, my State, and my country. If I try simply to be loyal to my town, State, and country, I may be disloyal to humanity. I will try above all things else to be loyal to humanity; then I shall surely be loyal to my country, my State and my town, to my school and to my family.

And those who obey the law of loyalty obey all the other ten laws of The Good American.

The Children's Code of Morals was the winner of a competition sponsored by the Character Education Association in 1914. It was widely adopted by schools in its original or modified form[3] and became very influential in the character education movement in the early twentieth century as reliance on the "codification" of virtues increased (see McClellan, 1992, Ch. 4).

Even though we are now witnessing a resurgence of virtue lists and codes, the language of the Children's Code seems out-of-date and naïve to many contemporary readers (although very appealing to many others). Today's codes are unlikely to emphasize so heavily health, hard work, patriotism, and duty. Yet, is it fair to say that the Code in its entirety is a good bit more balanced and sophisticated—see especially the last paragraph—than either detractors or supporters would acknowledge?

While we may object to some of the maxims in the Children's Code as peripheral to morality, it is also quite likely that its authors might find equally trivial some of the virtues we stress today. The next reading takes a critical look at such possible trivialization.

<hr>

Joan F. Goodman, "'Running in the Halls' and Moral Trivia"
(1998, 52)

I have been listening to fourth-grade children explain what it means to be moral. Being moral, they say, means being a "good person." And what is that? "Be nice, be kind, don't run in the halls, raise your hand, don't chew gum, don't pass notes, don't talk loud, don't be late, don't fight." This sort of value-lumping is hardly surprising. One expects children to merge the shoulds and shouldn'ts of their lives and not to have a highly refined hierarchy of values—some moral, some not. More surprising is that when I ask teachers the same question, they too fuse important, but, vague, values, such as "be kind," with idiosyncratic rules deemed necessary for managing children at school; no running in the halls is a favorite.

Now it is of course true that running in the halls causes excessive noise and possible accidents. It is, therefore, perfectly reasonable to forbid it. Rules that compel children to walk in a line, not stop until they reach their destination, lower their voices in corridors, and keep their hands to themselves may also be perfectly reasonable. But to call these rules "moral" stretches the term and not harmlessly so. Some would make the stretch: They argue that since morality concerns how we deal with, and demonstrate respect for, one another, running in the halls, with its potentially harmful consequences, is a moral violation. Or, that since the rule

<hr>

[3] The original Code contained these words (in "The Law of Kindness"): "In America those of us who are of different races, colors and conditions must live together. We are of many different sorts, but we are one great people. . . . I will not think of myself above any other girl or boy just because I am of a different race or color or condition." The version reprinted in the text, which was circulated in the *Journal of the National Education Association*, replaced the first sentence with "In America those who are different must live in the same communities" and deleted the last sentence.

against running is legitimate, even though merely a traffic regulation, the disobedience to the rule is itself immoral. I argue that turning rules-of-convenience into moral mandates cheapens morality, thereby lowering its inspirational and aspirational pull, and makes it unlikely that the moral dimension will become central to a child's personal identity.

By lumping "running in the halls" with "being nice," we overextend the meaning of morality and thereby trivialize it. Moral trivialization, linked closely to moral indifference, may be a more serious threat to our present society than moral ignorance. The problem is not that children don't know right from wrong—they know the distinctions full well; it is that they don't care. Indifference is a tough nut to crack. What is the appeal one makes to a child who, when criticized for a moral indiscretion, say cheating, replies with a shrug, "Sure it's wrong but so what, everyone does it"? One would rather avoid, and not have to remediate, moral indifference.

When a child disconnects the wrongness of an act from its prohibitedness, she removes the fundamental meaning of morality—its prescriptiveness. To say something is a matter of morality is to say it obliges behavior. Lying and stealing are not matters of preference to be practiced when convenient, rewarded, or self-serving. Moral values are not matters of taste and preference—you like jazz, I like rock—where personal discretion and interests may prevail; they are supposed to be binding imperatives. To feel a personal obligation, particularly in a culture that stresses personal choice, requires weighty and worthy objectives that merit abiding commitments.

One way we encourage children to be moral is by exposing them to great exemplars, Martin Luther King, Jr. and Rosa Parks, for example. We explain that they were great because they had a magnificent cause—the (to us) self-evident, eternal truth that all people are created, and must be treated, equally; they were great because they attacked wrongdoing nonviolently; . . . they were great because they could and did love even those who would destroy them; and they were great because for their cause they put their very lives at stake. We do not tell children they were great because they didn't run in the halls, pass notes, or chew gum.

Genuine morality is a hard sell. It demands self-denial, persistence, courage, and risk-taking. Almost by definition it means acting counter to our inclinations, making other's interests equal to our own. It means telling the truth when telling a lie would be more advantageous. It means refusing to go along with wrongdoing when the consequence may be loss of popularity. It means giving up opportunities for self-aggrandizement and pleasure. Moreover, the benefits of morality—purpose, direction, commitment, a deep sense of well-being, integrity, self-confidence, and self-fulfillment—tend to be neither obvious nor immediate. So why should a child bother?

In the short run, a child will bother because he fears punishment and seeks approval. In the long run, a child will bother only if he sees your interest as a form of self-interest, only if doing good translates into feeling good. What transforms moral knowledge into moral bindingness, in other words, is a moral identity, and that identity requires moral objectives worthy of incorporating into one's self-image. Thin gruel such as not running in the halls, chewing gum, or talking too loudly is not likely to be seized as constitutive of a self-image.

. . . I jaywalk. I'm not proud of doing so. I recognize the risk to my own and others' safety. I think it's wrong. I would stop jaywalking were I penalized with a stiff fine or, worse still, with the stares and disapproval of other pedestrians. I did, in fact, stop jaywalking when I lived in Berkeley, Calif. But giving up the habit then did not make me feel more worthwhile, or perhaps only slightly so. I certainly did not get up in the morning, look in the mirror, and say, "I am really becoming a good person." Not being a jaywalker did not become part of my identity. So when the sanctions were lifted, the bad habit resumed.

Similarly, a child might be pleased with herself when she walks, rather than runs, in the halls; nonetheless, her self-respect may remain inviolate if she reverts to running or raising her voice, even when reprimanded for so doing. We do not expect, and I dare say do not want, a child's moral identity and moral pride to have as its core obedience to local traffic rules. When we ask a child, "What sort of a person do you want to become?" we would not be satisfied if she said, "A person who does not run in the halls." Again, that is not to say the rule is inappropriate or even trivial, but it is a rule of convenience relevant to a particular situation, not a moral rule.

Children (ourselves as well) will make good and tough moral decisions, take pride in moral accomplishments, feel shame at moral lapses, and continually aspire to moral growth only if the moral act satisfies their self-definition. Lacking a moral identity, they will have little motive to resist daily moral threats and temptations, at least as long as discovery is unlikely or punishment minimal. Consider the following: An adolescent finds herself at a party with alcohol flowing freely. Plans are laid to trash another kid's yard because he is a "geek." The leaders proclaim that anyone who refuses to participate is a "jerk." Our student refuses. Why? Not from fear of discovery and punishment; she agrees that they will not be caught. Not because she is a friend of the victim; she, too, doesn't like him. It is simply that to commit the act defies her sense of self.

The next excerpt exemplifies a contemporary statement of virtues, not a code, written by a leader in the field. While it has a very modern ring, note how Lickona's notions of respect (which typically involve refraining from causing certain forms of harm) and responsibility (which often involves doing acts of beneficence) are similar to Kant's (and Mill's) "perfect" and "imperfect" duties, referred to at p. 94 in Chapter 4. Does this suggest there is more continuity in our notions of the moral good than a quick inspection of the language might suggest?

▼▼

Thomas Lickona, *Educating for Character: How Our Schools Can Teach Respect and Responsibility*
(1991, 43–48)

The natural moral law defining the public school's moral agenda can be expressed in terms of two great values: *respect* and *responsibility*. These values constitute the core of a universal, public morality. They have objective, demonstrable worth in that they promote the good of the individual and the good of the whole community. . . .

Respect and responsibility are the "fourth and fifth R's" that schools not only may but also must teach if they are to develop ethically literate persons who can take their place as responsible citizens of society. What are the concrete moral meanings of these foundational values?

Respect.   Respect means showing regard for the worth of someone or something. It takes three major forms: respect for oneself, respect for other people, and respect for all forms of life and the environment that sustains them.

Respect for self requires us to treat our own life and person as having inherent value. That's why it's wrong to engage in self-destructive behavior such as drug or alcohol abuse. Respect for others requires us to treat all other human beings—even those we dislike—as having dignity and rights equal to our own. That's the heart of the Golden Rule ("Do unto others as you would have them do unto you"). Respect for the whole complex web of life prohibits cruelty to animals and calls us to act with care toward the natural environment, the fragile ecosystem on which all life depends.

Other forms of respect derive from these. Respect for property, for example, comes from understanding that property is an extension of a person or a community of persons. Respect for authority comes from understanding that legitimate authority figures are entrusted with the care of others. Without somebody in charge, you can't run a family, a school, or a country. When people don't respect authority, things don't work very well and everybody suffers.

"Common courtesy" also derives from a basic respect for persons. I once spent time in the classroom of Molly Angelini, a gentle fifth-grade teacher in Moravia, New York, who made courtesy-as-respect a high priority. If a student banged a desk top shut, Mrs. Angelini paused to allow the student to say "Excuse me" to the class (they had discussed the fact that loud noises were an interruption if someone was speaking or a distraction if people were trying to think). Children were expected to apologize if they called someone a name. They were taught to say "Pardon me?" instead of "What?" when they wished something repeated. They were taught to say "Thank you" to the cafeteria workers who served them as they went through the lunch line. And they were taught that all of these behaviors were not mechanical gestures but meaningful ways of respecting other people.

Finally, just as the value of respect is involved in the smallest everyday interactions, it also underlies the major organizing principles of a democracy. It's respect for persons that leads people to create constitutions that require the government to protect, not violate, the rights of the governed. . . .

Responsibility.   Responsibility is an extension of respect. If we respect other people, we value them. If we value them, we feel a measure of responsibility for their welfare.

Responsibility literally means "ability to respond." It means orienting toward others, paying attention to them, actively responding to their needs. Responsibility emphasizes our positive obligations to care for each other.

Respect, by comparison, emphasizes our negative obligations. It tells us for the most part what *not* to do. This is sometimes called a "prohibitive morality." Lest we underestimate the "power of negative thinking," philosopher Jon Moline points out the importance of these moral prohibitions: They tell us our duty exactly. "Thou shalt not murder" has a precision that "Love your neighbor" does not.

A list of moral don'ts, however, is not enough. A responsibility ethic supplies the vital giving side of morality. Where respect says "Don't hurt," responsibility says

"Do help." It's true that the call to "love your neighbor" and "think of others" is open-ended; it doesn't tell us how much we should sacrifice for our families, give to charitable causes, work for our communities, or be there for those who need us. But a morality of responsibility does point us in the right direction. Over the long haul it calls us to try, in whatever way we can, to nurture and support each other, alleviate suffering, and make the world a better place for all.

What else does responsibility mean? It means being dependable, not letting others down. We help people by keeping our commitments, and we create problems for them when we don't. "I'm distressed," says a high school band instructor, "by the tendency I see in kids to think they can quit at any time." Responsibility means carrying out any job or duty—in the family, at school, in the workplace—to the best of our ability. . . .

▼▼▼▼▼

Respect and responsibility are the two foundational moral values that schools should teach. Are there others?

There are—such as honesty, fairness, tolerance, prudence, self-discipline, helpfulness, compassion, cooperation, courage, and a host of democratic values. These specific values are forms of respect and/or responsibility or aids to acting respectfully and responsibly.

Honesty is one such value. Dealing honestly with people—not deceiving them, cheating them, or stealing from them—is one basic way of respecting them. So is fairness, which requires us to treat people impartially and not play favorites.

Tolerance, too, expresses respect. Although tolerance can dissolve into a neutral relativism that seeks to escape ethical judgment, tolerance in its root meaning is one of the hallmarks of civilization. Tolerance is a fair and objective attitude toward those whose ideas, race, or creed are different from our own. Tolerance is what makes the world safe for diversity.

Other values help us respect ourselves. Prudence, for example, tells us not to put ourselves in physical or moral danger (the old idea of "avoiding the occasion of sin"). Self-discipline tells us not to indulge in self-demeaning or self-destructive pleasures but to pursue what is good for us—and to pursue healthy pleasures in moderation. Self-discipline also enables us to delay gratification, develop our talents, work toward distant goals, and make something of our lives. These are all forms of self-respect.

In a similar way, values such as helpfulness, compassion, and cooperation aid us in carrying out the broad ethic of responsibility. A helpful spirit takes pleasure in doing a kindness. Compassion (meaning "suffering with") helps us not only know our responsibility but also feel it. Cooperation recognizes that "no man is an island" and that, in an increasingly interdependent world, we must work together toward goals as basic as human survival.

Some qualities, such as moral courage, are an aid to both respect and responsibility. Courage helps young people respect themselves by resisting peer pressure to do things that are harmful to their own welfare. Courage helps all of us respect the rights of others when we face pressure to join the crowd in perpetrating an injustice. Courage also enables us to take bold, positive action on behalf of others.

▼▼▼▼▼

Democracy, in turn, is the best way we know of securing our individual rights (respecting persons) and promoting the general welfare (acting responsibly for the good of all). Teaching an understanding and appreciation of these democratic values—and how they are made realities through the laws of the land—is a central part of the school's moral charge. These values also help us define the kind of "patriotism" that schools should teach. In a democracy, patriotism doesn't mean "My country, right or wrong"; it means loyalty to the great democratic values on which the country was founded.

Even if a school begins with respect and responsibility—which I think are helpful starting points—and ends up with most or all of the values I've discussed, it's still important for people to go through the process of working up their own list of values they want to teach. . . . That process is a chance to bring together—or at least survey for their input—teachers, administrators, other school staff, parents, students, and community representatives—to get broad-scale support. Moreover, the actual list that a school or district comes up with in this way is likely to bear its own special stamp and distinctive priorities.

It's instructive—a way to identify our moral blind spots—to compare lists drawn up by different groups, especially groups in countries other than our own. For example, when the Ontario, Canada, Ministry of Education identified twenty values for schools to teach, its list included moderation, patience, and peace—three values less likely to show up on U.S. lists but obviously important for the well-being of both the individual and society.

Getting agreement about shared values does not, of course, guarantee that people will agree about how to apply those values in every situation. It's at the point of applying values, especially when values conflict, that differences of moral judgment or emphasis often arise. For example, what weight should be given to "respect for life" and "freedom of choice" in the abortion debate? What does "patriotism" mean in time of war?

However, disagreement at the level of application must not obscure agreement about the values (e.g., respect for life, liberty, responsible citizenship) themselves—or the fact that most of the time we do agree about how to translate moral values into social living. When it comes to the moral values we want our children to have, we can readily agree on the basics. We don't want them to lie, cheat on tests, take what's not theirs, call names, hit each other, or be cruel to animals; we do want them to tell the truth, play fair, be polite, respect their parents and teachers, do their schoolwork, and be kind to others.

In short, even in a society where values often clash, respect, responsibility, and their everyday manifestations are common moral ground. Recognizing that common ground is the essential first step in doing values education in our schools.

Is it fair to say that Lickona's approach, when read in even this summary form, is a substantial bit more complex than is signaled by a sound byte like "The Two R's"? To us, that complexity bespeaks an appropriate sophistication and balance.

Chapter 6

The Accountability of Teachers and Administrators

 ## At School

It's March. The weather teases, hinting occasionally of spring. Children, with their customary restless bravado, abandon winter jackets prematurely. The topics of the day are cliques—who's in, who's out—and sports. Observant teachers realize that it requires fresh engaging activities to take this frisky energy at full tide.

Hardie, ears perked as always, overheard several girls planning a burial for two recently deceased hamsters. A couple of students—even at this age unwilling to admit grief—announced that it is stupid to bury stupid animals. Who cares about stupid guinea pigs! What they want in class are real animals, a dog or cat. But of course, they complained, for the school to give permission for that would be too much like encouraging fun. Hardie interrupted and called for a class discussion on animals. He explained that, although school rules almost certainly prohibited dogs and cats in the class, there was an animal shelter next door to the school that would welcome the children's help. He was certain that the owner would provide work for a few children once a week.

The students were enthusiastic but questioned who would get to go and what would happen to those left out. During the conversation, other suggestions for "helping" were raised: xeroxing in the secretary's office, reshelving books in the library, cleaning up the yard, getting seeds planted, tutoring "little kids" in kindergarten and first grade. Hardie made copies of the list for the now revved-up children to take home. He then went to Principal Helter and told him of his idea to use one afternoon a week for "helping" activities.

Helter responded with enthusiasm: "Great idea, Hardie. Just the way to show parents we're taking their gripes seriously—you know, about how badly behaved the kids are. Also, no other elementary school in the district has started 'service learning,' so this project should make the school look good to the Super. If you begin on a small scale now we might be able to get a little cash and some other teachers to join next year." As Hardie moved to the door, Helter added, "Thanks, Hardie, for taking the initiative. You're a rare one; don't know how the place would get along without you."

The project moved ahead swiftly. A few parents responded with favorable comments to Hardie's note requesting parental permission. The school groundsperson, librarian, and secretary readily pledged their cooperation. Then, just a week from the planned starting date, trouble erupted. A group of parents, ignoring Hardie, protested directly to Helter. They argued that school service activities were inappropriate for children, certainly for their children. Teachers should be raising math and reading scores, not wasting children's time on tutoring. Let the little kids who can't read get outside help; fourth-graders need to be prepared for the more demanding academics ahead. Furthermore, if the school is to do "moral education" it should be about building character, not shelving books in the library. Hardie does a fine job at keeping the kids in line, making them courteous, and insisting they develop disciplined work habits. Indeed, many parents requested him because of his reputation for high standards and child productivity. Let him stick to that agenda.

Helter tried to appease the parents. He asked them to suggest alternative activities; he offered to make the service learning voluntary and to provide academic alternatives for those who chose not to participate. Nothing doing. The parents were adamant. They stalked out of his office with the warning that, if this was not resolved quickly, they were off to the superintendent and then to the school board.

When Hardie was summoned to the principal's office the next day he knew what was coming, for one of his students had already relayed ruefully his father's strongly negative reaction: "My good tax money," Fred reported the parent asserting, "going to that rinky dink school so you can care for animals? No way! I won't permit it! If I want you to shovel shit from a dog cage that's my business. I thought better of Mr. Knox. I thought he knew shoveling shit doesn't get you a decent job."

But Hardie *was* surprised when five minutes into their conversation Helter received a call from Ralph Senter, the superintendent, to say that the angry parents had contacted him as well. Though "of course" he personally thought the project was a terrific initiative, he didn't want the parents further antagonized: "Just not worth stirring up a lot of dandruff over this one, Fred, so take care of it, please," he cheerfully ordered.

"What do you think, Hardie?" asked Helter with an abject look.

"What do I think? What do you think I think? Tell Senter that I have notes from a bunch of parents who like the project. I'm sure we can get more support, too. Don't let a few outraged folks stop us."

"Look, Hardie, it's not that simple. Yeah, we probably could have a plebiscite and get a lot of votes, maybe hold a parent meeting and get a majority (though I doubt it because you know which parents would show for the meeting), but think of the publicity. It would definitely become a school board topic. The press would love to get their hands on it. Soon we'd be hearing about our school imposing 'liberal' values on children and neglecting their education."

"Fred, you're getting too scared too fast," replied Hardie, attempting a soothing voice. "You know I'm not exactly a card-carrying liberal. Schools all over the country are encouraging children to practice what *we* preach—responsibility for others, care for the weak, respect for work. These parents talk about the need for discipline. Well, what takes more discipline than cleaning out one dirty cage, then another, then another? Shoveling shit; yeah, exactly. I hadn't thought of it, but it's a good idea, very character-building.

"My bet is that the school board might well support the project; certainly there's a fighting chance that they would. But if they nix it they nix it; at least we won't have done their dirty work for them. What's the point of you and Senter pulling the plug now? If it's politics that concerns you—though, Fred, I know you're an educator at heart—then think about the points you'll lose with the faculty if you rescind your endorsement."

"This is one hell of a mess," replied a clearly troubled Helter. "You know I think the idea is great. I believe in it. And you're right, any principal worth his salt should support his teachers, especially when they're showing initiative in a way that fits with the district's own guidelines.

"I'm also used to parents griping, but it's a different ballgame these days. Once the spotlight gets turned on us, all hell can break loose—a blizzard of press coverage, e-mail, faxes, legal threats; pressure, pressure, pressure. Let's both think it over. I'll get back to you in a day or two."

Leaving the principal's office, Hardie was dejected, and not a little angry. It seemed pretty obvious that, no matter how much he rallied the troops, Helter would never oppose Senter. Head sunk down on his chest, he was startled by Maria's familiar voice:

"Hardie, but for that ancient screaming red tie I wouldn't have known you—shuffling walk, bleak expression, what gives? How about *me* buying *you* some coffee?"

"You're on, Maria. There's no one I'd rather be with right now."

Maria listened to the troubling story with disbelief. How could Helter interfere without at least calling a faculty and parent meeting? Didn't Hardie have a "right" to initiate his service project? Didn't teachers have any autonomy? If there was widespread opposition, that "right" *might* have to give way; they were after all in a public school. But not yet, not before more opinions were gathered!

Observing her troubled look, Hardie continued, "You know, Maria, it's not that I really believe one afternoon a week of shelving books will change the course of a child's life; very likely it will have no impact at all. What galls me is the hypocrisy of the administration. Here, Helter throws bouquets at me one minute because my class wants to do volunteer work and the next minute he pulls the rug out. If he'd been against it from the start, OK. If he had wanted me to do a more searching survey of parent attitudes, fine, no problem. But this kowtowing to a splinter group because of the potential for political trouble, and not because he agrees with them, that's a killer."

"Hardie, for once I absolutely agree with you," said Maria, "and the hypocrisy goes further. You notice the buckling under to authority; I notice the message it gives the children. We read them stories about heroes, we stress the importance of doing the right thing even when it means a loss of popularity, basically we tell them to speak truth to power, and now this. Hardie, we can't just roll over and play dead."

Hardie, touched by Maria's "we," asked, "How would you handle it, Maria?"

"I'm not sure as to strategy, only that we have to help Helter resist Senter."

There was a moment of sober silence between them. Then, just as Hardie thought he noticed a "something more" look in Maria's expression, she went on: "Actually, my coffee invitation this afternoon was less than wholly altruistic. I was looking for you. I have my own story to tell, and I think it's even more disturbing."

"Misery loves company. Let's hear it."

"You might say my problem is in some ways the opposite of yours," Maria began. "Helter is restraining your actions. He's coercing mine, through the good offices of Connie Comfort."

"How so?"

"You know Connie's in charge of the achievement testing. Last week she came to me with a copy of the Stanford Achievement Test that will be given to the fourth-graders at the end of the year. She told me, what we all know, that Helter wants the scores to go up. Apparently he wants it badly. On a list of average scores for the district, we're pretty low, and there are rumors that if we don't improve the school may be "consolidated" out of its present existence as the district's consolidation movement gains momentum. Now you can guess what Connie asked me to do. Maybe *told me* what to do is more accurate."

"Uh, oh."

"Yeah, you got it. She wants me to go over the questions from the test to be administered this year, and 'tutor' the kids."

"Wait a minute, Maria. Are you saying that Connie has a copy of the actual test we're giving this spring?"

"It surprised me, too. Apparently the test booklets are costly, and they're only reissued every so many years. In between, they're kept in the guidance office of each school."

"So Connie gives you a copy of the test and you give the kids the questions and answers?"

"Not exactly, but too close for comfort. She wants to be sure I have 'covered' all the material that they will be tested on, more or less item by item. When I objected, explained that I've followed the curriculum guidelines, used the assigned text and that's enough, she said she didn't like to ask this of me and neither did Helter but the bottom line is scores have got to go up.

"To justify the request she pointed out how awful it would be if the school were closed. She let me know what a good thing we have going here: It's one of the very few truly integrated elementary schools around. We're a model of interracial harmony and we've taken large steps towards developing a more inclusive curriculum. We also have an unusual degree of income and political diversity. If they consolidate us with another place, all that may be lost. What she didn't say, but didn't have to, was that she and Fred might lose their jobs, or at least their status.

"Then, to clinch her argument Connie threw in the fact that 'prepping' for achievement tests is commonplace in the district, now that scores are so closely tied to teacher, child, and school standing. That sounded like a not-so-gentle reminder that my own status around here would be hurt if the kids were to perform poorly."

Hardie moaned, "And what are you going to do about her 'request'?"

"Thus far, I haven't gone beyond considering my options. I guess I could tell her, 'no way.' But that would have bad repercussions on my kids' scores and, as you know, I don't exactly have the cream of the crop. I understand that these scores not only go into their records, in case any of them should apply to magnet middle schools, but may well influence their opportunities for advanced work next year and beyond. You know how, once low expectations are established, it just gets tougher and tougher for them. So, if I limit my thinking to the kids' (and my own) welfare, I should go along with Connie. But cheating is cheating. You can't have a rule that says, 'Don't cheat until it hurts you.'"

"So, what else can you do?" Hardie asked, impressed with Maria's wrestling.

"Well, I considered fudging. Say 'yes' to Connie but just don't do the 'tutoring,' or *really* keep it indirect. But that seems to me a bad choice: I'd be deceiving Connie, it wouldn't help the kids, it wrecks my spring teaching plans, and I will have run away from the issue.

"I also thought of a more political approach. Maybe you were hinting at that, Hardie."

"Yeah. What were you thinking?"

"Well, we might bring up the issue for the faculty to discuss. . . . No, we couldn't call a faculty meeting without even telling the principal; it'd have to be just getting a few folks together informally, have a meeting on the ethics of coaching for a test, and if we get enough support then send a delegation to Helter. At least that's what I thought until you told me your story. Now I think we'd lose with Helter.

"I also thought of getting word out to the parents or even the press. But I don't think we could do that. It would make the school look awful. Anyway, it's not clear to me how the parents would react. Some, I assume, would be appalled at the hanky panky, others would rather not know and let it happen, and some, I suspect, would be delighted and would push hard on the every-one-does-it argument. Why should their children's scores and future opportunities be sacrificed at the altar of honesty?"

"You're absolutely right, Maria."

"Right about what? I haven't even staked out a position."

"You're right that we can't play dead. There is no way we can ask children to respect us, or maintain our own professional (and personal) self-respect if we don't do something about these matters—both problems, but especially yours. Without question, you are being asked to behave unethically. In my case, I'm merely running into resistance trying to initiate an ethical act. If I can recall my old friends Kant and Mill, there's a difference between not being able to do something beneficial and having to do something wrong. If we bow down to Connie on the coaching, she to Helter, he to Senter—who it seems would rather bow to every political tremble than risk dissension within the school board—it's good-bye democracy, good-bye character education."

"And what, brave soul, do you think we should do?"

"It's not entirely clear to me, Maria. You painted some very unattractive but realistic options. With so much riding on scores the long-run solution might be to have the entire testing administration outsourced. Leaving test booklets that will be reused in some building closet or file is not a tenable policy. We are just not a sufficiently honorable community. When the stakes are this high, there will be cheating—by students, by teachers, or as a matter of covert school policy."

"But that's futuristic. What about now?"[1]

"I think we start by talking quietly to the other fourth-grade teachers, Aggie and maybe a few other reliably strong members of the faculty. Then, as a small group, we could go privately to Helter and let him know we're serious about refusing to cheat and prepared to stand with him against pressures from 'the system.' I'm not so sure your pessimism about his reaction is warranted on this one. It's really a serious matter."

"And if you're wrong? If he claims there is nothing he can do about it, that the schools' scores just have to go up?"

"I wish we knew someone who could talk some sense into these guys, but we don't; at least, I don't." Maria's nod signaled her agreement. Hardie went on: "Maria, maybe then it'll be time to tell him we'll have to go public—at least inform teachers, and maybe parents. He knows that, although many par-

---

[1] The "future" may be less far off than Hardie's term suggests. As we were preparing the manuscript for publication, *Newsweek* ran a "Special Report" titled, "When Teachers Are Cheaters," asserting that "an alarming number of teachers and principals face charges of fixing the numbers" on standardized tests, by practices ranging from the form of coaching urged on Maria by Connie Comfort to telling students the right answers during a test and simply excluding low-scoring students from the test altogether (Kantrowitz and McGinn 2000).

ents would support him, once it got into the newspapers it'd be a scandal. I have tenure, Maria. You don't. I'll gladly be the heavy if one is needed, but that's a bridge we don't have to cross right now."

"I like your plan to involve others, Hardie. We teachers so rarely act like a community, though of course we preach to the kids all the time about being a community, that the school is a community, that our neighborhoods are communities. Your service project, too, is about building community, and I want to see it happen. First my problem, then yours. OK?

"And speaking of joint projects," Maria smiled, "how about overcoming our problems with another round of coffee and us each taking half of that last piece of chocolate cake on the counter?"

❄❄ At the University

In this chapter, we shift our focus from the moral significance of the actions and motives of students to those of teachers, administrators, and school board members. We do this, not simply because they are in the school community, but in response to our belief that their actions and perceived motives are a powerful part of the students' moral learning environment.

This is the idea of the *implicit curriculum* (sometimes referred to as the "hidden" curriculum). Its premise is that what a school teaches is more than the subjects contained in class notes, assignments, and examinations; it includes the unspoken messages about how one should live, embedded in the way teachers and administrators carry on their work. A teacher who is deferential to department chairs and principals, but curt and dismissive with students and younger colleagues, will not get very far teaching students to be respectful of others. A teacher who does not grade student work promptly and thoughtfully will not succeed at teaching students responsibility. A teacher may emphasize self-discipline as a means of teaching students to balance the interests of others fairly with their own, but students will not learn that lesson if they observe the teacher consistently placing first priority on advancing his or her career. Students have a keen, even a vigilant, set of antennae for hypocrisy. The message, "Do as I say, not as I do," whether delivered explicitly or otherwise, is not likely to be heeded, for what the speaker *does* bespeaks a lack of commitment to what he or she has *said*. As educational theorist Clark Power puts it, "[s]tudents quickly become cynical of approaches to character education which advocate ideals in the classroom which seem unrelated or even contradictory with practices in the school" (Power 1987, 168).

Education professor Gary D. Fenstermacher has placed this idea in context, in words that bear including here at some length:

> There are several different ways teachers serve as both moral agents and moral educators. They can be quite directive, teaching morality outright—a form of instruction often called didactic instruction. When

it becomes heavy-handed or highly ideological, it is often considered in-
doctrination. Rather than specific instruction in morality, teachers can
teach *about* morality, as might be the case in courses on world religions,
philosophy, civics, or sex education. A third way to undertake moral education is to act morally. . . .

The first two forms of moral education are generally well known and
much discussed. Depending on the teacher and the content, these two
forms of moral education can be powerful influences on certain children
at certain times in their development. Neither of the first two forms,
however, has the potential to shape and influence student conduct in
such educationally productive ways as the third form. . . . Nearly everything that a teacher does while in contact with students carries moral
weight. Every response to a question, every assignment handed out, every
discussion on issues, every resolution of a dispute, every grade given to a
student carries with it the moral character of the teacher. This moral character can be thought of as the *manner* of the teacher.

Manner is an accompaniment to everything teachers do in their classrooms. Chemistry can be taught in myriad ways, but however it is taught,
the teacher will always be giving directions, explaining, demonstrating,
checking, adjudicating, motivating, reprimanding, and in all these activities displaying the manner that marks him or her as morally well developed or not. Teachers who understand their impact as moral educators
take their manner quite seriously. They understand that they cannot expect honesty without being honest or generosity without being generous
or diligence without themselves being diligent. Just as we understand
that teachers must engage in critical thinking with students if they expect
students to think critically in their presence, they must exemplify moral
principles and virtues in order to elicit them from students.
(Fenstermacher 1990, 134–135) (emphasis in original)

The power of the "school climate" is heightened by the implicit quality of
the message it carries. Open discussion of a moral problem explicitly invites
student reflection and judgment; even a fairly didactic moral lesson leaves
children free to reject it. However, when the message is unspoken it is experienced simply as background matter to be taken for granted, its truth so obvious that it is not even worth putting on the table—"*of course*, we all look out
for Number 1"—if indeed it is consciously noted at all.

We therefore ground our inquiry into the morality of the actions that
Maria Laszlo, Hardie Knox, Fred Helter, and Ralph Senter are considering,
with a realization that, in making and acting on their decisions, they are engaging in moral education of their students.

We begin with the teachers, Hardie and Maria. Each is experiencing some
pressure from "above."

In Hardie's case, it is to drop the community-service idea at the insistence
of the superintendent—even though Hardie, his students, and the principal

think it educationally valuable—to avoid a contentious airing of the question before the school board by a small group of militant parents. Notice that Senter has not said that the idea is a bad one, nor even that dissenting parents should have the right (perhaps in the name of pluralism, discussed at p. 99 in Chapter 4 and developed further at p. 194 in Chapter 7) to have their children excused from a program to which they object. Nor has Senter taken the position that Hardie should hold off until the issue can be decided by a higher authority than an individual classroom teacher. Rather, he sees it as his chief responsibility to keep controversy off the board agenda, to protect its members from having to engage with a strongly disputed idea. Had the parent group merely complained, and not threatened to "go public" with their objections, he might well have left the matter to Helter.

Maria is being urged by a senior faculty colleague, on behalf of the principal, to teach in a way that she thinks is dishonest and educationally impoverished, in order to help maintain her school's standing within the school system. Dishonest, because she believes that "teaching to the test," when she knows not only the subject areas to be tested but the precise questions, is morally equivalent to giving students the answers; educationally impoverished, because she believes that, since a test can address only a portion of what a student should have learned (and that portion distorted by the requirement that it be readily measurable), her students would benefit far more from spending the time in a broader or deeper engagement with the subject matter.

In each case, the primary question we consider is whether it would be wrong for them to act as they have been asked, or told, to act. To one who would say "no, it would not be wrong" to that question, the further question arises, whether the teachers not merely *may* obey (and still be acting morally), but *should obey*, that it would be wrong for them to refuse. In coming to grips with these questions, we encounter the concepts of *integrity*, *accountability*, and *professionalism*.

INTEGRITY AS A "MASTER VIRTUE"

The contemporary philosopher Gabriele Taylor speaks of integrity as having a "rather peculiar status" among the virtues (Taylor 1981, 151). It is not easily defined or described, for unlike such virtues as honesty, loyalty, or respect, "nothing whatever can be deduced about any kind of particular behavior . . ." from the fact that one has acted with integrity (ibid.). Were we to conclude that if Hardie agreed to drop the community-service idea he would lack integrity, we would not be suggesting that a teacher who had never desired to adopt it also lacked integrity. "[W]hat matters is not so much adherence to [a specific decision], but rather that the person of integrity should do what he himself thinks is right. . . ." (id., 143). Lack of integrity would be suggested by one speaking of Hardie or Maria as "going along" or "knuckling under," suggesting a want of steadfastness.

A classic description of this quality of steadfastness is Robert Bolt's portrayal of Sir Thomas More in *A Man for All Seasons* (1962). Bolt describes More as "a man with an adamantine sense of his own self" (xi). He goes on:

> He knew where he began and left off, what area of himself he could yield to the encroachments of his enemies, and what to the encroachments of those he loved. It was a substantial area in both cases, for he had a proper sense of fear and was a busy lover. Since he was a clever man and a great lawyer he was able to retire from those areas in wonderfully good order, but at length he was asked to retreat from that final area where he located his self. And there this supple, humorous, unassuming and sophisticated person set like metal, was overtaken by an absolutely primitive rigor, and could no more be budged than a cliff.
> *(Ibid.)*[2]

This sense of the inviolability of the core of one's self, which seems central to the idea of integrity, is an essential support to other virtues. To be thought of as honest, for example, one must adhere to the precepts of those values, not merely in the abstract, but when there is a cost to be paid thereby. A person lacking integrity may claim to be honest, but will fail to respond to its call in the face of even mild counterpressures on his or her acts or speech. It is in this sense that integrity may be thought of as a "master virtue," a condition of having others.

Steadfastness, however, can also appear as a failing rather than a virtue. In Taylor's words, the attitude of a person of integrity is that "there are certain things he cannot bring himself to do, and certain other things he feels he must do, irrespective of consequences" (Taylor 1981, 154). Against such a person, she continues, we may level "the charge of self-indulgence": Because a powerful sense of integrity may lead one to refuse to do what is actually the more beneficial course of action, and choose the more harmful of the available courses of action, integrity "comes to be regarded as a specific form of weakness" (ibid.) We will consider below the salience of this insight in the context of Hardie's and Maria's circumstances. For the moment, note Robert Bolt's recognition that it is only in "that final area" where continuing to yield to the "encroachments" of others is at the cost of one's self, of one's integrity.

In the present instances, the motive for "going along" that first comes to mind is self-protection, the fear of reprisal of various sorts or injury to one's standing with one's superiors. Although few might blame either teacher for doing what he or she is told, we believe it essential to consider explicitly the

---

[2] Sir Thomas More was Lord Chancellor to King Henry VIII of England. He was executed (on false testimony of treasonable statements) for refusing to take an oath acknowledging the authority of the Archbishop of Canterbury, the highest clerical official in England, to declare void the King's marriage to Queen Catharine (and thereby leaving him free to marry Anne Boleyn). Such an acknowledgment would have constituted a denial of the authority of the Pope as the divinely ordained successor to St. Peter.

relation between that judgment and the question whether the teachers would be *morally* justified in acquiescing.

It is not only those who believe in original sin who recognize (or should recognize) that the demands of everyday life at times will prove stronger than our moral resolve. An authentic humility about one's rectitude requires that when, whether because of lack of social support or the magnitude of the adverse consequences, we decide not to act according to the demands of morality in a particular case, we acknowledge that we are unable in that instance to live by its requirements. We may deserve the sympathy more than the censure of others, but it is important to our future capacity to act rightly that we not distort our moral compass in the process.[3] Even, therefore, if one were to conclude that one or both of the teachers realistically "had no choice," we would still insist on considering whether their action was right or wrong.

This is not to say that self-protection always lacks moral salience. First, prudence in choosing the occasions thought to be worth making substantial sacrifices or running serious risks is a virtue, not a vice: We are not called upon to risk or surrender our lives, except for the highest cause, and lesser dangers may also be weighed against the seriousness of the wrong being considered. Today, "prudence" has something of a pejorative moral ring to it; perhaps "discretion" or "judgment" is a better word. In Aristotelian terms, however, prudence is neither cowardice nor its opposite, rashness, but the mean between the two. (Again, Bolt's words are apt.)

It is essential, however, to the moral viability of prudential considerations that the claim, "I'll lose my job," or other feared consequence not be invoked as a talisman, to preempt the weighing process or as a rationalization to excuse a simple desire not to "make waves." Not every refusal has serious adverse effects, and it is just as much a mistake to assume *a priori* that every challenge to authority will be met with stern reprisal as it is blithely to presume that one is invulnerable to reprisal.

In the present case, Hardie notes that his tenure gives him substantial protection; even that protection is not unlimited—he could be charged with insubordination or other offense thought to warrant removal of tenure, and may be wholly unprotected from lesser forms of punishment—yet he quickly saw himself as significantly less vulnerable than Maria, who not only lacks tenure but is a first-year teacher whose contract could easily simply not be renewed. Even so, she is apparently willing to take at least initial steps toward engaging her colleagues around the issue (raising the question with some colleagues, preliminary perhaps to seeking a meeting with their principal). Although she might decide that she could not afford to go further than that, she

---

[3] Law teacher Warren Lehman wrote, with respect to the situation of a young lawyer intimidated at the prospect of speaking candidly to an older client: "If because of youth we have nothing to say, it is no problem to us that we do not say it. If because of youth it is harder to say what we have to say, we had better confess it than pretend to ourselves that we ought not say it because that is not our role or our duty" (Lehman 1979, 1096).

does not take refuge in her vulnerability to support a generalized fear to do anything at all but obey.

Second, the call of self-protection may be grounded in responsibilities to others. Chief among these are families dependent on the teacher for financial support. Again, this is a situational factor, which in some cases may be overwhelmingly strong, but in others may be significantly attenuated. There is a difference between honestly fearing to inflict significant deprivation on one's family and using that idea as a ready rationalization, or to justify endless self-aggrandizement. Moreover, one's children may reasonably expect support that goes beyond the financial. In sharing with them the conflict he or she is facing, a parent may find an important opportunity to foster their appreciation of what is to be gained and lost in each resolution of the question—indeed, even to give them the option of supporting the risky course.

Perhaps honest and conscientious reflection would lead one to decide either that "going along" is morally justified in a specific case, or that one "must" adopt a morally compromised stance on account of obligations to oneself or others. In such a case, although going along would be judged on balance to be the right thing to do, more would remain to be considered. In the words of contemporary philosopher Gerald Postema (1980, 70), "morality is not merely a matter of getting things right[,] as in solving a puzzle or learning to speak grammatically. . . ." Martha Nussbaum articulates this idea in these terms:

> The fact that events have produced a situation in which we cannot do justice to all the claims to which we are committed does not mean that we are no longer committed to all of them. . . . [T]he ethical life . . . means that we will seek ways to make good on our commitment to a value that has lost out, for example, by making reparations, or by devoting particular care to that area of our lives at other times. Second, it means that we will seek to remake the world in such a way that such conflicts more rarely arise. . . . If the conflict is never seen as a conflict, the rethinking is less likely to take place.
> *(Nussbaum 1994, 213–214)*

For Maria to seek to "remake the world" might mean that, even if she concluded that on balance she would be justified in doing as she is told in this instance, she would continue to work with colleagues and the principal, talking as a group about the question of justification, and seeking to reach agreement on a more satisfactory approach to the question next time around. Outside the immediate context of "obey or defy," she may find such an approach within reach. Hardie, too, should he decide to drop his service idea, might continue to give thought to its shaping, perhaps seeking the principal's advice, suggesting that parental input be sought more broadly, or researching what other schools or school systems are doing. At an appropriate later time he might present a more finely tuned proposal designed to meet at least some of the objections previously voiced.

Concerns about integrity and self-protection aside, the factors bearing on the morality of the choice Hardie and Maria will make are complex. More fundamental, in our view, is the question: To whom (or to what) is a teacher accountable? Two competing paradigms claim to point toward the answer.

ACCOUNTABILITY AS EMPLOYEE

The first paradigm sees the teacher as an *employee*, albeit a fairly skilled one, of the school system in which he or she works. Such discretion as Hardie and Maria have in carrying on their work exists at the explicit or implied leave of their "superiors," initially the principal, who is in turn accountable to the superintendent, an official in some ways analogous to a CEO, whose "board of directors" is the school board. "Board members are considered public school officers with sovereign power, in contrast to school employees, who are hired to implement directives" (McCarthy and Cambron-McCabe 1992, 385–386). (Even the "sovereign power" of the school board exists only by delegation from the state legislature, which in turn operates under authority given it by the state constitution and the voters, in whom ultimate sovereignty resides.)

Under this paradigm, a teacher may of course remonstrate, seek to dissuade the other, and the like, but obedience is not "giving in" to anything other than the proper order of things. It is a recognition of the fact that the teacher has no authority to decide a matter contrary to a lawful directive, specific or general, of the principal. It should not be surprising that this view, which reflects the prevailing consciousness of the employment relation, is reflected in the reasoning of many courts. As one leading case put it, "a public employee generally can be discharged for refusing to follow administrative policies and directives, even those they contend are misguided" (U.S. Court of Appeals for the Eighth Circuit 1986, 675 [*Cox v. Dardanelle Public School District*]).

Where the claim is that "administrative policies and directives" are not merely "misguided" but encroach on a teacher's (or student's) constitutional rights, the judicial response is a bit more varied, but in recent years at least has largely mirrored the *Cox* approach. (See the excerpts from several judicial decisions beginning at p. 175 in the next section of this chapter). Our purpose in citing legal authority, however, is not to describe the legal rights that Hardie and Maria might have should they be discharged or disciplined for refusing to do what they have been asked to do. The legal principle in our view mirrors, rather than is the source of, a societal sense of the deference owing a "superior." A teacher is, in this paradigm, *morally* obligated to carry out lawful orders of the principal; "insubordination" is not merely imprudent, it is wrong.

Character-education specialists Edward Wynne and Kevin Ryan support this view on two bases. The first sees a positive moral valence in hierarchy itself: "The acceptance of hierarchy has been an important theme pervading traditional values. Indeed, without appropriate hierarchy among the adults in a school, how can pupils learn to observe discipline?" (Wynne and Ryan 1997,

192). They also rely, however, on an argument based on accountability of the school:

> In important institutions, there must be clear points of account-
> ability, not merely an amorphous group of faculty members. Without
> focused responsibility, the clarity of decision making will be greatly
> impaired. We do not suggest that principals, as human beings, are
> necessarily wiser or more moral than individual teachers. . . . Our
> argument is that in education, the stakes are high. There must be one
> person clearly in charge.
> *(Id., 193)*

From within this perspective, Hardie's case is a simple one. Whether his idea is a good one or not, he certainly should accept the principal's judgment that it is not worth pursuing in the face of the parents' vigorously combative stance and the superintendent's desire to avoid an open conflict before the school board. While it is easy to criticize the "gutlessness" of these officials, it is not for an individual teacher—or for outsiders—to judge whether Helter and Senter acted discreditably in light of the entire set of complex relations between principal and superintendent, and between superintendent and board. Even if that were somehow determined to be the case, it would not be appropriate for a teacher, unable to persuade his "superior" to reverse or change his position, simply to disregard it.

Maria's case is significantly more complex. She has two reasons for resisting "teaching to the test" by going over specific questions that she knows will be on it. One is that she deems it a form of cheating, in effect giving her students the answers (albeit without telling them that). The other is that she regards it as an educationally impoverished way of spending class time better devoted to a broader form of learning. The specific questions on a test are meant to illustrate the learning acquired, and a valid review teaches underlying principles (for example, of sentence structure, grammar, or reading comprehension), with the concreteness of specific examples serving to aid the student in apprehending, and being able to apply, the principles.[4] Recollection of the answers to the specific examples taken from the test does not assure that a student will be able to work out answers to a range of similar questions.

In an "employee" consciousness, the second ground alone is probably not significantly different from Hardie's position. The fact that she sincerely, and perhaps correctly, believes that the students' time would be better spent in another way does not justify her acting on that belief in the face of the

---

[4] For example, the Stanford Achievement Test (SAT-9) (1996) for the spring semester, Fourth Grade, and fall semester, Fifth Grade, asks students whether the sentence, "Add more spise to the soup," contains a spelling error, as an application of the ability to apply "phonetic principles" to consonant sounds; and, in order to test principles of grammar, asks whether the sentence, "She soon discovered it were a bunch of rattlesnakes," is correct, and, if not, whether "were" should be changed to "was" or "are," or "discovered" changed to "discovers."

principal's contrary wish. But what of the first, her objection to participate in what she regards as a plainly wrongful act? (Recall the discussion of "perfect" and "imperfect" duties in Chapter 4, p. 94. Refraining from cheating is obligatory in a sense that teaching at its best is not.)

The initial question is whether it *would be* plainly wrong to go over specific questions that she knows, but does not tell the students, will be on the test. There is a continuum of actions designed to improve student performance on a test: reviewing the subject matter to be covered by the test; emphasizing, in that review, specific areas that are ordinarily given particular attention by those designing the test; reviewing—this is the present case—precise questions in the knowledge that they *will* appear on the test; reading out to the students some or all of the questions and telling them that they will be on the test; and, finally, adding the answers that she believes best. In today's world, most people would probably regard the first and second variants as not only educationally justifiable but morally acceptable as well, and the two last as plainly unethical.

Maria regards what she has been asked to do as morally equivalent to these last, but in an "employee" consciousness her sincere and reasonable belief would probably not suffice: the question is whether she is *right.* If so, she can claim the status of a "whistle blower," who is sometimes protected by law from retaliation and would in any event probably be regarded as doing something deserving praise rather than blame. If she is not right, she is simply one who is insistent on placing her own moral judgment above that of her superiors.

There are two important ways in which the conduct Maria is asked to engage in is an exercise in deception. First, those posing test questions to students impliedly assert—to students, parents, teachers, and any others who are interested in the test results—that doing well in the test evidences a good understanding of the area involved. As suggested above, the score of one who has gone over the specific test questions does not accurately reflect his or her understanding of the subject. Moreover, students taking a test (and their teachers) are reasonably understood by others to be asserting that they do not know in advance the specific questions they are being asked. Indeed, disclosure of the action that the school is contemplating would probably create something of a scandal; the "outside" world, in particular, newspapers and their readers among the citizenry, would in all likelihood quickly characterize the practice as "coaching" rather than preparation, a form of cheating not essentially different from simply supplying the answers.

Within the school system, however, and among parents, there would be a justifying impulse beyond—although probably including—that of narrow self-interest. It would be claimed that the deception was legitimated by the oversimplified, excessive use of a school's average test scores to judge the quality of the education it provides, both in absolute terms and—worse yet—in comparison with its peer schools. Accordingly, prepping students is necessary, and therefore appropriate, to protect them and the school from undeserved harm. Moreover, given the prevalence of "coaching" throughout the school system, Maria's action in acceding to Connie's request, far from giving her students an unfair advantage, would simply correct for the advantage that others are getting.

In an "employee" consciousness, this reasoning might not need to ground the claim that the practice in fact *was* legitimate; it would suffice if it established only that the principal's decision to have the teachers engage in it was reasonably arguable. In those circumstances, an individual teacher should recognize that her responsibilities are narrower than the principal's, and would not be morally justified in clinging to her parochial stance.[5]

The question remains whether the asserted justification *is* reasonably arguable. Whether a self-serving rationalization or a regretful acknowledgment of an unhappy state of affairs, the argument is essentially that moral judgments regarding personal honesty and fairness may be ruled out of bounds because of the wholesale corruption of the entire process of testing students and schools. In our judgment, the argument must be rejected. Whatever the justification for such a stance regarding, for example, modern warfare, teaching school is a different matter. We would assert in this context what Supreme Court Justice Robert Jackson observed in a very different (perhaps more compelling) context: "No one can make me believe that we are that far gone."[6]

ACCOUNTABILITY AS A PROFESSIONAL

The competing paradigm sees a teacher as a *professional*. As such, a teacher stands in a fiduciary relationship to his or her students, to whom primary accountability is owing, just as a physician's primary accountability is to the patient, and a lawyer's to the client. In those professions, the fact that someone else may at times sign the check or pay the bill is, under professional codes of ethics, not supposed to dilute that loyalty.[7] It is only the systemic obligations of a professional that can limit responsiveness to client, patient, or student desires: In a lawyer, the obligation is to the law itself; in a doctor, to the primary principle, *do no harm*; in a teacher, to pedagogic practices that support the intellectual and moral growth of students.

---

[5] A response similar to this reasoning characterizes the norms of the legal profession. According to the American Bar Association's Model Rules of Professional Conduct, a version of which is in effect in most states, an employed attorney is said to be *bound* by the rules "notwithstanding that the lawyer acted at the direction" of a supervising attorney, but a "subordinate lawyer" is held not to have *violated* the rules "if that lawyer acts in accordance with a supervisory lawyer's reasonable resolution of an arguable question of professional duty" (American Bar Association 1983, Rule 5.2).

[6] Supreme Court of the United States 1953, 228 [*Shaughnessy v. United States ex rel. Mezei*]. The case involved national security needs at the height of the Cold War.

[7] For example, the Model Rules of Professional Conduct, cited in note 5, specifically prohibit a lawyer from "accept[ing] compensation for representing a client from one other than the client unless . . . there is no interference with the lawyer's independence of professional judgment or with the client-lawyer relationship" (Rule 1.8(f)).

A professional can carry out these obligations only if his or her *independent professional judgment* is honored. One text expresses the idea of a profession in these terms: "By its nature a profession involves both considerable autonomy in decision making and knowledge and skills developed before entry and then honed in practice" (Goodlad 1984, 194). The requisites of entry into a profession include the special knowledge, skill, judgment, and character it calls for (which the educational and licensing requirements are meant to assure). For Hardie and Maria to be told that they must set aside their professional judgment would tend to cripple their growth as conscientious, mature, imaginative, reflective, and responsible teachers, leading them instead in the direction of becoming clock-watching, time-serving, order-taking subordinates. The conclusion of education professor Roland Barth is telling:

> Many schools perpetuate infantilism. School boards infantilize superintendents; superintendents, principals; principals, teachers; and teachers, children. This results in children and adults who frequently behave like infants, complying with authority because of fear or dependence, waiting until someone's back is turned to do something "naughty." To the extent that teachers become responsible for their own teaching, they not only help become responsible for their own learning, they also become professional.
> *(Barth 1989, 234)*

The Report of the influential Carnegie Forum on Education and the Economy (1986) advocated professional autonomy for teachers on the ground of students' educational needs:

> [Students] must be active learners, busily engaged in the process of bringing new knowledge and new ways of knowing to bear on a widening range of increasingly difficult problems. The focus of schooling must shift from teaching to learning, from the passive acquisition of facts and routines to the active application of ideas to problems. . . . [T]o support the learning of those students, [teachers] should have . . . the ability to work with other people in work groups that decide for themselves how to get the job done. They must be able to learn all the time, as the knowledge required to do their work twists and turns with new challenges and the progress of science and technology. Teachers will not come to the school knowing all they have to know, but knowing how to figure out what they need to know, where to get it, and how to help others make meaning out of it.
>
> Teachers must think for themselves if they are to help others think for themselves, be able to act independently and collaborate with others, and render critical judgment. They must be people [who can] create environments in which young people not only get a taste for learning but build a base upon which they will continue to learn and apply what they know to the lives they go on to lead.

In schools where students are expected to master routine skills and acquire knowledge, the necessary skills and knowledge can, to a degree, be packaged in texts and teachers can be trained to deliver the material in the text to the students with reasonable efficiency. But a much higher order of skills is required to prepare students for the unexpected, the nonroutine world they will face in the future. And a still higher order of skills is required to accomplish that task for the growing body of students whose environment outside the school does not support the kind of intellectual effort we have in mind.
(Carnegie Forum on Education and the Economy 1986, 57–58)

To say, however, that Principal Helter and Superintendent Senter should not remove the ultimate decision from the teachers in question is not to say that, even in a "professional" consciousness, Hardie and Maria should not reflect seriously on their proper course of action. They must consider, and perhaps be guided by, the unintended harms that their actions may cause others.

In Hardie's case, the principal shares his judgment about the value of his service project, but is faced with an order from *his* superior. That Senter's act may be reasonably judged adversely by Hardie does not alter the bind in which Helter would be placed if Hardie were to insist on going ahead with his plans despite the superintendent's expectation that Helter will "handle" the problem effectively. Moreover, the fact that both principal and superintendent have a wider accountability, and a broader experiential base, than he has (which under the "employee" paradigm would be given controlling weight) should in any event be taken into account by Hardie in exercising his professional judgment.

Maria, for her part, needs to consider what weight she should give to the fact that, because of the expectable misuse of test scores, her students (and the school) may suffer undeserved harm; students in other classes, and at other schools, will appear, misleadingly, to be doing better. Again, that public reliance on such measures of effectiveness seriously corrupts the learning process is a fact that neither she nor her principal can change. While recognizing the corrosive effect of so smoothly adjusting to "working the system," she nonetheless must also recognize the concrete harms that might attend her refusal.

In considering the balance to be struck in these cases, recall the discussion in Chapter 3 (p. 54) of the relative merits of consequentialist and deontological moral reasoning. To some, the ease with which the factors described in the two preceding paragraphs support "going along" is a major failing of consequentialism—the ready availability of plausible, but speculative, general harms that are thought to offset the reluctance to act in a cowardly or dishonest way. It disregards or reflexively dismisses the possibility that Maria's attempt to uphold the integrity of the educational process might have positive consequences for her students and colleagues as well. Deontology seems made of sterner stuff, less susceptible to the siren song of plausible, self-interested rationalization. To others, however, as the discussion of integrity earlier in this section illustrates, the very spurning of appeals to consequences is a repellant self-indulgence, which, in the name of one's moral purity, actually leads one to act wrongfully.

A "professional" paradigm, then, differs from an "employee" paradigm mostly in the *locus* of primary decisional authority and responsibility. A professional should certainly take counsel from the judgment of his or her peers, and recognize the complexities of the dynamics of accountability. At the same time, a supervisor of one deemed "merely" an employee should (except perhaps in a most authoritarian consciousness) permit, perhaps even encourage, the employee to remonstrate vigorously when he or she believes that important educational or moral considerations are being given insufficient weight. Beyond that, each perspective has its limits of applicability: A superior order to do an act that is unquestionably illegal, or (somewhat more controversially) flatly contrary to the employee's conscience, carries no moral imperative; a professional judgment that is wholly impervious to the pain that its implementation is causing others, especially students, is simply a rationalization for irresponsibility.

Yet an important difference remains, and it is one primarily for the leadership of a school system or school to choose between. A superintendent or principal can effectively choose what to expect of his or her teachers: do as I say (and, where I don't say, do what I *would* say), or develop your professional judgment as teacher (albeit, under my general supervision). Educators, and citizens, will differ as to the correct direction in which to lean.

Where they agree, however, is in the judgment that the choice has an effect on the *moral climate* of a school or school system. Recall Wynne's and Ryan's explicit avowal that a hierarchical model of principal–teacher relations has a *positive* effect on students, in light of the major role they give "discipline" as an aspect of good character: "The acceptance of hierarchy has been an important theme pervading traditional values. Indeed, without appropriate hierarchy . . . , how can pupils learn to observe discipline?"(Wynne and Ryan 1997, 192). To them and like-minded others, a major justification for the "employee" model is precisely the fact that students learn what is right from observing the unspoken messages of the way in which a school is run, the influences by which their teachers are expected to guide their actions.[8]

One whose idea of character sees "discipline" as a value that, though necessary, is dangerous as well, tends to regard this message as undermining more than reinforcing sound moral education. The students will not miss the

---

[8] Recall that Wynne and Ryan also maintain (as quoted at p. 166, above) that an appropriate hierarchy is supported on the ground that, independent of its moral lesson, "clear points of accountability" make possible "clarity of decision making." "There must be one person clearly in charge."

significance of the *grounds* of the administrators' actions, and of the reinforcement of the norm requiring Hardie and Maria to go along with their desires. With the "higher-ups" so evidently not giving the teachers the respect that their professional judgment calls for, their effort to teach their students to accord *them* proper respect will surely falter. Moreover, moral character is said to involve a fair degree of steadfastness, of courage, of willingness to risk; yet, the lesson of the experience is that, when the crunch comes (even a mild one), everyone—teacher, administrator, . . . student?—protects his or her flank, not only tacking with the prevailing winds, but not even waiting to be reasonably assured that the adverse winds will actually prevail. Moral character is primarily, all agree, about remaining honest, avoiding the temptation to lie or cheat to gain an advantage; yet, *of course* the school will cut corners and glibly embrace self-justifying rationalizations, when (as with respect to its test scores) there is a price to be paid.

Beyond that, the very breath of responsibility that in one sense gives principals, superintendents, and school boards a perspective and judgment that classroom teachers cannot fully appreciate is a two-edged affair. They do not know the students as individuals; the superintendent probably does not even know the teachers involved. The board is a group of lay people, responsive more to citizen (read, taxpayer) and mayoral (read, political), than to educational, priorities. The fact that Hardie's plan arose spontaneously, out of his students' reactions to a specific teaching opportunity in his classroom, gives to his proposal a tangible value that the abstract issue of "community service" cannot capture. The administrators are occupationally disabled from judging accurately the loss to that classroom in forcing Hardie to drop the idea. The more the priorities that define their position are given controlling weight, the less educational values will receive their due. For a compelling illustration of this phenomenon, see the opinions in *Lacks v. Ferguson Reorganized School District R-2* (U.S. Court of Appeals 1998), and the Note following, at p. 175 in the next section of this chapter.

This critique *can* take on an excessively polarized cast, so that the only "right thing" to do is to go down in flames, flags flying, over every "real world" pressure on an ideal curriculum. There is precious little danger, however, that school boards, superintendents, and principals will rush to this position; the more realistic outcome is that they will reject it entirely. The better course of conduct is for these actors to leaven their natural attraction to the "employee" model with a genuine apprehension of the loss attendant on it, and to leaven the rigor by which that model is enforced, so that opportunities to respect a teacher's professional judgment are not reflexively or unnecessarily dismissed.

One way in which this limited but significant change can occur is for authority not to be too quickly asserted at the higher level. Perhaps, if Senter's board would recognize more often that a major part of *its* accountability is to stand up for its superintendent, he in turn would more readily recognize the need to check his inclination to overrule his principal's supportive response to Hardie's service-learning project.

Maria's case is more intractable. The true source of wrongfulness in that situation lies outside the school system altogether, in the propagation of a notion of educational effectiveness that places excessive faith in outcomes quantifiable in "sound-bytes," readily convertible to a ranking of schools. The newsmedia, public officials, and the citizenry itself bear the responsibility for the corrosive effect of this impoverished notion of teaching success, not only on the academic enterprise of the schools, but on its ability to carry on a credible program of moral education. Parents, hyperresponsive to the interest in their children's success, are both victims of this state of affairs and contributors to its infirmities. Victims, because as individuals they feel powerless to insulate their children from the harms done by a flawed system of evaluation and its use in a manner that magnifies those flaws; contributors, because their protective responses strongly reinforce the feeling that at the systemic level the problem is insoluble and all one can do is work the system to one's own (and one's children's) maximum advantage.

We have noted (see p. 164) that Hardie's decision to "go along" with his principal's request, should that be his course, need not be the end of his engagement with the question. Similarly, whatever Maria's ultimate options are or should be, we can only endorse her determination to *begin* by seeking to consult more broadly among her teaching colleagues, rather than see her choices only as, right now, simply obeying or placing her job on the line. For the problem is not hers alone, and even a tentative step toward encouraging her peers to recognize the dilemma they are in is a constructive move toward resisting the sense of pervasive helplessness and nonresponsibility that characterizes the mindset of all of the relevant actors—teachers, who have little power; administrators, who must please the school board and the public that elects it; newsmedia, whose only accountability is to the public's asserted "right to know"; public officials, whose only accountability is to the electorate, impatient with complexity and demanding simple measures of assurance of "better schools." One teacher, a group of teachers, a single school cannot turn this situation around; the more pertinent question is how she, they, or it respond to the choices that *are* present.

✦✦✦ At the Library

The following excerpt argues for a greater recognition of the professionalism of teachers on the ground that the "deprofessionalization" of the job impairs the quality of education, both by reducing the appeal of the work to those who might contribute the most to it and by undermining the ability of teachers to do their best with their students. The second excerpt uses a judicial decision (albeit the dissenting opinion) to make a similar point.

▼▼▼

Theodore R. Sizer, *Horace's Compromise: The Dilemma of the American High School*[9]
(1992, 195–196, 198, 205–206)

It will require an unprecedented leap of faith for Americans to trust their teachers. They never have, not very much. Furthermore, the current public mood is punitive, albeit with some justification. Much teaching in high schools is abysmal. While some of this clearly is due to teachers' incompetence, insensitivity, and carelessness, some also flows from the conditions of work giving rise to Horace's compromise—and the demeaning attitudes, and the policies that flow from them, with which the public treats the profession. America and its teachers are in a cul-de-sac of attitudes and practice. Reversing direction will therefore be difficult. As effective teaching absolutely requires substantial autonomy, *the decentralizing of substantial authority to the persons close to the students is essential.* "Downtown" continues to set goals, but decisions over how teacher and student time is organized, the materials and the approaches used, and the way staff are deployed must be at school level, or, in large schools, at house (or other subschool) levels.

I have listened to many concerned school board members and central office administrators agree with this recommendation in theory, but emphatically not in practice. They argue that many teachers are not competent enough to take responsibility and that some principals are unable or unwilling to lead an autonomous school. I have seen enough inept teaching and mindless leadership in American high schools to understand their concern.

But we are caught in a vicious circle. Constant control from "downtown" undermines the ablest teachers and administrators, the very people whose number should be expanding. These top professionals are discouraged and frustrated, often to the point of cruel cynicism. With few exceptions we observed this sad fact in all sorts of schools in all parts of the country. The system is organized with an eye on the incompetent rather than the competent. All are shackled, to "protect" students from the bad teachers. Many of these ablest folk will leave or have left teaching—or will never enter the profession in the first place.

Excellent schooling requires excellent teachers and principals. Excellent people have self-confidence and self-esteem, and expect reasonable autonomy. Therefore, if we want excellent schools, we must give more power to the teachers and principals.

▼▼▼▼▼

Most difficult of all to accomplish will be a change in attitude toward and of teachers and principals. The professionals cannot see themselves or be seen as interchangeable "service delivery systems." The leaders among them, at the least,

---

[9] *Horace's Compromise* (Sizer 1992) is a famous portrayal of the ways in which insufficient resources and bureaucratization have constrained the work of conscientious teachers.

must be creative, flexible people, much as are the leaders of the other scholarly and academic professions. One sees groups of these people in some schools (too few) now, usually academically oriented "magnet" schools in the public sector or some independent schools. . . .

▼▼▼▼▼

Learning is a human activity, and depends absolutely (if often annoyingly) on human idiosyncrasy. We can arrange for schools, classes, and curricula, but the game is won or lost for reasons beyond these arrangements. The readiness of the students, the power of the incentives they feel for learning, and the potency of teachers' inspiration count more than does any structure of any school. . . .

▼▼▼▼▼

Unfortunately, . . . twentieth-century Americans' breathless belief in *systems* to run their lives tilts the scale markedly toward predictable order. . . . [The result has been] systems of schools, in both public and Catholic sectors, organizations arranged in pyramidal tiers, with governing boards and administrators at the peaks and classrooms at the base. Directions—"governance"—flowed from top to bottom, in the fashion of all hierarchical bureaucracies.

These pyramids stolidly survive. Indeed, they have become so familiar that any other form of providing for the schooling of young Americans seems unimaginable. While there are obvious advantages to hierarchical bureaucracy, it has its costs, and these are today paralyzing American education. The structure is getting in the way of children's learning.

▼▼▼

U.S. Court of Appeals for the Eighth Circuit, *Lacks v. Ferguson Reorganized School District R-2*
(1998)

[This lawsuit arose out of the discharge of Cecilia Lacks, a high school teacher of English and journalism, and the sponsor of the school newspaper. In upholding the discharge by the School Board, the Court of Appeals described the case as one involving "a school district . . . disciplin[ing] a teacher for allowing students to use profanity repetitiously and egregiously in their written work." It described the facts of the case in the following language.]

Lacks divided her junior English class into small groups and directed them to write short plays, which were to be performed for the other students in the class and videotaped. The plays written by the students contained profanity, including the repeated uses of the words "fuck," "shit," "ass," "bitch," and "nigger." When the plays were videotaped, these words were used more than 150 times in approximately forty minutes. Lacks later admitted that the plays contained an unusual amount of profanity, and one of her witnesses later described the use of profanity in the plays as "extreme," "disgusting," "upsetting," and "embarrassing." . . .

The following January, as a result of complaints by one of Lacks's students, the existence of the videotapes came to the attention of Vernon Mitchell, the principal of [the] High School. Mitchell initiated an inquiry into the matter. . . . Following the investigation, Dr. Robert Fritz, the district superintendent, formally charged Lacks with "willful or persistent violation of and failure to obey [the school district's] policies." . . . The school board found that Lacks was aware of the school board's policy preventing profanity, that she could have chosen teaching methods which prohibited profanity, and that her failure to do so constituted a "willful and persistent practice violative of Board policy to a degree that cannot be . . . tolerated." Based on its findings, the school board terminated Lacks's teaching contract. . . .

[The court majority held that there was no constitutional barrier to the discharge. In dissenting from the denial of a petition to rehear the appeal before the entire court, Judge McMillian asserted that the majority opinion presented "only a one-sided, fractional portion of the evidence." Judge McMillian pointed out that "the context in which they were read to the class . . . revealed that those two poems—vulgar and shocking as they were—were the first utterances in the class by a boy named Reginald, who previously had refused to participate in class and had repeatedly been sent to the principal's office because he did nothing but put his head on his desk during class. [A]fter he wrote and read aloud those two poems, Reginald went on to write several more for her class, the last of which, entitled 'Alone,' won academic awards." Asserting that these facts were entirely ignored by the Board, the dissenting opinion deemed it important to set forth the teacher's full testimony regarding Reginald's story. (Questions are by Ms. Lacks' attorney; some questions and answers are omitted without notation.)]

Question: I would like to show you, Cissy [Lacks], what's been marked as Exhibit 18, and ask if you can identify this document.

Answer: Yes.

Question: What is it?

Answer: This document is a series of poems that I showed to the administrators in my District that was done by one of my students, Reginald McNeary, when he was in ninth grade.

Question: What do they illustrate, Cissy?

Answer: They illustrate how a student can grow in a very short period of time using the student centered teaching method. They illustrate that a student can learn a lot of techniques in a very short time if he or she cares about what he is doing, and they show that what a student says in the beginning is not at all the way a student might want to express him or herself, but it's what they start with because they may not have had the experience to do or say anything else.

Question: First of all, tell us the story of Reginald. When he came into your class, what did you observe about him?

Answer: Reginald came into my class and he wanted to do absolutely nothing but put his head on his desk in the back of the room. He did not talk to anyone. He did not talk to me. He wouldn't do assignments. I would send him to the guidance office, he would throw away the sheets of paper. I would send him to the principal, I would get a note back saying that I should send him during my class but he wouldn't go. I continued to send—nothing worked for Reginald. He was totally silent, totally disengaged, totally disconnected from me, from school.

Question: How did you organize physically the classroom when you began the poetry writing?

Answer: The class was in a circle so we could talk to each other and share work.

Question: And did Reginald sit in the circle?

Answer: No.

Question: Where did he sit?

Answer: He sat in the back of the room with his head on his desk.

Question: What did the other students do?

Answer: They told me that if they had to sit in the circle, Reginald would have to sit in the circle, I should force Reginald into the circle.

Question: What did you tell them?

Answer: I told them there was no way I could force Reginald in the circle short of picking up the desk, but that they could get him in the circle by doing things so interesting to him that he would be jealous and come into the circle.

Question: Did that happen?

Answer: It did.

Question: How soon after did it happen?

Answer: Two days after we started doing things in poetry, he started moving into the circle.

Question: Okay, and this first poem that is listed on Exhibit 18 was written you say about three weeks after he moved into the circle?

Answer: Yes.

Question: Okay, would you read it for us, please?

Answer: Sure. It's called "Alone."

> *I'm all alone in this world today.*
> *No one to laugh with, no one to play.*
> *It's been like that since the age of three.*
> *No one to love care or hold me.*
> *I guess that's why I'm the way I am.*
> *No one loved me so I don't give a damn.*
> *No one to pick me up when I fall.*
> *No one to measure growth or how tall.*
> *Alone, how it hurts inside.*
> *If I were to die, no one would cry.*
> *I never gave a damn about any other.*
> *I love my shoes more than I love my mother.*
> *You might think I'm the devil or call me Satan.*
> *I have no love, I'm so full of hating.*
> *I guess that's why I have low self-esteem.*
> *The only time I show love is in my dreams.*

Question: Let me ask you Cissy, did this poem win any awards?

Answer: This poem, a somewhat corrected one, won awards. This poem won the first place in the poetry contest at Berkeley High School, and then I believe it also won the district-wide poetry contest.

Question: Okay, and then can you explain to us the process that you went through with Reginald to get him to this award-winning poem?

Answer: . . . Reginald wrote a poetry exercise for us when we were reading out loud in the class, and he asked if he could read it out loud. It was the first time Reginald said anything in the class to any of us.

Question: How did this poem come to be read to the class?

Answer: When we were doing the poetry exercises, we're just experimenting and nobody knows what anybody else has written, but when asked if they would like to share it, Reginald said that he would like to share what he had written.

Question: So he stood up and read it?

Answer: Yes.

Question: What did you say to him after he read these poems to the class?

Answer: Well, I was a little taken aback because it was also read with a lot of anger, and I told him in the class that I thought that his writing had a lot of anger in it, and that sometimes you can use anger to write extremely effective poems, and that he should listen to what we were doing in the rest of the classes when we talk about technique and process, and see if he could use some of that technique to express his anger in other ways.

Question: You did not criticize him for the street language in here?

Answer: No.

Question: Why not?

Answer: . . . I was so pleased that Reginald did something, that he made an effort to talk, it was the first time he shared anything with anybody and did anything at all in the class, I was not going to shut him down, I was going to take that and work with it. . . . [F]inally I had something that he had done that I could work with, and the class could see him somewhat as part of the class and begin to respond to him. I thought it was a good moment in teaching.

Question: Did he write any poems immediately after those two?

Answer: Yes.

Question: Can you tell us what the next poem was in the series?

Answer: The next poem was called "Hate."

Question: Could you read "Hate" for us?

> *There is so much hate in the world today.*
> *We are so busy hating we don't even pray.*
> *Some whites hate blacks and some Germans hate Jews.*
> *But they are wrong because no one can choose.*

How dark or bright or fat or light people are to be.
If it was up to me I would love all my brothers, white, Jews or any other.
For Christmas instead of begging for jewelry, instead I'm going to pray for
*   peace.*

Question: Did you see any progress then between those first poems and this one?

Answer: Yeah, Reginald was beginning to use all the techniques and styles we had talked about. He had opened up. He was beginning to talk about the feelings that he had, but in a way, I think, that he thought other people would listen to him and that was what he now thought was effective poetry.

Question: Did he write any other poem in that three-week period of time?

Answer: Yes.

Question: What was the next poem he wrote?

Answer: He wrote a poem called "Why."

Question: Could you read "Why" for us?

Why do they stare at me when I'm [maxin']?
Is it cus I'm not the color that they are [axin'].
They whisper in silence.
I guess they think I'll cuss.
Violence, why, why couldn't God make us one color
Instead of black and white, and many others?
Why, why when you look at me you look in fear
When I have never beat you up or made you shed a tear.
Why can't we all just get along living in harmony.
Is that too wrong? My sisters are labeled hooker and whore bangin',
And they have got my brothers dope and gangbangin'.
Why are my people living in poverty and the rich don't care how they be?
Now I know this is the worst poetry you [ever heard] but it comes from the
*   heart.*
I wrote every word.

Question: Did you see any progress here?

Answer: I saw incredible progress. He is starting to use a certain style now and a rhythm to his writing, and it's real clear that he also has a position and he wants the people to know what it is and when he read it he told us what this poem came from.

Question: And then the last poem in the series was the "Alone" poem you read to us? And how would you evaluate "Alone" as a piece of poetry?

Answer: I think that the person who wrote this poem is not a student poet but a poet. I think he is like Langston Hughes. He has an incredible way with words, and it makes people cry, in class, or just [be] so moved by what he is saying [and] doing, it's, you know, it's really amazing as a poem.

Question: And by the way, the poem "Alone" which won the district-wide poetry contest, does that have any street language in it?

Answer: Yes, it does.

Question: I never gave a damn about any other?

Answer: Uh-huh, twice.

Question: Considerably less than that what Reginald included in his first two poems, would you agree?

Answer: Yes.

Question: And how do you explain that progress?

Answer: Well, to me I see it all the time, that once a student opens up and starts expressing himself or herself and then learns the process or the techniques and they hear people listening to them, they just want to begin to change what they are doing, so it's quite, it just seems to me it is a quite natural learning process, it's part of the student centered method.

Question: You also talked to us about peer critique, and I'm interested to know how did the class respond to Reginald's first two poems? . . . Did the class respond to Reginald's first two poems?

Answer: The class as I recall was taken aback. They just listened, but at the same time said, "Reginald, good, you talked," that's what I remember. "Reginald, you said something."

Question: Okay, and how did they react to the poem "Alone"?

Answer: They actually cheered and clapped for him when he read it.

Question: Did the administrators show the Board Reginald's award-winning poem?

Answer: No.

Question: What did you think about that?

Answer: I was so discouraged, I didn't even know what teaching was about anymore. They showed the first two poems that Reginald wrote and didn't show anything else, somehow seemed to have lost or forgotten all the other poems. Very discouraging for a teacher and also for the student who had written the poems.

The outcome of this appeal [Judge McMillian went on] does not affect only the parties to this action. It affects all innovative and well-meaning teachers like Lacks and students in need like Reginald. When good educators are scared away or driven from our schools because they cannot trust the system to treat them honestly and fairly, we are all affected, most especially our children. . . .

[The opinion concluded:] I am not condoning the use of profanity in our schools or every aspect of Lacks's teaching methodology. . . . In this day and age, while our children are being exposed to the worst aspects of society through the media, entertainment, and sometimes even in their own homes, we expect public school teachers to erase the effects of that environment and make even the most uninspired children learn and achieve. Meanwhile, we require our teachers to pick their way through a mine field of competing and conflicting expectations, and changing and elusive legal standards. This case stands for the proposition that, for all her hard work and devotion to all her students, this teacher was in the end fired for stepping on a political land mine—one which she never even knew was there.

———————————

The division within this court of appeals mirrors one within the federal judiciary. Some three decades ago, Judge Frank Johnson[10] held unconstitutional the discharge of a teacher who directly refused an order by her principal and an associate superintendent that she no longer assign Kurt Vonnegut's *Welcome to the Monkey House,* which her junior English class had been given as outside reading *(Parducci v. Rutland)* (U.S. District Court for the Middle District of Alabama 1970). Judge Johnson, noting Vonnegut's reputation, described the administrators as displeased "with the content of the story, which they described as 'literary garbage,' and with the 'philosophy' of the story, which they construed as condoning, if not encouraging, 'the killing off of elderly people and free sex.'" The judge observed without comment that both men "later testified that neither of them was much of a reader, had any special expertise in the field of literature, or had ever taught an English course."

The court acknowledged, but termed a "platitude," the fact that "school officials should be given wide discretion in administering their schools and that courts should be reluctant to interfere with or place limits on that discretion." The case, to the court, illustrated:

> how easily arbitrary discrimination can occur when public officials are given unfettered discretion to decide what books should be taught and what books should be banned. While not questioning either the motives or good faith of the defendants, this Court finds their inconsistency to be not only enigmatic but also grossly unfair. With these several basic constitutional principles in mind it inevitably follows that the defendants in this case cannot justify the dismissal of this plaintiff under the guise of insubordination.

The currently prevailing temper of the federal courts is illustrated, not only in the *Lacks* decision, but in a somewhat similar recent decision of the U.S. Court of Appeals for the Fourth Circuit, *Boring v. Buncombe County Bd of Education* (1998).

Margaret Boring chose the play *Independence* for four students in her advanced acting class to perform in an annual statewide competition. As she described the play, it "powerfully depicts the dynamics within a dysfunctional, single-parent family—a divorced mother and three daughters; one a lesbian, another pregnant with an illegitimate child." Although the play won seventeen of twenty-one awards when performed in a regional competition, when the play was performed for an English class in the school a parent of one of the students in the class complained to Principal Fred Ivey, who then asked Boring for a copy of the script.

After reading the play, Ivey was inclined to prohibit Boring from using the play in the state competition, but was persuaded to allow it if certain portions

---

[10] Frank Johnson, of the U.S. District Court in Alabama, became widely known—admired by many, reviled by many others—for his decisions seeking to enforce the Supreme Court's invalidation of state-mandated school segregation.

were deleted. In June, however, Ivey requested the transfer of Margaret Boring from Owen High School, citing "personal conflicts resulting from actions she initiated during the course of this school year." The superintendent approved the transfer stating that she had failed to follow the school system's controversial materials policy in producing the play. The board of education upheld the transfer, and Ms. Boring sued, alleging that prior to the hearing there was considerable public discussion of the transfer, including assertions that the play was obscene and that she was immoral. Ms. Boring claimed that she was transferred in retaliation for "expression of unpopular views through the production of the play and thus in violation of her right to freedom of speech" under the Constitution.

In rejecting her suit, the court asserted that "plaintiff's selection of the play *Independence,* and the editing of the play by the principal, who was upheld by the superintendent of schools, does not present a matter of public concern and is nothing more than an ordinary employment dispute." A government employer, the court of appeals reasoned, "no less than a private employer, is entitled to insist upon the legitimate, day-to-day decisions of the office without fear of reprisals in the form of lawsuits from disgruntled subordinates who believe that they know better than their superiors how to manage office affairs."

Again, the court was divided. Judge Hamilton insisted that the case was far from an "ordinary employment dispute. Instead," he concluded:

> this is a case about a school principal . . . and a county school board . . . , who targeted Margaret Boring as a scapegoat and used her to shield them from the "heat" of the negative outcry resulting from the performance of *Independence.* This is also a case about a dedicated teacher . . . who in no way violated any aspect of an approved curriculum; who followed every previously required standard set forth for the selection and approval of the school production; who, when requested to do so, redacted certain portions of the production and only permitted its performance after that performance had been explicitly approved by her principal, Mr. Ivey; yet, who nevertheless lost her position as a result of the production, all for the sole purpose of shielding the principal and the Board from the wrath of the public outcry.

Judge Motz likewise dissented:

> When a teacher steps into the classroom she assumes a position of extraordinary public trust and confidence. She is charged with educating our youth. Her speech is neither ordinary employee workplace speech nor common public debate. Any attempt to force it into either of these categories ignores the essence of teaching—to educate, to enlighten, to inspire—and the importance of free speech to this most critical endeavor.

Chapter 7

When Values Collide

At School

It's easy to kill a project, harder to kill an idea. When Fred Helter quashed the service learning proposal after a handful of parents objected to the superintendent, a different group of parents, Hardie learned, met to get the initiative back on track. Though pleased by their activism, Hardie was worried. He foresaw factions and friction in the making. These activist parents, many of whom were relatively well-off and politically liberal, would surely confront resistance, both from the objecting parents, who were also fairly wealthy but conservative, and from at least some of the working-class parents. Like the original group of objectors, the latter's opposition reflected a desire to have the school focus single-mindedly on academics, but not because "do-goody projects" stood in the way of bringing their children high SAT scores, a classy college credential, and an investment banking career. Rather, they saw an unwavering emphasis on traditional academic skills and knowledge as their children's only passport to higher education and a decent job.

Hardie didn't want to sit still while matters escalated. His impulse was to participate in the conversations before they became a lightening rod for acrimonious bickering among parents. How, though, to proceed? He needed advice on strategy: Who better to consult than his smart, experienced colleague, Aggie Cerine.

Aggie, ever indifferent to standard greeting conventions, took one look at Hardie at the door of her classroom, and exclaimed, "I know just why, after all these months of invisibility, Hardie Knox is paying me a visit today!" She went on quickly, interrupting what would have followed his skeptical look: "I may be an old-timer but I still hear the scuttlebutt. So the service learning project just won't roll over and play dead, Hardie. I suppose you're worried, as well you should be, that trouble may be brewing in the community."

"How in blazes did you hear?" asked Hardie, reassured by Aggie's blunt manner.

"From the kids, naturally. It was a pretty ugly scene. Before class I overheard one of your students' brothers sounding off about 'what a lousy school this is, what a stupid principal we have,' because he wouldn't give permission for 'the one decent idea a teacher has had all year.' He went on indignantly with an explanation of your service learning project and how it had been rejected. I think he was astonished when his friend, a kid from the flats, responded: 'Oh, you think you're so great going to clean up an animal shelter. Maybe you should try cleaning your own house instead of having a maid do it for you.'

"Mr. Indignation shot back, 'I do keep my room neat, fatso, which I bet is more than you can say,' and the other kid replied, 'As a matter of fact I clean the whole house, every room including the kitchen, every week, but I'd be real pleased if you'd come over and do it for me. Why not give the dogs a break?'

"Your student's brother finished it off with, 'No, thanks! I'll stick to the dogs and leave you to your pigsty.'"

"Good God, Aggie," said Hardie, "this matter could really get out of hand. I dreamed of a project that would unite kids in common worthy pursuits; I sure didn't want it to degenerate into an activity that pulls children and families apart, and certainly not one that separates them along class lines. Do you think I should contact the enthusiastic parents and tell them they may be triggering a heavy political storm?"

"Hardie, I don't think you should be mediating among groups of hotblooded parents. Before we push for any policy, we need to put our heads together. It's an important matter for the whole school. Our peerless leaders moved too fast on this one—assuming they'd preempt a political fight in front of the board—and Senter is getting what he deserved. He didn't think beyond the hotheads yelling at him, and now he and Helter may have to backtrack. How about we talk to Fred, and see whether he's open to bringing the issue to the faculty and then, if the faculty likes the idea, to a Home and School meeting?"

"Great idea, Aggie! You should bottle that wisdom and spread it around."

To their pleasure, the teachers found Helter favorable toward the proposal. He confided to them that he realized he and the superintendent had acted precipitously; he regretted it and, assuming he didn't run into trouble from Senter, would welcome the chance to "backtrack." He couldn't just support the parents who wanted service projects in the school, in the face of Senter's instructions on the subject, but as a first step he was willing to see what the faculty as a whole thought.

It became clear at the faculty meeting that the teachers were of many minds. At one end were those who thought that, given the controversial nature of the issue, with all its political overtones, things should be left as they were. It was not a suitable project for one classroom to take on and there was too much opposition for it to be adopted school-wide. Maybe some day service learning would get institutionalized, but only if it became a requirement of the school district's central office, and carried the school board's endorsement. Until then, they had more than enough on their plates and should let this one go.

At the other pole were a number of teachers solidly lined up behind Hardie. To them, it was a great idea and should be adopted immediately by the upper-grade classes. Helter should try to squeeze funds out of central office so they could carefully monitor the children's experiences and assure the project's successful outcome. He could sell Senter on the idea of announcing it as a "pilot," and saying a substantive decision would be made only after a good trial. There was time enough to evaluate pros and cons after that.

These teachers rejected arguments that the political resistance should be allowed to settle the matter. For them, service learning was obviously the good and right thing to do; it transcended political considerations. One afternoon a week would hardly derail a child's rise in the global economy, nor interfere with his or her mastery of the 3Rs. Instead it might make students feel a smidgeon more useful, expand their worldview, give them new enthusiasms—for animals if they worked at the shelter, for books and computers if they worked at the library, for the elderly if they worked at a nursing home. Schools had an obligation to enlarge students' consciousness, especially their moral sensibilities, and develop their openness to spending a *little* of their time on some altruistic activity. This was a powerful hands-on way to meet that obligation, and it was suitable for all children regardless of ability, social background, or beliefs. It should be required.

Occupying a middle ground in the dispute were a set of teachers basically favorable to the proposal, but hesitant. They did not want to take the plunge unless support from parents was strong—not universal support but a large majority behind the proposal. They too suggested beginning immediately, but clearly conceived of the project only as a pilot, and they thought that, at this stage at least, participation should be entirely voluntary for both teachers and students.

Recalling Hardie's account of the emerging antagonisms in his classroom, Aggie cautioned against embracing a volunteer program as a wise compromise. "I suppose it's fine for teachers to volunteer, at least at the start of a new initiative, and I would be glad to do so, but the idea of kids volunteering really bothers me. Think about the possibilities. If the parents who opt their children out tend to be the more politically conservative or the poorer ones, we'll end up exacerbating the social differences that we try so hard to break down. And if parents give their kids freedom to make their own decisions—which is unlikely—I can imagine the names that will start flying around. Unless we luck out and the 'cool' kids volunteer, those who sign up will be labeled goody-goody or 'teacher's pet,' and their parents 'limousine liberals.' Not exactly what we want to accomplish."

The faculty meeting ended inconclusively, but with a majority obviously ready to endorse the middle position. Helter said he'd wait for broader parental input before going back to Senter. He told the teachers to make sure all parents were informed of the Home and School meeting at which the question would be discussed.

The Home and School leadership was glad to have an issue that might help get a good parent turnout, and notices were sent home to each family, posted in the halls, published in the local newspapers, and included on the school's Web page.

Attendance at the Home and School meeting was good but (as always) skewed toward the more well-off families. Many parents from the flats, some working in the evening and others lacking access to a car, could not get to school at night even if they were so inclined. Those not accustomed to speaking up often, or not having strong feelings about the issue, tended to support what the teachers proposed.

As a result, a substantial majority of those present voted to endorse the idea that the project should start promptly, in as many classes as possible, with participation voluntary for both teachers and parents in this first round. It was clear, however, that, given the degree of support in the room, the service learning advocates intended to seek approval from the superintendent's office for a broader mandatory program. It was also obvious that the opposing parents found both the proceedings and the decision unacceptable. As the group broke up, an angry parent hissed to one of the pro-project leaders, "See you at the next school board meeting."

Approaching the exit door, Maria joined Hardie and Aggie. "Congratulations Hardie, you sure seized victory from the jaws of defeat."

"Looks to me like a pyrrhic victory, Maria. With such thick hostility, I don't see how we can go forward."

"Hardie, you've got to be kidding. Sure, we could have done with a broader consensus, but no child will be *forced* to participate."

"That's true," Aggie jumped in. "No one *has* to join, at least not immediately, but there is a larger concern here than freedom to opt in or out. We can't just dismiss the objecting families as caring only for their kids' progress toward CEO-dom. There are thoughtful parents who sincerely and strongly believe that schools should not have service projects as part of the school day. These parents don't share our ethic of benevolence; at the very least, they want to choose the time and manner of their altruism. It's one thing, they'd argue, to stand for honesty and decency and fairness in day-to-day classroom exchanges among children and teachers, quite another to set aside school time to let children leave the premises in order to talk with the elderly, shelve books, or clean dog cages."

"But their kids don't have to do it," Maria again protested.

"No," Aggie continued, now with a trace of irritation, "we've established that fact for the present, but these parents realize that, once the project gets under way, it's likely to be played up in the press and begin to expand. Their fear is that it may not stay all that voluntary. Anyway, even if none of these things materialize, the kids who opt out are not going to receive the same instruction that they'd get if there were no such project. What can a teacher do, other than homework, when a substantial number of children are out of the classroom, even the building?"

"And then there's the other, more or less silent group," Hardie chimed in, knowing that what he was about to say would prick Maria's sympathies. "The parents from the flats, who were pretty badly underrepresented tonight, are going to complain that once again 'middle-class values' triumphed, that once again the more assertive, wealthier parents won the day—just as they do when it comes to picking teachers, moving into advanced classes, avoiding (or getting) special education, getting the discretionary goodies that we distribute.

"We may think, at least subconsciously, that their missing voice is unimportant. Let's face it, we don't believe that one afternoon a week without traditional instruction will affect the kids' academic growth; we may even think the service opportunities will contribute to that growth, but they think otherwise. What we see as altruistic, they see as, at best, just plain nutty. Why should their children spend time during school on what these folks perceive to be ordinary chores? Their kids do plenty of cleaning, plenty of talking to the elderly, in their own homes. More ominously, a couple who couldn't come tonight called me to say that this initiative is yet another act, *perhaps* not a deliberate one, to foster a consciousness of servitude in their children."

At Maria's quizzical look, Hardie reiterates, "You got it. For that parent, we're encouraging servitude not service. We're telling the kids, implicitly at least, that school work doesn't matter for them; that they're not really fit for academic learning and we don't expect it of them; that what they should be learning is how to do menial work. No one actually went on to say this over the telephone, but it wouldn't be off the wall to connect the reaction to the service idea with a criticism of how *soft* we are—you know, how quickly some of us back down when a child doesn't turn in his homework or gives us a half-assed excuse for not completing a test; how palsy-walsy almost sycophant-like, we are with youngsters; how easily we let ourselves be manipulated by them."

Noticing that they had meandered to a near-by coffee bar, and finding that as they talked the matter had gotten only more complex, the three colleagues went inside and settled in for some serious conversation. Maria, picking up on Hardie's last comments, but not feeling comfortable either agreeing or disagreeing with them, decided to broaden the topic. "Those complaints about us as softies, I get a lot of them, sometimes from kids whose parents or grandparents were immigrants (Asians, Latinos, Africans), from African Americans, but also from some whom we used to call "white ethnics"—working-class families, many of them Catholics, of European ancestry. They have the same objection; what we see as *engaging* children they see as *pandering* to them."

"Can you say more about that, Maria?" Aggie asked. "It may well be part of a much bigger picture."

"Well, let's see, one parent—and I gather she thinks many are like-minded—told me she objects to the conversational way I run the class; you know, always trying to get kids to participate, voice their opinion, disagree with my interpretation of a book or event. She said children should respect their elders, and especially their teachers. When I replied that was my wish as well, she said her child would never respect an adult who acted as I did. Her child, and she as well, expected teachers to be smart, know a lot, and make sure they taught it *to* the kids, not try to extract knowledge *from* them. If the kids already knew as much as I seemed to think, she asked, why should they bother coming to school?

"And, she went on, it was particularly hard for her to accept the way I encouraged children to argue—with each other, with me. How could a child respect a teacher as an authority figure and at the same time challenge her all the time? That was the opposite of respect; respect means deference—as she had to make very clear when her son tried arguing with *her* at home. What the parent was too polite to add was that my teaching practices undermined her own child-raising ethic."

"Do you think she had a point there?" Hardie asked kindly, sympathetic to all the challenges Maria was facing in her first year of teaching.

"No, not much of one, Hardie. I suppose I have no right to judge her parenting, though I'm not certain, but I'm clear that her ways of teaching and disciplining are wrong. By 'wrong' I mean that they won't work, they will backfire. Her kid is one of the most cowed, unimaginative, frightened, sullen kids in the class. In fact, I was planning to talk with her about his excessive inhibition, his turned-off attitude, but after our conversation I realized the kid was behaving just as she would have wished. And he does do well on tests, especially the objective ones."

"That kind of reaction could just be the tip of an iceberg," Aggie suggested.

"For sure! Some parents have been critical of my approach to evaluating student work. One parent was upset when I wrote on her son's test paper that I would not count the 'F' as part of the semester grade because I knew that he had recently taken on—actually, had laid on him—substantial domestic obligations (a lot of baby-sitting for his niece), which probably interfered with his test preparation. The mother did not interpret my gesture as an act of kindness; rather she accused me of holding a different set of standards for rich than for poor kids. How would her child accomplish anything if I wasn't more demanding? Then she started in on . . ."

"Enough already, Maria, we all get complaints like that," Hardie interrupted, concerned that too many criticisms of his friend were piling up. "They even come to a tough guy like me. The way to handle them is to . . ."

"Just a minute, Hardie," now it was Aggie interrupting, "I didn't hear Maria asking for advice. We need to think more deeply about the significance of these differences, not just how to 'handle' them."

"Actually, Hardie," said Maria, smiling, "you may be stunned to hear, these parents' complaints don't get to me. I just have this unshakeable conviction that a big emphasis on obedience and authority is wrong, and while I suppose I can't convince these parents, neither can they convince me. What does trouble me, and maybe you two can be of help on this one, is the parent's request that I 'toughen up.' Specifically, that last mother said she wants every grade to count, she wants any excuse the child gives for incomplete work to be checked with her, and she wants serious penalties when work is turned in after the due date. And she means serious—a week of detention the first time an assignment is late, two weeks the second. Now that is something I simply cannot do."

Now Hardie was smiling. "Maria, do I hear a wee bit less understanding and sympathy toward these parents than toward those kids a while back who were beating up on one another after class?[1] You turn somersaults to 'join' with a *child's* mindset, but you cavalierly reject the notion that maybe you should join his *parents'*."

"Oh, come off it, Hardie," Maria replied, with equal measures of irritation and playfulness. "I do sympathize with the parents. They live in a pretty harsh world, and don't have much experience of any but 'tough' approaches to whatever problem they're facing. It's not that I am judging them, certainly not harshly, but I am convinced that, understandable as their attitudes might be, their solution is no solution at all. Anyway, the parents are trying to make me *act* like them."

"Well, Maria, at the least you are proving that you're a complicated person. I can't share your assuredness that the parents are wrong, certainly not wrong given their circumstances. When a poor kid living in dangerous surroundings—and the danger may come from neighbors or from cops—starts arguing with and disobeying the rules of adults, he may end up in real trouble. It's fine for physically secure kids to speak their minds, take risks, not be held strictly accountable, what's the harm? But there are environments where if you take a risk—even be on the wrong street at the wrong time—you sure won't take another one very soon."

"Good Lord, we've been talking for an hour," Aggie noted. "We're into such deep waters that, despite my years at this job, it's starting to make my head spin. Listening with my ears peeled to you two, I long ago gave up on finding an acceptable resolution; just clarifying the contested issues has kept me busy. Before we call it quits, though, let me see if I've got anything straight.

"Going back to tonight's Home and School meeting, Maria liked the outcome because our tentative decision—assuming it isn't reversed up the line—permits a service learning project to get started but doesn't coerce it. She liked

---

[1] See Chapter 4.

it because she thinks it's good moral education; end of story. Hardie and I had a couple of worries: The first is that the decision wasn't made by a true majority. On the merits, the proposal is more coercive than meets the eye, and it is not so clearly, at least not so universally, thought of as good moral education. There are legitimate objections to it, which may relate to parents' social circumstances. I'm not as sure as the enthusiastic parents that the idea is so plainly right that it should be required, and I still have a lot of concerns that calling it voluntary has a big downside.

"A bunch of more general questions emerge from all this: When should a decision be binding on folks who seriously disagree with it? What sorts of decisions should be put up to parents? When subgroups disagree, is it a sufficient response to let each do their own thing? If the faculty is clear on what's right for the kids—and remember they did support the initiative—should their professional views trump parental views, again assuming for the moment that service learning is a realistic possibility?

"Then, we got onto some parental complaints that perhaps cannot be 'handled' by a live-and-let-live tolerance. Some of the parents strongly disapprove, *morally* disapprove, one might say, of how we relate to their children. What we see as creating respectful and productive interchanges, they see as disrespectful and destructive. So what do we do? Move over and do it their way, at least with their children? That strikes me as impossible. How do you run a classroom being forgiving with one child, and punitive with another? Or do we tell the parents, 'Look! At school I'm in charge, at home you are'? That may be OK for minor matters like raising your hand before speaking—yes at school, no at home—but how do you tell a kid that the freedom to speak your mind honestly can be dishonored outside school?

"Can we instead ask parents to find common ground with us, recognizing that circumstances—theirs and ours, one group versus another—will keep us from reaching full agreement? If we seek common ground, how do we get a conversation going? How broad should the participation be? Do we include members of the wider community? Members of the administration and school board? Where, and with what essential concerns, do we start?"

"Phew," said Hardie, as he went for the jackets, "what an agenda you've laid out for us to tackle, Aggie! It should keep us going for a good couple of years or so. Meanwhile, will you permit me to assert an old-fashioned male prerogative and walk you to your cars?"

At the University

"When values collide," when *A* thinks right what *B* deems morally wrong, or when two values regarded favorably by *A* (or *B*) pull in opposing directions, what is to be done? We encountered an instance of this problem in Chapter 4, arising out of the specific question whether Maria should condemn or deter students who justify fighting in response to verbally aggressive, disrespectful acts. Our analysis addressed enduring questions regarding the existence and discernment of right answers to questions of morality, and the propriety of a pluralist position, one which forbears to require that *others* act in accordance with one's own moral judgment, even though one might deem that judgment in fact correct and the others' morally deficient.

In this chapter's scenario, we come upon similar questions, but in a far more complex setting, implicating the values and moral judgments of a wide variety of potentially relevant actors operating at different levels of decision making within a school system: an individual teacher, faculty or faculty group; a principal, superintendent, or school board; and parents or parent groups.

The issues were posed by two aspects of the teachers' activities, Hardie's service learning proposal and Maria's approach to student–teacher interaction: her encouragement of student's active participation, including disagreement with her opinions, and her willingness to overlook substandard student performance on the ground of unusual home responsibilities. (We will call these approaches her teaching methods.) Three sets of questions arise:

1. Are programs of service learning, and Maria's teaching methods, valid and important parts of moral education?
2. If so, should individual parents nonetheless be permitted, in Hardie's case to have their children exempted from participation, and in Maria's to expect that their child be treated as *they* think proper?
3. Should authority to decide these questions—whether at the level of individual classroom, school, or school system—reside in teachers, administrators, or parent groups?

Before we consider these questions, it is important to recognize that the problem is one that could have arisen only in the modern era, and has such "bite" because of continuing reactions to relatively recent changes in prevailing moral thinking. According to Isaiah Berlin, for most of its history Western thought was dominated by what he characterizes as a "Platonic ideal":

> In the first place . . . all genuine questions must have one true answer and one only, all the rest being necessarily error; in the second place, . . . there must be a dependable path towards the discovery of these truths; in the third place, . . . the true answers, when found, must necessarily be compatible with one another and form a single whole, for one truth cannot be incompatible with another.
> (Berlin 1959/1992, 5–6)

Early in the nineteenth century, this set of premises, sometimes termed moral absolutism, was completely undermined by a "reversal of values" (id, 12). Values came to be seen as "not discovered but created. [Accordingly,] no system of propositions [could] be constructed to describe them, for they are not facts, not entities in the world" (Berlin 1996, 186). As a result, "values can clash—that is why civilizations are incompatible. . . . Some among the Great Goods cannot live together. . . . We are doomed to choose, and every choice may entail an irreparable loss" (Berlin 1959/1992, 12–13).

The idea that supportable values might not be reconcilable with one another added "the conception of tragedy" to political thought. Tragedy, previously attributed to "avoidable human mistakes" (id, 185), now was understood as unavoidable. It is therefore not a person's adherence to truth in his values that earns our admiration, but "his spiritual attitude—the sincerity, the intensity, the dedication with which he seeks to follow the light within himself" (Berlin 1996, 186).

Berlin's biographer, Michael Ignatieff, has noted how these developments "led easily to relativism, to the proposition that human conduct could only be judged by internal, variable or contextual standards" (Ignatieff 1998, 285). If that were so, however, "Berlin's liberal tolerance rested on nothing more than a queasy live and let live" (ibid.). Out of this development arose a distinction between relativism and pluralism, which we considered in Chapter 4 (p. 99). Our scenario illustrates the continuing shock waves in our culture produced by the clash between the earlier worldview and the newer one, and by the attempt, of which Isaiah Berlin's thought is a premier instance, to maintain the viability of pluralism as a "middle way" between absolutism and relativism in morality. The excerpt by Berlin, see p. 206, in the next section of this chapter, is in our judgment a brilliant analysis of several interrelated questions dealt with throughout this section.

SERVICE LEARNING AND MARIA'S TEACHING METHODS: THE MORAL STAKE

Is service learning a valid and important part of moral education? Hardie's positive answer to this question arises from his judgment as to the priorities among goals of moral education and as to the preferred pedagogic methods of achieving them. In order, therefore, to indicate the thinking that might inform Hardie's judgment, we will both look back to themes already encountered and briefly foreshadow the subject of Part IV, "The Pedagogy of Moral Education."

Hardie's stance rests in part on a conception of moral action and character that goes further than simply avoiding wrongful acts. It requires devoting at least a portion of one's energies to pro-social acts, responding in some way to the needs and suffering of others. It requires an amelioration of the self-regarding, "get ahead" focus of most of our efforts. It values this outlook not only for its own sake, for the good acts that it prompts, but also in the belief that developing habits of pro-social action will make a person more disposed to take the concerns of others seriously into account in decision making.

Beyond that, Hardie's approach has a pedagogical premise as well—a commitment to experiential learning as a necessary teaching method. Children can, to be sure, learn the value of "good deeds" by reading about moral exemplars, whether heroic figures of history or ordinary folks like those around them. Yet, proponents of service learning maintain, the lesson is far more powerfully brought home by actually carrying out thoughtfully designed, age-appropriate service projects, *and* by engaging in focused reflection on the experience, the insights and perspectives it yields, and the questions it raises.

On this view, time spent in service projects is hardly "wasted," for it is as much moral instruction as is reading of George Washington and the cherry tree, or even of Rosa Parks and Martin Luther King, Jr. As Jesuit teacher William J. O'Malley observes:

> Trying to make a person in a nursing home smile, or feeling the palpable need for love in an injured child, or reading to someone blind can be a more profoundly educative experience than getting through "King Lear." It opens your horizons, which is what being human is all about. *(O'Malley 1998, 18)*

More deeply, however, the answer to the "waste of time" fear implicates several central ideas about learning and achievement. There is not so tight a connection, this answer asserts, between the quantity of effort put into, say, math and the extent to which it is learned. A child whose school day is balanced among several modes of learning activity, and balanced as well between "work" and "play," will in this view learn more than one whose teacher relentlessly keeps the child's nose to the grindstone. The contemporary phenomenon of subjecting young children to an entire school day without recess for the sake of greater academic achievement is not only an atrocious restraint, but academically self-defeating as well.

Specifically relevant to the moral aspect of education is the idea that an ethical stance toward others in the world requires a certain moderation of anxiety about "falling behind" in the race of life. Unalloyed, this fearfulness is a major source of antisocial conduct. Indeed, academic values too are best served, in this view, by reining in anxiety to succeed or excel. Time spent in service learning teaches a student that he or she can do well *and* do good, that these ends are not in wholly unyielding competition.

Maria also grounds her approach to teaching in premises about the nature of moral action and about effective pedagogy as well. Her thinking exemplifies the concept of "disinterestedness" (discussed at p. 52 in Chapter 3). To her, living a moral life calls for a developed ability to exercise moral judgment, to reflect on choice and experiences, to stand outside one's own opinions and priorities and imagine how they appear to others.

Expressing doubt, asking questions, and questioning answers are vital means of acquiring this skill. Again, Father O'Malley:

> [H]uman life begins to die when we stop asking why. Children begin to feel it is somehow impolite to be too inquisitive. [T]hat a child . . . keeps pestering, badgering, asking unsettling questions, intruding on the lesson plan . . . is what learning, as opposed to schooling, is all about. *(Id., 14)*

Authority usefully frames the question and the approach, but simply looking to authority (including the authority of the teacher) for answers inhibits rather than facilitates learning. Knowledge is not absolute and wholly given, but emergent and partial. "Mistakes" are an essential part of the learning process, so long as students are encouraged to acknowledge them, to learn from them (and from one another), and to try again; "getting it right" is a life-long process, not a daily pedagogical objective.

What students most need, as they grow, is to learn to struggle productively with hard questions; to Maria, this learning is of moral as well as academic significance. It teaches that having right answers to important questions reflects the quality of a person's thinking, not simply his or her credentials or authority. Equalizing (somewhat) the teacher–student relation encourages students to support more egalitarian relations throughout life, whether they find themselves on the "high" or the "low" end of an inequality. To Maria, this is a major moral virtue, and a valid source of "respect." Honoring a person for his or her office alone—whether that of position, age, or power—is a morally hazardous form of respect.

Maria's commitment to the individualization of expectations, another aspect of her morality-driven pedagogy, is seen in her approach to the student who failed to pass a test and complete certain homework because of household responsibilities. To Maria, it is simply wrong to judge the work of a student ignoring that it was carried on under unusual pressures. Beyond her own moral sense, she is educating the students' as well, for she believes that an individualized view of equity is morally preferable to "one size fits all" expectations. By learning to make similar contextualized judgments, her students will enlarge their sympathies, alert to the actual life-situation of those with whom they deal, those whom *they* will be judging. She believes that younger children treated with empathic individualization will turn out stronger and more self-reliant than if they are made to "toe the mark" prematurely.

At bottom, however, this prediction is as much a statement of hope as of expectation. Her (and, she hopes, their) outlook is aspirational, oriented toward the world as it could be, rather than simply grounding normative directives in what is. She will not allow her teaching methods to be driven by such folk wisdom as, "It's results that count," "You're either a winner or a loser," or "You can't count on getting by in the world on sympathy."

Responses to Parental Objections: Pragmatic and Pluralist Considerations

It is obvious that nearly every premise, perception, and priority that we have hypothesized as the bases of Maria's and Hardie's positions is deeply contested, often fiercely so, in our culture. Many parents listen to the sounds of very different drummers when it comes to what morality consists of, what makes for good pedagogy, and how they (and their children) should deal with the imperfections of social life. The question thus arises: How should a school or school system (in the case of Hardie's service learning proposal) or an individual teacher (in the case of Maria's teaching methods) respond to sincerely held, and vigorously asserted, parental objections?

Whether the school affirms or rejects parental requests, it is important at the outset to distinguish *pragmatic* grounds (prudence or "statesmanship") from those of *principle*. It is often easy for a school or teacher to resist, or to accept, parents' claims on practical grounds. In *yielding* to parental objections, teachers or a principal might abandon the idea of service learning, or make participation optional, in order to diffuse controversy and criticism. A teacher in Maria's position might accede to a parent's demand that her child's work be judged on a "no excuses" basis to avoid it becoming an issue with the principal. Alternatively, a school might *resist* parents' request to exempt their child from a mandatory service program by responding, "We can't do that. What would we do with them during the time the other children are at their service project?" Maria might object, "I can't teach a class with one student graded on criteria different from the ones I use with all the others."

The same outcomes (yielding to and resisting parents) could be reached on grounds of principle. Service learning might be made optional because the school *believed* that in this area one ought to respect parental educational priorities and pedagogical premises that differ from Hardie's *even if thought wrong*; Maria might accede to a parent's wishes because she *believed* it important not to subject a child to conflicts of philosophies between home and school. Such decisions would rest on the principle of tolerance or pluralism. Similarly principled would be the opposing conclusion, overriding the pluralist claim: If service learning was believed to be so clearly central to moral education, or the harm to a child from excessive expectations thought sufficiently great, a teacher or school would be wrong to abandon those judgments willingly in the face of parental objection.

It is tempting for schools and teachers to invoke pragmatic considerations reflexively, as a barrier to further discussion, because to do so may seem simpler than to confront the question whether the objectors' claims should in justice entitle them to have their own way. We believe, however, that the greater complexity of principles does not warrant evading them, and that the temptation should be resisted.

This is not to say that pragmatic considerations are morally objectionable merely because they are pragmatic. To say that a response is not *based* on a moral principle, but only on prudential considerations, is not to say that it is *un*principled, that it *violates* a moral principle. Whether it does or not depends on the specifics of the matter. By the same token, to say that a decision is based on principle does not establish that it is right; the moral validity of the relevant principle remains to be judged.

A pluralist position, as we suggested earlier (Chapter 4, p. 80), is one that forbears to require that *others* act in accordance with one's own moral judgment, even though one might deem that judgment in fact correct and the others' morally deficient. Pluralism rests on the belief that there *is* a right and wrong at stake, and that one may believe that he or she *knows* what it is but nonetheless think it right not to *insist* on having others act in accordance with that view. Even where there are significant differences in moral beliefs, we frequently do not think it appropriate to require that all conform to the view we regard as right.

Forbearance to insist on the priority of one's own moral outlook is a form of what has been termed "epistemic modesty." This phenomenon, giving rise to an obligation to respect the moral views of others, is the basis for pluralism, and has several sources. The broadest, perhaps, is the recognition that one's judgments, however clear they may seem to their holder, might in fact be wrong, that a person with whom one is in serious disagreement might be correct. It might also rest on a recognition that, even if wrong, the other person is nonetheless to be respected, that he or she has come to a differing conclusion responsibly and with integrity. (For a development of this thought, see the excerpt from the British philosopher David Heyd at p. 210 in the next section of this chapter). Finally, one might be inclined toward a pluralist position by a recognition that the other person has a special stake in the answer; the complaining mother (in Maria's case) is, after all, more intimately and enduringly responsible for her child's welfare and development than is an individual teacher.

In its more extreme forms, this "modesty" becomes (in philosophical terms) more metaphysical than epistemological, that is, closer to a claim that there is in reality no truth of the matter, but only differing points of view, different "tastes." This is ethical relativism. (See p. 80 in Chapter 4 for an elaboration of this distinction.)

Neither the parents nor the teachers or school in the present scenario is making a relativist claim. Relativism tends to be employed today as an epithet, used by those who, holding tightly to their opinions regarding moral truth, have difficulty imagining that others, who reject their views, disagree not about the *existence* of moral truth but about its *content*, thinking wrong what the first group thinks self-evidently right (or vice versa). Pluralism responds to such diversity of moral judgments by not insisting that one side's answer bind the other. The objecting parents, for example, are asking the school (or teacher) to forgo acting on its (or her) moral judgment regarding service learning, out of deference to the differing judgments of the objecting parents. The school or teacher might concur on pluralist grounds.

The question of pluralism does not arise when a conflict between beliefs has little or nothing to do with morality. Not everyone has to be equally devoted to music, math, or muscle building. We each make our own choice of hobbies, time allocation, friendships, or aesthetic preferences. Here variety is a positive good; it adds to life's vitality and nudges us out of complacency. A diversity of flowers makes for a more colorful array.

At the same time, when a conflict is over a moral question it is obvious that there are limits to the proper role of pluralist considerations. Although those limits differ in people's minds, it is not difficult to postulate easy cases, where *in*tolerance of another point of view is plainly called for. The torture of children to learn the location of money, for example, cannot seriously be presented as a case for not "imposing" prevailing views on nonconformists. Isaiah Berlin's words (quoted in Chapter 4, p. 85) make the point well:

> [I]f we meet someone who cannot see why (to take a famous example) he should not destroy the world in order to relieve a pain in his little finger, or someone who genuinely sees no harm in condemning innocent men, or betraying friends, or torturing children, then we find that we cannot argue with such people, not so much because we are horrified as because we think them in some way inhuman—we call them moral idiots. *(Berlin 1992, 203–204)*

Between these poles—the irrelevance of pluralism because of the absence of a serious moral question and the inappropriateness of a pluralist response because of the absence of any legitimate moral disagreement—is a large area of uncertain boundaries. (The excerpt by David Heyd, referred to above, seeks to examine this problem.)

We turn now to the central questions raised by the case at hand: First, would it be wrong for the school or teachers to stand their ground, to *refuse* to defer to the contrary judgments and priorities of the objecting parents? Second, would it be wrong for them to *agree* to defer to parental objections, by making participation in service learning optional or (in Maria's case) by changing her teaching methods? We consider each question in turn.

THE CASE FOR DEFERENCE CONSIDERED

Should school personnel defer to parents? In a school setting, the boundaries of pluralism are neither self-evident nor clearly legislated. There is a loose, largely implicit, consensus that parents defer to educators in core matters of "schooling," while educators defer to parents in core matters of "child rearing." Thus parents do not normally expect a school to exempt children from reading or math requirements, and teachers do not ask parents to prohibit children from watching particular television programs. Both requests are "out of bounds." The division of authority between school and home may wobble under trying circumstances—if the teacher thinks the family very misguided in their child-rearing methods, if a parent strongly objects to a particular text or to required participation in after-school activities—but there is normally a mutual expectation that the domains are separate. Both teachers and parents may have to put up with what they do not like, even what they consider immoral.

This separation of powers is an easy form of live-and-let-live pluralism. The boundary markers between the domains are less a wall than a membrane, permeable yet real. A teacher who has good grounds to believe that a parent has physically abused a child is rightfully expected to override parental authority and intervene in some way. But a porous boundary can be the source of legitimate dispute. Suppose, for instance, that a teacher believes a parent is likely to "overreact" (but short of real abuse) to a child's poor performance, and decides to withhold such information, although parents generally receive it. While in both instances the teacher has rejected a pluralist response, in the latter case the parent has a greater basis to retort that the teacher should have exhibited some "epistemic modesty," respecting parents' authority to judge what is appropriate discipline even when she is strongly critical of their actions.

Parents too might test the boundary. For example, when a teacher's discipline is perceived as inappropriate or ineffective—either because it is too harsh or too lenient—or when a school adopts a text that is deeply offensive to many, parents may not willingly accede to the implicit boundaries. In these instances parents might object to the teacher's actions, or ask that their own child be removed from the class or exempted from reading the book, putting the teacher to the necessity of choosing between resistance and deference to parental viewpoints.

There is no clear answer to these instances. The unpalatable reality of life is that at every level of human relationships one must, for the greater good of social harmony, sometimes put up with what one finds deeply objectionable. But it is also true (as in the instance of clear abuse) that such tolerance is not boundless. There are times in which "intolerance" is called for. (For a recognition of these realities and an attempt to respond to the difficulties they present, see p. 208 of the excerpt by Isaiah Berlin in the next section of this chapter.)

In our scenarios, concluding that Hardie's service learning proposal and Maria's pedagogy were clearly matters for the school to decide would require some parents to tolerate what they do not like; if they were clearly matters of parental discretion, then some teachers would have to tolerate what *they* do not like. (The first case is like math, the second like television-watching). If, however, the case is one where both parties may rightfully claim authority, the school personnel would not be off-base in declining to defer. As professionals, a school or school system, acting at times through teachers, may justly insist on "imposing" its view on the entire student body. The decision to hire Maria and Hardie bespeaks a certain (perhaps provisional) judgment as to the discretion that they should have in the form and style of the classroom, and it may be appropriate for teachers and principals to turn aside individual parent demands for a different approach.

A judicial decision rejecting a challenge by parents and students to a high school's community-service requirement sheds some light here. The plaintiffs grounded their objection in the fact that approval of the program by school board members expressed "a favorable view of altruism," a "matter of opinion not shared by all," and that students working in such a program would naturally be thought by others to support the idea "that helping others and serving the community are desirable." The court noted that "the gamut of courses in a school's curriculum necessarily reflects the value judgments of those responsible for its development," but requiring students to study the course materials does not compel them to subscribe to those values (U.S. Court of Appeals for the Third Circuit 1993, 993 [*Steirer v. Bethlehem Area School District*]).

What of the converse question: Would it be wrong for the teachers and school to *choose to defer* to the objecting parents? Put another way, would the school or teachers be morally obligated to *refuse* to defer to parental objections or requests? We believe that the question whether the teachers *should*, no less than *may*, refuse to surrender their positions out of a pluralist respect for the dissenting parental views is governed by considerations of professionalism and its implications. In the present context those considerations are triggered only if the faculty believes that to omit service learning from the required curriculum is (as we will suggest below) close to "educational malpractice," or if Maria believes that deference to the parent will place an unjustifiable burden on the child—that he will "fail" on tests or assignments repeatedly, become discouraged, fall further behind, and increasingly "turn off" schooling—or that restraining a child's classroom responses will prevent him from developing a necessary intellectual curiosity and self-confidence. Where, but only where, such conditions are honestly thought to be present, the school personnel will, we believe, be obligated to try to act in accordance with their professional judgment, despite the friction this may bring about and despite the uncomfortable counter-pulls the decision may place on some students.[2]

Opposition to Hardie's and Maria's ideas would probably not focus on the question of deference and the force of pluralist values. Those who tend to be hostile to service learning (and experiential methods of learning generally) and to Maria's teaching methods might also be unsympathetic to the idea that we live in a world of moral diversity. They might support their negative view of service learning and individualized teaching simply on the ground that their view is *right* (as indeed it was widely assumed to be), and would tend to presume that one can disagree with them only by espousing ethical relativism. They might bridle at the suggestion that they are "really" asserting a pluralist claim, which has something of the air of a generous concession to odd, out-of-date ideas rather than a reaffirmation of tried and true beliefs.

The dissatisfied parents would therefore probably invoke the concept of democratic accountability, the idea that educational priorities should be set, not by the "educational establishment," but by the lay community, whose (presumably sympathetic) input would come from parents individually or as a group, the school board as the representative of community values, or the

---

[2] Ideally, Maria and the parent would seek to work out a realistic accommodation about homework, perhaps involving some willingness on the parent's part to take account of the pressures that are interfering with the child's progress. In specific circumstances, the ideal may be out of reach, but a teacher should not reflexively presume that such would be the case, and shrink from making the effort.

voters themselves. As we saw in the last chapter (see p. 171), that concept of accountability is in tension with the concept of professionalism, which tends to see teachers as accountable primarily to the students, as informed by their independent professional judgment. We turn to the effect of that tension in the present context.

WHO SHOULD HAVE THE SAY?

There is a host of plausible decision makers in the situations presented in the scenario:

> individual teacher (as in Chapter 6)
> a school's faculty
> a school's principal
> individual parents
> the parents of a school as a group
> the superintendent of schools
> the school board

We considered the allocation of discretion and authority within the system (that is, between and among teachers and administrators) in Chapter 6. In focusing here on the participation of parents and parent groups, we are again concerned, not with the legal answer—which vests authority to answer these questions in the school board, and in the superintendent as its delegate, subject to (limited) legislative and constitutional constraints—but with the normative question, what practices *should* the board and the superintendent require or permit, in order to enhance rather than undermine effective teaching and, more specifically, a viable program of moral education?

In most cases, a decision at the level of the board or superintendent will be more to permit than to require. That is, although in theory any policy decision can be made at the system level, in most cases the decision (general or specific) will often be to allow an individual principal to use his or her discretion. Similarly, principals will often leave particular decisions to teachers, whether as a group or individually. The initial normative question for each of the higher echelon people will therefore be whether to assert their authority to overrule a teacher, group of teachers, or (in the superintendent's case) principal, or to decide not to intervene in the decision.

A like analysis applies to interactions with parents. In one sense, of course, parents have no decisional authority over what goes on in school, except as they are given it—by the board, superintendent, principal, or teacher. (Of course, they have *influence*, which may succeed in inducing a person or body with authority to mandate a result they seek.) Our question, however, is whether any of the educational authorities should defer to parental objections or requests, and in that sense allow the parents to make the decision. We turn first to the question of the disagreement between Maria and the parent of one of her students.

We suggested earlier that as a rough guide teachers should have and assert the greater say in matters of curriculum and pedagogy, and should more readily defer to parents in matters of child-rearing. This principle points fairly strongly toward reinforcing Maria's reluctance to defer to the parent's objection to her classroom style—her encouragement of students to raise questions, form and express their points of view, and engage critically with what they read and hear. She has presumably come to her view as a result of her study and experience, and has concluded that, at least for her, it is a preferable way of teaching (in the case of this student as well as generally). Maria should give the parents' objections a serious hearing, but she must feel free, if her professionalism is to have any salience, to follow her conscientiously derived decision. (Were the parent to take her objections to the principal, he would be obliged, we believe, to decline to overrule Maria.) Beyond these matters of principle, it is not practically feasible, except at the margins, for Maria to individualize her instructional methods in the classroom.

Maria's second issue is whether she should accept the parent's earnest request that she not "customize" her evaluation of a child's performance in recognition of the student's home responsibilities. Here too, there is a strong argument in favor of the teacher's professional autonomy. However, it is a much closer call, and we can see the rightfulness of acting in accord with the wishes of the parent. Maria's judgment is based on her perceptions about the child's domestic life, what he does and does not have time for outside of the school day. This is pushing the limits of the school boundary and moving more into the parental domain. Despite Maria's belief that the parent is in error, epistemic modesty may require her to acknowledge that she "might in fact be wrong," and that even if she is right, Maria should defer to a parent's "special stake." Moreover, parents may have a greater claim when asking the teacher *not* to make an exception for their child than when (as with respect to service learning) they are asking *for* an exception.

As for the service learning issue, the faculty's and principal's decision to put the question before the Home and School Association seems a sensible exercise of practical judgment. Even if service learning is as good, as compelling, an idea as the faculty thinks, getting the support of a majority of those who attend and vote at a meeting of parents will lend it the strong legitimacy that in our culture comes from a democratically adopted practice. "Majority rules" has a talismanic appeal, and a favorable vote strengthens the hand of those who have to deal with objecting parents. Contrariwise, if a majority of parents opposed it, the faculty would be asking for trouble if it were to impose it.

Do these pragmatic considerations regarding a service learning requirement pass moral muster? One might conclude so, in two senses. First, acknowledging that the service learning issue is plainly curricular and squarely within the school's rather than the parents' domain, and also that (as we believe) it is a valid and important part of a program of moral education, one might still conclude that it would not be warranted to go so far as to assert that a school is morally obliged to have service learning; the question might appear more as one of good educational practice than morality itself. Second, the deference to a parental majority in opposition has a grounding that is not merely prudential. Epistemic modesty counsels that a substantial group of parents might have access to information about their children, and the world in which they are growing up, superior to that of the faculty. Thus, had the parents voted *against* a service learning project, the faculty might be right to decide to withhold implementing its own contrary judgment.

The issue surrounding the legitimacy of the actual voting process—questioning whether "real" majority support was manifested—presents different considerations, however. Despite its wide appeal, any majority vote is always open to challenge on grounds relating to the information supplied, the attendance at the meeting, or the decision to ask for a show of hands. Voting at a meeting inevitably favors those able and willing to attend, deeming irrelevant whatever pressures cause some parents not to do so. While it is possible, therefore, that a more truly representative poll would have gone against service learning, a mail ballot, although giving a voice to all who wish to be counted, has its own limitations. It eliminates the possibility of a fuller exchange of ideas and information and a more reflective decisional process prior to the vote. It also permits resort to misleading and inflammatory appeals, which have the effect of skewing the presumed randomness of those who vote and those who do not. Finally, most organizations typically act on the basis of a majority vote taken at a meeting, so long as a quorum is present.

No matter how a group resolves these important tensions, some will be disaffected and suspicious. We do not find any violation of principle regarding the vote that would impose a barrier to going forward.

More fundamentally, despite the contrary arguments reviewed above, we believe that the considerations counseling *against deference* to parental opposition are decisive. As we develop in the next chapter, service learning seems central to a sound program of moral education; it is the major vehicle for moving a student's consciousness to a more inclusive sense of "we." Parental disagreement with the content of the moral lesson of service learning is no more entitled to carry the day than in other curricular areas.

Moreover, a decision to make participation mandatory (with or without an "opt-out" provision) would not preclude extensive parental involvement in the design and evolution of the program—how much service, what kinds, etc. It does not even preclude an occasional exemption, but the threshold should be high, an opt-out option for compelling individual reason, and certainly not an opt-in arrangement. In general, lay persons tend to be more skeptical than teachers toward many forms of experiential learning, and the idea that service learning is a diversion from "real school" will find an attentive ear at parent–teacher meetings. Yet, as professionals, teachers are not only justified in "imposing" their view on the entire student body, as they do about all of the other decisions that go to make up a curriculum and pedagogy, they have an obligation to exercise their best judgment of students' educational interests.

Toward Reconciliation of Conflicting Values

The conflict between and among individuals over values, on which the scenario has focused, has its counterpart in the thinking of individual teachers and principals, and in the decisional processes of superintendents and school boards. Much of the enduring controversy that attends public education today reflects the fact that schools, like each of us as individuals, must repeatedly choose between competing values, where each has some substantial claim for respectful attention.

Examples abound. An excellent text, Kenneth A. Strike's and Jonas F. Soltis' *The Ethics of Teaching* (1992), is built around a large number of these, of which the following are illustrative:

- Should a teacher impose a serious punishment on a student anonymously accused of deliberately causing a laboratory explosion, toward whom circumstantial evidence supplies some reasonable grounds for suspicion but who earnestly denies his guilt?
- Should the faculty advisor of a student literary magazine censor a student's high-quality and thought-provoking short story about the seduction (and subsequent pregnancy and abortion) of a student by a teacher, who will be readily identified by everyone as two specific people in the school?
- Should a principal listen in on classes through the public-address system without disclosing his presence?

Note a certain parallelism in the "face-off" between values that competing responses to these examples reflect:

A (yes)	*B (no)*
importance of not letting seriously wrongful acts go unpunished; willingness to act on balance of probabilities	"due process"; reluctance to punish one protesting innocence without some sort of trial or proof
desire to prevent irresponsible student acts from causing harm to student and teacher	appreciation of importance of encouraging talent; reluctance to override student editorial judgment, to censor student publications
importance of teacher accountability; commitment to enforcing standards	concern about privacy; fear of inhibiting teacher initiative

Many, perhaps most, of us would tend consistently to favor either an *A* or a *B* in all of these examples. Those in the first camp, generally the "conservative" or tradition-oriented side, tend to find salience in a certain confidence that authority will be used responsibly, and are less concerned about the possibility of abuses creeping in than that wrongful acts will go unresponded to and reinforce tendencies toward an atmosphere of moral lassitude. Those in the second group, the "liberal" or critical side, are quick to see moral failures in the exercise of legitimate authority, and insistent on maintaining in force safeguards against abuses of authority; that social harms may result tends to be regarded as a necessary price to pay.

In our view, the same dynamic is at work in a large number of "hot button" issues generating public controversy in education today. Those who oppose the distribution of condoms in school, for example, fear the legitimation of casual sexual relations; those who favor it tend to believe that decision making about sexual activity is an individual or family responsibility, and in any event, primarily want to discourage unwanted pregnancies and the spread of sexually transmitted diseases. In truth, most people probably would not want to encourage *either* outcome, yet it has been difficult to get past denigrating one of these harms in the cause of protecting against the other.

Although these differences cannot be wholly reconciled, we believe that some progress can be made. First, all must acknowledge that these problems present conflicts, not between good and evil, or between moral standards and relativism, but between real goods. The underlying premise must be a recognition that, contrary to the premodern philosophy, values are not fully reconcilable. We again find relevant wisdom in words of Isaiah Berlin:

> What is clear is that values can clash. . . . You believe in always telling the truth, no matter what; I do not, because I believe that it can sometimes be too painful and too destructive. . . . Values may easily clash within the breast of a single individual; and it does not follow that, if they do, some must be true and others false. Justice, rigorous justice, is for some people an absolute value, but it is not compatible with what may be no less ultimate values for them—mercy, compassion—as [they arise] in concrete cases.
>
> Both liberty and equality are among the primary goals pursued by human beings through many centuries; but total liberty for wolves is death to the lambs, total liberty of the powerful, the gifted, is not compatible with the rights to a decent existence of the weak and the less gifted. . . .
>
> These collisions of values are of the essence of what they are and what we are. . . . We are doomed to choose, and every choice may entail an irreparable loss.
> (Berlin 1959/1992, 12–14)[3]

---

[3] The quotation in the text is a portion of a fuller statement of Berlin's view, set forth at p. 206 in the next section of this chapter.

This lesson needs to be taken to heart by those conservatives who act as if they really do yearn for the collapse of the modernist insight of which Berlin speaks, who write as if once relativism is rejected the merit of their policy initiatives is plainly established. But liberals too must acknowledge their share of the demonization game. Their aversion to the conservatives' monopoly-of-virtue stance does not justify a refusal to acknowledge that the social ills that are so troubling to conservatives *are* real and serious. If you insist on handing out condoms to teenagers, what *do* you propose we as a society do in the face of our failure to speak sensibly to teenagers about irresponsible sex? More importantly, perhaps, what do you as individuals and groups plan to do yourselves, if you have only scorn for those who commit their time and effort to the promotion of "abstinence" programs?

The challenge is to embrace fully the realization that values which to us are not ordinarily controlling are nonetheless (in Berlin's term) "intelligible to us." From that point of departure, we can hope to begin to respond with sympathy, imagination, and understanding to those fellow humans who find some values far more compelling than we do. This response is to us the beginning of a way out of the dilemma of irreconcilable values, because it suggests that the answer is to be found, not in an answer—a result, a "winner"—but a process, one that may not lead to agreement on a result (although at times it will), but that in any case informs and guides each participant in his or her engagement with an issue.

The process is what political philosopher John Rawls calls "considered judgement in reflective equilibrium" (Rawls 1971, 46). In describing that process and its possibilities, Strike and Soltis (1992, 74) emphasize that "we must make clear and explicit the rules and principles that underlie our moral intuitions." But "our" moral intuitions differ, and a major purpose of this book has been to "make clear and explicit" the differing principles and premises that, in our view, underlie those differences.

The point of this unearthing process, however, goes (in Strike's and Soltis' words) "even deeper":

> Sometimes a deep understanding of the principles of [our premises] can lead us to revise our initial opinion about what is meaningful or correct. Understanding the principle can make an expression that seemed obscure or ambiguous clear and comprehensible, or it can lead us to see the awkwardness or obscurity of something that had appeared clear and simple. Likewise, a moral theory can change or overrule our intuitions about moral phenomena. Once we see more clearly what is assumed by our moral intuitions, we may wish to change them. Thus, there is an interaction between moral theory and moral intuition in ethical reflection, each influencing the other. The trick is to achieve some point of reflective equilibrium between our moral sense and our moral theory. By reflective equilibrium we mean reaching a point in our deliberations where we feel that our moral intuitions and the moral

theory that accounts for them are satisfactorily consistent and where the decisions we reach and actions we take can be justified by our moral theory.

*****

How, then, do we settle ethical arguments? We proceed first by trying to discover the moral principles that underlie our differing senses of right and wrong. When we see what it is that our moral intuitions assume, perhaps some will change their minds. If not, then we must test our conflicting moral principles by seeing what else follows from them. If we find that some proposed principle leads to an abhorrent result in certain cases, that is a reason to abandon it. Perhaps some will change their minds when they see what else they must agree to if they are to hold consistently to their current principles.
(Id., 74–75)

This process is obviously easier to describe than to carry out in the world we live in, easier for an individual to struggle over with sometime success in his or her mind than for disputing individuals to achieve, let alone for contending groups to reach for. We do not romanticize the likelihood of major or sudden progress. We do espouse the fundamental validity of Strikes's and Soltis' insight. If there is another, surer way, we do not know it.

At the Library

Isaiah Berlin, *The Crooked Timber of Humanity: Chapters in the History of Ideas*
(1959/1992, 2–6, 12–14, 17–19)

When I was young I read *War and Peace* by Tolstoy, much too early. The real impact on me of this great novel came only later, together with that of other Russian writers, both novelists and social thinkers, of the mid-nineteenth century. These writers did much to shape my outlook. It seemed to me, and still does, that the purpose of these writers was . . . essentially moral: they were concerned most deeply with what was responsible for injustice, oppression, falsity in human relations, imprisonment whether by stone walls or conformism—unprotesting submission to man-made yokes—moral blindness, egoism, cruelty, humiliation, servility, poverty, helplessness, bitter indignation, despair, on the part of so many. . . . And conversely they wished to know what would bring about the opposite of this, a reign of truth, love, honesty, justice, security, personal relations based on the possibility of human dignity, decency, independence, freedom, spiritual fulfilment.

Some, like Tolstoy, found this in the outlook of simple people, unspoiled by civilization. . . . Others . . . put their faith in scientific rationalism, or in social and political revolution founded on a true theory of historical change. Others again looked for answers in the teachings of the Orthodox theology, or in liberal western democracy, or in a return to ancient Slav values. . . .

What was common to all these outlooks was the belief that solutions to the central problems existed, that one could discover them, and, with sufficient selfless effort, realize them on earth. They all believed that the essence of human beings was to be able to choose how to live: societies could be transformed in the light of true ideals believed in with enough fervor and dedication. . . .

When I became a student at the University of Oxford, I began to read the works of the great philosophers, and found that the major figures, especially in the field of ethical and political thought, believed this too. Socrates thought that if certainty could be established in our knowledge of the external world by rational methods . . . the same methods would surely yield equal certainty in the field of human behavior—how to live, what to be. This could be achieved by rational argument. . . . The Stoics thought that the attainment of these solutions was in the power of any man who set himself to live according to reason. Jews, Christians, Muslims (I knew too little about Buddhism) believed that the true answers had been revealed by God to his chosen prophets and saints, and accepted the interpretation of these revealed truths by qualified teachers and the traditions to which they belonged.

The rationalists of the seventeenth century thought that the answers could be found by a species of metaphysical insight, a special application of the light of reason with which all men were endowed. The empiricists of the eighteenth century, impressed by the vast new realms of knowledge opened by the natural sciences based on mathematical techniques, which had driven out so much error, superstition, dogmatic nonsense, asked themselves, like Socrates, why the same methods should not succeed in establishing similar irrefutable laws in the realm of human affairs. With the new methods discovered by natural science, order could be introduced into the social sphere as well. . . .

The rational reorganization of society would put an end to spiritual and intellectual confusion, the reign of prejudice and superstition, blind obedience to unexamined dogmas, and the stupidities and cruelties of the oppressive regimes which such intellectual darkness bred and promoted. All that was wanted was the identification of the principal human needs and discovery of the means of satisfying them. This would create the happy, free, just, virtuous, harmonious world which Condorcet so movingly predicted in his prison cell in 1794. This view lay at the basis of all progressive thought in the nineteenth century, and was at the heart of much of the critical empiricism which I imbibed in Oxford as a student.

At some point I realized that what all these views had in common was a Platonic ideal: in the first place that, as in the sciences, all genuine questions must have one true answer and one only, all the rest being necessarily errors; in the second place, that there must be a dependable path towards the discovery of these truths; in the third place, that the true answers, when found, must necessarily be compatible with one another and form a single whole, for one truth cannot be incompatible with another—that we knew *a priori*. This kind of omniscience was the solution of the cosmic jigsaw puzzle. In the case of morals, we could then conceive what the perfect life must be, founded as it would be on a correct understanding of the rules that governed that universe.

True, we might never get to this condition of perfect knowledge—we may be too feeble-witted, or too weak or corrupt or sinful, to achieve this. . . . But even if we could not ourselves reach these true answers, . . . the answers must exist—else the questions were not real. The answers must be known to someone. . . .

[Berlin goes on to describe his exposure to the idea that the "supreme values pursued by mankind" were not "necessarily compatible with one another," that "there are many different ends that men may seek and still be fully rational, fully men, capable of understanding each other and sympathizing and deriving light from each other."]

What is clear is that values can clash—that is why civilizations are incompatible. They can be incompatible between cultures, or groups in the same culture, or between you and me. You believe in always telling the truth, no matter what; I do not, because I believe that it can sometimes be too painful and too destructive. We can discuss each other's point of view, we can try to reach common ground, but in the end what you pursue may not be reconcilable with the ends to which I find that I have dedicated my life. . . .

Both liberty and equality are among the primary goals pursued by human beings through many centuries; but total liberty for wolves is death to the lambs, total liberty of the powerful, the gifted, is not compatible with the rights to a decent existence of the weak and the less gifted. An artist, in order to create a masterpiece, may lead a life which plunges his family into misery and squalor to which he is indifferent. We may condemn him and declare that the masterpiece should be sacrificed to human needs, or we may take his side—but both attitudes embody values which for some men or women are ultimate, and which are intelligible to us all if we have any sympathy or imagination or understanding of human beings. Equality may demand the restraint of the liberty of those who wish to dominate; liberty—without some modicum of which there is no choice and therefore no possibility of remaining human as we understand the word—may have to be curtailed in order to make room for social welfare, to feed the hungry, to clothe the naked, to shelter the homeless, to leave room for the liberty of others, to allow justice or fairness to be exercised.

. . . We are all aware of the agonizing alternatives in the recent past. Should a man resist a monstrous tyranny at all costs, at the expense of the lives of his parents or his children? Should children be tortured to extract information about dangerous traitors or criminals?

These collisions of values are of the essence of what they are and what we are. . . .

We are doomed to choose, and every choice may entail an irreparable loss. Happy are those . . . who have, by their own methods, arrived at clear and unshakable convictions about what to do and what to be that brook no possible doubt. I can only say that those who rest on such comfortable beds of dogma are victims of forms of self-induced myopia, blinkers that may make for contentment, but not for understanding of what it is to be human.

*****

If the old perennial belief in the possibility of realizing ultimate harmony is a fallacy, . . . if we allow that Great Goods can collide, that some of them cannot live together, even though others can—in short, that one cannot have everything, in principle as well as in practice—and if human creativity may depend upon a variety of mutually exclusive choices: then . . . how do we choose between possibilities? What and how much must we sacrifice to what? There is, it seems to me, no clear reply. But the collisions, even if they cannot be avoided, can be softened. Claims can be balanced, compromises can be reached: in concrete situations not every claim is of equal force—so much liberty and so much equality; so much for sharp moral condemnation, and so much for understanding a given human situation; so much for the full force of the law, and so much for the prerogative of mercy; for feeding the hungry, clothing the naked, healing the sick, sheltering the homeless. Priorities, never final and absolute, must be established.

The first public obligation is to avoid extremes of suffering. . . . We may take the risk of drastic action, in personal life or in public policy, but we must always be aware, never forget, that we may be mistaken, that certainty about the effect of such measures invariably leads to avoidable suffering of the innocent. So we must engage in what are called trade-offs—rules, values, principles must yield to each other in varying degrees in specific situations. . . . The best that can be done, as a general rule, is to maintain a precarious equilibrium that will prevent the occurrence of desperate situations, of intolerable choices—that is the first requirement for a decent society. . . . A certain humility in these matters is very necessary.

This may seem a very flat answer, not the kind of thing that the idealistic young would wish, if need be, to fight and suffer for, in the cause of a new and nobler society. And, of course, we must not dramatize the incompatibility of values—there is a great deal of broad agreement among people in different societies over long stretches of time about what is right and wrong, good and evil. Of course traditions, outlooks, attitudes may legitimately differ. . . .

But, in the end, it is not a matter of purely subjective judgement: it is dictated by the forms of life of the society to which one belongs, a society among other societies, with values held in common, whether or not they are in conflict, by the majority of mankind throughout recorded history. There are, if not universal values, at any rate a minimum without which societies could scarcely survive. Few today would wish to defend slavery or ritual murder or Nazi gas chambers or the torture of human beings for the sake of pleasure or profit or even political good—or the duty of children to denounce their parents, which the French and Russian revolutions demanded, or mindless killing. There is no justification for compromise on this. But on the other hand, the search for perfection does seem to me a recipe for bloodshed, no better even if it is demanded by the sincerest of idealists, the purest of heart. No more rigorous moralist than Immanuel Kant has ever lived, but even he said, in a moment of illumination, "Out of the crooked timber of humanity no straight thing was ever made." To force people into the neat uniforms demanded by dogmatically believed-in schemes is almost always the road to inhumanity. . . .

Of course social or political collisions will take place; the mere conflict of positive values alone makes this unavoidable. Yet they can, I believe, be minimized by promoting and preserving an uneasy equilibrium, which is constantly threatened and in constant need of repair—that alone, I repeat, is the precondition for decent societies and morally acceptable behavior, otherwise we are bound to lose our way. A little dull as a solution, you will say? Not the stuff of which calls to heroic action by inspired leaders are made? Yet if there is some truth in this view, perhaps that is sufficient.

ⲧⲧⲧ

David Heyd,[4] *Toleration: An Elusive Virtue*
(1996, 4–5, 10–12, 14–15)

[Heyd begins by pointing out that tolerance is an elusive concept because it rests between notions of moral "absolutism"—disagreements that should not be tolerated (e.g., torturing the innocent)—and moral indifference—disagreements that are easily accepted because they implicate no moral question (e.g., holiday celebrations). As he explains:]

There are, on the one hand, cases in which the firm commitment to a moral truth restricts the scope of application of the concept of toleration. For instance, any mode of restraint in the attitude to anti-Turkish incitement by German skinheads would hardly be considered "tolerance," because the object of the restraint is patently immoral. In other words, some actions are straightforwardly "intolerable," and any conciliatory attitude toward them could at best be based on *pragmatic* considerations (of fear or the need for compromise), but never on the idea of tolerance. On the other hand, there are cases in which the belief in moral pluralism calls for the acceptance of ways of life (or beliefs) different from my own, either because I acknowledge their legitimacy or because I simply do not care about them. Refraining from a hostile reaction to members of other religions, or from persecuting homosexuals, is accordingly hardly to be considered as displaying tolerance under contemporary pluralist conceptions.

So it seems that the idea of toleration has undergone a gradual process of compression between the demand not to tolerate the immoral (absolutism) and the requirement to accept the legitimacy of the morally different (pluralism). On the theoretical level, this means that toleration in the strict sense must be clearly distinguished from pragmatic compromise with the otherwise "intolerable" as well as from moral indifference. That is to say, the concept of toleration must be narrowed down in its philosophical use so as to refer strictly to cases in which restraint in the response to another's belief or action is based on some specifically *moral* grounds (thus excluding both compromise and indifference). But what are the typical examples for such a narrowed-down idea of toleration?

The history of the idea of tolerance provides us with good examples, from religious toleration in Locke to the modern toleration of minorities, such as Jews, African Americans, homosexuals, and so on. But these are typically historically outdated examples, because today we would expect people to abstain from hostile behavior toward all these groups, not as a matter of toleration but as a matter of the rights of others or the recognition of the value of their ways of life, or because it is simply "none of our business" to interfere with the beliefs and most of the actions of other human beings.

Classical liberalism, such as Locke's or Mill's, rested on the principle of tolerance more than does today's form of liberalism, which is closer to skeptical pluralism. Locke's argument for tolerance was based on the counterproductiveness of

---

[4] Professor Heyd is the editor of this book and the author of its Introduction, from which the excerpt in the text is taken.

the compulsion of religious beliefs; Mill's was based on the value of personal autonomy. The shift from these views to the modern conception, which rests on easy acceptance of the heterogeneity of values and ways of life, pushes the concept of tolerance dangerously close to that of indifference. And even if this moral
development is welcomed by the moral pluralist, it must be clear that much of the
original intrinsic value of tolerance is put under threat.

*****

The distinction between tolerance and indifference is an important constituent
in any theoretical attempt to delineate the contours of the former. . . . In seven-
teenth-century England, people's religious practices were hardly treated as lying
beyond the legitimate concern of their fellow citizens. In nineteenth-century England, people were rarely indifferent to their neighbors' sexual practices. But in pre-
sent-day England, most people do not feel very strongly about either the religious
faith or the sexual preferences of others. One could even generalize and say that
the scope of indifference is growing in the field of value judgment, and that liberalism today means less the toleration of other ways of life than the cool acceptance
of the very plurality and heterogeneity of lifestyles. If that is the case, toleration
might prove in the future to have been "an interim value," that is, an attitude that
characterized political morality between the age of absolutism, in which every deviation from the only truth was suppressed, and the age of pluralism, in which nothing
is considered a deviation.

*****

[The concept of toleration includes] the condition that its object be not only
thought to be morally wrong, but *justifiably* thought so. The homophobe's restraint
toward homosexual behavior cannot, accordingly, be defined as a case of toleration, because there are no good reasons to object to the behavior in the first place.
The same applies to restraint in interracial relations and attitudes. . . . This leaves
only a narrow space for toleration, namely, the scope of beliefs and actions justifiably disapproved of yet not to the event of being "intolerable."

*****

[T]he indeterminacy of the concept of toleration is due to its being "com-
pressed" between two spheres: phenomena that by no means should be tolerated
(like cruelty and murder) and phenomena that should not be objected to in the first
place (like gender or racial identity). The remaining sphere left for this narrow (but
morally valuable) concept of tolerance consists of beliefs and actions that are justifiably (and maybe morally) disapproved of and yet are said to be immune from negative interference. The duality of conflicting reasons for rejecting and accepting certain beliefs and actions creates the so-called paradox of toleration, which is
obviously more pointed in the case of morally objectionable phenomena. . . .

*****

The conception I wish to outline can be called "perceptual." It treats toleration
as involving a perceptual shift: from beliefs to the subject holding them, or from actions to their agent. . . .

The essential element in this perceptual shift might be called "personalization."
When opinions and beliefs, actions and practices, are judged on their merit, they
are considered impersonally, that is, in abstraction from the subjects holding,
choosing, or acting on them. Opinions and practices can be judged for their validity, truth, and value irrespective of the way they have been adopted, chosen, and

followed. But opinions and actions do not float subjectless in the air; they can also be viewed as held with integrity, chosen freely, or followed authentically. This personal dimension introduces a categorically different kind of judgment, to which tolerance belongs. The intimate relation as well as the distinction between beliefs and believers, actions and agents, has been the cornerstone of all theories of toleration from Locke, through Kant and Mill, to Rawls, Dworkin, and Raz.

Some contexts typically require an impersonal judgment of beliefs and practices, that is, in abstraction from the person holding them. Obvious examples are the evaluation of scientific beliefs or of legal rules. In these contexts, ad hominem considerations are rightly thought of as fallacies. But in the sphere of interpersonal relations, particularly when actual interference in another's life is considered, the personal index of beliefs and actions becomes highly relevant; it is never strictly with beliefs or actions that we are interfering, but with individuals and their lives. . . .

I call toleration a perceptual virtue, because it involves a shift of attention rather than an overall judgment. Tolerant people overcome the drive to interfere in the life of another not because they come to believe that the reasons for restraint are weightier than the reasons for disapproval, but because the attention is shifted from the object of disapproval to the humanity or the moral standing of the subject before them. . . .

▼▼▼▼▼

How can we bring up children to become tolerant of others without weakening their commitment to their cherished beliefs and preferences? How can we expect people to grow up to have a sharply defined political or religious profile, a well-defined aesthetic and moral personality, and yet be tolerant of incompatible sets of beliefs and values? If we adopt the perceptual model, this difficulty looks slightly less menacing. Training children to look at people without regard to some of their convictions and behavior might not be easy, but it is fully compatible with implanting strong personal convictions and principles. . . .

[T]he perceptual view frees tolerance from its dependence on relativism and multiculturalism. Toleration of the practices and beliefs of other peoples and cultures involves recognizing the intrinsic value of the human beings who are committed to certain cognitive systems or who autonomously choose and follow certain systems of rules and values. It does not require any weakening of certainty, confidence, or commitment to our own beliefs and values.

Part 4

The Pedagogy of Moral Education

Chapter 8

Pedagogical Preferences and Their Sources

 ## At School

Children do not stand and wait while schools figure out best practices for instructing them. Remember Tony from Chapter 2, the boy whom classmates considered "weird" because with his cap, stained clothes, and muddy shoes he looked more farmer than suburbanite? The boy who habitually withdrew with a stack of books into a corner of the room? Well, those days have vanished.

Under Maria's persistent gentle prodding, Tony has begun to "socialize"—but with a vengeance. A month ago, trying to ingratiate himself with a couple of students, he began to pass notes to them during class, not just now and then but on a regular basis. Then, when confronted by Maria, he denied having done so. The bald denial got to Maria more than the note passing, which was annoying enough. She was at her wit's end with his constant lying, but worse than the notes and lies were the smirks and laughing-eyed looks he'd toss the other children while he lied, saying in effect: "We're in control now, she can't stop us, she can't touch us," a real we-against-her mentality. Yet, except to confiscate the notes without reading them, Maria largely ignored the disruption, on the assumption that the children would lose interest in Tony's antics. Given the nascent spirit of cooperation and good will in the class, she thought she could count on her students to reject these disruptive forays. Better that they give Tony the corrective "feedback" than that she prematurely interrupt a natural piece of social learning. At first her approach worked; the kids were increasingly uninterested in Tony's notes and the frequency of their appearance steadily declined.

After a few days, however, not getting the amused attention he sought, Tony upped the ante. One morning, presumably inadvertently, he let out a loud burp that set off a paroxysm of giggles in the class. Pleased by the reaction, Tony began manufacturing burps at ever-shorter interludes. Sometimes he would go over to another child and burp in his face. It was worth annoying the few—and several children were obviously disgusted with this prank— to tickle the fancy of many. Maria's instinct was still to ignore Tony to the extent possible. She reasoned that serious discipline would only rally his support and heighten the children's we-against-you sentiment that Tony had ignited. But she was concerned about the acceleration of attention-seeking and she no longer could count on the children as allies. So she tried a light-handed use of authority. Going up to him in front of his classmates she said after a loud burp, "I know, Tony, you think that what you're doing is pretty neat, but save it for after school please; for obvious reasons, it's not permitted during class time. You need to cut it out now."

No response from Tony. After the next series of burps, Maria took him into the hall for a talk. "Tony, let's say you were teaching this class. Would you let a child burp?"

"Dunno."

"I think you do know, Tony. It's obvious to us both that I can't teach when the children are laughing at you, right?"

"Guess so."

"And maybe that's what you want—me not to teach and you to get the kids' attention."

Silence from Tony.

"OK, Tony, I see you don't want to talk. If you don't stop, Tony, I'll have to send you to the principal's office."

He didn't stop, she did send him. Whatever scolding was meted out by Helter, however, made no impression. In fact, Tony's repertoire of antics grew. He got bolder, even as Maria began giving him demerits. Added to the burping were incidents of farting and saliva bubble-making. Increasingly, too, he seemed to be getting his jollies from mocking Maria. For example, he drew funny faces on the blackboard before class and on his jacket. She was pretty sure the portraits were caricatures of herself. Still the kids said nothing to Tony. They were now clearly enjoying both his outlandish behavior and his willful disobedience. Maria realized that she needed to stop it once and for all.

She spoke briefly to the entire class: "I understand that some of you think Tony is funny. Let's talk about why he is funny to you and not funny to me." She had hoped they would note that farting and burping, like all bathroom humor, is not intrinsically amusing but becomes so because of its forbiddenness in the classroom context, and that it is this very inappropriateness, the breaking of social inhibitions, that makes it disrespectful to her as proprietor of the classroom. But the children couldn't (or wouldn't) answer except to say Tony was just obviously funny and then giggle some more in the telling. Failing to get any significant student participation, Maria simply told the children to attend to the class activities, not to Tony, but she had scant expectation of significant compliance.

So what next? After years of being a misfit he was reaching out; he was an outsider wanting to be an insider. Given his initial isolation, one could look at this behavior, despite its inappropriateness, as a significant bit of progress. The class clown routine was Tony's way, and a not uncommon way, to affiliate with his peers. Tony was like a five-year-old trying to make social points by clumsily showing off. ("My Dad is the strongest man in the world.") Maria had conjectured that with time these infantile bids would yield to more age-fitting behaviors. But while Tony was making halting efforts to socialize, the class was becoming desocialized. They were abandoning the hard-won courtesies that had lately characterized their relationships. With the other children collaborating and abetting Tony, this now had become a whole-class problem.

It was largely the disrespect that got to Maria. She had been performing somersaults for Tony because he, more than most others, triggered her sympathy. She knew what it was like to be a loner, to be rejected by your peers, to be discounted. She had been a bookish, brainy nerd for years and it had cost her psyche plenty. Sensitive to Tony's unhappiness, Maria had spent much "free" time devising strategies that might ease him into his peer group—pairing him off with a suitable buddy for various class assignments, featuring him in "sharing" time by requesting his description of the birth of a calf, asking him to be the class co-photographer and chronicle their field trips, even preparing a unit on power tools so that Tony could look "cool" explaining how they were used on a farm. Now he was turning on her. She felt unsuccessful, unappreciated, scorned.

As Maria mused over next moves, Tony brought events to a climax. It started out as just another school day of burps and farts until suddenly, when Maria went to the board to write down some arithmetic problems, the class broke out into a hilarious bout of laughter. The indignity of being the clueless object of this raucous outbreak pushed Maria over the edge: "For God's sake," she bellowed, smashing the chalk onto the floor, "what is going on here?" The children were startled and chagrined. One of the girls blurted out, "It's your skirt, Ms. Laszlo; there's a lot of white stuff on the back of it." Sure enough, her rear was covered white. She glanced at her desk and saw that the chair, where she just had been sitting, was generously dusted with powder. She glared at Tony: "So this is your idea of a good joke?" Silence. "Are you, or are you not, going to admit to doing this, Tony?" No response. "OK class, right now you are going to tell me. Was it Tony?" After a pause, the girl who had pointed out the powder on Maria's skirt shyly nodded affirmatively.

Under the circumstances, it was sufficient evidence. "Tony, come up here." No movement. Maria stalked over to his chair, grabbed his arm, and shoved him onto her powdered desk chair. Then she lifted him up, turned his backside to the class, and said, "Good, now you look like me." Returning him to the chalky chair she continued, "You'll sit here until recess. Don't move, don't grin, don't open your mouth. Then, at recess, you'll clean this chair spotless and every other chair in the room. What you don't finish today, you'll complete tomorrow. As for the rest of you," Maria turned to the class, "you may have your recess and then we are going to talk this matter out once and for all, and put an end to it. Right now you will all sit absolutely still and absolutely silent while I get Tony the sponges and cleaning equipment he'll need."

She stalked out, adrenaline flowing, heart racing, yet knowing no one in that class would disobey her orders—not this time. When she returned silence reigned; the kids had never looked so meek or intimidated. On her command they did the arithmetic problems faster and with more concentration than she had ever witnessed. A fleeting thought: Was there something to this power-wielding, as much as it went against her grain?

When the recess bell rang, Tony, without a reminder, began his clean-up. He was good at this! Clearly a child used to cleaning. Not just wiping but scrubbing. As he worked hard first on her chair, then systematically on the others, Maria felt her old sympathy beginning to percolate and with it regret for her actions.

Anxious to undo her assault on Tony, Maria tried another tack. "Tony, I know that not having friends in the class has really bothered you a lot. You've tried to get the kids to like you by being funny, but you just forgot that I have feelings and get hurt too. Remember how you didn't like it when the boys made fun of your clothing and hat? That hurt you. Well, when you make fun of me, drawing those chalk caricatures and now the practical joke with the powder, that hurts me—a lot. Do you understand, Tony?"

"Guess so."

"I bet you thought of how the other kids would laugh at the powder on the rear of my skirt, but did you think of how it might really upset me, even make me cry?"

"Cry? No, I didn't think of that."

The children returned from recess and Maria, more confident than before, settled them down for a talk. She started by asking them what a parent would do if one child in the family, assigned to set the table, deliberately omitted the forks and then his sister, amused by the omission, got a bunch of forks and put them on the chairs instead of the table. Maria's students were in agreement; parents would find both kids at fault. Now, Maria hypothesized, supposing the sister had merely laughed and egged on her brother to keep setting places without forks. Most of the students still thought that the sister should get punished (accessory to the crime argument). Finally, Maria asked, what might the sister do that would contribute to a positive family dinnertime.

One suggested, "The sister should tell on her brother. He's goofing off."

"No," another disagreed, "it's wrong to be a tattler. She should just go get the forks herself and put them on the table where they belong."

"But that wouldn't be fair," a third jumped in. "It's not her day to set the table. It's her brother's day and he has to do it. Otherwise she is doing more than her share."

"OK, you're right," admitted the second. "How about the sister talks to the brother and tells him to stop being stupid? Doesn't he know they won't be able to eat until the table is set right and he's just making everyone suffer by being so goofy? That way there is no tattling and the brother still has to do the work 'cause it's his turn."

It went on. Maria was pleased. Now she could use this domestic scenario to help the children make the appropriate translation to Tony and his shenanigans.

A familiar rat-a-tat-tat on her classroom door was followed by the good-natured face of Hardie with a bag of delicious smelling popcorn in hand. "Have you taken up permanent residence in this room, Maria?"

"Lost in thought, Hardie. No, not composing the great American novel, just sorting through a rough day. Sit down if you have the time and save yourself a long evening telephone call."

"Battle-fatigued Hardie, ever ready to serve and take up your cudgels."

"No cudgels this time, Hardie, but definitely much to discuss with you."

Maria described the Tony-related events in full detail, including her guilt for having disparaged Tony in front of his peers. Would he venture forth to make friends again or give up on his obvious wish to give and receive friendship? What a disaster if that was the result of her temper!

Hardie interrupted her reflections. "Maria, how very different we still are in how we think about children and work with them. I applaud the acts that you regret; I regret the acts that you approve. The punishment of Tony was entirely appropriate. You had tried more modest means—talking to him, sending him to Helter, even detentions. Given his nasty little prank, losing your temper, embarrassing him, making him sweat—all that was called for. My goodness, he was begging you to break into his escalating mischief. The mistake, as I see it, was in not clamping down sooner. In my class the first note passed would have been the last one. And as for your anger, well, it's not something I'd recommend as a daily prescription, but it's good for kids to see you're made of flesh and blood, just like them, that you're not some mechanical automaton—all programmed responses and no feeling.

"But, forgive me, I don't approve of all the talking that you so value. Your effort to get to the bottom of behavior—why the kids find Tony funny while you don't, what Tony is trying to accomplish with his foolishness, whether or not this is the child's or group's responsibility—seems to me misguided. Maria, we are not in the "talking cure" business. We are educators, not therapists. Besides, you can't expect nine- and ten-year-old children to understand the motives of their behavior and then, based on their insights, to change. Would we even expect that of one another?"

"Hardie, you sure are predictable. Isn't this the same conversation we've had since the fall? You think I'm hopelessly naive and I think you seriously underestimate children's capacities. Here I had thought, maybe merely hoped, that our differences were narrowing."

"Not hopelessly naive," objected Hardie, "just a little naive."

"Well, suppose we go over the Tony issues one more time and see just where we disagree," Maria suggested.

"You need to understand," she continued, "that I'm an unregenerate believer in the cooperative "constructivist" model of education. That means a lot of things: First, I am loathe to impose rules based on the "because-I-say-so" rationale. Most rules should arise from class experiences and make sense to the children. I'd go further and not accept a "because-the-school-says-so" or "because-the-class-requires-it" rationale for rules. Children need to have input into the rules that oblige them if they are to genuinely accept them.

"Second, I do not think a bit, OK a good bit, of unruliness is a very high price to pay for the opportunity to work out social and moral issues collectively. I know it looks bad to see a child passing notes, worse to see him burping, but wouldn't it have been great if the kids had turned Tony's antics off, better yet if they had figured out a way to include him as a peer so that he didn't have to resort to clowning? Instead I forced obedience by shaming him. Now what does that accomplish except a deflated sense of self and the possible abandonment of any desire to affiliate? I want the children to become moral agents, not obedient rule-followers. That objective can be accomplished only if the kids think and talk about the motives behind (and fallout from) Tony-like incidents.

"Also, Hardie, so often behavioral problems are collective, not individual. Tony would not have passed the notes had there been no receiver for them. He would not have mocked me if the students had been outraged. We've got a ways to go; they disappointed me a lot, but Rome wasn't built in a day, as they say. I know, Hardie, you look narrowly at the behavior while I try to look at the conditions that propelled the behavior."

Hardie, straining with impatience, registered his protest: "Hey, Maria, not so fast. Let me describe my own thinking."

"One last word, Hardie, and the floor is yours. I do, unlike you, think talking is critical. It is by talking about what's fair that children become fair, care about fairness. I should think at least some of the kids were genuinely outraged, at least by the powder incident, but were afraid to speak out. If we don't talk these things over as a group, how can we help children develop a conscience, a conscience that will not permit them to be a bystander when others are humiliated? Yes, matters went badly today, but it wasn't a totally lost learning opportunity. Except, of course, for my eruption. Punitiveness, shaming a child—there's no growth to be had from that.

"Maria, you have changed. I'm impressed. That was a powerful defense of a reasonable position. Not naive, but maybe wrong on your pedagogy. Let me try to explain. We're not far apart in our goals. I also want children to be considerate of their teachers and one another and I agree that respect doesn't mean blind obedience to imposed rules, though children should favor adult judgments as the default position. And, like you, I want children to be skilled analysts of a moral situation, to figure out the just solution and to care a lot about pursuing it. Moral anesthesia may be our greatest social problem. Like you, I want children to have the guts to resist group pressure and speak out against wrongdoing.

"Where we part company is on how to reach those ends. I am absolutely convinced that "talking through" misbehavior or, as you might further insist, talking about what behaviors constitute misbehavior, is not a useful tool to accomplish our shared goals. Children acquire virtues by experiencing rightful conduct. That means living in an ordered classroom with reasonable rules regularly enforced. We adults provide a model of fairness for them; they do not construct the model. They are just not capable of doing that. OK, I trust them less than you. The little Tonys of the world always keep accelerating their antics because they speak for the rebellious spirit of their classmates. The more outrageous they are, the more they successfully defy authority, the more the other children enjoy it. True, a few kids may be offended on your behalf (not on behalf of some moral system they've constructed), but I would never rely on that sentiment, particularly when it is a group, not a single child, you are trying to influence. Groups have a particularly nasty way of seizing onto and relishing destructive behavior. Tony acts out his classmates' forbidden instinctual resistance to being contained, to being civilized.

"Part of a fair, ordered classroom is making sure that each child is well informed of the limits within which he must operate. When he tests the limits, as he surely will, there have to be appropriate consequences. Moderate punishment—I like to think of it as a corrective experience—will inhibit him when temptation arises again. Once he pays the price for wrongdoing, he is forgiven, a new equilibrium has been established. That's justice. Talking over the infraction may not be inappropriate, but it's icing on the cake. The child will never have the sense of expiation and rightful restoration of a moral order if he is simply asked what went wrong and what should be done.

"I mean, think of it! One kid wallops another. You ask him, what made you do it, while the victim goes off to the hospital in an ambulance? That route just invites the perpetrator to rationalize, to disregard the interests of others, to lie in the service of himself. I agree that you become just by experiencing justice, but justice is not an infraction followed by a series of probing questions about whys and wherefores.

"What goes for correcting Tony goes for the group. I wouldn't have them dig into familiar domestic activities and extract from them appropriate norms for a well-functioning classroom. I'd tell (not ask) them: As a group we must respect the teacher and each other. I'd elaborate on what respect means, and disrespect, too. Then, having supplied the frame, I'd have a group discussion on the topic—ask them to write an essay giving examples, maybe post the best ones, and explain why they were the best. Finally, and only after all the parameters of respect and disrespect were clear, I'd invite them to look at how respect gets played out in families."

Hardie couldn't seem to stop. He paused awkwardly, and got Maria's nod to finish.

"Look, Maria, I understand your fear that teachers impose lots of arbitrary rules signifying nothing of moral importance. They do. I understand how that coerciveness threatens the development of a true moral identity in children.

We rule-makers must be very careful that we select for worthwhileness, for the good of all, according to principles of justice and benevolence. Children should understand the order to which they must submit; we want their buy-in. But, Maria, they must habituate to the rules, they must feel the pinch of inhibiting themselves, feel the natural deprivation in exercising control, before they responsibly can invent and impose a moral code on themselves and their classmates."

The two friends looked at each other with appreciative smiles, silently acknowledging their mutual wish for common ground and their shared earnestness about this subject. Given that understanding, the still considerable disagreement between them mattered less than it once had.

"Maybe we're getting there, Hardie," sighed a weary Maria, "and maybe we'll go to our graves with different opinions. Either way, thanks for hanging out with me."

"Maria, we will go to our graves with different opinions because there is no completely right solution. If it weren't so, I would have missed one of the liveliest conversations I've had since I became a teacher."

At the University

The practical import of Maria's and Hardie's earlier rhetorical skirmishes is now manifest. Hardie believes that Maria blundered in not stopping Tony when he first signaled his intention to sabotage classroom decorum. She should have known that matters would only escalate, for Tony obviously relished the prospect of seriously disrupting the classroom. Moreover, having intervened much too late, Maria should not have compounded her surrender of authority by attempting to engage Tony in peer-like conversation and then turning to other children for aid in redirecting Tony's behavior.

Maria disagrees. She is repentant only for losing her temper; Hardie's assertion of superior power to enforce child obedience is repugnant to her. While force might have curbed the act (though at best only temporarily), it would have further alienated Tony and thwarted his minimal social progress to date, progress that in her view is critical for his future moral growth. Maria is committed to long-term goals with Tony: to bring him into the classroom society, to help him feel a valued stakeholder in a collaborative community. For that she is willing to put up with what to Hardie is simply unacceptable insolence.

How do we judge the choices of these two conscientious people? Which one has their teaching right? To what extent may both be right? One might respond that there is no judgment to be cast here. Each teacher probably acted out of native temperament, and did not exercise real choice—or each acted as his or her conscience directed, out of a common goal (for Tony to become a responsible and respectful member of the community). In any event, why cast judgment?

Though this position has some merit, we disagree with the conclusion that there is therefore nothing worth mulling over. Conscientiousness, while necessary in a teacher, is insufficient, for the grounds of conscience must be subjected to critical judgment. Teachers can and do influence what we become, especially if there is consistency of message and method across a school system. Moreover, while personality will likely bias the choices one makes—Maria is by nature soft-hearted and psychologically minded, Hardie firm and action-oriented—each teacher could, and if convinced probably would, lean against that inclination and, in at least some cases, select the opposing option.

More fundamentally, it is important to recognize that, although a divergence of means may at times appear to be merely incidental to a commonality of ends when they are stated in general terms, the divergence may reflect differences in the more specific articulation of hoped-for ends. Hardie and Maria, for example, may share a commitment to the end that Tony "become a responsible and respectful member of the community," but as each gives specific content to that outcome divergences would likely appear. An example is two teachers who uphold the value of aiding children to become "excellent students," although one has in mind breadth of subject-matter knowledge and another mastery of the close reading of texts or enhancement of independent thinking.

Before making *our* judgments of the teachers, however, it is important to appreciate the premises of *their* judgments. In what follows we examine the teachers' disagreements over how to "read" Tony's morality, for we believe that these differing readings are the foundation of their differing pedagogic responses. Specifically—and here we play out distinctions developed in preceding chapters—we examine relevant differences between these teachers in several areas:

1. their *attribution of moral significance* to actions;
2. their *moral priorities;*
3. their conceptions regarding the *moral nature of children.*

We also consider contrasting traditions of

4. *learning and teaching,* and of
5. *moral development* (emotion, cognition, and moral identity), which give additional ballast to their pedagogical preferences.

Through this review we intend to illustrate how pedagogical positions are based on underlying moral and psychological convictions. If we are right about this, it is a mistake to judge a pedagogy without uncovering, articulating, and assessing its more fundamental worldviews.

INTERPRETING (MIS)CONDUCT

In *Habits of the Heart* (1996), Robert Bellah and his colleagues tell the story of the Puritan leader John Winthrop, first Governor of the Massachusetts Bay Colony, who, when informed that during an "especially long and hard winter" a poor miscreant was stealing from his woodpile, summoned the man and instructed him to take whatever amounts of wood he needed whenever he wished for the rest of the winter. "Thus, he said to his friends, did he effectively cure the man from stealing" (id., 29).

Just as removing the wood was no longer theft once permitted by its owner, so note-passing, even burping and farting, are moral offenses only if likely to be thought objectionable by those present. Maria, while upset and angered by Tony, and not disputing that his motive was to disrupt her class, is not willing (unlike Hardie) simply to condemn his antics as "sabotage," "insolence," or "insurrection." She has none of Hardie's moral outrage because, like Winthrop, who looked past the wrongfulness of an act to see a man pressed by hunger, Maria responds to her perception of Tony's motives, both his immediate ones—what he is trying to accomplish with his peers through these annoying behaviors—and, more essentially, his longer-term ones, the quality and content of his developmental progression and goals.

Despite her previous objections to virtue-education programs, such as those presented by Jan Bonham at their in-service training session (see Chapter 5), Maria is drawn to the virtue-ethic emphasis on the person, or the person-in-being—on who one *is* rather than what one *does*. Given such eyes, she is relatively indifferent to the note-passing (though less so to its sequelae). She regards the acts, or at least wants to regard them, not so much as a threat to her authority or an effort to embarrass her as a bid for attention. That the acts do deeply embarrass her, make her feel helpless and out of control, and give Tony undeserved notoriety, troubles Maria, but despite her explosive surge of anger she would prefer to respond to them simply as annoying distractions, which she can put aside.

Beneath the mischief-making, beneath what appear to be hostile, mocking acts, Maria sees a lonely boy deprived of healthy social experiences, who now, for the first time, is struggling to earn peer group status and friendship. Drawn to appraising motives instead of acts, Maria reacts to Tony primarily with compassion and understanding, seeking to place in the background her moral judgment and condemnation. Doing the wrong thing just does not have the same moral sting for her as for teachers who take primary account of, and demand accountability for, the acts students commit.

Out of this orientation emerges, as well, a fairly fluid notion of what *is* correct behavior, and a broad tolerance for deviance—again, more tolerance than we would find in one whose views of right and wrong were focused on acts. She can turn her head and disregard the note-passing, not define it as wrongful. She can ignore outspoken children, somewhat excessive noise, spontaneous outbursts, even burping. Maria wants children to enjoy maximum freedom and minimum restraint at school, for she views the class as an experimental laboratory where, through the press of social demands, children, encouraged to be themselves, can become better selves. She finds the usual school climate unnecessarily stuffy and too intolerant of "oddballs."

Maria sees her task in dealing with this difficult student primarily in relational terms. Attracted to oddballs, to lost souls, she wants to influence Tony's behavior by being what might be termed a "friendly presence" in his life at school. To be sure, she would hold out to him a standard of proper behavior toward another person and toward a teacher, but would do it in a manner that makes clear her regard for him as a person and her concern for his emotional and moral well-being. She is not content simply to see to it that he knows what behavioral change is expected of him and suffers whatever consequences are appropriate should his responses fall short. Realizing that she might fail to reach him, she acts, not in light of that knowledge, but rather in response to her more hopeful, optimistic core.

Maria is thus predisposed to sympathize with a philosophical stance responsive to the appeal of liberty, and is unwilling to sanctify (moralize) traditional constraints. She would find attractive the teaching of John Stuart Mill: "The despotism of custom," he protests, "is everywhere the standing hindrance to human advancement, being in unceasing antagonism to that disposition to aim at something better than customary, which is called, according to circumstances, the spirit of liberty, or that of progress or improvement" (Mill 1859/1993, 138).

Or, again:

> Eccentricity has always abounded when and where strength of character has abounded; and the amount of eccentricity in a society has generally been proportional to the amount of genius, mental vigor, and moral courage it contained.
>
> ▼▼▼▼▼
>
> The same mode of life is a healthy excitement to one, keeping all his faculties of action and enjoyment in their best order, while to another it is a distracting burthen, which suspends or crushes all internal life. . . .
> Why then should tolerance, as far as the public sentiment is concerned, extend only to tastes and modes of life which extort acquiescence by the multitude of their adherents?
> *(Id., 135, 136)*

Maria's response is thus grounded partly in her hospitality to behavioral experimentation, and her belief (with John Dewey) that morality develops through the particularity of experience. She allocates fewer behaviors to the clearly obligatory, categorizes fewer as universalizable independent of the situation and more as transient or conventional. (See Chapter 3 for a fuller discussion of these distinctions.) Rules of courtesy, of what is deemed considerate behavior, are prime examples of contextual evaluation. Even a practical joke, such as the chalk incident, may be understood as license a child would take only if trust and mutual regard are well-established, rather than merely an expression of lack of respect.

Maria also wants children to participate as a group in generating moral norms. It is in group situations that children collectively experiment with behaviors in a safe place, sort out together what matters to them a lot, a little, or not at all, what is tolerable and what is hurtful to their mutual well-being. The feedback they offer one another, and the norms they collaboratively generate, are for Maria the surest ways for children to establish a moral community and their own moral identity. Values generated by children will stick because they engage their will, their deep desires, their essential sense of self; values "imposed" do not because they engage only children's compliance with the will of others and are likely to fade when those others vanish.

For this process to work, however, the group must not be permitted to become simply another external force, imposed on the Tonys of the class. The teacher must be vigilant to see to it that the group in fact remains a safe place, that feedback not become ridicule or ostracism, and that collaboration not degenerate into imposition. The difficulty of guiding a group of children to work in this way does not impair Maria's belief that it is well worth the effort.

Hardie has an altogether different "read" on Tony. For him, conduct is central, motive incidental; adult judging is essential, understanding peripheral; and values express enduring truths rather than evolving truces worked out by a classroom group. Although Hardie also considers himself committed to virtues, virtues for him are made manifest in actions, not intentions. For the sake of Tony and for the sake of the moral order in which Tony lives—which extends far beyond the classroom—the teacher must sharply distinguish moral and immoral acts.

In making those distinctions, Hardie is (perhaps inadvertently) a Kantian. The categorical imperative asks: Were we to justify Tony's behavior—objectively disruptive, hurtful, and impudent as it is—would we be content if others in the class, in the broader society, were to act as he did? The answer is obvious. Just as lying cannot be universalized (one can lie only when there is a norm of truth-telling; lies are parasitic on honesty), so too does disorderly conduct fail as a norm (one can be allowed to be disorderly only when there is a norm of orderliness; disorder is parasitic on order).

Moreover, in his disrespectful and abusive behavior to Maria, Tony has violated the Kantian principle that each person is to be treated as an end, never as a means to the actor's ends. The notion that Tony's violation of Maria (the chalk incident) can be overlooked because it is premised on an understandable motive—to establish a closer relationship with his classmates—is, for Hardie, an appalling, "ends justify the means" argument. He finds deliberate mistreatment of one person by another flatly inexcusable.

To judge the deed, however, is not to act without compassion. On the contrary, Hardie believes, it is the overly permissive, "let's try to understand you" orientation that lacks compassion, for we *become* our deeds; it is our deeds that form us. If Tony, controlled by an adult authority holding the line, does the right thing frequently enough, he will find a gratification in righteous behavior that is not available through the reactions of other children or talking things over. Doing right will become habitual.

Hardie would find his (literary) hero in George Eliot's *Adam Bede* (1859/1985). Adam is a man of infinite fortitude, exacting rectitude, and a rigorous sense of duty—to skilled and honest work, to family, to burdensome responsibilities and commitments. He does not let analysis of motives or consequences deflect the demands of duty.

> "Good come out of it!" said Adam, passionately. "That doesn't alter th' evil: *her* ruin can't be undone. I hate that talk o' people, as if there was a way o' making amends for everything. . . . When a man's spoiled his fellow-creatur's life, he's no right to comfort himself with thinking good may come out of it: Somebody else's good doesn't alter her shame and misery."
> *(Id., 459) (emphasis in original)*

Mindful of just how self-serving reflection after the deed can be, George Eliot observes:

> The action which before commission has been seen with that blended common-sense and fresh untarnished feeling which is the healthy eye of the soul, is looked at afterwards with the lens of apologetic ingenuity, through which all things that men call beautiful and ugly are seen to be made up of textures very much alike.
> *(Id., 315)*

Hardie also finds no contradiction between punishment and compassion. Tony, obedient to the strictures of a moral community, enjoys the privileges of membership; disobedient, he is punished, pays his dues, and is readmitted. When a child understands the moral point of punishment rather than seeing it purely as coercion, "being punished for wrongdoing will seem like having the existence of a moral order of things, and of one's place in it, confirmed" (Wilson 1971, 116). Hardie's endorsement of punishment echoes a theme eloquently expressed by Simone Weil (in an essay quoted at greater length at p. 141 in Chapter 5):

> Punishment is a vital need of the human soul. . . . Just as the only way of showing respect for somebody suffering from hunger is to give him something to eat, so the only way of showing respect for somebody who has placed himself outside the law is to reinstate him inside the law by subjecting him to the punishment ordained by the law.
>
> ▼▼▼▼▼
>
> Punishment must . . . not only wipe out the stigma of the crime, but must be regarded as a supplementary form of education, compelling a higher devotion to the public good.
> *(Weil 1986, 102–103)*

While Hardie would prefer that Tony respond to punishment by learning to "fly straight," rather than continuing to pay the price of incorrigibility, unlike Maria he does not find that being a teacher warrants his having an emotional stake in Tony's choosing the first rather than the second path. In this stance, he is supported by a less optimistic sense than Maria has of what is possible in a teacher–student relation.

Hardie would certainly not turn to the group, Tony's classmates, to make and bring home to him moral judgments about his behavior. Values, being universal, need not be freshly minted by young children, whether individually or collectively. Group-generated or -reinforced norms have utility in some contexts—e.g., to rally support for established values, to infuse them with spirit, energy, and loyalty—but to extend their authority further is counterproductive at best. A group of children is especially unlikely to impose discipline on itself, to promote the virtues of temperance, humility, fortitude, or prudence. Indeed, it is at least as likely that groups operating mostly under their own authority will turn in very wrongful directions. Collective norms of "coolness" may include taunting the weak, cheating, stealing, lying, truancy, and the like. The chillingly murderous morality of the freely self-governing boys in *Lord of the Flies* may simply be gripping fiction, but its lesson commands sober attention.

Group norms should not arise from an autonomous freestanding collectivity but from the larger society. When a child identifies with a group committed to meritorious causes, when aroused by vital social purposes, his spirit will be justifiably uplifted. Consider this account many years later of childhood participation in joint patriotic enterprises during World War II:

> Shortly after Japanese planes bombed Pearl Harbor, plunging the United States into World War II, Ray Doyle of Philadelphia enlisted in his country's defense—as a can-smasher. It was important work for a five-year-old. "We collected tin cans and stamped them—crushed 'em, flattened 'em—and piled them up in the local air-raid warden's garage. . . . We were told that we were helping to build weapons."
>
> All over America, from 1941 to 1945, kids contributed to the war effort. They gathered and bundled newspapers. They carried kitchen grease to the butcher shop to be turned into glycerin for gunpowder. They saved their pennies to buy war savings stamps at school. . . . Looking back participants remember feeling that they were "members of a special group, a special generation."
> (Infield 1996, 116–117)

For Hardie and others like-minded, the challenge is to inspire groups with worthy goals (hopefully, not dependent on wartime spirit), having the power to stir the energy, excitement, mutuality, and joy of group effort.

There is, however, more to Hardie's and Maria's differing pedagogic impulses than their interpretations of Tony's act. The discrepant values most cherished by each teacher, what we will term their *moral priorities*, also fuel their pedagogical controversies.

ARTICULATING MORAL PRIORITIES

Hardie is attracted to the "hard" virtues: diligence, hard work, obedience, self-denial, and fortitude. Raised from childhood on the teachings of Benjamin

Franklin, he often posts for students lists of the qualities that patriot valued: temperance, silence, order, resolution, frugality, industry, sincerity, justice, moderation, cleanliness, tranquility, chastity, humility (Franklin 1963, 90–91). Maxims such as these from Franklin's *Poor Richard's Almanac* are as relevant to Hardie today as to eighteenth-century Americans:

> "He that cannot obey cannot command."
>
> "Great good nature, without prudence, is a great misfortune. . . . "
>
> "Blessed is he that expects nothing, for he shall never be disappointed. . . . "
>
> "'Tis easier to suppress the first desire than to satisfy all that follow it."
>
> "Let no pleasure tempt thee, no profit allure thee, no ambition corrupt thee, no example sway thee, no persuasion move thee, to do anything which thou knowest to be evil. . . . "
>
> "Nothing brings more pain than too much pleasure; nothing more bondage than too much liberty."
>
> *(Id., 194–197)*

These stern and dour admonitions are not for Maria. She is attracted to the "soft" virtues, arising from our attachments to one another, which today are often summed up as the virtue of "caring." The softer virtues, notes the contemporary English philosopher David Carr, include such "other-regarding" qualities as "unselfishness, considerateness, sympathy, benevolence, kindness, generosity, courtesy, respect, charity and possibly patience and tolerance, . . . modesty and humility" (Carr 1991, 200). What makes these virtues "soft" is that they tap the natural desire for affiliation.

The preferred loyalties of our teachers go a long way towards explaining their pedagogical strategies. To develop a caring ethic, Tony must be attached to his teacher so that he can dare to attach himself to others. Maria, through her own caring, gives him the requisite ego-stamina to face social rejection. Recall our first encounter with Maria (Chapter 2, p. 10) when she proclaimed to Jan Bonham, "I'm going to be kind and caring towards the children, provide a good model, and expect them, with occasional reminders from me, to be kind to one another." This remains her credo. She was then, and continues to be, a relation-oriented virtue ethicist of the Nel Noddings persuasion (see p. 72 in Chapter 3). And she is still convinced that strict discipline, punishment, repression, adult laying-on of duties and obligations, inhibit the growth of a natural, joyful, committed, caring community.

Such qualities as frugality and prudence have been termed the "little virtues" by Philip Hallie.[1] The "little virtues" serve our self-interest. "They protect our hides—that is their main function" and a minimally admirable one,

---

[1] Although originally meant as the quality of good judgment—Aristotle's "practical wisdom"— today prudence often has the meaning of self-protection, reluctance to risk. See the discussion at p. 163 in Chapter 6.

in his judgment. "If all we do for our children is pound into their heads reasons for protecting their own hides, their [acquired] nature will be as wide as the confines of their own self-seeking skins." Vastly superior, to Hallie, are the "great virtues" of compassion and generosity which, though antithetical to cautious self-interest and "often impractical," are those virtues of the heart that make for true altruists (Hallie 1997, 40).

Hallie is well-known for his book, *Lest Innocent Blood Be Shed* (1979), an account of the heroism of the inhabitants of the French village of Le Chambon under Nazi occupation. One such hero described by Hallie was Magda Trocmé. Such virtues as thrift and prudence hardly characterized her life. From one day to the next, the family cash box was as available as her home to anyone in need, while her repeated efforts to rescue desperate strangers were the height of incautiousness. As Hallie recounts:

> During the first terrible winter after the fall of France, the first refugee came to the door of the presbytery of Le Chambon. . . . When Magda asked the mayor to give her the necessary papers, he—quite rationally—said, "What? Do you dare to endanger this whole village for the sake of one foreigner? Will you save one woman and destroy us all? I am responsible for the welfare of this village. Get her out of Le Chambon tomorrow morning, no later."
>
> The voluble and eloquent Magda was wise enough not to argue against the little virtues. . . . From that winter's night on, she never tried to justify the saving of refugees to the custodians of the welfare of Le Chambon or of France. She worked closely only with people who had more in their hearts than protecting their hides.
>
> *(Id., 42)*

Hardie would note that Magda's great courage was not likely to have been the result of a childhood spent in caring classrooms filled with kind classmates and teachers. He admires Magda (as well as Ben Franklin), not for her compassionate feelings, but (borrowing famous words of Rev. Martin Luther King, Jr.) for "the content of [her] character," for her daily unflinching risk-taking that resulted in life-saving acts. As a teacher, Hardie is not concerned whether a child is attached to him or to others; nor is he much interested in the internal workings of a child's psyche—his or her self-esteem, social-esteem or loving motives. It is not right relationships but right commitments that concern him, commitments that are often grounded in the "little virtues" that Hallie scorns. Self-esteem (assuming that there is such a thing) will emerge from the doing of good deeds; it will not be the source of them.

Indeed, while Hardie's priorities are no less emotionally grounded than Maria's, he is "turned off" by a focus on soothing, stroking talk. Adam Bede had it right when he said: "I like to keep my breath for doing instead o' talking" (Eliot 1859/1985, 44). Hardie would find an emphasis on caring, kindness, and consideration insipid, pallid, thin—devoid of real (rigorous) moral content. Of course, by virtue of their humanity all people deserve respect and protection from the abuse of fundamental rights, but they do not each deserve praise. Approval should be earned; there must be a *there* there to approve of. As C.S. Lewis observes, friendship has to be about something:

> The very condition of having Friends is that we should want something else besides Friends. Where the truthful answer to the question *Do you see the same truth?* would be "I see nothing and I don't care about the truth; I only want a Friend," no Friendship can arise—though Affection of course may. There would be nothing for the Friendship to be *about*; and Friendship must be about something. . . . [T]hose who are going nowhere can have no fellow-travellers.
> *(Lewis 1960/1988, 66-67) (emphasis in original)*

The notion of a "caring community," where care is turned inward, focused on one another, rather than turned outward to the issues of the world— e.g., the environment, animal rights, poverty, disease, illiteracy—has about it a group narcissism distasteful to those of Hardie's orientation. It is all just a little too cozy, too comfortable, too easy. This feel-good therapeutic morality that imposes no demands beyond "being nice" makes for selves stripped barren, what Robert Bellah and his colleagues call the "radically unencumbered and improvisational self" (Bellah et al 1996, 81). If we are to care for one another regardless of performance, if our worthiness is not a precondition of another's approval, who will be motivated to take the risks of resisting injustice? The awe we feel, the inspiration we receive from greatness, is flattened by expending vast sums of approval on fairly ordinary expectable "niceness."

These differences between Maria and Hardie, in both their "reading" of morally significant conduct and their moral priorities, are reinforced by their differing presuppositions about human nature. It is the confluence of all three of these factors that in our judgment best explains their pedagogical preferences.

INTERPRETING HUMAN NATURE

Maria, like David Hume (see p. 86, in Chapter 4), believes in our "natural sympathies." For her, human nature is predominantly inclined toward benevolence and cooperation; it becomes corrupted when children are psychologically inhibited and socially indoctrinated by adults. Children will treat others as they have been treated: the abusing parent often has been an abused child, the loving parent a well-loved child. Bad behavior is often the manifestation of bad treatment; it is "unnatural."

This belief in natural goodness motivates Maria to explain carefully the reasons for specific rules and the consequences of infractions, to invite student participation in (and even student acceptance or rejection of some) significant decisions, and to maintain respectful attention to student reactions. And it strongly inclines her to keep to a minimum criticism, punishment, and repression.

In some of her responses to Tony's provocations, Maria found herself violating her own principles. Cleaning chairs was a menial and unnecessary task. She deliberately humiliated him, exacting obedience through the forceful use of authority, a squelching not an enabling act. What bothers Maria is not so much the temporary pain she inflicted by making Tony comply with a punishment—after all, such transient pains are unavoidable in growing up—but the possibility that in having humiliated this child, she broke faith with him and put at risk his natural drive to affiliate. Maria's belief in a child's natural but fragile goodness echoes another theme of Simone Weil: "[W]hen a man's life is destroyed or damaged by some wound or privation of soul or body, which is due to other men's actions or negligence, it is not only his sensibility that suffers but also his aspiration towards the good" (Weil 1986, 204).

Hardie's "take" on human nature is more hardened. Like G.J. Warnock (see p. 92, in Chapter 4), he is impressed by our "limited" rather than by our "natural" sympathies, by our willingness to abuse others to satisfy them. The temptation to increase pleasure is limitless—from grabbing the biggest portion of food in the cafeteria or taking advantage of others as a child, to hoarding riches in later life. Resisting temptation and subjugating desire are the heart and soul of morality. If one believes human nature is disposed to "self-interested and antisocial attitudes," explains David Carr, it makes sense to assert that children must be "controlled externally by imposed law or internally by the inculcation of a conscience informed by principles of altruistic self-control" (Carr 1991, 185). The task of education then becomes "systematic socialization or acculturalization of the young with respect to the customs and values of their social group" (id., 177).

To acculturate means to constrain. This viewpoint is an echo of Emile Durkheim:

> Our sensibilities . . . incline us toward individual, egoistic, irrational, and immoral ends. Between the law of reason and our temperaments, there is a genuine antagonism, and, consequently, the former can impose itself upon the latter only through exercising a very real constraint. It is the sense of this constraint that gives rise to the feelings of obligation. (*Durkheim 1925/1961, 112*)

When Hardie looks out into the world, he sees more callousness toward others than empathy. The card sharks in Maria's class amassed their booty just as CEOs and investors do; there is no natural socialism in corporate America.

Thus, while Maria's values of caring and kindness promote the celebration of human passions that, if followed, will naturally direct us towards loving attachments, Hardie's values of restraint and self-control call for the repression of human passions that, let loose, tend to destroy social well-being. To Hardie, avoiding improper behavior requires that children submit respectfully to rightful authority—among which one's teacher tops the list. Once that respect, that leverage, is lost, a child is no longer instructable. To Maria, it is as children become sensitized to the feelings of others that their sympathies become less limited, that they supplement self- with other-regarding interests, and come "naturally" to consider the needs of classmates before scooping up the most and best, whether of the cafeteria food, baseball cards, or other material goods.

We have sought to show how pedagogy is something more than a set of technical choices driven solely by considerations of effectiveness and efficiency. We (once again) find helpful in this regard the work of Lawrence Kohlberg, who offers a highly developed framework seeking to connect the teaching of morality to moral priorities and assumptions about human nature, which are at the base of what he terms "educational ideologies." While we will conclude that the connections he asserts are too tightly drawn, we believe that his framework has great value.

THEORIES OF LEARNING AND THE TEACHING OF MORALITY

To Kohlberg,[2] an ideology is close to what we have called a worldview, a set of beliefs about human nature, human development, morality, and learning. He maintains that a teacher's choice of pedagogic approaches manifests, consciously or otherwise, one of three educational ideologies, which he terms "romantic," "cultural transmission," and "cognitive-developmental." The *romantic* ideology accepts Rousseau's belief (which we have quoted at p. 22 in Chapter 2) that "Everything is good as it leaves the hands of the Author of things; everything degenerates in the hands of man" (Rousseau 1979, 37). The best pedagogy, therefore, is a "null-pedagogy," one that leaves children to their natural inclinations. To cultivate the natural (which is also the good), educational objectives should center around self-actualization, including an assortment of "mental health" qualities such as self-confidence, self-esteem, spontaneity, and self-discipline. Although the romantic view had a strong influence on the progressive movement, in its pure libertarian form it has few current adherents. Certainly neither Maria's nor Hardie's positions seem to take any account of it. We leave it aside.

The *cultural-transmission* ideology, according to Kohlberg, rests on the premise that the young child lacks both reason and understanding. The mind of the young child is a blank slate, and accordingly must be (in the words of John Locke) "made obedient to Discipline, and pliant to Reason, when at first it [is] most tender, most easy to be bow'd" (Locke 1693/1927, 21). Until maturity children should be "under the absolute Power and Restraint of those in whose Hands they are" (id., 26). They "should look upon their Parents as their Lords, their absolute Governors, and as such stand in awe of them," for fear and awe are the means by which unruly minds may be brought under control (id., 27). "He that is not us'd to submit his Will to the Reason of others *when* he is *young*, will scarce hearken to submit to his own Reason when he is of an Age to make Use of it" (id., 23) (*emphasis in original*).

---

[2] We draw in this section principally on Kohlberg and Mayer 1972 and Kohlberg 1987.

This approach fits easily with a behaviorist understanding of learning. At the core of behaviorism—a theory that stretches from Locke to B. F. Skinner—is the belief that all learning comes from positive and negative reinforcement of emitted behaviors. There are no innate ideas; indeed, classic behaviorism asserts that humans lack an innate propensity to acquire skills or understanding, an innate capacity to select and order stimuli or to take intrinsic satisfaction from doing so. Accordingly, reinforcement is a most powerful inducement to learning.

While to behaviorists educational goals, including moral ones, are understood as objective in the sense that they do not arise out of individual feelings or dispositions, they are not seen as possessing universal or eternal truth-claims. To think that they do would be to commit the naturalistic fallacy (inferring an *ought* from an *is*; see the discussion at page 83 in Chapter 4). Rather, behaviorists, understanding all standards to be relative to a culture or nation, unabashedly accept existing social standards as the source of the moral goals of education, and they are entirely comfortable with the educational objective of qualifying children to take their anticipated positions in the reigning status system. "[T]he cultural transmission school is society-centered. It defines educational ends as the internalization of the values and knowledge of the culture" (Kohlberg and Mayer 1972, 454).

The *cognitive-developmental* ideology (a theoretical justification of progressive education, and Kohlberg's own choice) subscribes to the Dewey/Piaget tenet that children attain knowledge—both cognitive and social—through active participation with their environment as they resolve problems and conflicts of everyday life. Because in this view knowledge is "constructed," not received, it is often referred to as "constructivism." According to Piaget (see, for example, Piaget 1952), a child knows an object only when she acts upon it; mere looking does not make it hers. Knowledge simply "laid on" by teachers (or parents) is thought to wash away because it fails to bring about an active change in a child's thought patterns. External reinforcement of adult-chosen objectives, therefore, is not an effective pedagogical tool; absent a child's interest, there is no learning. As Dewey put it:

> Save as the efforts of the educator connect with some activity which the child is carrying on of his own initiative independent of the educator, education becomes reduced to a pressure from without. It may, indeed, give certain external results, but cannot truly be called educative. Without insight into the psychological structure and activities of the individual, the educative process will, therefore, be haphazard and arbitrary. If it chances to coincide with the child's activities it will get leverage; if it does not, it will result in friction, or disintegration, or arrest of the child's nature. *(Dewey 1897/1959, 20)*

Interest peaks when the subject of inquiry is perplexing and the child has the available cognitive structures to make sense of it; making sense is stimulated by a challenging teacher and environment. The teacher's mission is not to give instruction, to impose rules, and coerce obedience, but to facilitate construction, to guide the development of a child's autonomous making of meaning. He or she is to stimulate inquiry (rather than give the right answers) and encourage reflection and rational discourse, by giving students the opportunity in the classroom to reach cooperative decisions about their moral lives.

Children "construct" their moral ideas largely through group interaction. A social perspective is stimulated when children rub up against the desires and ideas of others. Democratic classroom discussions are therefore critical to the enhancement of moral reasoning. Discussions are held to resolve specific conflicts, to establish general rules, to consider hypothetical or real-life dilemmas in which values compete—for example, telling a lie versus helping a friend, injuring one to save many, stealing goods that will otherwise be used for bad ends. Democratic discussions are morally worthy in themselves because they promote equality (one person, one vote), respect (consideration of the views of others), rationality (appeal is to reasoned analysis of conflicts), and deliberation (in-depth reflection on problems). They are also the most effective method of enlisting children's ownership of moral decisions and stimulating stage progression. While collective loyalty and identity can be achieved without democratic discussions, the infusion of these practices into the group protects it from becoming abusive to individuals both within and outside its confines.[3]

Does Hardie belong to the cultural-transmission camp? Sort of. Hardie, we have seen, cares about virtuous behaviors (acts) more than motives or intentions, and is clear on the objective existence of those virtues. One gets to virtue, he believes, through the build-up of habits, to habits through practice and drill, and to practice and drill through control exercised by an authority actively intervening with rewards and punishments. He thus shares with the cultural-transmission ideology the premise that standards are objective, that is, they have a reality independent of the consciousness of the actor, and in large measure are transmitted by reinforcement, both positive and negative. However, like other traditional moral educators, he would differ sharply with the morality and educational objectives of the cultural-transmission model. He would insist on *judging* prevalent social mores, and his support of "conventional" values extends only to those that he judges are in fact *right*. Indeed, the voices of those who think like him today are seeking to rally the country to resist the decline of morals in contemporary society. Their educational objectives are not to swim with the prevailing tides, but to oppose them where

---

[3] This approach led Kohlberg to establish the "Just Schools" program, which sought to create the following classroom conditions:

(1) Open discussion focusing on fairness, community, and morality; (2) Cognitive conflict stimulated by exposure to different points of view and higher-stage reasoning; (3) Participation in rule making and rule enforcement and the public exercise of power and responsibility; (4) The development of community or group solidarity at a high stage. (Higgins 1991, 121). See further p. 282 in Chapter 9.

they find those values incompatible with values that they deem true, but "out of fashion." Morality, in this view, is not something that responds to passing cultural changes in society.

Hardie might also take exception to the underlying "blank slate" description of the child's mind, and with it the Lockean notion that knowledge comes only from experience—from outside to inside. He is sympathetic to Kant's categorical imperative, and to the role of reason in discerning and applying moral standards; he probably believes in the existence of an innate reasoning capacity—though one perhaps not to be counted on in the moral decision making of ten-year-olds.

The question is whether, and under what conditions, children will employ their reasoning ability. To the Hardies of this world, that has a lot to do with what one is reasoning *about*. Children may reason well in aid of their self-interest, yet falter when it would call for them to repress their desires. Morality requires vigorous and persistent adult instruction, not because children lack rational capacities, but simply because to follow reason's leadings is hard. Were it not hard, had it nothing to do with renunciation, Hardie could leave it to natural maturation, much like such attainments as curiosity and physical development.

We see, then, *contra* Kohlberg, that one can without self-contradiction subscribe to a "human nature" that is not wholly inclined toward the good, believing that the good has to be cultivated through rigorous behavioral practices, and yet stop short of adopting a relativist morality. One can believe that human nature has its inherent worthy thrusts—to attach oneself to others is surely a prime contender—and that many good qualities will mature in the child without adult intervention, yet still believe that morality is not such a thrust and cannot be left to nature.

It is the difficulty of moral attainment that, according to Wynne and Ryan, justifies "upping" the incentives:

> The more profound—the more important and difficult—a thing is to learn, the more profound the learning pressures that must be applied. [L]earning to prefer right over wrong is perhaps the hardest thing for humans to learn. Obviously, strong learning pressures must be applied to transmit such knowledge. We learn easy things—tomorrow's weather, who won the ball game—simply by casual listening and reading. But the greater effect a particular learning has on our lives, the more substantial the relevant pressures or incentives must be.
> (Wynne and Ryan 1997, 39–40)

Because successful moral instruction requires rigorous behavioral incentives, schools, they suggest, should thoughtfully and generously reward children for their prosocial conduct. There are many such incentives, of which the following are examples:

1. *Conspicuous praise*: notes or phone calls to parents; announcements over the school public-address system; names listed on the black-

board or the class or school bulletin board; photographs prominently displayed; mention in the school paper; notations on report cards; certificates on award occasions; bumper stickers for parents ("My child is a character-award winner at the _____ school"); invitations to a special party; names on a plaque or poster place on the school wall.

2. *Symbolic recognition* (like athletic letters): pins, ribbons, badges, jackets, medals, trophies.

3. *Publicly recognized titles*: school president, team captain, member of the honor society (where character is one requirement for membership).

4. *Contacts with prominent people*: breakfast with the principal.

(Id., 67) (emphasis in original)

Does Maria belong to the cognitive-developmental school? Sort of. She shares with its members the belief that judging morality by actions is not as sound as judging by motivations or intentions; that morality is highly contextual and evolves in response to the social problems of group life; that a behavioral pedagogy of reinforcement is ineffective; that authority should be shared and children's decision-making capacities should be respected.

But where the Piaget/Kohlberg tradition emphasizes rationality and justice (more appealing to Hardie than Maria), she emphasizes emotions (particularly compassion and empathy) and community. Maria believes that the internalization of morality comes less from rational analysis of problematic situations than from an interest in, and identification with, the well-being of others. She is skeptical of Kohlberg's notion that children are naturally inclined to philosophy, eager to think about moral conundrums and to apply intellectual resolutions to daily life; she believes rationality will always be bypassed or distorted unless aligned with psychological wishes and needs (not, however, reinforced, as Hardie would have it, by behavioral incentives and habit).

Moreover, Maria does not see individual autonomy as a prime developmental goal. She is distrustful of judgments that individuals make apart from the norms of their community and emotionally disengaged from peer reactions; she is partial to decisions made by individuals engaged in and searching for group harmony.

Here, then, is another unraveling of Kohlberg's tapestry. While Maria's theories of learning and teaching make her a card-carrying constructivist, she, like Hardie, departs from Kohlberg's moral objectives. A sense of justice born of principled, rational, and impersonal thought is, for her, much less a good than concern for others born of compassion and emotional attachments.

Hardie and Maria, as *we* have "constructed" them, do not have the ideological purity often found among theoreticians. Rather, they are an amalgam of several competing underlying premises. It is our judgment that there is no necessary self-contradiction here, that the value of attending to underlying premises, priorities, and paradigms is not to align our practical judgments with theoretical single-mindedness, but to encourage reflection and facilitate a more defensible synthesis. We elaborate on this judgment after a necessary detour through those psychological features of development—emotion, cognition, and personal identity—that bear on the teaching of morality, for they channel a child's receptivity to *any* pedagogical method.

DEVELOPMENTAL CONSIDERATIONS: EMOTIONAL

Psychologists customarily separate cognitive from emotional development while simultaneously recognizing the artificiality of the distinction. Both the distinction and the overlap seem intuitively obvious. We recognize that genuinely to "feel your pain" is not the same as to *understand* your pain, yet I do not feel your pain without simultaneously knowing something about it, and knowing something about it is likely to elicit my sympathy.

In the young child, distinctions between the cognitive and emotional systems are virtually nonexistent; indeed, development is often described as a process of increasing differentiation and organization both within and between these systems. However, if we read development backward, from when the distinctions are plausible, it is apparent that preschool children lead with their feelings, not their reason, and that their feelings are suffused with moral sentiments, however unbounded. As the educational psychologist Kieran Egan points out, "children's major intellectual tools and categories are not rational and logical but emotional and moral" (Egan 1979, 15).

Over the course of years, the moral component of the child migrates towards independent self-conscious status. Along the way, the cognitive element grows in importance and forms with the emotional elements an increasingly complex, differentiated, and stable structure. Ideally, an integrated cognitive-emotional moral system takes up final lodging in, and becomes critical to, the adolescent's (and adult's) self-image.

But there are obvious hazards on the journey: The child's morality, undernourished by caretakers, may fail to develop or, insensitively nourished, may grow askew, tilting excessively to the cognitive or emotional. Why is tilting a hazard? Because, if one only *knows* the interests of another without *feeling* them, there will be no will to act, while if one merely *feels* for someone else's interests, without *understanding* the basis of their call, there will be moral blundering. Blending the cognitive and emotional, therefore, is a prime objective of moral education; indeed, we think that the extent to which an adult persistently and consistently accentuates moral considerations in his or her life has much to do with the successful unification of these two sources, as well as the prominent residence of the moral in one's self-image.

Because children habitually assemble experiences into emotional polarities, good and bad are easy distinctions. As Egan observes, "Before children can walk or talk, before they can skate or ride a bicycle, they know joy and fear, love and hate, power and powerlessness" (Egan 1988, 28). In the morality of the young, what gets to be characterized as good or bad is closely tied to desires and fears. Anything we want, get praised for, aspire to, is a candidate to be regarded as good, and the reverse for the bad.

A conversation with a grandson of one of the authors gives the flavor of this initial-stage protomorality, equating (at age three) goodness with (much wanted) power. In elaborating on his infatuation with Superman, he explained: "Superman is a good guy, he can fly." Kohlberg, describing his young son (Kohlberg 1987, 22), makes similar observations: The good was what he liked, what brought him satisfaction, the bad, what he did not like. Thus, good guys and bad guys were not distinguished by acts of aggression or the righteousness of their causes, but by the coveted qualities of success in a struggle or competition.

The natural tendency to order the world in sets of emotionally charged moral polarities is fostered by the child's internal capacity for empathy. Empathy appears to be another "given" of the human mind. As a global reaction of distress to the distress of others, it is apparent long before a child can appraise the basis of the distress.

Another "grandson" incident demonstrates the raw power of this reaction. The child, then age four, and his much-loved uncle were driving in heavy traffic. Stopped from their slow crawl by a red light, the uncle burst out, "Oh, fuck! Stupid light, turn green." The child echoed this admonition: "Stupid light, turn green," but after a short pause, added, "Sorry, light. I didn't mean to hurt your feelings." Much as the child identifies with and emulates his uncle, there is momentarily a more powerful urge, identification with the injured party—the inanimate traffic light.

Initially the motive force behind the child's concern for others, empathy, if properly supported, continues as a powerful moral motive. As the primatologist Frans de Waal writes:

> Despite its fragility and selectivity, the capacity to care for others is the bedrock of our moral systems. It is the only capacity that does not snugly fit the hedonic cage in which philosophers, psychologists, and biologists have tried to lock the human spirit. One of the principal functions of morality seems to be to protect and nurture this caring capacity, to guide its growth and expand its reach, so that it can effectively balance other human tendencies that need little encouragement.
> (de Waal 1996, 88)

With age, empathy is modulated by cognitive understandings; it becomes a more refined response, with more carefully chosen targets. Self-regarding distress shades into other-regarding sympathy. Further, a child comes to feel more empathy for those who suffer enduring rather than temporary life-insults, and for those who are close rather than remote. It is, however, an inconstant force, frequently failing in competition with egoistic drives and dependent on pressure from the adult world for its robustness.

Another "given" of the human condition, fortunate for the socialization of morality, is the strong attachment that children develop to those responsible for their gratifications. Because they love and seek love from the hand that feeds them, they eagerly respond to parental approval and disapproval. Parents, aided by the leverage of attachment, can sensitize even the prerational child to what is morally most critical by meting out their strongest approbation and disapprobation for the values they most cherish or reject.

At first the child is obedient in order to avoid triggering disapproval or jeopardizing attachment. But accompanying a growing separation from parents is a deepening identification with them: the child comes to share and incorporate parental values as his or her own. Thus, resisting the temptation to steal a cookie, at first motivated by fear of being caught and suffering the attendant disapproval, becomes around school-entry age—and to varying degrees depending on situational forces (conspicuously, that of self-interest)—a self-addressed directive against violating one's own conscience. Obedience from fear becomes obedience from guilt.

Guilt, the more mature emotion, is also the more bedeviling, harder to avoid or to shuck off. If a theft goes undetected, mere fear no longer stands in the way of enjoyment of the cookie, while guilt over eating the forbidden fruit persists. At the same time, equilibrium is harder to reestablish, requiring reconciliation through apology, restitution, or a substantial passage of time.

Adults stroke children's guilt by drawing on that ready standby, a child's empathy. They point to the child's responsibility for harm caused to another—"You just pushed Billy, that wasn't nice"—and stress the feelings of the injured party—"How would you feel if Sally took your toy, if Sally didn't give you a turn?"

The young child, then, largely *feels* his way into an early quasimorality. He starts with a strong tendency to slot experience into moral-emotional polarities. In his own mind, the good is what feels good. It is what he desires and admires, what is desired from him and admired in him, what nurtures his empathic feelings and avoids generating feelings of guilt. It is a start to his moral journey, but, without benefit of more cognitive maturity, it is a whimsical and unpredictable start.

DEVELOPMENTAL CONSIDERATIONS: COGNITIVE

Until approximately ages seven to nine, young children are prelogical, in the state that Kohlberg calls "preconventional" and Piaget calls "moral realism." Rules are immanent in the world and are transmitted through adult authority. Like natural objects, they have existed forever, exert a powerful presence, and are not to be tampered with or ignored, but their existence has no explanation or purpose.

What is the problem with younger children's reasoning? According to Piaget, the limitation lies in the self-centered or "egocentric" nature of their thinking. This is not a conventional self-centeredness, which presupposes knowing others' interests but privileging one's own. It is rather a simple inability to see the world through the eyes of another, to understand the likeness between other minds and one's own. Although acts such as stealing and lying are perceived as wrong, the wrongness lies in rule-breaking, not in hurting others. The younger child treasures her own property, but simply is not aware of the property interests of others, and a lie is not understood as injurious to others.

Until a child can perform what Piaget calls "mental operations," he or she cannot genuinely understand the reciprocity principle of the Golden Rule. An "operation" is an exercise in reversibility—knowing that $2 + 2 = 4$ implies $4 - 2 = 2$—the principle at the core of the admonition, "Do unto others what you would have them do unto you." A "preoperational", "egocentric" child cannot perform the reversals, and therefore, though able to voice and even at times to obey the Golden Rule, cannot make it an operative principle.

The younger child is above all a literalist. She judges the seriousness of an offense by its material results, not by the perpetrator's intentions. For example, the young child believes—and, again, these views fade only gradually, hanging on under some circumstances until late in elementary school—that the rule "don't bite" does not apply to "don't hit," the rule "don't lie to a parent" does not mean "don't lie to a friend," and breaking one dish on purpose is not as bad as breaking a lot of dishes by accident.

The impact of this "realism" on judgments of culpability is illuminated through Piaget's inquiries into children's responses to clumsiness, stealing, and lying. One such inquiry (Piaget 1948, 118) concerned two accounts involving children's responsibility for breaking cups. The first concerned a little boy who, called to dinner, opened the dining-room door not knowing that behind it was a chair with a tray containing fifteen cups, which broke on impact. In the other story, a boy, trying to get some jam from a cupboard while his mother was out, climbed onto a chair and stretched out his arm in a vain attempt to reach it. But in reaching he knocked over a cup, which fell and broke.

Investigators asked children to assign appropriate guilt and punishment in the two cases. A typical six-year-old answer was of this sort:

> What did the first boy do?—*He broke eleven cups.*—And the second one?—*He broke a cup by moving roughly.*—Why did the first one break the cups?—*Because the door knocked them.*—And the second?—*He was clumsy. When he was getting the jam the cup fell down.*—Is one of the boys naughtier than the other?—*The first is because he knocked over twelve cups.*—If you were the daddy, which one would you punish most?—*The one who broke twelve cups. . . .*
> *(Id., 120–121) (italics in original, here and in quotations from Piaget following)*

Children reached similar "objective" judgments regarding stealing and lying. In one experiment, children were asked to say who was naughtier, a boy who stole a roll for a friend who had missed dinner or a girl who stole a ribbon from a shop because it would nicely adorn her dress. A six-year-old decided that, although the boy who stole was kind, and not naughty, he deserved greater punishment because (as he believed) rolls were costlier than ribbons.

As for lying, although children below the ages of seven or eight have grave trouble sticking to the truth (because they confuse desire with reality), they are nonetheless very concerned about lying. They regard mistakes as the equivalent of intentional falsehoods. The bigger the discrepancy and the more unlikely the false statement, the more evil the perceived lie. Thus, saying you saw a dog twice the size of a cow is, to a six-year-old, worse than saying the teacher gave you a good grade when you got no grade. Because there is nothing unusual about receiving good grades, the lie about grades is insignificant; such an event could happen and parents are likely to believe it is true. "It is therefore only a little lie, all the more innocent because a mother is taken in by it," whereas there is no such thing as a dog bigger than a cow (id., 151).

By age ten a reversal has occurred. The credibility of the lie is now a ground of condemnation rather than exculpation; the naughtier child is he who deceived his mother by saying that the teacher was pleased with his work. "Why is he the naughtiest?—*Because the mother knows quite well that there aren't any dogs as big as cows. But she believed the child who said the teacher was pleased*" (id., 154).

To the younger child, morality is obedience. As autonomous thinking increases, children begin the process of critical rationality: moving from a view of obedience as an inherent obligation, to a growing concern for fairness—first, a recognition that, although the command is unjust, obedience nonetheless trumps fairness, and finally to the belief that fairness trumps obedience.

Piaget again illustrates the shift with children's story responses. A mother asked her young son and daughter to help with the housework. The girl was told to dry the dishes and the boy to gather wood, but because one child went into the street and played, the mother asked the other one to do both chores. Younger children deemed fairness to reflect obedience. Asked how the child should respond to the mother's request, an eight-year-old said: "*He ought to have done both things because his brother wouldn't.—*Is it fair?—*It is very fair. He is doing a good deed*" (id., 278).

The response of a nine-year-old recognized that the command was unjust, but evidenced a belief that obedience trumps fairness: "*She ought to have gone at once.—*Why?—*Because when you're asked to, you must go at once.—*Was it fair?—*No, it wasn't her turn.—*Why did she go?—*To do as she was told.*" (id., 280).

By the age of twelve, a child had come to the view that fairness trumps obedience. "*She shouldn't have done it. It's not fair that she should work twice as hard and not the other.—*What was to be done?—*She should have said to her mother, 'It's not fair. I ought not to do double the work.'*" (id., 281).

Piaget discerned a similar evolution in children's understanding of what constitutes fairness. It is only around ages eleven or twelve that sense of fairness changes from sameness—all goods are distributed equally—to a fuller consideration of circumstances, from justice-as-equality to justice-as-equity. When questioned, for example, why it is wrong to cheat on a test, children moved from a perspective of obedience (because it is prohibited, because you will be punished), to one of equality (because you are stealing from or harming another person, unbalancing the equilibrium). It is only in preadolescence, when the child can appreciate the need to take account of those *unlike* oneself, that there is a response from the perspective of equity. A child age eleven, for example, responded to a question regarding the fairness of cheating on a test: *"For those who can't learn they ought to be allowed to have just a little look, but for those who can learn it* [cheating] *isn't fair.—A child copied his friend's sum. Was it fair?—He ought not to have copied. But if he was not clever it was more or less all right for him to do it"* (id., 288).

A parent or educator may respond with skepticism to Piaget's description of the child's long apprenticeship in moral rationality. After all, we urge quite small children to give way (turn over a toy, let pass an act of aggression) to younger ones on the ground that the smaller child cannot understand rules of fairness, which we presume the slightly older child does understand. When we get compliance we assume our argument was accepted. But this assumption may be wrong. A six-year-old probably does not understand why her parents get angry when she throws an object or hits another child, but tolerate the same behavior from her three-year-old sibling. The child obliges because she is obedient to authority, perhaps also because she has empathy for the younger child. Eventually she will come to understand that compensation for age differentials is a form of equity, but even then she might resist unless being fair is becoming part of her emerging moral identity.

To demand that one act righteously requires more than empathy and rationality; it requires also a feeling that one's selfhood is on the line. Unless participation in wrongdoing pinches a moral identity, children, like adults, are not likely to resist the pull of self-interest. As William Damon elaborates:

> [P]ersons with the same moral beliefs may differ in their views on how important it is for them to be moral in a personal sense. Some may consider their morality to be central to their self-identities, whereas others may consider it to be peripheral. Some may . . . consider morality to be a force outside of the self, a socially imposed system of regulation that [constrains] or even obstructs one's pursuit of one's personal goals. In such cases, morality may . . . be viewed as antagonistic to one's "real self," at least at times.
> *(Damon 1984, 110)*

At day's end, the extent to which we gravitate to, ignore, or avoid the moral is a matter of its centrality in our self-identification. When morality is prominent in this structure, moral violations will cause very unpleasant feelings of self-derogation, self-alienation, and loss of integrity. When unimportant or absent, we are psychologically immune to our own immorality. William Damon and Daniel Hart conclude:

> There are both theoretical and empirical reasons to believe that the centrality of morality to self may be the single most powerful determiner of concordance between moral judgment and conduct. . . . People whose self-concept is organized around their moral beliefs are highly likely to translate those beliefs into action consistently throughout their lives. . . . Such people tend to sustain a far higher level of moral commitment in their actual conduct than those who may reason well about morality but who consider it to be less pivotal for who they are.
> *(Damon and Hart 1992, 455)*

We turn, therefore, to consideration of the development of moral identity.

DEVELOPMENTAL CONSIDERATIONS: MORAL IDENTITY

Despite its impossible vagueness, the concept of selfhood is honored in psychology because it reflects the widespread perception that such a psychological structure is real and serves as a master control system (much as we described integrity as a "master virtue," see p. 161 in Chapter 6). The notion of self explains why two people with identical aspirations—to be recognized in their jobs and respected by their peers; to earn and spend money; to be a good parent, friend, and lover; to have a nice home, prepare and eat good food, enjoy sports; to contribute to a religious and community life—have vastly disparate responses to their relative successes and failures. Augusto Blasi, a major theorist of moral identity, captures the importance of the construct:

> The self is not simply a collection of characteristics, traits, or [precepts]; it is an organization of self-related information in which the various elements are brought together according to certain principles of psychological consistency. The organizing principle, varying from person to person. . . . defines what could be called the essential or the core self, namely, the set of those aspects without which the individual would see himself or herself to be radically different; those so central that one could not even imagine being deprived of them; those whose loss would be considered and felt as irreparable.
> *(Blasi 1984, 131)*

Moral identity, along with religious identity, is probably at the core of the core. It alerts us to the moral much as an aesthetic sensibility alerts us to the beautiful (and ugly). In part it is a cognitive filter monitoring our reactions; in part it is an emotional instigator, pushing us into action. It guides our choices so that what should not be done we cannot do and what should be done we must do. It explains why Maria, unbidden, spends several evenings each week dining with her cranky widowed mother and why Hardie volunteers each weekend at a homeless shelter. Ultimately, it explains why our behavior, though seemingly spontaneous and reactive, is reliable and steadfast. Moral identity transmutes moral judgments into moral obligation and wills us into action. Without moral identity one may easily turn away from a problem without even noticing the obligation that was shrugged off. (The excerpt by Clark Power at p. 252 in the next section of this chapter elaborates on this moral indifference.) In a best-case scenario the sense of self is integrated with concern for others, so that "unselfishness" loses its meaning—to care for oneself is to care for others.

Such a confluence of interests characterized the rescuer, Magda Trocmé: "Only the mysterious virtue of taking other people's needs to be the motive of her own actions was natural to her. Still, important as it was in her life, she hardly ever noticed it. It was part and parcel of her psychological anatomy" (Hallie 1997, 42).

If moral identity is so vital, can educators give it a jump-start? Perhaps, but not easily, for once again we have a structure that arrives late in development (if at all) requiring as it does a degree of self-awareness ("I am the kind of person who must do x and cannot do y") not generally possessed by the preadolescent. William Damon, an astute investigator of the topic, noted that even though some six-year-olds "believe" in justice-as-equality, and a few years later "believe" in justice-as-equity (those in greater need or with greater merit should get more), such judgments are usually external to their self-image. They rarely respond to identity questions—asking what sort of people they are, what sort they want to be—with morally cast statements, "either of a direct sort (such as a wish for improvement in the lot of others) or in terms of one's own makeup (such as a wish for a stronger moral character or a finer set of moral beliefs). Nor do children see morality as one of the features of themselves that changes or that makes them the way they are" (Damon 1984, 117). Not until adolescence, when morality may have been incorporated into their identity, do some children describe themselves or others in terms of belief systems (ibid.; see also Damon 1977).

The absence of a moral identity also explains why in "real life" (not hypothetical) situations children's self-interest rises above their moral principles. For example, in repeated trials Damon gave children ages four to ten the task of distributing ten candy bars among four children who had been making bracelets. The younger ones kept as many as seven candy bars each, with the justification that they wanted them. Older children made more generous distributions, but nonetheless gave themselves extras. They rationalized their greed with an equity principle—"I made more; I worked harder"—while never finding another child's work better (Damon 1984, 117).

An obvious source of resistance to the development of moral identity is its demand that we overcome our "limited sympathies." That effort requires a determined will, and so our question becomes, How do we jump-start the will? Again, this is not the stuff of childhood. Willpower is needed when temptation and duty conflict. To possess willpower under such circumstances, a child has to recognize the conflict and resist the temptation; he or she must be able and willing to force a weaker tendency (duty) to triumph over a stronger (pleasure) (Piaget 1967). In cognitive terms, willpower requires a child to step back from an egocentric perception of the world and subordinate immediacy claims to more durable but less readily available value claims. In emotional terms, willpower requires bringing an affective charge together with a moral judgment so that what was initially perceived as aversive, at least in the near term, is recast as satisfying, at least in the long term. An altogether tough assignment.

Although we do not expect the child to have a generalized moral will connected to a moral identity, nor to be able to think completely rationally about moral questions, we do not mean to suggest thereby that he or she is incapable of self-restraint or moral goodness. As we have suggested, these qualities are frequently, if not systematically, expressed. They are motivated by a child's empathy, desire for approval, internalization of standards, and concepts of fairness. Teachers can and do foster them. It is time to return to pedagogy.

PEDAGOGY REVISITED

We have examined the developmental underpinnings of morality that need to be factored into the differing worldviews focused on initially in this chapter— the teachers' attribution of *moral significance* to action, their *moral priorities*, and their conceptions regarding the *moral nature* of the child. In that effort, we first considered the differences and the connections between *cognitive* and *emotional* development, and then focused on the idea of *moral identity* as a critical aspect of development. We elaborate here some of the lessons for teaching derived from these concepts.

The elementary school teacher's task, as we see it, is to cultivate the *foundations* of a moral identity. Although he or she will also want to ensure "right" behavior, that objective alone is too limited; little is gained by a moral education, indeed, by any education, that shapes actions without shaping the person.

Aiding a child to grow a moral identity is not an easy task. Above all, those who work with children must claim for themselves, if they are to be able to help develop it in others, strong moral identities. Educators need to commit to the goal, while appreciating the magnitude and duration of the effort required. Exemplars of moral excellence impress others because their achievements are difficult, because resisting the excessive pursuit of self-interest is the distillation of a prolonged apprenticeship. It follows that moral education cannot succeed when it is merely the pet project of a few teachers or a few activities mandated by the principal. It must (unobtrusively) saturate all teaching, all administration—the stated curriculum, the hidden curriculum, the extracurricular curriculum, the buzz in the corridors, the conversations with parents. If it is experienced as an "add-on" to the "real" curriculum, even one encountered regularly in the students' week, it will fail to beckon children, to arouse their admiration, to find a foothold in their fantasies, and, so failing, children will be hard put to resist the countermoral choices they confront daily.

The idea that moral education must pervade the educational environment has a "vertical" no less than a "horizontal" dimension. That is, in addition to not being relegated to a specified hour in a classroom day or week, it needs to be encountered repeatedly (but differentially) as students move from grade to grade.

In this effort, especially in the early grades, one appeals to the feelings of children—empathy, attachment, identification—and to their impressionability, so that the moral life is seen as warm, vital, splendid. At every grade there should be a balance of techniques. One steps forward and enforces rules, steps back a little and exemplifies, steps back further and defers to children. Within a grade and from one grade to another, the processes of stepping forward and stepping back are themselves a complex mix of dogmatic, emotional, and rational appeals. How much of each—forward and back, emotional and rational—depends first on age, with the rational lagging behind the emotional. It depends as well on the issue—more forward for more serious matters—and on the personality and comfort levels of the people involved. Given this complexity, we can offer a framework but not prescriptions.

A focus on values must be implemented with an awareness of a child's developmental access to them. That means moral education must be staged. A child who at twelve has come to appreciate principles of equity will be more likely to put them into practice if she has become habituated to repressing greedy impulses. Having practiced restraint, she is also more likely to value it, for we are biased in favor of the behaviors we possess; a neat person believes that a person's mind is only as ordered as her desk, while a sloppy person rejects the analogy, finding no merit in order.

As R. S. Peters notes: "Habituation may . . . help to lay down a pattern of response that may be used in the service of more appropriate motives at a later stage," when the child is called to resist "social threats and pressures such as ridicule, disapproval, ostracism" (Peters 1974, 328). It is then that Hardie's habit training will come in handy; habits become duties and they, too, foster voluntary obligations.

Habits are also more easily cultivated in the early school years, when children are heteronomous, oriented to identifying the right with authority. They accept, even seek, Hardie-type rules without needing much rational justification. Indeed, Joel Kupperman, a thoughtful character-education philosopher, advocates dogmatic instruction as the dominant form of moral education in the primary grades:

> The central norms should be presented as assuredly correct; this does not mean, of course, that teachers need be heavy-handed, should refuse to take questions seriously, or refuse to regard what is taught as subject to reflective thought. [But] it is absurd to suppose that very young children

generally are in a position to understand, and to weigh reflectively, justifications for considering, say, murder and theft to be wrong.

❦❦❦❦❦

To suppose that there can be effective moral reflection without a first stage in which categories are learned and habits and attitudes are formed is . . . naive. . . .
(Kupperman 1991, 175, 176)

While there is certainly merit in Kupperman's analysis, we take issue with his advocacy of dogmatic instruction as the *exclusive* form of early moral training; young children lead with their feelings, and appeals to the emotions are effective as well. Too many rules, too much authority, quash spontaneous empathy, just as too few rules and too little authority cheat the child of moral direction. Maria appreciates the superiority of self-chosen to imposed values, but she is apt to overdo discussion because she exaggerates children's reasoning skills and their capacity for disinterestedness. Recall her effort to get the class to tell Tony that farting and burping were disrespectful and unacceptable in a classroom context, and her hope that they would analogize fairness in a domestic setting-the-table scene to fairness in the student–teacher incident.

Hardie is apt to overrate habit training because he is convinced that submission to rules, any rules, is a step towards self-discipline. We know intuitively (and research supports the intuition[4]) that excessive authority is less likely to promote self-direction than defiance or a calculated obedience responsive only to the actual presence of a credible threat of sanction. Hardie also underestimates the propulsion that fellow-feeling gives to moral behavior. He believes that one "crafts" caring children by requiring the performance of good deeds; he is excessively skeptical of natural empathy mutating into social responsibility. (For a statement of the importance of not polarizing habit-oriented and reflection-oriented pedagogic approaches, see the excerpt by William Damon at p. 254 in the next section of this chapter.)

Discipline is an example of the importance of attending to the developmental aspects of a moral identity. Discipline can serve differing (although related) goals: It can mark the morally important, it can serve as a deterrent, or as a punishment.

But before any discipline is inflicted, the wrongdoing must be understood. R. S. Peters makes the point well:

> Parents often punish children for stealing without appreciating that the child has not yet the grasp of concepts such as property, ownership, lending, giving and the like which enable him to understand that it is stealing for which he is being punished. . . . it is impossible to conceive

---

[4] For a summary of the relevant research, see Kohn 1993, 1998.

how [such extrinsic reinforcers] could be sufficient to bring about understanding.
(Peters 1974, 325)

As understanding grows, discipline can play a morally educative role, aiding the still-young child, whose moral compass is heavily reliant on the evaluations of others, to sort out the morally relevant and important from the rest. A natural-consequence discipline—"You took something that wasn't yours, now you must replace it"—is an association grasped by the young. When the child masters the more abstract principle of reciprocity, an appeal to the Golden Rule is appropriate: "Think how you would feel if someone took your _____." Later still, with the increased autonomy and internalization of values that accompanies the approach of adolescence, the older child can, in addition, handle an appeal to moral identity—"You know better than to steal. You need to think this over. Does what you did fit who you are?" At this point discipline may retain its capacity to deter or punish, but has scant influence on a child's moral reasoning or identity.

An overdisciplined child will focus on the correction, not on what is being corrected, with the likely outcome of generalized fear and defensiveness. Similarly, the overly rewarded child will transfer her motivation from the deed, initially seen as an intrinsic pleasure, to the praise that she garners. It is for this reason that those wholeheartedly committed to intrinsic motivation oppose reinforcement altogether (see e.g., DeVries and Zan 1994; Kohn 1993). An underdisciplined child will have difficulty learning both the centrality of morality and what is perceived as morally imperative. Her morality will be halfhearted at best. The risk of Maria's child-affirmation strategy is that in promoting self-esteem by praising the person, rather than the acts, she undermines the deeper self-esteem that comes from genuine accomplishments.

The necessary balance between disciplining and "understanding" wrongdoing is mediated by individual and circumstantial considerations. One would not mete out the same punishment to Tony as to a more conventionally socialized child; to a child with innocent as to one with self-aggrandizing intentions; to a child's wrongful act that had no consequences as to one that was substantially harmful; to an uninstructed as to a morally educated child.

In discerning the proper choice here, between "building" character by transmitting traditional values through a directive approach (Hardie) and "constructing" character as children grapple with their ongoing social problems in a democratic classroom environment (Maria), developmental considerations, although critically important, do not supply the sole guide. It is obvious to us that children must be taught certain rights and wrongs—e.g., stealing, lying, cheating, cruelty to people and destruction of property—and that they must be taught in advance of a fully autonomous understanding, for that is a very late developmental milestone. Appropriating a cultural transmission ideology and a behavioral methodology is suitable for those values, at least in part. When children do what is plainly wrong they should be so informed and held to account.

But some questions have answers that are more deeply contested: Should children be allowed to exclude one another from social activities, to express their fury at each other, to receive recognition and privileges for excelling, to report on others, to accept collective responsibility and participate in collective work? Further, the precise parameters of the conduct described as stealing, lying, cheating, cruelty, or destruction are not always plain, nor is it wholly clear what the appropriate discipline should be. Is it stealing when a child has no concept of property? Is it destruction when unintentional? Should a child be punished if provoked?—if instructed by a parent to do something wrong?

In these instances a constructivist approach seems more apt. Questions of fairness about particular events—equality regardless of merit, equity that takes merit or handicaps into consideration—may call especially for group discussions and individual reflection. Construction of some classroom rules by group action also is appropriate at any age, *provided* they concern matters that the teacher deems appropriate for decision by the children. Facilitated discussions among children should not be a device used to insinuate adoption of the teacher's values. It is a bad idea, therefore, to select topics—violence, for example—where decisions of the children may be vetoed, or to lead a discussion to a predetermined resolution (see Goodman 2000).

We note again that differing approaches, such as Hardie's and Maria's, are each incomplete without the leavening provided by the other. In contrast to Kohlberg, we believe that Maria's and Hardie's methods are complementary, not contradictory. To some extent the soil must be kept soft and pliable, inviting children to shape it. The approach of Maria—gentle, welcoming, caring, child-deferent—serves that end. Recall (again) her first statement of intention as she prepared to begin teaching: "I'm going to be kind and caring towards the children, provide a good model, and expect them, with occasional reminders from me, to be kind to one another."

There is merit here. Kindness is catching; it feels good to get and good to offer; it stokes empathy. Voluntary feelings of obligation are likely to emerge out of gratitude for kindness received. Kindness also fosters identification. The children, liking Maria, will want to be like her. And the opportunity to be heard, what Hardie deprecates as "talk therapy," will encourage increased reflection and rationality.

But to some extent the soil must be made firm, its contours set by adults for children to follow. Hardie's drills in habits of restraint (not talking out of turn), respect (removing hats), and good deeds (volunteering at the animal shelter) also have merit. It is true that when a student's action is plainly wrong a purely admonitory or punitive response will probably fail to foster development of moral identity in the student. However, a more sympathetic response, which leads a teacher to understand the roots of the behavior, but is not accompanied by action intended to stop or redirect the behavior, will also fail to engage the child's potential for moral development. In this instance, the development of moral identity must wait a bit and decent acceptable behavior be insisted upon until it becomes habitual, even in the absence of internalization.

By contrast, when students have said or done something that a teacher *believes* is wrong, but recognizes that others might reasonably think otherwise (for example, a group's refusal to choose a child for recess teams because he or she is just not skilled enough), a preemptive intervention to force the child onto one team—like its opposite, a relativist, "who can judge" attitude—does not constitute moral teaching. What is required of the teacher is that he or she facilitate the students' engagement (probably in the classroom later on, rather than in the school yard during recess) with the moral element, and the moral complexity, of their actions.

In many ways, moral education is more art than science. We suspect Hardie and Maria are both effective moral educators because they are committed to the enterprise and to the children, because they know what reasonably can be expected of fourth-graders, because they are superb role models, and because, though they "lean" to particular approaches, they show a pedagogical balance and respect one another despite their differing priorities.

Perhaps the most salient lesson is the centrality of the classroom teacher. Given the goal that we have suggested (growing a personal moral identity) and the variety of means to that end (appealing to the emotional and rational, staging the instruction, combining differing pedagogies), it seems clear that moral education requires, perhaps more so than other aspects of the educational program, a teacher's enthusiastic commitment.

Implementation of even the soundest program is not a ministerial act. It cannot be wholly scripted, for it cannot displace the need for individual teacher judgment and situation-sense in response to the varying dynamics of individual classroom moments. Genuine respect for the professional discretion and judgment of individual teachers in carrying out the program should therefore be built into the design of the program. Similarly, teachers should find in the specifics of a program's manner of execution significant opportunities to learn from and support one another.

Above all, a program must seek, and prove able, to tap the teachers' aspirational side, however that may have become obscured by the many dispiriting aspects of daily life as a classroom teacher. To accomplish this end, it is necessary for the central administration to strengthen its supportive input—as, for example, by making resources available to teachers as they begin to take on a new program—and lighten the extent to which it prescribes details. It is also necessary, however, for individual teachers, often harried by multiple demands upon them and struggling with issues of "burnout" and related ills, to rise to the occasion, to take seriously the goals and demands of moral education, and to resist the ever-present voice that would mock a positive response to aspiration. A school administration may make this response harder or easier, but the ultimate responsibility to decide whether to engage with the program lies with each teacher.

In reading the next (and final) chapter, we ask you to keep these thoughts in mind as we consider the construction and implementation of a specific set of curricular interventions in the name of moral education.

✱✱✱ At the Library

F. Clark Power, "School Climate and Character Development"
(1987, 157–159)

[The need for students] to develop a sense of responsibility for the welfare of the school community . . . is illustrated in the following excerpts taken from a class discussion about making an agreement that would require students to enforce a rule against stealing. This discussion is particularly revealing because high school students in general recognize that stealing is a serious, intrinsically immoral action, while they generally regard such actions as class cutting and marijuana and alcohol use as less serious, conventional violations. The adult discussion leader presented the class with a situation which had recently occurred in the school. A student left his portable tape recorder in his locker and forgot to lock it. Another student passing by stole the tape recorder and later bragged about it to his friends.

Leader: Should his friends express their disapproval?

Mary: I'd say you'd better not brag about it. You'd better shut your mouth or you'll get caught.

Sally: If somebody is going to be dumb enough to bring something like that into the school, they deserve to get it stolen. If you aren't together enough to lock your locker, then what can you expect. If somebody is going to steal, then more power to them.

Leader: Is that what other people think? It's OK if you can get away with it?

Mary: No, stealing is wrong.

Leader: Well then, do you have a responsibility in a situation like this to try to talk the thief into returning the stolen goods?

Mary: You can't put pressure on students like that.

Bill: You can't ask that.

Mary: This school is responsible for enforcing rules.

Bill: Yeah, the kids come here to learn, not to patrol the hallways. They come here to go to school.

Mary: We are the ones who are teenagers. The teachers are grown up. They are the big people. They are supposed to control the students in the school. We are here to learn.

Todd: You shouldn't steal. But the way society is, everybody does it. . . . [Expressing disapproval] depends on a lot of things—[like] who is whose friend. It depends on what they want to do. . . . Let them take the risk of losing a friend or let them not say anything.

This exchange is quite revealing and by no means atypical. I would like to call attention to four points. First, there is a gap between students' acknowledgment that stealing is wrong and their passive acceptance of its occurrence. Since, as Todd put it, "everybody steals," few members of the school . . . feel a sense of moral outrage or disappointment when stealing occurs. Second, . . . the students reacted in ways which protected the thief; and Sally even condoned stealing, as a fitting response to the foolishness of bringing something of value to school. Third, Sally's willingness to excuse the thief while blaming the victim illustrates the strength of the privatistic norms of self-protectiveness and mistrust and the lack of any collective sense of mutual trust or care. Fourth, the students refuse to accept responsibility for rule enforcement, as incompatible with their status as teenagers and students and as destructive of their friendships. While we may feel sympathy for Mary's claim that asking students to share responsibility for enforcing rules places great pressure on them, are we to maintain that adolescents should feel no responsibility in this area? Moreover, need there be a conflict between adolescent loyalties to their peer friendship groups and loyalty to the school as a whole? For Aristotle such a conflict would indicate that something was lacking in their conceptions of friendship and the school society. He viewed the bonds of friendship as necessary for making the *polis* or larger societal associations possible.

[The incident illustrates the] failure of schools to develop in students a habit of active, democratic participation. The fact that the staff generally make the significant decisions about school life and discipline leads students to develop habits of passivity and acquiescence. Such habits may be functional within certain bureaucratic contexts. However, such habits run counter to the principle of democratic participation, which underlies our society, and to our conception of the developed moral conscience, as one which actively seeks to discern the right and the good in active collaboration with others. Unfortunately, in many of our schools we teach about political democracy in the social studies class but our practices of schooling are far from democratic. John Dewey pointed out that this segmentation of democracy into a narrow, political realm posed a great threat to our democratic political structures:

> Whenever democracy has fallen it was too exclusively political in nature. It had not become part of the bone and the blood of the people in the conduct of life. Unless democratic habits are part of the fibre of a people, political democracy is insecure. It cannot stand in isolation. It must be buttressed by the presence of democratic methods in all social relationships.[5]

---

[5] John Dewey, "Democracy in the Schools," in *Intelligence in the Modern World: John Dewey's Philosophy,* ed. Joseph Ratner (New York: Modern Library, 1939), pp. 720–721 (footnote by author).

The context for these remarks by Dewey is a plea for greater teacher participation in decision making as well as for student participation. How are teachers to help students to form democratic habits, if their workplace, the school, discourages the faculty's exercise of democratic participation? How is democracy to become a part of the "bone and blood" of our youth if it is not a vital part of their school experience?

As we have emphasized throughout this book, competing schools of pedagogical thought, although often viewed as exclusive of one another, can and should be integrated. To partake of multiple practices is neither inconsistent nor unprincipled; indeed, a multipronged approach reflects and respects the complexity of children's motives and learning processes, as the following reading suggests.

William Damon, *Greater Expectations: Overcoming the Culture of Indulgence in America's Homes and Schools*
(1995, 155-159)

Socialization practices that focus on the character side of children's development must foster good habits as well as the capacity for careful reflection. We must not allow ourselves to become distracted by those who would polarize the two. It is indeed true that habit and reflection are two distinct psychological systems, with distinct developmental roots. In order to integrate the two systems, we must recognize the differences between them; but in no way does this imply that we should set the two in opposition.

Habit is deeply embedded in the child's emotional and behavioral reflex system, whereas reflection derives from cognitive schemes of abstraction and is closely linked to the child's intellectual competence. Habits are based upon natural dispositions that are bolstered over years of actual practice; whereas reflection derives from advances in insight that can be hypothetical or speculative. Habit grows on the plane of action, whereas reflection grows on the plane of consciousness. Habit is automatic, whereas reflection is subject to decision (and indecision). Habit is spontaneous and embedded in one's immediate experience; whereas reflection draws on notions that are distant in time and place from the situation that one finds oneself in.

Both habit and reflection can be sources of moral action, though of very different kinds. Habit rules over the vast territories of moral behavior that most of us simply assume. In general, the vast majority of human social life is harmonious and well-regulated, beginning early in childhood. Children do not routinely rob, kill, or lie: such behaviors are exceptional even among troubled populations. The reason that children normally do not deviate from our social norms is that they acquire, through nature and practice, habitual patterns of emotional and behavioral responding. For most children most of the time, such patterns trigger prosocial acts such as helping or sharing and prevent antisocial responses such as violence or theft.

But on some occasions, children's normal patterns of behavior fall short of the situation's demands. Conditions change, and unexpected new circumstances suddenly appear. Strong new temptations may arise. Old habits become tested, or they no longer apply. At such junctures, children must turn to reflection in order to appraise their alternatives. These periods of reflective awareness can be crucial during key turning points in life. The deliberative choices that they engender can lead children to whole new levels of moral awareness and commitment.

▼▼▼▼▼

The impassioned civil rights leader Virginia Durr, for example, threw off her own habitual racism in a series of incidents that began when she turned seven. During Virginia's birthday party, a cousin insulted a black child that Virginia was fond of. Virginia protested vehemently. With her protest began a whole new critical perspective on the system of discrimination that Virginia had grown up with and had taken for granted. Later, when at college, she still struggled with her own disinclination to sit at the same dinner table with black students. It was not until she began working side by side with black women on joint political causes that Virginia was able fully to shed her early prejudicial views and adopt a wholehearted belief in racial equality. Virginia's perspective grew over decades of similar observations, experiences, and reflections. It came to fruition when, in middle adulthood, she became a leader in the struggle to give voting rights to all Americans.

New choices of action based upon self-conscious moral reflection are both important and noteworthy, because they often disrupt the prior flow of development. Still, they are relatively rare in the course of human life. Habitual responses, in contrast, generate moral actions frequently, in ways so common that they usually go unnoticed. All the acts of moral commission and omission that we often take for granted—a mother watching over her child, a dedicated teacher helping her student, a man declining to steal from a beggar—represent moral acts that are commonly conducted through habitual emotional and behavioral processes. This is why the moral life is built on a foundation of habit; even though, as in the case of Virginia Durr, its design at times may be modified through flashes of reflective insight.

▼▼▼▼▼

Young people must learn to act right habitually, as a matter of course. The moral life is built primarily on good habits. It is important that young people learn to resist immoral temptations in the same automatic way that most people refrain, without hesitation, from robbing a helpless beggar or hurting their loved ones. But reflection, when grounded in good values, supports rather than deflects the habitual moral response. Moreover, reflection is one way to guard against that periodic human tendency to blindly stumble into horrendous moral mistakes. Only when habit and reflection marry does sustained moral commitment become possible. It is such commitment, and no less, that we must aim for in our children. It is this goal that must drive our socialization practices.

Both reflection and habit are essential ingredients in the final mix that defines a child's moral character. This point for those concerned with the moral character of young people is not to weigh their importance but to find ways of advancing them both. It is not enough to promote reflection and habit on separate developmental tracks. We must help children find ways to integrate the disparate psychological systems that reflection and habit represent. For the main part of moral growth is not simply acquiring good habits or insightful reflectiveness; rather, it is developing the capacity to move easily between the two. This capacity requires a conscious awareness of one's own habits; and, even more importantly, it requires coherence between one's theoretical moral beliefs and one's deep-seated emotional and be-havioral response systems.

♥♥♥♥♥

There is no single way to promote such coherence. To the contrary, only a vari-ety of experiences can help children integrate moral habit and reflection and ulti-mately to develop their capacities for sustained moral commitment. Variety in moral experience is as important for the growth of character as balance in instruction is for the growth of competence. The variety may include direct engagement in moral activities such as serving others in need, observations of moral behavior on the part of others, discussions of moral issues with respected peers and adults, and reflec-tions about the meaning of moral activity for one's own sense of identity and pur-pose in the world. Formal instruction in a religious or spiritual tradition also plays a key part, as does guided awareness of transcendent moral concerns in the world at large.

Chapter 9

Forging a Moral Identity

✳ At School

What with all the politicized skirmishes over service learning, Helter opted for a postponement. Anticipating their protest, he called Connie, Aggie, Hardie, and Maria to his office.

"Look," he began awkwardly, "I have a lot of respect for what you've been up to this semester. I want you to know that. Not just the service learning project but all the talk about morality that you've stimulated. Maria, your agitation over "coaching" children for the achievement tests, you had a legitimate gripe there. And Hardie, your service plan just took me by total surprise—true, a pleasant surprise, but surprise nonetheless. I just wasn't prepared to do battle. As principal I should have gotten out in front, but it's not too late; my announcing a postponement isn't a subterfuge."

"Who knew?" Hardie began, as always irresistibly drawn to anyone suffering guilt pangs. "Who could possibly have guessed the reactions of all the parties? And you say it's not a dead duck yet?"

"No, not at all," Helter continued. "I've got a request and a promise to put to you today."

"Let's skip right to the promise," Aggie suggested in her brusque, bemused way. "I get real nervous about requests, especially when they are tethered to rewards."

"You're free to say no, Aggie, but here's the suggestion," continued the now more relaxed principal. "The clamor over service learning made me realize that we need to have a better sense of what we're about in this school—morally about, that is. What do we stand for? What sort of people do we want our students to be when they graduate? How do we help them get there? I don't mean we need a 'vision thing'; not one of those vacuous statements schools put out. I mean a direction and a program to get us there. Hardie's proposal, as I see it, was merely an element of a program. One element for one class—that's not the way to go."

"We should be able to cook you up a program this evening," said Aggie. "And then the promise?"

Ignoring Aggie's tease, Helter continued. "I have sufficient funds squirreled away to pay you for a little released time these last few weeks of school and more for some time over the summer. What I'd like you to consider together is how we might do moral education in our school."

"*Do* moral education?" Maria asked, more of herself than the others. "Hardie and I have been squabbling all year about what moral education *is*, never mind how to *do* it."

"I know you've had your disagreements, but now it's time to move on. Find areas of agreement and room to agree on disagreeing. Find out what other teachers think and want. Talk to parents. Do more reading. Go visit programs. You want this to happen. So do I."

"And the promise part?" Aggie insisted again.

"I promise that, although of course your plan will be modified as we get more input, I will support the process all the way. I will stand behind it with the parents, the administration, and the school board. I know the final product won't please everyone, no one completely, but as long as you consider the interests of all parties, I'll back it. I will go up against Senter if need be, though I think he too was thrown off balance and is sympathetic at heart. But if necessary, politics be damned!"

Hardie responded swiftly: "I'll sign on the dotted line. How about you three?"

"Absolutely," said Maria. "An impossible and impossibly wonderful assignment. Right, Aggie?"

"Not so fast, you guys! I want to hear a bit more. What exactly is the 'product' we four are to produce, Fred?"

"Well, I don't want this killed in advance with excessive formatting instructions—the five goals, ten objectives, and twenty implementations sort of approach—but we do need something that will explain what, overall, we're trying to achieve, and how we're going to achieve it; you know, something about curriculum and pedagogy. I suggest that you work out general objectives while school is still in session, run them by a few teachers and parents from different constituencies, and then work up the fuller plan over the summer. If you want more input from a consultant, the budget can handle a little of that. Aggie, as you have the most seniority, I'd like you to take the lead."

"By which you mean that I'm sufficiently crusty to put up with angry phone calls as the initiative leaks out, sufficiently detached to put up with our own internal squabbling, and sufficiently docile toward principals' 'requests' that by fall you'll have a report on your desk come what may."

"Something along those lines," Helter said with a grin as he thanked them and closed the meeting.

The three classroom teachers were in fact very pleased with their assignment. Helter had abundant choices: He easily could have walked away from the commotion over moral education and done nothing; he could have tossed a sop at the problem with a small gesture, something like a canned goods drive at Christmas or a hallway exhibition dedicated to morality; or he could have asked Jan Bonham to write up a proposal for the school. They were lucky in Helter; at bottom he identified with them, not with out-of-the-building authorities, and he respected them. With that wind at their backs they agreed to an immediate meeting for brainstorming.

It was Connie Comfort, however, who began the conversation. "I guess my total silence in Helter's office was pretty noticeable. Let me make up for that by being first with my initial reaction to his idea. I've been watching events this year from the sideline—which, after you hear what I have to say, is where you may wish I stayed. With one foot in the school and the other foot in the community, I know how touchy this moral education business is, and it's clear to me that we need to move very gingerly or we're in for a full-scale parental eruption, far bigger than Hardie's service learning idea caused."

Hardie, put off by Connie's habit of reducing moral education to service learning and service learning to his problematic project, as well as by her usual don't-stir-the-waters mentality, asked a bit gruffly, "What would 'very gingerly' look like, Connie?"

"If we are to get support from parents and teachers, we should have a program that concentrates on the school's big ticket problems, the ones that bother everybody. We should stop children's general rudeness to teachers and each other, stop their outright disobedience when given explicit instructions to do or not to do something (from throwing away food wrappers to bringing in homework), stop the bullying and fighting—and, yes, Maria, stop the swearing."

"What, nothing about drugs, booze, and sex?" asked Hardie, increasingly irritated.

"Those issues haven't hit us hard as yet, but maybe, as a prophylactic," Connie answered. "But first, we establish a uniform discipline code that makes sense and is enforceable. The kids learn that each time they are rude—talk back, fail to follow an instruction—there are immediate consequences; you know, one or two demerits depending on the offense, a detention after a certain number get accumulated. Then we also put in place a beefed up dispute resolution process, along with training of kids and teachers to deal with the bullying and violence. Although, come to think of it, central as they are, I'm not sure we can deliver teachers for training."

Now, it was Maria's turn to jump in. "Connie, I wish you could hear yourself. You sound so dreary, discouraged, and dispirited. Your proposal is so limited. Moral education has to be more than a set of techniques to quiet kids so we can get through the day with minimal disruptions."

"Maybe so, Maria, but as far as I'm concerned a calm atmosphere and obliging children would go a long way to lift the sinking morale and growing teacher burn-out in this place. Don't sell it short unless you've got better goods."

Hardie was glad to take up this invitation to move beyond Connie's ideas. "Fair enough, Connie. I've been peddling my preferred brands to Maria all year, so I might as well put a few on the table for us now. Yes, Connie, kids are rude and many are driving teachers nuts. I have zero tolerance for children's insolence, as Maria knows; I took her on pretty strongly for being tolerant of a child's out-of-bounds behavior. But the solution must be more indirect. We don't get kids to behave—or perhaps I should say we will at most get them merely to behave—by making our primary target an assault on their misbehavior. We underrate children and undermine the grand appeal of morality if our goal is so meager, if it's only that children should learn to refrain from rudeness and not engage in violence. If we are to hook them on the moral, we need to provide greater inspiration."

"What's uninspiring about not fighting? I think it is a worthy and wonderful goal for a child," Connie retorted.

"Come on, Connie," Aggie now weighed in. "Hardie's clearly right about that. When was the last time your self-image got pumped because you avoided a fight? Even if it's true, which I doubt—by my lights you're a scrappy (and effective) woman—not fighting is a narrow goal, it's situationally specific, and it's negative, hardly a grand motivator."

"So what would 'grand motivators' look like?"

"Well," Hardie answered, "a lot of folks talk about organizing moral education programs around the virtues of 'respect' and 'responsibility.' We might consider them, but to me the terms are a bit wimpy, or maybe I mean too flexible. Hell, Connie, you might adopt them to cover the don't-fight, don't-be-rude goals. Selecting a few virtues for our program is fine, but I'd prefer courage, fortitude, temperance, persistence—traits we aspire to and never fully acquire."

"Hardie, I see you can keep the man out of the Marines but you can't keep the Marines out of the man," rejoined a now animated Connie. "You don't really believe that the kids in this school, most of whom watch TV at least four hours a day, complain if they have to wash the dishes, and moan over homework, are nurtured, as you were by your ex-Marine Dad, on honor, duty, and patriotism?"

"And besides, Hardie," it was Maria entering the conversation, "ex-Marine or not, you romanticize what touches children. They are into playing and giggling and talking together, into gaining approval and acceptance, into their baseball-card collections and video games, into hanging out and eating junk food, and, sometimes, into doing their work. Our program should concentrate on helping them behave considerately and decently during these activities."

"Oh no, Maria!" exclaimed Hardie, as usual piqued by her outlook. "If their lives are so humdrum, it's our fault. Romantic, maybe I am, but not unrealistic. Look at the stories kids love: They go for victories by the small and righteous over the large and loathsome—Moses felling Pharaoh, David against Goliath, Jesus against the money changers, Jack against the giant, Hansel and Gretel against the witch. They go for courage against adversity—Dorothy and her companions conquering fear, Huck Finn placing his life at risk to save Jim, the girls of *Little Women* overriding poverty and illness to provide for their family. They go for adventure stories filled with risk, bravery, self-sacrifice, and generosity—Tolkien's *The Hobbit* and C. S. Lewis' *The Lion, the Witch and the Wardrobe*."

"You *are* a romantic!" Maria shot back, although with a smile of admiration and recognition to go with her exasperation. "*The Wizard of Oz* is only superficially about courage. Really it's about friendship among an unlikely collection of characters. So is *Little Women*—four sisters lovingly supporting each other and their parents. So is the Hansel and Gretel story. The bonds between siblings may have been forged in danger and terror, but it's their attachment to each other that's gripping. That's what makes *The Mill on the Floss* so memorable. "

"Well, George Eliot may be memorable to you . . . ," Hardie began, then quickly desisted in favor of Aggie's forceful intervention.

"Let's take a breather," she suggested, "and try to give ourselves some direction. I think I see where each of you is going, or at least coming from. Connie is proposing a targeted approach concentrating on critical school problems that fall in the moral domain. Hardie wants a program that taps lofty aspirations and, knowing him as I do, Connie's everyday courtesy and decency will surely get folded into these high-minded virtues. Maria wants to concentrate on the positive side of Connie's negative agenda—how we get children to be kind and caring to one another. Instead of our pitting each approach against the others, can we each be a bit more specific about how we'd meet our goals? Connie, how about if you start us off by elaborating on what you've already said about discipline?"

"Look," said Connie, eyeing Hardie, "I know you think this is the same old boring classroom-management stuff. But can't you see we've got to start with what's workable? Put aside the fact that it would be no small achievement if teachers behaved more uniformly and consistently, and if children clearly understood limits and consequences. With the diversity of families in this school, we have to worry about ruffling sensibilities. We all know that teachers complain when Senter and Helter tell them what to do; well, parents don't like it either when they and their kids are told how to live. You can only work on this stuff around the edges.

"But I didn't mean to sound as though all I favor is tighter discipline. I don't want to be a martinet, and I don't want kids to be marionettes. I'd like to have more student participation in decision making. I'd like them to think about what's right; how they, how we, should all treat one another. We could get representatives from each upper-grade elementary class to join the faculty in discussions on rules, as well as on discipline. Students might also be part of a group charged with resolving disputes and monitoring the rudeness-civility business. Service learning might be useful too, but let's keep it simple and local—cleaning the classroom and school grounds, helping out in the cafeteria and library. It better be modest and voluntary or there will be an uproar."

"All right, I think we're getting somewhere," said Aggie. "Connie suggests meeting her targets with a clear discipline code, student participation in developing and perhaps implementing that code, and a modest voluntary service learning project. Hardie?"

"I'm against a uniform discipline code for a couple of reasons. For one, it's too prescriptive; you're never going to get my friend Maria to give demerits for rudeness, and I'd give more than demerits. For another, it overly emphasizes violations and punishment. Without meaning to brag, I don't have a rudeness problem in class. My kids know what's off-limits. Maybe it's my emphasis on habit training, but anyway, they know from their first day that I expect civil, polite behavior at all times, no exceptions.

"Furthermore, I've come to think that cleaning—the classroom, the cafeteria, the school grounds—should not be classified as 'service.' We must routinely expect that much of our kids, just as they do in Japanese schools. We should make such chores a regular part of the school day—and I'd extend the chore list to helping the janitors, the secretaries, the crossing guards, the librarians, etc. 'Service' is helping others, not caring for our own school community. That's no more 'service' than the chores children perform, or should be performing, in their own homes."

"Just a minute," Aggie broke in. "The maintenance employees union would have a name for 'helping the janitors'—*scabbing*. They'd surely see it as a move to lay some of them off. But for the rest, Hardie, you've told us what you're against, now tell us what you're for."

"Glad to. Once you accept my 'grand' virtues, I'm not too concerned about how we implement them. When it comes to methods, we don't need to reinvent the wheel. I'd be content adopting one of those programs we heard about in Jan Bonham's in-service day,[1] such as Josephson's Six Pillars of Character or the Character Education Curriculum. But we also could do it ourselves, borrowing the standard common methods—discussions with children and parents, workshops, speakers and assemblies, recognition of outstanding character (I prefer out-of-school heroic types to in-school people), posters and spirit-engendering school events, careful selection of required and optional books (especially in language arts and social studies classes), genuine community service. But most of all we need to have a committed faculty willing to give a lot of themselves."

"Maria, could you turn your scowls into a statement of your own views?" Aggie asked.

"Sure. Given the hour, though, I'll make it short and to the point. I agree with just one of Connie's points: parents *are* squeamish on this subject. And I agree with just one of Hardie's points: 'most of all we need to have a commit-

---

[1] See Chapter 5.

ted faculty willing to give a lot of themselves.' What I'm for, therefore, is moral awareness, moral conscientiousness, and *no* moral education program in any formal sense, none of the stuff Hardie went through except for his last sentence, which I totally agree with. We insinuate morality. We keep the talk flowing—with each other, with kids, with parents, with our friends, with the media, with our own community groups. We look for opportunities to raise questions with children about the implications of their behavior. When appropriate, we point out better ways, fairer ways, more caring ways of behaving.

"But to formalize moral education is to kill it. Morality isn't math after all, although that too could do with more insinuation and less formal instruction. However earnest and morally conscientious the teacher, she cannot impose morality onto a reluctant child, she can only impose obedience. Hardie does a great job not because of his lofty goals or his habit training, but because the kids observe his own character. Do you know he calls every sick kid every day, and he visits them, too? He stays after school and tutors without charge, he takes up every fallen bush and flower on school property, and he slips kids pencils and papers, books, whatever they might need. *That's* why he doesn't have a 'rudeness problem.'"

Aggie, content that the group had so readily and fully aired its differing views, concluded that the next step in this thorny job was for each member to explore the issues independently. "Friends," she said, "this is proving to be an even harder task than I expected. I've been persuaded by each of you in turn. It's late. I suggest we mull over what's been discussed, talk to colleagues, and reconvene next week. I'm going out to hunt for some big goal that might cover the diversity among us. Wish me well." The others gladly assented, and the group adjourned.

▼▼▼▼▼

Aggie opened the next meeting. "This afternoon our time is limited, so I'd like to omit the chitchat and present one idea for your reactions. I've paid Jan Bonham a visit. Naturally, she wouldn't say anything until I gave her a summary of our meeting. It turned out that where we heard discord, she heard agreement. We'd all veto a program aimed at creating obedient automatons—marionettes is what Connie said. Each of us wants to see kids who, at graduation, have internalized an appetite for goodness. We may not agree on what qualities best exemplify goodness—I suspect, although Bonham isn't so certain, that Maria and Hardie would select different ones—but we all see this quality of striving after goodness as essential. Maria spoke of moral conscientiousness, Hardie of aspiring. Bonham calls this quality having a moral identity; she is convinced that it's the umbrella for sheltering all moral education programs."

"Pretty woolly term, if you ask me," Hardie burst in. "Isn't she just trying to mask our disagreement? Sounds tautological, too—the goal of moral education is for kids to internalize moral education."

"Hold on, Hardie. That rush to cynicism, does it come from hanging around me too long?" Aggie asked. "Actually, I think she's on to something.

Moral identity, says Bonham, means that when kids begin to picture what kind of grownup they want to be, what jobs, what lifestyle they seek, they will use moral criteria along with the familiar ones—family approval, money, status, power, pleasure, aptitude. And they will put their daily choices through the same filter, asking questions like: Is it (the choice) socially useful or harmful?—in the short run?—in the long run? Will I have to make moral compromises? If so, of what sort? Will I be able to hold onto my integrity?"

"Hmm," from Hardie. "My sort of language."

"Mine too," from Maria and Connie simultaneously.

"She made several other good points," Aggie continued, "that now seem obvious. If one's morality is central to one's identity, it isn't so easy to know what's right and do what's wrong. In my own case, for example, even when I disapprove, I usually follow Helter's orders—the textbooks he wants, the grade distribution he wants, the frequency of parent conferences he wants—but I won't do social promotions. Why not? Because I think it's a form of lying, because I think it sets kids up for more failure, and because I think it cheats those who deserve promotion. Helter knows that and gives way. There are plenty of good people who disagree with me but, nonetheless, it's something I will not do. I guess you could say it's part of my moral identity.

"Bonham also pointed out that moral identity is an aspect of oneself that takes a long time to develop; the process only starts in elementary school. And it's intricate. It should include Connie's rule-setting and discipline, Hardie's lofty virtues, and Maria's social sensitizing. How much of which and when depends on what values you are trying to get across, the child's developmental status, and his or her individuality. She was also very big on the critical importance of teachers' reflection and commitment, something you all mentioned as well. So Hardie, Bonham isn't ducking or papering over controversies. She says moral identity is complex and we've got to figure out the details."

"And, of course, she would be glad to lend a hand on the details, for a nice fee," Hardie said, only partially facetiously.

"Oh, come on, Hardie," protested Maria, "give her a break. I still like what Aggie is saying and I gather Connie does, too. She's at risk for a neck-ache tomorrow from all that nodding."

"It does sound good," agreed Connie. "I'm especially attracted to the developmental part. That's something we haven't thought nearly enough about, and by 'we' I mean parents as well. What's right for the first-grader differs from what's right for the fifth. I can see selling that approach. Everyone, regardless of child-rearing philosophy and methods, deals differently with younger than older kids; the younger are more supervised, more corrected, more directed. However, I share Hardie's concern about 'woolliness.' How do we determine what goes under the umbrella?"

"This is not bad," sighed a relieved Aggie. "If we agree that moral identity can serve as an embracing goal, I can write up a short summary for Helter and include your different slants—we'll call them objectives. Then, oh joy, we can spend the summer months together working on Connie's question as we compose a fuller, more concrete document. Does hard-to-convince Hardie agree?"

"Whatever possessed me to select a career in elementary school teaching? Against three strong women all I can do is pocket my doubts, for now anyway, and surrender to you."

"You can't fool us, Hardie, you just want out of here," said Aggie as she stood up. "It's too beautiful an evening not be with your significant other."

"Afraid not. We're history."

Hardie, turning away quickly—perhaps in embarrassment—missed Aggie's knowing glance at Maria. Only the two women saw Maria's blush and her hastily averted gaze.

Report of the Faculty Committee on Moral Education
Agatha Cerine, Constance Comfort, Hardie Knox, Maria Laszlo[2]

GOAL: BUILDING A MORAL IDENTITY

The Centrality of Teachers to a Moral Education Program
Teachers attentive to their own morality
Teachers attentive to a moral curriculum
Teacher authority to individualize curriculum
Teacher training and support

The School as an Open Moral Community
A serious commitment
A broad commitment
Required participation in targeted moral activities

Core Values: Rights and Reaches
Protecting rights
Encouraging the reach
The value of doubt

Shared Teacher–Student Responsibility
Teacher enforcement of primary values
Participation of students in rule-making and rule-enforcement
Open discussion of moral issues

A Developmental Pedagogy
Staging pedagogies
Staging accountability
Staging construction of moral identity

End/Beginnings

Supplementary Statement of Professor Jan Bonham

❡❡❡❡❡❡❡❡❡❡

We begin with a confession. The disagreement among us has been keen; but for our common commitment to moral education we might well have abandoned this effort. We have disagreed across the board: What are the components of a good program? How should they be taught? By whom? Under what circumstances? Nor did a careful review of other programs, further reading, and considerable consultation appreciably diminish those disagreements.

In frustration, and with our due date looming, we considered ducking by submitting an inoffensive report of broad generalizations. Each of us, for example,

---

[2] We acknowledge with gratitude the consultative services of Professor Jan Bonham, of the State University School of Education.

could advocate the virtues of respect and responsibility as critical to any program. But we soon realized that each of us attaches quite different meaning to those words. Hardie Knox links them to the child-as-student, with an expectation that primary respect is due to school authorities and primary responsibility to school's imposed obligations—conscientiously following the rules and expectations, "going along." Maria Laszlo links the words to the emergent child-as-agent, with the expectation that primary respect and responsibility go to the individual conscience, which sometimes requires questioning authority and resisting go-along pressures. Connie Comfort links the words to the family, with the expectation that they, not the child, are obliged to give (and receive) respect and responsibility; it is their accountability that should be the first concern of the school, for the child will fall in line behind his or her parents. A report consisting of vaguely self-evident and innocuous generalizations, we realized, would bury such complexities and might, on balance, obscure and oversimplify more than it enlightened.

In the end our dilemma—how to write a useful report, while giving voice to legitimate differences—has been resolved (as we have learned it could be) only partially. Our moral education program (at the elementary school level) turns out to be more a set of criteria, of guideposts, than a blueprint. For some readers even this much detail will be too restrictive. They will object to the impositional, top-down suggestions, and to our assumption that schools can determine, at least in part, what values to teach and how to teach them. For others, the report will be excessively general, equivocal, and impractical. We understand their frustration. Although it was our intention to write a manual-like document, over time we came to believe that even if we could, we would not.

It seems right to preserve the disagreements this topic provokes. For some

twenty-five centuries philosophers have disagreed over every aspect of morality: the nature of a moral value, the instantiation of morality in acts, motives, and consequences, the justification for placing one value over another, the source and variability of values, the prerogative of judging, the cultivation of morality in the young. While there is (we believe) a consensus within our society on core values, we also recognize that moral values inevitably can conflict—justice with mercy, discipline with freedom, honesty with loyalty, persistence with compromise. Beyond these hurdles we face contentious pedagogical conflicts. We would be unfaithful to the depth and richness of the topic if, in the name of utility and practicality, we lost sight of just how tough and uncertain the practice of moral education can be.

The first requisite of a moral education program is that in making choices one remain alert to the alternatives rejected. Maintaining awareness of alternatives, though burdensome, emancipates the decision-making process from reflexive swiftness and is essential to a thoughtful tolerance. In that spirit we have set out minimal criteria for a moral education program against the background of contending positions. The criteria we have settled on are sometimes a compromise between polarities, sometimes a choice between them, and sometimes a synthesis of their commonalities. Assuming these criteria make sense, they should be construed as benchmarks for an educator charged with developing, carrying out, and evaluating a program of moral education.

GOAL: BUILDING A MORAL IDENTITY

A person's morality, as we have come to understand it, is more distillation than accumulation. Morality is not *merely* an accretion of disciplined habits, one layered on top of another until a child automatically and reliably becomes right-acting at school. It is not *merely* the nurturing of compassion, sufficient in amount so that a child will respond predictably with care and generosity in class. And it is not *merely* the cultivation of a knowledgeable, deliberative stance toward decision making, enabling a child eventually to weigh the moral implications (and ambiguities) of everyday choices.

The "moreness" of moral identity—that which is beyond good habits, compassion, and reflection—is partially captured by words like will, resolve, and aspiration. It is as much searching and striving as coping and adapting; it is a way-of-being-in-the-world rather than just a response-to-the-world.

Moral identity shares features with our other identities, such as our identity as an athlete or as a parent. It is true of at least our positive identities (and each of us has many) that we are *preoccupied* by them, that we *monitor* their adequacy, and that we *resist* challenges to them. For example, someone with a genuine athletic identity, as compared to someone who merely enjoys exercise or engages in sports for the adulation or profit it brings, is on the lookout for opportunities to play his sport. He expresses his athleticism off as well as on the field by staying in shape and avoiding temptations. He monitors his skill level and seeks to improve. Faced with a setback, such as an injury, he goes through rehabilitation eagerly and earnestly. Someone with a parental identity, as compared to someone who just happens to be a parent (even a conscientious one), steals time from nonparenting activities to be with his children. He thinks about parenting when not doing it, watches others and compares his style to theirs. He monitors and evaluates his skills, trying always to do better. When he makes a mistake or is rejected by his child, rather than withdrawing he redoubles his efforts. And someone with a strong, as compared to a weak, moral identity is alert to opportunities for expressing moral statements and actions, sees the moral implications in seemingly neutral situations, questions the adequacy of his responses, and courageously resists invitations to be amoral or immoral, despite the cost to his self-interest (as perceived by most).

If any doubt the centrality of moral identity, consider an example, extreme to be sure, of the effect of its absence. Adolph Eichmann, a Nazi S.S. officer, was executed in Israel in 1962 after conviction of the crime of organizing the deportation of millions of Jews to death camps with (in the words of the indictment) "the intent to destroy the [Jewish] people." Yet he was not without good habits, compassion, and deliberation. As described in Hannah Arendt's classic study, *Eichmann in Jerusalem: A Report on the Banality of Evil* (Arendt 1964; for the indictment, see p. 244), Eichmann bore no hatred for Jews. Indeed, for several years he prided himself on facilitating the emigration of many. His feelings towards his family and friends, according to psychiatrists who examined him at his war crimes trial, were highly "desirable." He was a persevering honest worker who equated conscience with duty, and duty with a meticulous obedience to orders. It was not for him to question policy or evaluate propaganda. His self-perception as a "little cog" in a vast enterprise left him totally insensitive to his own wrongdoing. What he lacked altogether was any independent moral core that might speak against his participation in the atrocities and any life purpose save self-advancement. He allowed himself to be fully defined by others and to accept whatever identity they thrust upon him. In Arendt's words:

> Except for an extraordinary diligence in looking out for his personal advancement, he had no motives at all. And this diligence in itself was in no way criminal; he certainly would never have murdered his superior in

order to inherit his post. He *merely*, to put the matter colloquially, *never realized what he was doing. . . .* He was not stupid. It was sheer thoughtlessness— something by no means identical with stupidity—that predisposed him to become one of the greatest criminals of that period. *(Id., 287–288) (emphasis in the original)*

In this deficiency Eichmann was like many others who, under orders, mindlessly commit acts that they would avoid but for such orders. As a member of the Hitler Youth put it: "The ghastly thing was just the fact that it was not gangsters and roughnecks, but decent, intelligent and moral people who allowed themselves to be induced to acquiesce in something deeply evil and to serve it" (Maschmann 1964, 221).

The famous experiments by Stanley Milgram (1969) on the psychology of obedience demonstrate that ordinary people readily administer what they believe to be extremely painful shocks to innocent subjects. (In fact, there were no shocks and the subject was a confederate feigning pain.) Once people perceive an authority (in Milgram's experiment, the "scientist") as legitimate, they surrender their autonomous conscience and do the unconscionable. As Milgram reports:

> Specifically, the person entering an authority system no longer views himself as acting out of his own purposes but rather comes to see himself as an agent for executing the wishes of another person.

▼▼▼▼▼▼▼

Morality does not disappear, but acquires a radically different focus: the subordinate person feels shame or pride depending on how adequately he has performed the actions called for by authority. *(Id., 133, 146)*

Children are particularly vulnerable to acquiescence, yet we would have them withstand powerful moral counter-pulls from peers and the larger society—pulls toward simple pleasures, popularity and power, material goods and respect. We ask children to treasure their moral identity so highly, to find its pursuit so gratifying, that they will turn from strong temptations, for who does not want to be successful and well liked? The major challenge for schools is how to implant *within* children the moral autonomy that allows them to question, monitor, and judge their acts (and failures to act), and if necessary to stand apart, while simultaneously grafting from *without* the enduring wisdom of our moral heritage.

On this our committee agreed: More important than a child's conformity to a set of rules or virtues is a lifelong moral alertness central to their self-definition. We also agreed that pursuit of this goal compels a school to make these commitments:

- The Centrality of Teachers to a Moral Education Program
- The School as an Open Moral Community
- Core Values: Rights and Reaches
- Shared Teacher–Student Responsibility
- A Developmental Pedagogy

The Centrality of Teachers to a Moral Education Program

Children will not become (and remain) morally alert and centered if teachers are bored, indifferent, and unengaged with morality. That much is obvious. But what more precisely do we mean by moral engagement? How high a priority must the moral hold in the teacher's teaching and in her personal life?

Some of us believe that no character-building program can succeed unless the faculty collectively makes it the center of its professional work. The faculty is obliged to be full-fledged ongoing participants in developing, maintaining, and evaluating the curriculum. Moreover, as instructors, teachers should infuse the moral dimension into all subjects wherever feasible and be sensitive to the moral aspects of all decision making. As influential persons, teachers should be moral exemplars; the standards they hold for themselves must at least equal the standards they hold for children. When there is personal moral slippage, as is inevitable, the school is obliged to have programs available for rekindling moral alertness. This entails providing teachers with administrative and curricular support, significant and regular amounts of in-service programs, and ample opportunities for formal and informal discussions among themselves. In addition, teachers' moral alertness should be assessed in the hiring and promotion process.

Others among us are of the view that growing moral identity in children, like growing other skills and interests, requires neither a major curricular investment nor a faculty of moral paragons. Indeed, grave dangers lurk along that path. Teachers mounted on white chargers may easily trample the rights and views of others. Just as one can be a good coach without being an athlete, and can give useful advice to parents without having children, so too one can be a good moral educator, yet a flawed person. Better to tread lightly in this area by gently drawing children's attention to moral issues as they come up in the existing curricular materials and children's ·social interactions. In fact, better not to have a formal "program" at all lest it become captive to oversimplified pronouncements, posturing, and self-righteousness.

To consider these positions more deeply, we asked ourselves how morality is like and unlike another academic discipline, mathematics. We agreed that to be an effective elementary-school math teacher one does not have to co-construct the math curriculum, insist that math permeate all subjects, or be preoccupied with the topic in one's nonteaching life. While effectiveness may be boosted by

such conditions, they are not mandatory. Is a moral educator properly to be held to a different standard?

According to the maximalists, the threshold of commitment for teaching morality is much higher than for teaching math. Although both subjects require an instructor to convey knowledge (both of facts and rules) and analytic skills, morality requires that he or she convey moral *desire* as well. Although we want children to use their mathematical skills in the world as well as in class, they need not seek and pursue math voluntarily, enthusiastically, and forever; they need not define themselves as one for whom math is important. The moral educator has to engage children in constructing a morality they can live by; the math teacher can more easily "lay on" the knowledge.

Because children imitate what they see, moral desire can be passed on, the maximalists argue, only if the teacher herself possesses a goodly supply and displays her wares to the children. While the math teacher need not be a mathematician, the moral educator must be a moralist: She must read the world through moral (among other) lenses, see herself as a moral agent, clarify the bases of her decisions, and be willing to pass judgments on events and the people responsible for them—while recognizing that (and explaining why) others disagree with her judgments.

It is a teacher's obligation not to mute her moral judgments and to help children formulate their own. The contemporary British philosopher Mary Warnock puts these points powerfully:

> You cannot teach morality without being committed to morality yourself, and you cannot be committed to morality yourself without holding that some things are right, others wrong. You cannot hold that, and at the same time sincerely maintain that someone else's view of the matter may be equally good. . . . No one needs much education to know that there are dif-

fering views as to what is right and wrong. They need to be educated, however, in the matter of defending their own position; and to this end, they need, from an early age, *examples* of people who are ready to do this with passion and integrity. They also need to see before their eyes people whose theoretical opinions actually make a difference to their own lives and practice. *(Warnock 1992, 164) (emphasis in original)(the first two sentences of this passage are quoted by Warnock from an earlier work of hers)*

Child psychiatrist Robert Coles emphasizes the centrality of a teacher's *actions:*

We grow morally as a consequence of learning how to be with others, how to behave in the world, a learning prompted by taking to heart what we have seen and heard. The child is a witness; the child is an ever-attentive witness of grown-up morality—or lack thereof; the child looks for cues as to how one ought to behave, and finds them galore as we parents and teachers go about our lives, making choices, addressing people, showing in action our rock-bottom assumptions, desires, and values, and thereby telling those young observers much more than we may realize. *(Coles 1997, 5).*

Assertions like these make mininimalists squirm. Moral education, they point out, has much more in common with math education than the maximalists appreciate. Like moral education, math requires applying a set of principles to the unfamiliar. Moreover, a good math teacher, like a good teacher of any subject, will want to cultivate an autonomous interest in the subject, as well as knowledge and judgment about it. Without an attraction to math, children will miss opportunities to resolve everyday problems by using these skills, just as, lacking an attraction to the moral, they will miss opportunities for making moral choices. Cultivating interest is obviously

enhanced by a teacher's sincere enthusiasm. When she clarifies why she cares for the subject, and backs up her declarations with real stories (of everyday problems solved, for example), children are more apt to take heed than when their exposure is confined to workbooks. Interest is also enhanced when the teacher illuminates the surprising relevance of mathematical ideas to other subjects.

But just as math need not be, probably should not be, a central preoccupation of teacher or student, for there is much else to teach and learn, so too with morality. To be aware of the moral angle in one's decisions and sensitive to the moral implications of others' decisions does not require a Herculean teaching effort. It is a state of mind that grows gradually in a child, is nurtured more at home than at school, and is profoundly influenced by one's peer group and the wider culture. Yes, children should hear the judgments of teachers, but teachers must hear the judgments of children and parents. It befits teachers to be modest in their ambitions, lest their efforts in this domain swamp other, equally central, educational obligations.

The differences among us suggest that even if a school is committed to building moral identity, as we recommend, teachers will vary on how much they want to "front" the enterprise. That is to be expected and respected. However, if teachers are to be engaged in this pursuit, we agree that a number of program components, to which we now turn, are indispensable.

Teachers Attentive to Their Own Morality

To be credible to children, teachers must attend first to their own morality. It is true of morality, as it is of literature or math, that one is forever an apprentice in search of deepening awareness. How does a teacher model awareness so that it is accessible to children? We believe that children catch their teacher's values by experiencing the fair, sometimes firm, sometimes fun-loving, sometimes forgiving, always caring manner he has with them; by his conscientiousness in preparing instruction and responding to student work; by his genuine interest in their families and extended lives; by his attentiveness to the special circumstances of individual children; by his efforts to foster supportive relationships among students. We add to such lists—which struck some of us as a bit too perfectionist—the imperative that teachers reveal, to themselves as well as to children, their *moral mistakes*. If the growth motif is to control the educational process then, as with any form of growth, we must look to false starts, errors, and backsliding for instruction. A teacher who can share wrongdoing and weakness in the context of renewed effort is, we believe, a powerful moral force for children.

Teachers Attentive to a Moral Curriculum

Teachers need also to find moral "lessons" (questions as well as answers) in the curriculum. For some this is a simple matter of self-consciously exploiting what already exists. As David Purpel and Kevin Ryan (1976) point out, the ordinary curriculum is morally laden: from debates about abortion in biology, to the justification for insurrection in history, to career education programs (id., 44–54).[3] Ted Sizer elaborates on the thought:

What a teacher selects to "tell" in a class is an exercise in values. If one refers in a social studies lesson to Native Americans as "them" and implies that the first settlers of the American West were Europeans, one is saying a great deal. Describing the Indians as the (likely) first of many human immigrants to these continents sends a quite different message. The way a biology teacher treats life in class—whether, for example, live frogs are purchased and pithed in quantity for students to dissect—signals important

values. Mocking the squeamishness and reserve of students who do not want to kill frogs can deeply affect a young student.... Can I take this frog's life so that I can learn about reptilian innards? The adult who impatiently rejects the legitimacy of a student's confusion teaches a value. One cannot teach at arm's length: the world does not allow it. The issue of life is in the middle of every biology class, and most other classes too. To pretend it is not there is to say something about it; in that sense is the vacuum dangerous. Value issues infuse every classroom. *(Sizer 1984, 123)*

Some teachers will rely on "moral moments" that occur spontaneously in the lives of children—a fight, a theft, an exclusion, an opportunity to help. Still others may prefer to turn to one of the published moral education programs. These range considerably in the values covered and the explicitness of the teaching. Whatever the merit in any such material,[4] there is a danger, where the "moral curriculum" is based wholly on externally generated material, that their lessons will be undermined by a teacher's neglect of the moral moments that arise at other times during the school day. This concern informs the next consideration especially.

Teacher Authority to Individualize Curriculum

More critical than what curricular vehicle teachers select is that they be given the authority to select. Too much management by higher-ups of what to teach and how to teach weakens the likelihood that the lessons will come to roost in the lives of teachers and therefore of children—at school and beyond. To be effective, a teacher must have the opportunity as well as the motivation to notice and seize occasions for reflection, for moral growth does not come without much mulling over. Without their signature on the in-

---

[3] [See also Benninga 1991; Jackson, Boostrom, and Hansen 1993; Lickona 1991; Ryan and Bohlin 1999.]

[4] [For discussion, see Chapter 5.]

struction, teachers are not likely to be successful.

Teacher Training and Support

Schools should recognize that the success of a moral education program is dependent on teacher sophistication as well as teacher enthusiasm. Neither comes for the asking. Because there are enormous complexities at the what-to-teach and how-to-teach levels, ongoing formal and informal support is required if teachers are to become comfortable with the subject matter. Teachers will benefit from ample opportunities for collaborative study and discussion as well as for contact with "experts" and administrators.

The School as an Open Moral Community

Important as teachers are (a fact this group was not likely to overlook), the larger collectivity is also responsible for the morality children learn. "The school itself must embody good character," say Thomas Lickona and his collaborators:

> It must progress toward becoming a microcosm of the civil, caring, and just society we seek to create as a nation. The school can do this by becoming a moral community that helps students form caring attachments to adults and to each other. . . . The daily life of classrooms, as well as all other parts of the school environment (e.g., the corridors, cafeteria, playground, and school bus), must be imbued with core values such as concern and respect for others, responsibility, kindness, and fairness. *(Lickona, Schaps, and Lewis 1997–1998, Principle 4)*

To manifest its good faith, a school should be up-front about its values and priorities in the self-defining (and self-promoting) statements it makes to the extended community, most particularly parents. It should provide safe opportunities for discussion that are inclusive of parents, staff, children, administration,

and faculty and, where feasible, join forces with other child-serving community groups to construct a moral climate beyond the classroom.

So far so good. We all liked the words that came up in this discussion: moral community, moral atmosphere, infusion, commitment, saturation, pervasiveness, and loyalty—at least until one of us asked the simple question, "What exactly is *meant* by a moral community, and how is loyalty to such a community expressed?" With that innocent inquiry our unity was fractured.

Those of us who had been uncomfortable with "programming" moral instruction now saw the downside to "saturation" and "pervasiveness": school authorities monitoring children's every move, curbing their spontaneity, self-assertion, and experimentation; the educational objective of moral awareness transmuted into an authoritatively enforced moral conformity. Don't be blind, these teachers warned, to the harm done by banner-waving moralists: A child spills his food (perhaps on purpose, perhaps not), he is called "irresponsible"; a child objects to an assembly presentation (perhaps tactfully, perhaps brusquely), he is called "disrespectful"; a child is indignant or angry (perhaps justifiably, perhaps irrationally), he is called "uncooperative"; a child is delinquent in an assignment (perhaps negligent, perhaps not), he is called "disobedient." Better, they argue, to be straightforward: Inform the child he must clean up the spill, must inhibit his objection to an assembly, cannot openly express anger in class, has to complete his assignments, but do not turn rule-breaking into moral offenses.

The skeptics also objected to elevating school loyalty into a moral good. Loyalty to a community, they argued, is at least in tension with—if not opposed to—the pursuit of moral identity. A child developing an autonomous moral consciousness should be encouraged to consider carefully and perhaps resist the group's values, even to stand apart from "school

spirit." Loyalty to a community, like loyalty to a team, can be superficial, transient, and morally insignificant, merely a
temporary boost to one's self-importance.
Furthermore, it easily falls prey to an us-
against-them mentality. Before extolling
the virtues of loyalty, therefore, one must
ask what is it about the school that *merits*
a child's loyalty? Notions of "we-ness,"
even a very moral "we," are not worthy
claims *per se*.

Schools are not self-enclosed, self-
defining, or self-sustaining collectives.
They exist, to be sure, to initiate children
into the traditions and knowledge of a
culture, but also—one hopes—to provide
a forum for ongoing revitalization and re-
assessment of those traditions. Loyalty is
contingent on the school's honorable discharge of this mission, not alone on its
internal climate. As a government agency,
a public school may command obedience, but loyalty—which is after all akin
to devotion—it can only inspire, and can
do so only insofar as it brings to children
"an intellectual, imaginative, moral and
emotional inheritance," equipping them,
as they depart, "to look, to listen, to
think, to feel, to imagine, to believe, to
understand, to choose and to wish"
(Oakeshott 1972, 24, 22).[5]

---

[5] C. S. Lewis' remarks about an analogous
virtue, friendship [quoted in part in Chapter 8, p. 231], are worth recalling here:

The very condition of having Friends is
that we should want something else besides Friends. Where the truthful answer to
the question *Do you see the same truth?*
would be "I see nothing and I don't care
about the truth; I only want a Friend," no
Friendship can arise—though Affection of
course may. There would be nothing for
the Friendship to be *about*; and Friendship
must be about something, even if it were
only an enthusiasm for dominoes or white
mice. Those who have nothing can share
nothing; those who are going nowhere can
have no fellow-travelers.

(Lewis 1960/1988, 98) (emphasis in original)

Others in our group, while appreciating the possible hazards of "saturation"
and "pervasiveness"—moral policemen
stalking the corridors and promoting an
empty "rah rah" school spirit—find the
fear vastly exaggerated. When moral educators talk of saturation and pervasiveness, they mean no more than the creation of an environment that, to quote
Lickona and his colleagues again, "helps
students form caring attachments to
adults and to each other" and embodies
"core values such as concern and respect
for others, responsibility, kindness, and
fairness" (Lickona, Schaps, and Lewis
1997–1998, Principle 4). Enveloping
children in such an atmosphere is worthy
of loyalty apart from what else the school
is doing. Loyalty to a school is much like
loyalty to a family. We do not expect children to condition regard for their family
on how family members have positioned
themselves in the world; we are loyal to
our parents because they are our parents,
our caretakers. Beyond minimal standards, they do not have to prove themselves worthy; so too with a school.

Loyalty can be thought of as a series of
concentric circles, starting with the family, then moving to the classroom, the
school, and ever outward to embrace the
neglected and suffering—people, animals, the environment. A school concerned with its moral mission will continuously *want* to enlarge its nexus, but
there are limits as to what we can routinely *expect* a school to embrace.

Moreover, although moral identity
eventually becomes an autonomous and
interior conscience, it is first the (heteronomous) expression of family and
community values. While it is true that
children need encouragement to resist
their peer group, they also need to belong to it, or at least to define themselves
through (and then against) a group identification. Someone who from the outset
stands outside the group will not develop those sympathies, loyalties, and
convictions that at a later date he or she

may choose to prune or discard. The more a school stands for a set of strong social ideals and instantiates a set of values in daily life, the richer the palette of values for students to draw from. But even when schools see their mission narrowly, better that children take on whatever coloration the peer group provides than to be colorless, stripped of any identifications.

Belonging is the first step on the way toward independence. As the contemporary American philosopher Michael Sandel reminds us, "where the self is unencumbered and essentially dispossessed, no person is left for *self*-reflection to reflect upon" (Sandel 1982/1998, 179).[6] In the absence of "constitutive attachments" (Sandel's term) to others, our choices will result from personal preferences devoid of moral consideration. Being part of a group—caring about it, sharing its interests and values—is as important to a maturing sense of self as the freedom to resist it and the system of justice to regulate it. A caring moral community gives children that sense of belonging which is particularly central to the early moral life.

The duality of belonging and independence is well captured in these words of Terrence Des Pres:

> Human beings need and desire to be part of a larger whole, to [join] with their fellows and even, in moments of great passion, to lose the sense of self entirely. That is the basis of sex and religion, of politics and society. But just as much, men and women yearn for solitude, they struggle fiercely for an existence apart, for an integrity absolutely unbreachable.

That is the basis of dignity, of personality, of the egoism which fuels creation and discovery, and finally of the sense of individual "rights." *(Des Pres 1976, 202–203).*

Belonging to a community instills a sense of collective responsibility and encourages our moral emotions. A child sees a paper on the floor and automatically picks it up: He doesn't want *his* school to be littered. A child feels under the weather but comes to choir practice anyway: He doesn't want *his* group's performance to suffer. A child takes umbrage when *his* schoolmate is subject to ethnic slurs: *He* feels insulted. In his school and with his friends he does what he would do in his home and for himself. According to Durkheim, it is affiliation with a community that:

> draws us out of ourselves, that obliges us to reckon with other interests than our own, it is society that has taught us to control our passions, our instincts, to prescribe law for them, to restrain ourselves, to deprive ourselves, to sacrifice ourselves, to subordinate our personal ends to higher ends. *(Durkheim 1956, 76)*

As the "I" stretches toward an inclusive "we," values also get compromised and homogenized. Again, Durkheim: "Society can survive only if there exists among its members a sufficient degree of homogeneity; education perpetuates and reinforces this homogeneity by fixing in the child, from the beginning, the essential similarities that collective life demands" (id., 70).

Stark though the gulf between these two approaches appeared, it was quite surprisingly narrowed by adding the requirement that a *moral community* be an *open* one. If a school is genuinely open to disagreement, if it finds within the maxim, "we care for one another," the commitment, "we care for opinions not to our liking," then narrow parochialism

---

[6]See Robert Bellah's discussion of a similar point, the moral vacuity of the "radically unencumbered and improvisational self," the person who has no ties or identifications with others beyond "being nice" (Bellah et al 1985, 81).

is avoided. An open community will open children to the clashes of the day. Its porous walls will encourage teachers to bring the world into the classroom for examination and debate, and encourage students to reach out into the world, thereby preparing them for citizenship. We consider the following to be essential components of an open moral school community.

A Serious Commitment

The school administration must make known to teachers and children that its commitment to moral education is serious. For some schools the commitment is displayed in a structured form—promoting a particular value-of-the-week or -month, rewarding children for their character attainments, evaluating children's moral growth, conducting "character" assemblies, bringing moral exemplars to visit, using press releases to celebrate the school's moral activities and accomplishments. Other schools, equally serious, prefer a more embedded or implicit morality, a softer sell. Their approach assumes that values surface in the way we are, the way we do things here, rather than from praising moral behavior, singling out children, or searching for external controls more generally.

In this dispute we agree with Lawrence Kohlberg: techniques are secondary to an enthusiastic commitment. It is not:

> a matter of one or another educational technique or ideology or means, but a matter of the moral energy of the educator, of his communicated belief that his school or classroom has a human purpose. To get his message across, he may use permissiveness or he may use discipline, but the effective moral educator has a believable human message. (Kohlberg 1976, 213)

A Broad Commitment

An open moral community requires commitment from all the constituents of the school, better yet, of the entire school district. Engagement with moral education, as with any serious mind-shaping work, cannot be an optional curricular activity. In addition to teachers and administrators, the entire staff (including bus drivers, food preparers, and maintenance workers, who may be in the school very little) should have some input into, and responsibility for, the program. Children should know the staff by name (last name as well as first), know their responsibilities and respect their contribution to the operation of the enterprise, perhaps work at times with them (where feasible) as quasi-apprentices.

Teachers (and administrators) need candidly to share with parents the moral stances they are advocating and invite families to bring objections and suggestions to the table. Parents are the primary moral educators of their children; schools can disagree with them, can try to reach accommodations with them, but cannot ignore them. Without open discussions aimed at a shared language of the good, schools may become insulated moral islands. Children, then, will dismiss school standards as soon as *they* are dismissed or, worse, come to believe that morality is nothing more than arbitrary rules devised by "interested parties" to control them. The school, to avoid a within-these-walls morality, must also reach out to the nonparent community for its contributions. This foot-in-the-community effort needs to include children as well as teachers and administrators.

We recognize that all of this is easier to prescribe than to implement. In the short run, taking it seriously will complicate the work of teacher and principal. Some of what is needed may lie beyond the possible. Yet a program that dismisses the entire idea as "impractical," which does not make a serious and sustained effort in this direction, is itself impractical, and bound to run aground on its own timidity.

Required Participation in Targeted Moral Activities

We were less divided on the appropriateness of a service component to a program of moral education than on almost any other issue. While we appreciate the coerciveness of "requirements," a credible commitment to establishing a moral community is seriously undermined if, say, gym but not service is mandatory. We support the idea that, however much young people "obey the rules," they should learn that moral action requires committing some portion of their "work" life to aiding others.

In the implementation of service learning, there is room for wide divergences. Some might make it the program core, others are troubled by the time commitment involved. Schools will also vary in what they consider suitable service. They may choose within-school activities, especially for younger children—cross-age tutoring, assisting school staff, improving school property, raising funds for school drives.

We recommend, however, that, at least for the older child, schools also consider external activities, using this requirement to bridge the school/society divide by bringing home to children what they can do—eventually what they will take on as an obligation—to help to heal, to repair the world. In today's environment of instant global communication, it is valuable, even for younger children, to extend service activities to "causes" that go beyond the local level, to expand their awareness of need and their ability to respond.

The "learning" portion of a program of service learning should not be ignored. Although some important learning takes place simply from the experience of service, a reflection component is immensely valuable, even in the lower grades. An activity as simple as caring for pets in an animal shelter, for example, can give rise to discussions regarding the problem of neglected and abused pets, animal rights,

and the qualities that might attract one to a career as a veterinarian.

It is a mistake to regard a conscious effort to maximize the educational value of service as undermining its altruistic quality. While the needs of those served should be primary once an activity is undertaken, there need not be a dichotomization of the service and the educational payoff. So long as a program is alert to the danger of exploiting those in need to enhance the education of students, the fact that students find service to others educationally rewarding does not impair its character-building quality. Rather, students can learn to view their "self-interest" in a broader way.

Core Values: Rights and Reaches

None of us was disposed to compose a list of must-teach virtues; on this there was no dissent. The commonly listed virtues, we agreed, are murky and tend to merge. Furthermore, cultivating virtues competes with other approaches to moral education—e.g., an emphasis on acts and their consequences, or on moral alertness and sensitivity. Even among the die-hard virtue ethicists, there is a split: the softies stress caring and benevolence, the "hardies," courage and restraint.

Yet we could hardly submit a report without some attention to the content of moral education. Despite the battles waged over values, and the respect we owe to uncongenial perspectives, we believe, and think virtually everyone believes, that there are shared fundamental principles. These fundamental principles emerge from our human sympathies, from the requirements for a healthy, self-sustaining society not awash in discord or suppression, and from what it takes to live a "flourishing" life. More concretely, our sympathies are violated, our society troubled, and our lives diminished, when people are treated cruelly, when they possess no rights, when deception is tolerated, when there is no accountability for wrongdoing.[7] Philippa Foot has articulated this point of view convincingly:

> Granted that it is wrong to assume identity of aim between peoples of different cultures; nevertheless there is a great deal that all men have in common. All need affection, the cooperation of others, a place in a community, and help in trouble. . . . We are not, therefore, simply expressing values that we happen to have if we think of some moral systems as good moral systems and others as bad. . . . We do not have to suppose it is just as good to promote pride of place and the desire to get an advantage over other men as it is to have an ideal of affection and respect. These things have different harvests, and unmistakably different connexions with human good. *(Foot 1982, 164)*

All cultures concede the priority of basic moral values. The most frequently cited all-encompassing universal binding principle is probably the Golden Rule:

> "Love your neighbor as yourself," said Jesus. "What is hateful to you do not do to your neighbor," said Rabbi Hillel. Confucius summed up his teaching in very similar terms: "What you do not want done to yourself, do not do to others." The *Mahabharata*, the great Indian epic, says: "Let no man do to another that which would be repugnant to himself.". . . In each case, moreover, the words are offered as a kind of summary of all the moral law. *(Singer 1995, 230)*

Schools are justified in teaching these principles not just because they are at the core of an ethical life but because an ethical life, tugging as it does against narrow self-interest, is the path to a meaningful life and, finally, a life of contentment.

From virtuousness, said the ancient Greeks, comes *eudaimonia* or happiness:

> [T]he lives of those who have nothing to do but enjoy themselves are much less happy than we would expect them to be if human nature were suited to the unalloyed pursuit of personal pleasure. Perhaps, having developed into beings with purposes, we are naturally driven to seek larger purposes, which give meaning and significance to our lives. Perhaps the boredom and loss of interest in life, observable in many of those with no purposes beyond their own pleasure, are the result of neglecting this aspect of our nature. *(Singer 1981, 145–146)*

While there are many ways to find purpose beyond oneself—why not devote oneself to collecting stamps or playing golf?—the ethical life, perhaps because it demands self-transcendence, has a grandeur all its own. Singer elaborates:

> Footballers are constantly reminded that the club is larger than the individual; so are employees of corporations, especially those that work for corporations that foster group loyalty with songs, slogans and social activities, in the Japanese manner. . . . [L]iving an ethical life is certainly not the only way of making a commitment that can give substance and worth to your life; but for anyone choosing one kind of life rather than another, it is the commitment with the firmest foundation. The more we reflect on our commitment to a football club, a corporation, or any sectional interest, the less point we are likely to see in it. In contrast, no amount of reflection will show a commitment to an ethical life to be trivial or pointless. *(Id., 218)*

Protecting Rights

Liberty and equality, says the *Declaration of Independence*, are inalienable rights. For John Stuart Mill, these values stemmed

---

[7] [See Chapter 4, pp. 94, 111, for a discussion of universal values.]

from a simple imperative, the basis of all moral obligations: Do not do that which interferes with the rights of others; do no harm (his "perfect" duties, see p. 94 in Chapter 4). People have a basic "natural" right to pursue their lives as they wish constrained only by the natural rights of others to do the same. "[T]he only purpose for which power can be rightfully exercised over any member of a civilized community, against his will, is to prevent harm to others" (Mill 1859/1993, 78).

Translated into school practice, "Do no harm" is an insistence on fairness. Schools are enjoined to give everyone an equal bite of the apple, or at least an equal shot at reaching the apple. Behavior that illegitimately advances the interests of one child over another—cheating, stealing, lying, bullying, injuring—is forbidden. Behavior that fosters equality of opportunity—sharing, turn-taking, cooperation, tolerance, respect—is encouraged, at times required. The extent to which a school permits or supports "winners" and "losers" through competition and recognition for excellence will vary (and, again, we deem it a dangerous diversion to insist on debating polar responses to the question of the proper extent). No school, however, would claim that it may deliberately or heedlessly restrict or advance the opportunity of some over others; history may have done this, social circumstances may perpetuate this, but school personnel are not at liberty knowingly to play favorites.

Schools, of course, have rules based on other premises, such as being a responsible student or loyal to the community. Children are expected to demonstrate diligence, try their hardest to do their best, and persevere when it gets tough. They are expected to protect, or certainly not injure, school property, participate in school activities, and show respect to school personnel, but failure to meet these expectations is less abhorrent than injuring the rights of others. A child who is lax about his work is, or should

be, judged less harshly than a child who cheats on his assignments.

The fundamental commitment to protect individual freedom by guaranteeing equality of opportunity is bedrock, the ground of our political institutions and our way of life. Clearly it is the school's obligation to model these principles and convince children to respect and to practice them.

Yet, although fidelity to these rights is essential, it is an insufficient ambition. Constructing a moral identity requires more.

Encouraging the Reach

"Do no harm" values, to which children justifiably are held accountable, have a negative cast. They need to be supplemented with *aspirational* values, values for which one is rarely held accountable, values that are never fully realized, are always "*assumed,* not assigned, *undertaken* rather than imposed" (Babbie 1985, 27) (emphasis in original). These values constitute the reach beyond our grasp, the gap between "what one has already achieved and what one still ought to accomplish" (Frankl 1962, 106), the self-transcendent commitments we make, break, and remake. They constitute the majesty of morality; those who live by them fill us with awe. For the religious they mean drawing closer to God, for the nonreligious they mean leading a more caring, generous, and courageous life.

Perhaps for individuals, achievement of these aspirational values is not obligatory. A school, however, that fails to enlarge the aspirations of its students has shorted their potential. "Children will not thrive psychologically," according to William Damon, "until they learn to dedicate themselves to purposes that go beyond their own egoistic desires" (Damon 1995, 81).

In fact, inspiration for aspirational values is abundant throughout the standard curriculum, especially in history and literature. It is found not only in the moral examples of heroes, but as well in the modest, courageous, and altruistic lives of ordinary people. The Giraffe Project (based in Langley, Washington) supplies profiles of great historical heroes and also encourages children to find heroes in their midst, those of any age who have stuck out their necks to help others. The program culminates in children selecting a social problem of concern and developing a service project to address it. Some random examples of discovered heroes (The Giraffe Project 1997, No. 36) include:

- *Chitra Besbroda,* a social worker in Harlem who rescues abused pet animals by night.
- *Fred Boeger,* who found evidence of financial corruption in the California schools and risked everything to blow the whistle.
- *Michael Crisler,* who was born in 1988 with a chronic disease but who has raised tens of thousands of dollars for children's hospitals and for the Oklahoma City bombing victims.

A special "allure," says contemporary philosopher Robert Nozick, lights the lives of those who hold fast to principles:

> There are some individuals whose lives are infused by values, who pursue values with single-minded purity and intensity, who embody values to the greatest extent. These individuals glow with a special radiance. Epochal religious figures often have this quality. To be in their presence (or even to hear about them) is to be uplifted and drawn (at least temporarily) to pursue the best in oneself. *(Nozick 1981, 436)*

Children, especially young children who so love myth and fantasy, are sitting ducks for moral allure. They are attracted to stories of moral struggle that pit great good against evil, strength against weakness, courage against cowardice, generosity against stinginess, God against the Devil. Stories of risk-taking, endurance, steadfastness, compassion, honor, and self-sacrifice appeal to children of all ages.

The Value of Doubt

Efforts to inculcate virtues, however, need to recognize the virtue of *doubt.* An awareness of uncertainty, of the pervasive imperfection of all "solutions," is fundamental to morality—alertness, reflection, study, and reevaluation its antidote. Some would go so far as to say that without reflection and choice there is no moral action. Habitual goodness does not count. Although this is not our position—those acts of decency in which children constantly engage without premeditation, we consider moral—reflection and doubt are nonetheless too often undervalued in moral education programs. We should not forget the model of Socrates who, through his restless and unrelenting doubt of every presumed certitude, taught us how fragile is "truth" and how valuable the questions that probe it. When Meno asked if virtue can be taught, he responded, "I am so far from knowing whether virtue can be taught or not that I do not even have any knowledge of what virtue itself is." To Meno's incredulous, "[D]o you really not know what virtue is? Are we to report this to the folk back home about you?" Socrates replied: "Not only that, my friend, but also that, as I believe, I have never yet met anyone else who did know."[8] If humility and modesty are virtues (and, unlike doubt, they do appear on virtue lists), they are not sustainable without the ceaseless questioning of a doubting Socrates.

A fear that children tend to withdraw from ambiguity and are frustrated by uncertainty may cause educators to soft-pedal or disvalue doubt and disagreement. We believe that it should not. Doubt need be no more immobilizing for the young than for the old. In our experience even small children find it more ex-

---

[8] [For the colloquy between Socrates and Meno, see the epigraph to this book, p. xvii.]

citing when a teacher responds to a question with a question than with an answer. When confronted with a dilemma—and many questions are easily posed as dilemmas—a child does not have to be a logician to wonder and speculate (with an adult or other children) on the alternatives. This is not to suggest that every moral occasion should be greeted with doubt, nor that serious reflective discussion never dissipates it; sometimes right and wrong are, or become, clear. But children (like adults) often need to "feel out" various possibilities much as they feel out different political priorities, ways of acting with their peers, or approaches to their academic work. Often we must grope toward a right answer if we are to find it.

Shared Teacher–Student Responsibility

We all agree that children, key participants in the moral community, should have some voice in establishing and enforcing the morality to which they are subject. But the questions, how strong a voice and under what circumstances, evoked much difficult talk among us. Those who believe that morality emerges through the social life of school, and is more about intentions and feelings than approved behaviors, view teachers for the most part as first among equals. The teacher's task—to encourage children's social sensitivity, social responsibility, and moral determination—is best fulfilled by creating cooperative rather than authoritative relationships. In a cooperative relationship, the teacher facilitates children's thinking by participating in their conversations, posing questions and encouraging reflection. The teacher's method is the discussion—teacher with student, student with student, students together in formal and informal groups. According to the highly regarded Child Development Project, the class meeting is a crucial tool for productive discussions:

> Essentially, class meetings are times to talk—a forum for students and teacher to gather as a class to reflect, discuss issues, or make decisions about ways they want their class to be. Class meetings are not a forum for teachers to make pronouncements or impart decisions. Neither are they tribunals for students to judge one another. The teacher's role in these meetings is to create an environment in which students can see that their learning, their opinions, and their concerns are taken seriously. The students' role in these meetings is to participate as valuable and valued contributors to the classroom community. (*Development Studies Center 1996, 3*)

In class meetings, norms are generated and problems discussed. An example is a discussion of the formation of cliques: Children in grades 3–6 are asked to discuss whether they have ever been in, or excluded from, a clique. What might be the benefits and hardships of cliques? Why do people form cliques, given their inclusion and exclusion practices? What can teacher and students do to prevent cliques from forming, or to keep them from generating harmful effects? The goal is to reach "a shared understanding of when friendship groups can do more harm than good" (id., 111). It is one of the teacher's tasks to help students distinguish between asking each class member to be equally close friends with every other, and expecting them not to "forge the bonds of friendship at others' (painful) expense" (ibid.).

Entrusting substantial responsibility to children for governing their lives strikes others as irresponsible. Children are much too immature, self-centered, inconsistent, and irrational to be given grave decision-making responsibilities. If we refuse children a wide berth in deciding matters of curriculum—or even the foods they can eat and the TV programs they can watch—why do we think they can determine the moral rules that should govern them? To grant such an allowance is to trivialize morality.

Furthermore, democratic discussions, especially with elementary-school children, are often something of a ruse. Look again at the discussion of cliques. It is hardly open. The teacher, not the children, has determined that cliques are bad. The purpose of the meeting is to address a *problem*, to "look at the ways in which formation of friendship can degenerate into excluding, scapegoating, and other harmful practices" (id., 109). Although the leader asks the children to consider the benefits of cliques, it is the negative consequences that are emphasized and, note, before concluding the meeting the teacher asks what can be done to prevent them.

The discussion is hardly a democratic grappling with an issue on which reasonable people disagree. Compare, for example, the contrasting view that adults should not interfere in the "special attachments" of children:

> Sometimes teachers are concerned about cliques that form. We understand and agree with concerns about children feeling left out when excluded from a group's play. However, children's attachments are important to them and mark progress in social development. Stability in preferences reflects conservation of values that is necessary for moral development. Therefore, we suggest that teachers encourage children's special friendships. (DeVries and Zan 1994, 60–61)

If a teacher wants to take a moral stand against cliques, better and less manipulative to state her position clearly, then use class meetings to explain her reasoning and to request children's interpretations and reactions. If the discussion is to be "open," the teacher also should be open, willing to fine-tune or trim the rule, but also to take seriously the point of view that, given the benefits of "special attachments" and the difficulties of legislating friendships, the rule should be withdrawn and attention directed to moderating the harm done.

It is in the best of circumstances a challenge for students to manage wisely the authority entrusted to them. Lawrence Kohlberg's Just Community Schools provides a telling example. Speaking of high-school students, Kohlberg and his colleagues asserted that teachers should simply advocate for their favored positions, and should have no more say than students: "We believe that decisions involving discipline and student life ought to be made democratically, with students and teachers having an equal vote" (Power, Higgins, and Kohlberg 1989, pp. 30–31). At the first meeting of the first high school to practice Kohlberg's direct democracy, students were invited to choose from a number of electives offered in the last periods of the day. A student unexpectedly proposed, and the group concurred, that those who did not like any of the electives should be permitted to leave school early. "Caught" by a decision that was unacceptable to the school and in violation of city rules, Kohlberg announced that the vote was preliminary and a "real vote" would be taken at the subsequent meeting.[9]

Kohlberg came to realize that allowing a wide latitude for democratic decision making works best when students have already identified with the normative ex-

---

[9] Kohlberg himself understood that democratic procedures did not assure good outcomes:

> In arguing for democracy as a way of respecting and fostering the autonomous personhood of students, we by no means share the romantic assumption that all will be well once adolescents are delivered from the bondage of adult control. . . . Democracy means more than giving everyone a vote. It is a process of "moral communication" that involves assessing one's own interests and needs, listening to and trying to understand others, and balancing conflicting points of view in a fair and cooperative way.
> (Id., 32)

pectations of the larger social group. The example he liked to use was the collectivist *kibbutz* settlements of Israel. Here, long before they become decision makers, children have accepted the adults' collectivist egalitarian ideology and, emotionally attached to the group, willingly make personal sacrifices for its greater good. While many decisions are put in the hands of the youth, options are limited by collective needs. How many hours one works, for example (a parallel to the number of classes one attends in the Just Community Schools), is not optional. "If everyone is supposed to work for two hours in the afternoon on the kibbutz (on the farm or in a service branch) and someone is regularly playing her guitar during that time, she will soon enough hear about it from her friends. For in a collective living situation, everyone has a stake in everyone else's living by the same norms of conduct" (id., 40).

The Japanese elementary school also gives children considerable authority against a similar backdrop of strongly and widely held normative expectations. According to Catherine Lewis (1997), it is common in Japanese schools for young children to run class meetings at which important decisions are made about classroom rules and activities.

> By first grade, monitors . . . assembled and quieted the class before the teacher arrived for each lesson. In addition, they often led meetings, evaluated other students' behavior, and led the class in solving disputes or problems that arose. In fact, first-grade monitors—not teachers—managed much of the mechanics of classroom life, freeing teachers to teach. *(Id., 106)*

Teachers work more as consultants than authority figures. "The teacher was not so much a leader as a resource. . . . [She] shied away from authoritative statements that might short-circuit children's own problem solving" (id., 113). But it is

clear to all that group loyalty and attachment are prime values and that the well-being of the class (and school) depends upon everyone participating in a host of chores. The message of group responsibility is brought home to first-graders during the initial weeks of school when, although no demands are made of them, they observe the sixth-graders voluntarily cleaning their (the first-graders') rooms. The teacher "wonders" out loud whether "we'll soon be big and strong enough to clean the classroom ourselves" (id., 110). Not exactly an invitation to insubordination!

Caring in these schools is promoted through questions. Children are asked: What have you done for others this week? How can family members help one another? What would you do for your mother if she were sick? Values are also promoted by praise. After being "introduced" to the class by the monitors, the teacher relates "how happy she was that children helped one another spontaneously when a big wastebasket was spilled at lunchtime earlier in the week; how happy she was that children were including all their classmates in playground games rather than leaving some children to feel lonely; and how sad they would all feel if the children who continued to run in the hall were to fall and hurt their heads" (id., 112).[10]

Thus we see that, although democratic decision making characterized the Just Community Schools of Kohlberg, the life of the *kibbutz*, and the elementary schools of Japan, they operated under different constraints. What lessons are there here for schools that want to balance adult and child responsibilities in moral education programs?

Teacher Enforcement of Primary Values

Fundamental normative expectations, those basic moral values that constitute

---

[10] [See the fuller discussion by Lewis at p. 25 in Chapter 2.]

the backbone of the community, must be made clear to children and clearly enforced. Robert Howard, a Kohlberg-trained elementary school teacher, calls them the Big Rules:

> I had certain "Big Rules" that were nonnegotiable and not subject to the will of the class. These rules, including "We will treat others as we would like to be treated," "People are safe in this classroom," "Property is safe in this classroom," and "People are treated with respect in this classroom," were distributed to and signed by both students and parents at registration on the first day of school. . . . The existence of the Big Rules in combination with the social contract that the students and parents had entered into [through signing onto the rules] gave me the opportunity to exercise a veto if the students wanted to create a class rule or establish a punishment that I felt violated the Big Rules. *(Howard 1991, 61)*

Having the Big Rules eliminated the predicament of a fellow teacher:

> A student in her class was guilty of spitting on another student. In the class meeting, the students democratically decided that the "appropriate" punishment would be for the guilty student to stand in a circle made up of his fellow classmates and have each class member spit upon the offender in turn. Because such a punishment would have violated the Big Rules of my classroom, I would have argued against it in class meeting. Had it come to a vote and won, I would have vetoed it on the grounds that the punishment failed to treat the student with respect and dignity. *(Id., 62)*

It is critical not to obscure or minimize the Big Rules by adding to them what are merely school-based conventions. Equating Big Rules with fundamental moral values implies that they are uni-versalizable to all (or mostly all) human encounters and obligatory as a matter of morality. They form the community's backbone; other values stem from, and are justified by, them. To attach to this spine rules of convenience, as some codes do—not chewing gum, not bringing "Walkmen" to school, and not running in the halls—is to blur important distinctions. School-based conventional rules such as these may require adherence and enforcement (as do traffic laws), but they are not fundamental moral values constituting the backbone of the community. The scale of approval and disapproval for obeying and disobeying them should be distinguished so children learn that moral rules occupy a higher status.

Participation of Students in Rule-Making and Rule-Enforcement

Every school must decide upon the extent and form of children's input. Schools will vary on both dimensions. For some, decisions on all rules will be shared with students, others will invite participation only on peripheral issues or only by older students. The children's input can range from voicing an opinion, to sharing in decisions, to exercising decisional authority as a group; from direct one-person, one-vote participation to indirect participation through elected members of a student council.

There is no end to the possible permutations of who decides what and how. A good school policy should make clear—in advance of open discussions—the extent to which rules are set by students, and provide for periodic review. What is essential is that children feel they have a voice, and in fact do have a voice, in matters of importance to them; and that they also understand that some norms and practices are inviolable, and (at least in the higher grades) why this is so.

Within these simple requirements, a school can decide as it chooses the extent and manner of student participation in decision making. Variations reflecting differences in emphasis and priorities are not problematic, so long as the overall regime is respectful of the full gamut of relevant considerations. What must be avoided is a highly polarized stance, more interested mainly in caricaturing and ridiculing the disfavored pole, and driven largely by resentment and mistrust.

Children should also have some role in policies of enforcement and the consequences of transgression. Again, their role can range from expressing a viewpoint to the teacher, to the class, or to a representative governing body (which itself can have a small or large student voice), to more decisive authority. Whatever the students' role, they are likely to learn, simply from the act of participation, to temper their (often) harsh judgments and demands for retribution with a measure of understanding and forgiveness. In Japan, young children designated as "caretakers" have large responsibilities for resolving fairly serious problems—fights, teasing, rejection. Shouldering these responsibilities, it is found, strengthens their dedication to mutual helping and enlarges their notions of fairness.

Open Discussion of Moral Issues

Beyond participating in shaping the rules and the consequences of infraction, children need opportunities to discuss moral conflicts and their own moral difficulties. Even young children can grasp the conflict between what they want to do and what they should do, the problem of dual loyalties, and the plurality of values among people. To discuss such conflicts, whether they arise from invented moral dilemmas, literary or historical texts, or the children's own lives, requires support and encouragement.

Not every discussion need end in a resolution. There is a substantial yield, as Robert Nozick points out, simply from talking:

> To engage in a moral dialogue with someone is itself a moral act, whose moral character does not lie solely in being an attempt to get at the moral truth. . . . Rather, (sincere) engagement in moral dialogue is itself a moral response to the other's basic moral characteristic. . . . It itself is responsive to him; perhaps that is why openness in moral dialogue, considering carefully and responding closely to the concerns of the other, so often is an effective means toward resolution of conflict.
>
> When each is aware that the other is responsive to his or her own (valuable) characteristics in the very act of discussion and in the course the discussion takes, then this noticing of mutual respect is itself a force for good will and the moderation of demands. *(Nozick 1981, 469)*

Many topics—the exclusion of children (from cliques or team games), gossip, hurtful but somewhat subtly expressed "attitudes," the extent to which infractions and punishments should be collectivized—need airing and reflection before there is (or even if there is not) a resolution. It may often be sufficient if talk around such issues raises sensitivity, an awareness of complexity, and the desire to continue pursuing the issue.

A Developmental Pedagogy

There are important distinctions between first- and fifth-graders' moral perspectives and moral thinking. Basic requirements of moral deliberation—to take the point of view of others, to consider intentions and consequences as well as acts, to move back and forth between general principles and specifics, to behave consistently across similar situations, to restrain impulses, to maintain a disinterested mindset, to reason independently of authority—are all difficult to impossible (depending on age and maturity) for younger children. Some would claim that most of their "moral" behavior, at least until the double-digit years, is premoral, a matter of identifying with one's mentors, obeying rules (parental or social), and responding to sanctions and rewards. Children's understanding of justice and authority, according to William Damon, is characterized during the elementary-school years as a "series of unfolding mental confusions" (Damon 1977, 179).

Not surprisingly, opinions among us were divided on the pedagogical implications of children's immaturity. One view was that younger children needed clearer, firmer, and (many) more rules than older children, with fewer modifications based on situational considerations; intention and consequences should minimally be factored into judgments. Thus, if a child "steals," little weight should be given (in terms of the adult response) to whether he did not know it was wrong or lied to cover his tracks, whether this was a first offence or a repetition, whether the value of the possession or the effect of the theft on a specific victim was great or small. Because a child's understanding is limited and inconsistent, the sanctions in each instance should be correction through restoration of the goods, with perhaps mild disapproval that imparts adult concern—but no more serious discipline. Children are at this age too unsophisticated about psychological states—their own and others'—to "learn" much morality from explanations or punishment beyond "It's the rule."

According to this view, discussions are generally unproductive with young children. Take fairness: Children cannot be persuaded, in the face of their self-interest, to act according to the principle that equality is the best policy. Their advocacy of the equality principle is paper thin, and evoking it often takes so much "leading" by a teacher that the effort becomes, in reality, impositional.

Young children, whom Piaget called "moral realists," perceive obligations as objective and law-like. They want to know what is expected of them. "What characterizes the culture of childhood proper is rules," says developmental psychologist David Elkind, "rules for playing games and for not playing, for what to do when it rains or snows, when a siren blows, a black cat crosses your path, or you step on a crack" (Elkind 1976, 97). Educators should honor this respect for authority—it won't last!—by instilling good habits that are difficult to acquire, though easy to abandon, in later life. Habits, what R. S. Peters has called "settled dispositions," need cultivation; they cannot be summoned at will but, once established, they make willing easier. Although habits are usually thought of in terms of restraint—self-control, responsibility, obedience, and decorum (manners, tidiness, punctuality)—there is no reason, says Peters, not to include as well habits of reflection, sharing, and generosity (Peters 1974, 318).

"Don't short-shrift the children," insisted others in our group. Yes, children are self-interested and have rational limitations; yes, they equate morality and authority. But these features do not exhaust their dossier of moral resources. Children's rich empathic and imaginative capacities generate powerful identifications with those in need. Look at how they are drawn to suffering—from ants and bugs to faraway peoples—and how quickly they volunteer as "helpers" (that volunteering gets adult approval does not fully explain children's pleasure).

Teachers should not neglect such sensibilities. They should encourage children's participation in rule-making, in sharing each others' feelings, in thinking about solutions to dilemmas. They should exploit the chance to arouse moral sensibilities, moral alertness, and the child's own sense of agency. As with habits, the tender sentiments also need early cultivation if they are to become dependable components of a moral identity.

On reflection these positions, while seemingly opposed, are not *wholly* exclusive of one another; they can be integrated without contradiction, as we now suggest.

Staging Pedagogies

Effective moral education programs require the full pedagogical repertoire at each age. Children should have the opportunity to deliberate over choices, to exercise choice, and to discover the consequences of their choices. But the domain of their authority should reflect their cognitive stages—smaller during the "moral realism" stage, larger with increments in their social perspectives and rationality.

Similarly, as the child sheds her moral absolutism and realizes, for example, that fairness or equity is not always a matter of equality; as logical powers grow, sympathies broaden, and fluid imaginative identifications (with heroes and villains) decline, there should be a parallel increase in exposure to moral dilemmas, pluralist and conflicting values, and the subtleties of morality (for example, distinctions between behavior and motive, means and ends, voluntary and coerced acts).

The slope of the curves on which these increments could be plotted will vary somewhat with the individual or group. Again, those differences need not be beaten into the ground; exactly what "slope" is correct is of far less importance than that there *be* one, significantly upward-moving.

Staging Accountability

The level of children's cognition should guide our reactions to their behavior. We must understand that literal and imitative thinking may cause them to act, by our lights, inconsistently. They may sincerely maintain, for example, that it is wrong to take someone's *money*—so they have been told—but not wrong to take someone's *lunch;* or wrong to take anything at all from a *child,* but not wrong to take something from the *classroom*—the class is not a person. Concreteness may dimin-

ish the sensitivity of children to people's motives, causing them to judge a large accident more harshly than a small intentional wrongdoing. Blurred concept delineation may leave them confused as to boundaries: when, for example, an act is to be regarded as stealing and when as "borrowing"; when an object is "owned" and when available to them (don't we all question, when we find something, how far to go in search of the rightful owner?). Vivid fantasy may make it natural for them to distort—we call it lying—the recollection of an experience, especially in the service of self-interest.

Expectations of moral goodness, responsibility for moral infractions, and the administration of sanctions must be fine-tuned to the child's interpretations of events. In the early years, adults should tilt toward protecting children from undue temptations rather than holding them fully culpable for their wrongdoing. Just as one would babyproof a room against the onslaughts of an active toddler, so one must "morally-proof " the environment, at least against major hazards arising from the ignorance of children.

It is questionable, for example, to hold a young child accountable, even after instruction, for "stealing" money from a night table, for "borrowing" objects from school and not returning them, for "lying" about what he did or where he was. Better not to leave valuables around, not to allow borrowing without clear check-out and check-in procedures; better not to grill children about their whereabouts but to supervise them.

The fact that these are moral transgressions may justly prompt an adult's mildly expressed disapproval, but strong discipline, absent understanding, is ineffective; the child perhaps feels ashamed but does not know in what way to change or how to accomplish it. For the somewhat older child, whose mapping of a situation more closely approximates the adult's, stronger condemnation, rewards and punishment may spur learning. But these methods too run their course. Finally, the adult's appeal is largely to an individual's principles and self-concept.

Staging Construction of Moral Identity

It is important to bear in mind that the path to moral identity is long and crooked. Mistaken judgments, insensitivity, oversight, even deliberate wrongdoing are expectable and acceptable. Habits and compassion need to be encouraged in the young, but they will be recontoured with age. Adult values are initially accepted by children, then rejected, and later revisited.

Moral autonomy is an ambitious goal. A broad encompassing social perspective that overrides self-interest and a consistent application of moral principles that incorporates a flexible interpretation in altered contexts are extremely demanding achievements, intellectually and emotionally. On the way, a child will take his or her cues from others and will submit often to the siren song of the peer group, even when it is heedless of the call of conscience. As with human (as opposed to animal) development in general, a robust moral identity awaits a long incubation.

Educators need not be in a hurry; time is on their side.

End/Beginnings

We have no summary, no set of short, "punchy" prescriptions, no "bullets," quotations, slogans, or maxims, that will quickly give an interested reader an overview of our approach and its programmatic implications. In working our way through apparent major disagreements to a set of guidelines to which we all subscribe, we discovered a basic truth. *Most approaches to moral education are strong in what they focus on, weak in what they ignore or denigrate.* A univalued solution is an oxymoron, whether it is "Crack down on troublemakers," "Teach the two [or five] Rs," "Learn to be good by doing good," or "Morality is a matter of reflection on choice."

As individuals, we who worked together on this committee differ significantly in our priorities and dispositions. One tends toward the didactic and prescriptive, a second toward the ambivalent and interactive, a third toward a minimalism driven largely by a sense of irony, a fourth toward impatience with what appears impractical. What we learned in listening to one another was . . . to *listen* to one another: to listen for the concerns, even the fears, that our favored approaches generate in others; to listen for the emergent response that seeks to meet those concerns while holding faithfully—if a little less tightly—to our own priorities; to resist the temptation to caricature, even demonize, priorities and concerns, even people, different in viewpoint from ourselves. William Damon's insight about school reform generally bears keeping in mind as we think about moral education:

> [T]he oppositional ethos of many current school reform efforts has mitigated against [a] bridge-building sort of effort. When reformers argue about the virtues of play versus drill, phonetics versus whole language, encoding versus comprehension, self-esteem versus mastery, or school-as-fun versus school-as-work, they are standing on one side of the gap and placing their opponents on the other. If we are to help all our children realize their full academic potential, we must design school programs that build bridges across such gaps. *(Damon 1995, 155) (emphasis omitted)*

The resulting synthesis, we continue to insist, should not simply be dismissed as either a smorgasbord, to be sampled at whim, or as a stew, a pablum, that merely mixes together all contending points of view. The truth is that neither alone nor simply piled up together will service learning, moral exemplars, discipline, or discussion and reflection do the job. Each alone has a core value that needs to be leavened with a balancing insight, which significantly shapes its structuring and application:

- Service, it must be learned, benefits not only the one "served," but the one who serves as well;
- Moral exemplars are not distant heroes but people living among us, whose lives and choices illuminate our own;
- Discipline must be administered in recognition of the overarching goal of reintegrating the wrongdoer into the classroom community;
- Discussion and reflection are to be distinguished from merely "sounding off."

In choosing from the "menu" of moral education pedagogy as a whole, a certain comprehensiveness of approach is important. The urge to polarize, to oversimplify, to latch on to those approaches that one finds most appealing, to "get on with the job so we can turn to other things," must be resisted. But integration is more than aggregation, and it is important that each aspect of the program not be approached as giving contending approaches a "turn." Breadth, comprehensiveness, and balance are not matters of "giving in" to all contending political constituencies in the field, but rather a genuine commitment to the complexity of morality, to the truth that all sides have some portion of the truth, to the wisdom of Simone Weil's eloquent reminder [see Chapter 5, p. 141] that there is no real liberty without obedience, no deserved honor without discipline, no genuine submission without resistance, no legitimate authority without equality, no lasting security without risk, no authentic autonomy without belongingness.

At the same time, no amount of integration can possibly wring out of a sophisticated program the variations that inevitably will, and in our view *should,*

arise in both conception and application. The brute fact of differing views must be respected. But a program that tilts a bit too much in one direction is a far better program than one that takes (what even to us is) the right direction and runs downfield with it, inattentive to differences among children, schools, and communities, or among teachers.

Teachers: A fitting word with which to close. To us, it is the centrality of the teacher's part in the success or failure of any program that yields the prescription with which we will end. Off-the-shelf programs, and those centrally designed by outside experts or inside administrators, share a critical infirmity: Unless they are treated as, but only as, resources for individual teachers and faculties to draw on, they will inevitably let the students down. Considered as resources, they are valuable, often (for busy teachers) invaluable. Even so, a program can only benefit by having its initial structuring reflect substantial faculty involvement, and once instituted needs to be accompanied by additional aids to teachers expected to develop and execute it: serious and periodic in-service programs, opportunities for collaborative reflection, openness to revision in the light of experience.

Supplementary Statement of Professor Jan Bonham

It was a privilege to be permitted to participate in the deliberations of this group of elementary-school teachers. In my view, the *source* of the proposals contained in this report is as significant as its *content.* Principal Fred Helter deserves great credit for recognizing the talent and commitment of his colleagues, and for giving them the support needed to allow them to work together to engage with one another over a sufficiently sustained period of time that their differences became a basis, not of simple declamation and counter-declamation, but of collective wisdom and sophistication.

While the four authors of this careful, thorough, and sophisticated treatment are entitled to every credit for the abilities they brought to the job, it is important to realize that talents and motivations like those exhibited here are replicated in thousands of schools across the country. These four came to their task with differences in perceptions, priorities, and perspectives like those we find mirrored in every sector of contemporary society. I believe that it was from their immersion in the daily lives of their students—in the classrooms and hallways of their school, from the accumulation of incidents demanding a response, from their witnessing the range of variations in those responses that they "got" the complexity and grittiness of the problem. It was this process of constant learning that aided them in making of their presuppositions a point of departure, a viewpoint to be listened to and reflected on, rather than a banner to be proudly flown, firmly implanted, and fiercely defended.

Too often we read that teachers are the source of the problem; this report demonstrates that (as its text concludes) teachers are rather those to whom we should turn for informed and constructive responses to the vexing and important problem of moral education.

References

American Bar Association. *Model Rules of Professional Conduct.* Chicago: American Bar Association, 1983.

Anderson, Elijah. *Streetwise: Race, Class, and Change in Urban Community.* Chicago: University of Chicago Press, 1990.

Anderson, Elijah. *Code of the Street: Decency, Violence, and the Moral Life of the Inner City.* New York: W. W. Norton, 1999.

Annas, Julia. *The Morality of Happiness.* New York: Oxford University Press, 1993.

Arendt, Hannah. *Eichmann in Jerusalem: A Report on the Banality of Evil.* New York: Penguin, 1964.

Aristotle. *Nichomachean Ethics,* trans. J. E. C. Weldon. New York: Prometheus Books, 1987.

Babbie, Earl. *You Can Make a Difference: The Heroic Potential within All of Us.* New York: St. Martin's Press, 1985.

Barth, Roland. "The Principal & the Profession of Teaching." In *Schooling for Tomorrow: Directing Reforms to Issues that Count,* ed. Thomas J. Sergionvanni and John H. Moore. Boston: Allyn & Bacon, 1989.

Battistich, Victor, and Marilyn Watson, Daniel Solomon, Eric Schaps, and Judith Solomon. "The Child Development Project: A Comprehensive Program for the Development of Prosocial Character." In W. M. Kurtines & J. L. Gewirtz (ed.), *Handbook of Moral Behavior and Development, vol. 3: Application,* pp. 1–34. Hillsdale, NJ: Lawrence Erlbaum, 1991.

Bellah, Robert, and Richard Madsen, William Sullivan, Ann Swidler, and Stephen Tipton. *Habits of the Heart.* Berkeley: University of California Press, 1996.

Bennett, William. "Moral Literacy and the Formation of Character." In *Moral Character and Civil Education in the Elementary School,* ed. Jacques S. Benninga. New York: Teachers College Press, 1991.

Benninga, Jacques S. Moral and Character Education in the Elementary School: An Introduction. In *Moral, Character, and Civil Education in the Elementary School,* ed. J. S. Benninga, New York: Teacher's College Press, 1991.

Bentham, Jeremy. *An Introduction to the Principles of Moral and Legislation.* ed. J. H. Burns and H. L. A. Hart. Oxford: Clarendon Press, 1970/1996.

Berlin, Isaiah. *The Crooked Timber of Humanity: Chapters in the History of Ideas.* New York: Vintage Books, 1959/1992.

Berlin, Isaiah. "The Romantic Revolution: A Crisis in the History of Modern Thought." In *The Sense of Reality: Studies in Ideas and Their History,* ed. Henry Hardy. New York: Farrar, Straus and Giroux, 1996.

Birmingham Board of Education. *Something Better for Birmingham.* Birmingham, AL: Board of Education, 1936.

Blasi, Augusto. "Moral Identity: Its Role in Moral Functioning." In *Morality, Moral Behavior, and Moral Development,* ed. William Kurtines and Jacob Gewirtz. New York: Wiley, 1984.

Bok, Sissela. *Common Values.* Columbia, MO: University of Missouri Press, 1995.

Bolt, Robert. *A Man for All Seasons.* New York: Vintage Books, 1962.

Bonhoeffer, Dietrich. "What Is Meant by Telling the Truth?" In *Ethics,* ed. Eberhard Bethge, trans. Neville Horton Smith. New York: Macmillan, 1955.

Boring v. Buncombe County Board of Education. 136 F.3d 364 (4th Cir., 1998).

Brennecke, Fritz. *The Nazi Primer: Official Handbook for Schooling Hitler Youth,* trans. Harwood L. Childs. New York: Harper & Brothers, 1938.

Butler, Samuel. *Erewhon: Or Over the Range.* Newark, DE: University of Delaware Press, 1981.

Cahn, Edmund. *The Moral Decision.* Bloomington, IN: Indiana University Press, 1955.

Callahan, Sidney. "Self and Other Feminist Thought." In *Duties to Others,* ed. Courtney S. Campbell and B. Andrew Lustig. Boston: Kluwer Academic Publishing, 1994.

Campbell, James. *Understanding John Dewey*. Chicago: Open Court, 1995.

Carnegie Forum on Education and the Economy. *A Nation Prepared: Teachers for the Twenty-First Century*. New York: Carnegie Forum on Education and the Economy, 1986.

Carr, David. *Educating the Virtues: An Essay on the Philosophical Psychology of Moral Development and Education*. New York: Routledge, 1991.

The Character Counts Coalition. *Character Counts!* Marina del Rey, CA: The Josephson Institute of Ethics, 1995.

Character Education Institute. *Character Education Curriculum*. San Antonio: Character Education Institute, 1994.

Coles, Robert. *The Moral Intelligence of Children*. New York: Random House, 1997.

Cox v. Dardanelle Public School District. 790 F.2d 668 (8th Cir., 1986).

Damon, William. *The Social World of the Child*. San Francisco: Jossey-Bass, 1977.

Damon, William. "Self-Understanding and Moral Development, From Childhood to Adolescence." In *Morality, Moral Behavior, and Moral Development*, ed. William Kurtines and Jacob Gewirtz. New York: Wiley, 1984.

Damon, William. *Greater Expectations: Overcoming the Culture of Indulgence in America's Homes and Schools*. New York: The Free Press, 1995.

Damon, William, and Daniel Hart. "Self Understanding and Its Role in Social and Moral Development." In *Developmental Psychology: An Advanced Textbook*, ed. Marc H. Bornstein and Michael E. Lamb. Hillsdale, NJ: Lawrence Erlbaum, 1992.

Dawkins, Richard. *The Selfish Gene*. New York: Oxford University Press, 1976.

Des Pres, Terrence. *Survivor*. New York: Oxford University Press, 1976.

Developmental Studies Center. *Ways We Want Our Class to Be: Class Meetings That Build Commitment to Kindness and Learning*. Oakland, CA: Developmental Studies Center, 1996.

DeVries, Rheta, and Lawrence Kohlberg. *Constructivist Early Education: Overview and Comparison with Other Programs*. Washington, DC: National Association for the Education of Young Children, 1987.

DeVries, Rheta, and Betty Zan. *Moral Classrooms, Moral Children: Creating a Constructivist Atmosphere in Early Education*. New York: Teachers College Press, 1994.

de Waal, Frans. *Good Natured: The Origins of Right and Wrong in Humans and Other Animals*. Cambridge, MA: Harvard University Press, 1996.

Dewey, John. "My Pedagogic Creed." In *Dewey on Education: Selections*, ed. M. S. Dworkin. New York: Teachers College, 1897/1959.

Dewey, John. *Theory of Moral Life*. New York: Holt, Rinehart & Winston, 1908/1960.

Dewey, John. *Human Nature and Conduct*. New York: Henry Holt & Co., 1922.

Dewey, John. *The Moral Writings of John Dewey*, ed. James Gouinlock, rev. ed. Amherst, New York: Prometheus Books, 1994.

Durkheim, Emile. *Moral Education*. Glencoe, IL: The Free Press, 1925/1961.

Durkheim, Emile. *Education and Sociology*. Glencoe, IL: The Free Press, 1956.

Egan, Kieran. *Educational Development*. New York: Oxford University Press, 1979.

Egan, Kieran. *Primary Understanding: Education in Early Childhood*. New York: Routledge, 1988.

Elkind, David. *Child Development and Education*. New York: Oxford University Press, 1976.

Eliot, George. *Adam Bede*. New York: Penguin, 1859/1985.

Elson, Ruth Miller. *Guardians of Tradition: American Schoolbooks of the Nineteenth Century*. Lincoln: University of Nebraska Press, 1964.

Fenstermacher, Gary. "Some Moral Considerations on Teaching as a Profession." In *The Moral Dimensions of Teaching*, ed. John I. Goodlad. San Francisco: Jossey-Bass, 1990.

Foot, Philippa. *Virtues and Vices and Other Essays in Moral Philosophy*. Oxford: Blackwell, 1978.

Foot, Philippa. "Moral Relativism." In *Relativism: Cognitive and Moral*, ed. Jack W. Meiland and Michael Krausz. South Bend, IN: University of Notre Dame Press, 1982.

Frankl, Victor. *Man's Search for Meaning: An Introduction to Logotherapy*. Boston: Beacon Press, 1962.

Franklin, Benjamin. *Autobiography and Other Writings of Benjamin Franklin*. New York: Dodd, Mead, 1963.

The Giraffe Project. *The Giraffe News*. No. 36. Langley, WA: The Giraffe Project, 1997.

Goodlad, John L. *A Place Called School: Prospects for the Future*. New York: McGraw-Hill, 1984.

Goodman, Joan F. "'Running in The Halls' and Moral Trivia." *Education Week*, September 23, 1998.

Goodman, Joan F. "Moral Education in Early Childhood: The Limits of Constructivism." *Early Education & Development* 11 (2000): 37–54.

Griffin, James. "Virtue Ethics and Environs." In *Virtue and Vice*, ed. Ellen Frankel Paul, Fred D. Miller, Jr., and Jeffrey Paul. Cambridge: Cambridge University Press, 1998.

Hallie, Philip. *Lest Innocent Blood Be Shed: The Story of Le Chambon and How Goodness Happened There*. New York: Harper & Row, 1979.

Hallie, Philip. *Tales of Good and Evil, Help and Harm*. New York: Harper Collins, 1997.

Hare, R.M. *The Language of Morals*. Oxford: Clarendon Press, 1952.

Hartshorne, Hugh, and Mark May. *Studies in Deceit*. Vol. 1. New York: Macmillan, 1928.

Haugaard, Kay. "The Lottery Revisited—A Case of Too Much Tolerance?" *Chronicle of Higher Education*, June 27, 1997, B4. Reprinted as "The Lottery Revisited." In *Unriddling Our Times*, ed. Os Guiness. Grand Rapids, MI: Baker Books, 1997.

The Heartwood Institute. *An Ethics Curriculum for Children*. Pittsburgh, PA: The Heartwood Institute, 1992.

Heyd, David, ed. *Toleration: An Elusive Virtue*. Princeton: Princeton University Press, 1996.

Higgins, Ann. "The Just Community Approach to Moral Education: Evolution of the Idea and Recent Findings." In *Handbook on Moral Behavior and Development*. Vol. 3, ed. William M. Kurtines and Jacob L. Gewirtz. Hillsdale, NJ: Lawrence Erlbaum, 1991.

Hinman, Lawrence. *Ethics: A Pluralistic Approach to Moral Theory*. New York: Harcourt Brace, 1994.

Hoffman, Martin L. "Development of Prosocial Motivation: Empathy and Guilt." In *The Development of Prosocial Behavior*, ed. Nancy Eisenberg. New York: Academic Press, 1982.

Howard, Robert. "Lawrence Kohlberg's Influence on Moral Education in Elementary Education." In *Moral, Character, and Civic Education in Elementary Education*, ed. Jacques S. Benninga. New York: Teachers College Press, 1991.

Hume, David. *A Treatise of Human Nature*, ed. L.A. Selby-Bigge. Oxford: Clarendon, 1896.

Hume, David. *An Enquiry Concerning the Principles of Morals*, ed. Eric Steinberg. Indianapolis: Hackett Publishing Co., 1983.

Hunter, James Davison. *The Death of Character: Moral Education in an Age Without Good or Evil*. New York: Bantam Books, 2000.

Hursthouse, Rosalind. "Virtue Theory and Abortion." In *Philosophy and Public Affairs* 20 (1991): 223–246. Reprinted in *Virtue Ethics: A Critical Reader*, ed. Daniel Statman, pp. 226–244. Washington, DC: Georgetown University Press, 1997.

Hutchins, William J. *The Children's Code of Morals for Elementary Schools*. Washington, DC: Character Education Institute, 1917.

Hutchins, William J. "The Children's Morality Code." *Journal of the National Education Association* XIII (1924): 292.

Ignatieff, Michael. *Isaiah Berlin*. New York: Henry Holt, 1998.

Infield, Tom. *50 Years After the War*. Philadelphia, PA: Camino Books, 1996.

Jackson, Philip, Robert Boostrom, and David Hansen. *The Moral Life of Schools*. San Francisco: Jossey-Bass, 1993.

James, William. *Principles of Psychology*. Vol 1. New York: Dover Publications, 1890/1950.

Jefferson Center for Character Education. *Jefferson Fact Sheet*. Pasadena, CA, Aug. 1995.

Johnson, Paul. "God and the Americans." *Commentary* (January 1995): 25–45.

Kaestle, Carl. *Pillars of the Republic: Common Schools and American Society 1780–1860*. New York: Hill and Wang, 1983.

Kagan, Jerome. *The Nature of the Child*. New York: Basic Books, 1984.

Kamii, Constance, and Rheta DeVries. "Piaget for Early Education." In *The Preschool in Action: Exploring Early Education Childhood Programs*, ed. M. C. Day and R. K. Parker. Boston: Allyn & Bacon, 1977.

Kant, Immanuel. *Grounding for the Metaphysics of Morals*, with *On a Supposed Right to Lie because of Philanthropic Concerns*. 3rd ed, trans. James W. Ellington. Indianapolis: Hackett Publishing Co., 1785/1993.

Kantrowitz, Barbara, and Daniel McGinn, "When Teachers Are Cheaters." *Newsweek*, June 19, 2000, 48–52.

Kohlberg, Lawrence. "Education for Justice, a Modern Statement of the Platonic View." In *Moral Education*, ed. Theodore and Nancy Sizer. Cambridge, MA: Harvard University Press, 1970.

Kohlberg, Lawrence. "The Moral Atmosphere of the School." In *Moral Education—It Comes with the Territory*, ed. David Purpel and Kevin Ryan. Berkeley, CA: Mutchan, 1976.

Kohlberg, Lawrence. *Essays on Moral Development.* Vol. 1, *The Philosophy of Moral Development*. San Francisco: Harper & Row, 1981.

Kohlberg, Lawrence, with Rheta De Vries. *Child Psychology and Childhood Education: A Cognitive Developmental View.* New York: Longman, 1987.

Kohlberg, Lawrence, and Rochelle Mayer. "Development as the Aim of Education." *Harvard Education Review* 42 (1972): 449–496.

Kohn, Alfie. *Punished by Rewards: The Trouble with Gold Stars, Incentive Plans, A's, Praise, and Other Bribes.* New York: Houghton Mifflin, 1993.

Kohn, Alfie. *What to Look for in a Classroom.* San Francisco: Houghton Mifflin, 1998.

Kozol, Jonathan. *Death at an Early Age: The Destruction of the Hearts and Minds of Negro Children in Boston Public Schools.* Boston: Houghton Mifflin, 1967.

Kupperman, Joel. *Character.* New York: Oxford University Press, 1991.

Lacks v. Ferguson Reorganized School District R-2. 147 F.3d 718 (8th Cir., 1998).

Lehman, Warren. "The Pursuit of a Client's Interest." *Michigan Law Review* 77 (1979): 1078–1097.

Levi, Primo. *The Drowned and the Saved.* New York: Vintage International, 1988.

Lewis, C.S. *The Four Loves.* San Diego: Harcourt Brace & Co., 1960/1988.

Lewis, Catherine. *Educating Hearts and Minds: Reflections on Japanese Preschool and Elementary Education.* New York: Cambridge University Press, 1997.

Lickona, Thomas. *Educating for Character: How Our Schools Can Teach Respect and Responsibility.* New York: Bantam Books, 1991.

Lickona, Thomas, Eric Schaps, and Catherine Lewis. *Eleven Principles of Effective Character Education.* Washington, DC: The Character Education Partnership, 1997–1998. <<http://www.character.org/principles/index.cgi>>.

Locke, John. *Some Thoughts Concerning Education.* Cambridge: Cambridge University Press, 1693/1927.

MacIntyre, Alasdair. *After Virtue: A Study in Moral Theory.* 2d ed. South Bend, IN: University of Notre Dame, 1984.

MacIntyre, Alasdair. *Three Rival Versions of Moral Enquiry.* South Bend, IN: University of Notre Dame Press, 1990.

Mackie, J.L. *Ethics: Inventing Right and Wrong.* New York: Penguin, 1990.

Mann, Horace. *The Republic and the School,* ed. Lawrence Cremin. New York: Teacher's College Press, 1957.

Mann, Horace. "Lectures and Annual Reports on Education, 1867." In *The History of American Education Through Readings,* ed. Carl Gross and Charles Chandler. Boston: D.C. Heath & Co., 1964.

Maschmann, Melita. *Account Rendered: A Dossier on My Former Self,* trans. Geoffrey Strachan. New York: Abelard-Schuman, 1964.

McCarthy, Martha and Nelda Cameron-McCabe. "The Legal Foundation of Public Education." In *Educational Policy and the Law.* 3d ed., ed. Mark G. Yudof, David L. Kirp, and Betsy Levin. St. Paul: West Publishing Co, 1992.

McClellan, Edward. *Schools and the Shaping of Character: Moral Education in America, 1607–Present.* Bloomington, IN: ERIC Clearinghouse of Social Studies/Social Science Education, 1992.

Midgley, Mary. *Wickedness: A Philosophical Essay.* London: Routledge, 1984.

Milgram, Stanley. *Obedience to Authority.* New York: Harper and Row, 1969.

Mill, John Stuart. *Utilitarianism, On Liberty, Considerations on Representative Government,* ed. J. M. Dent. London: Everyman's Library, 1859/1993.

Mill, John Stuart. *Utilitarianism.* Indianapolis: Hackett Publishing Co., 1861/1979.

Moore, G. E. *Principia Ethica,* rev. ed., Thomas Baldwin. Cambridge: Cambridge University Press, 1993.

Moore, Michael. "Torture and the Balance of Evils." *Israel Law Review* 23 (1989): 280–344.

Morgan, Edmund S. *The Puritan Family*. New York: Harper & Row, 1966.

Morgenbesser, Sidney. "Approaches to Ethical Objectivity." In *Moral Education*, ed. Barry I. Chazan and Jonas F. Soltis. New York: Teachers College Press, 1973.

Nisbett, Richard E., and Dov Cohen. *Culture of Honor: The Psychology of Violence in the South*. New York: Westview Press, 1996.

Noddings, Nel. *The Challenge to Care in Schools: An Alternative Approach to Education*. New York: Teachers College Press, 1992.

Nozick, Robert. *Philosophical Explanations*. Cambridge, MA: Belknap Press, 1981.

Nucci, Larry P. "Challenging Conventional Wisdom about Morality: The Domain Approach to Values Education." In *Moral Development and Character Education*, ed. Larry P. Nucci. Berkeley, CA: McCutchan Publishing, 1989.

Nucci, Larry P. "Doing Justice to Morality in Contemporary Values Education." In *Moral, Character, and Civil Education in the Elementary School*, ed. Jacques S. Benninga. New York: Teachers College Press, 1991.

Nussbaum, Martha. "The Discernment of Perception: An Aristotelian Conception of Private and Public Rationality." In *Love's Knowledge: Essays on Philosophy and Literature*. New York: Oxford University Press, 1990.

Nussbaum, Martha. "Valuing Values: A Case for Reasoned Commitment." *Yale Journal of Law and the Humanities* 6 (1994): 197–218.

Oakeshott, Michael. *Rationalism in Politics*. New York: Basic Books, 1962.

Oakeshott, Michael. "Education: The Engagement and Its Frustration." In *Education and the Development of Reason*, ed. R. F. Dearden, P. H. Hirst, and R. S. Peters. London: Routledge & Kegan Paul, 1972.

Oliner, Samuel P., and Pearl M. Oliner. *The Altruistic Personality*. Glencoe, IL: The Free Press, 1988.

O'Malley, William J. "Curiosity." *America*, October 3, 1998, 14–19.

Parducci v. Rutland. 316 F. Supp. 352 (M.D. Ala., 1970).

Peters, R. S. *Psychology and Ethical Development*. London: George Allen & Unwin, 1974.

Piaget, Jean. *The Moral Judgement of the Child*. Glencoe, IL: The Free Press, 1948.

Piaget, Jean. *The Origins of Intelligence in Children*. New York: International University Press, 1952.

Piaget, Jean. *Six Psychological Studies*, ed. David Elkind, trans. Anita Taylor and David Elkind. New York: Random House, 1967.

Plato. "Meno." In *The Collected Dialogues of Plato*, ed. Edith Hamilton and Huntington Cairns. Princeton, NJ: Princeton University Press, 1961.

Postema, Gerald. "Moral Responsibility in Professional Ethics." *New York University Law Review* 55 (1980): 55–91.

Power, F. Clark. "School Climate and Character Development." In *Character Development in Schools and Beyond*, ed. Kevin Ryan and George F. McLean. New York: Praeger, 1987.

Power, F. Clark, Ann Higgins, and Lawrence Kohlberg. *Lawrence Kohlberg's Approach to Moral Education*. New York: Columbia University Press, 1989.

Purpel, David E. *Moral Outrage in Education*. New York: Peter Lang Publishing, Inc., 1999.

Purpel, David E., and Kevin Ryan. "It Comes with the Territory: The Inevitability of Moral Education in the Schools." In *Moral Education . . . It Comes with the Territory*, ed. David Purpel and Kevin Ryan. Berkeley, CA: McCutchan, 1976.

Raths, Louis, Merrill Harmin, and Sidney Simon. "Selection from Values and Teaching." In *Moral Education . . . It Comes with the Territory*, ed. David Purpel and Kevin Ryan. Berkeley, CA: McCutchan, 1976.

Rawls, John. *A Theory of Justice*. Cambridge, MA: Harvard University Press, 1971.

Roberts, Lani. "Duty, Virtue and the Victim's Voice." In *Duties to Others*, ed. Courtney S. Campbell and B. Andrew Lustig. Boston: Kluwer Academic Publishing, 1994.

Rousseau, Jean-Jacques. *Emile, Julie, and Other Writings*, ed. R. L. Archer. New York: Barron's, 1964.

Rousseau, Jean-Jacques. *Emile or On Education*, trans. Allan Bloom. New York: Basic Books, 1979.

Ryan, Kevin, and Karen E. Bohlin. *Building Character in Schools*. San Francisco: Jossey-Bass, 1999.

Russell, Bertrand. "A Free Man's Worship." In *Why I Am Not a Christian*. New York: Simon & Schuster, 1903/1957.

Sandel, Michael. *Liberalism and the Limits of Justice*. New York: Cambridge University Press, 1982/1998.

Sartre, Jean-Paul. "Existentialism and Ethics." In *Moral Education*, ed. Barry I. Chazan and Jonas F. Soltis. New York: Teachers College Press, 1973.

Schumacher, E. F. *A Guide for the Perplexed*. New York: Harper & Row, 1977.

Shaughnessy v. United States ex rel. Mezei, 345 U.S. 206 (1953).

Shweder, Richard A., Manamohan Mahapotro, and Joan Miller. "Culture and Moral Development." In *The Emergence of Morality in Young Children*. ed. Jerome Kagan and Sharon Lamb. Chicago: University of Chicago Press, 1987.

Simon, Robert L. "Suspending Moral Judgment: The Paralysis of 'Absolutophobia.'" *Chronicle of Higher Education*, June 27, 1997, B5.

Singer, Peter. *The Expanding Circle: Ethics and Sociobiology*. New York: Farrar, Straus & Giroux, 1981.

Singer, Peter. *How Are We to Live: Ethics in an Age of Self-Interest*. Amherst, New York: Prometheus Books, 1995.

Sizer, Theodore. *Horace's Compromise: The Dilemma of the American High School*. Boston: Houghton Mifflin, 1992.

Sizer, Theodore, and Nancy Sizer, ed. *Moral Education*. Cambridge, MA: Harvard University Press, 1970.

Sommers, Christina Hoff. "Ethics without Virtue: Moral Education in America." *American Scholar*, Summer 1984, 381–389.

Stanford Achievement Test. Reviewer's Edition. 9th ed. San Antonio, TX: Harcourt Brace, 1996.

Steirer v. Bethlehem Area School District. 987 F.2d 989 (3d Cir., 1993).

Stone, Lawrence. *The Family, Sex, and Marriage in England 1500–1800*. New York: Harper & Row, 1977.

Straughan, Roger. *"I Out to But . . . ": A Philosophical Approach to the Problem of Weakness of Will in Education*. Windsor, Berks: NFER-Nelson, 1982.

Strike, Kenneth A., and Jonas F. Soltis. *The Ethics of Teaching*. New York: Teachers College Press, 1992.

Taylor, Gabriele. "Integrity." In *The Aristotelian Society*, Supp. Vol. LV. London: The Aristotelian Society, 1981.

de Toqueville, Alexis. *Democracy in America*. London: Everyman's Library, 1835/1994.

Trollope, Anthony. *Orley Farm*. New York: Oxford University Press, 1861/1985.

Tyack, David, and Elisabeth Hansot. *Managers of Virtue: Public School Leadership in America, 1820–1980*. New York: Basic Books, 1982.

Warnock, G. J. *The Object of Morality*. London: Methuen & Co., 1971.

Warnock, Mary. *The Uses of Philosophy*. Oxford: Oxford University Press, 1992.

Warnock, Mary. "Moral Values." In *Values in Education and Education in Values*, ed. J. Mark Halstead and Monica J. Taylor. London: Palmer Press, 1996.

Weil, Simon. "Draft for a Statement of Human Obligations." In *Simon Weil—An Anthology*, ed. Siän Miles. New York: Weidenfeld and Nicolson, 1986.

Wilson, James Q. *The Moral Sense*. Glencoe, IL: The Free Press, 1993.

Wilson, P. S. *Interest and Discipline in Education*. London: Routledge and Kegan Paul, 1971.

Wright, Robert. *The Moral Animal*. New York: Vintage Books, 1994.

Wynne, Edward A. "Character and Academics in the Elementary School." In *Moral, Character, and Civil Education in the Elementary School*, ed. Jacques S. Benninga. New York: Teachers College Press, 1991.

Wynne, Edward A., and Kevin Ryan. *Reclaiming Our Schools: Teaching Character, Academics, and Discipline*. 2d ed. Upper Saddle River, NJ: Merrill, 1997.

Yudof, Mark G., David Kirp, and Betsy Levin. *Educational Policy and the Law*. 3d ed. St. Paul: West Publishing Company, 1992.

Yulish, Stephen. *Search for a Civic Religion: A History of the Character Education Movement in America, 1890–1935*. Lanham, MD: University Press of America, 1980.

Credits

Isaiah Berlin, *The Crooked Timber of Humanity: Chapters in the History of Ideas*. Vintage Books, 1959/1992.

Sissela Bok, *Common Values*. University of Missouri Press, 1995. Copyright by the author.

William Damon, *Greater Expectations: Overcoming the Culture of Indulgence in America's Homes and Schools*. The Free Press, 1995.

Emile Durkheim, *Moral Education*. Translated by Everett K. Wilson and Herman Schnurer. The Free Press, a Division of Simon & Schuster, Inc., 1961, 1973.

Joan F. Goodman, "Running in the Halls' and Moral Trivia." *Education Week*, Sept. 23, 1998. Reprinted with permission from Education Week.

James Griffin, "Virtue Ethics and Environs." In *Virtue and Vice*. Eds. Ellen Frankel Paul, Fred D. Miller, Jr., and Jeffrey Paul. Cambridge University Press, 1998.

Kay Haugaard, "The Lottery Revisited," first published as "Suspending Moral Judgment: Students Who Refuse to Condemn the Unthinkable," in *The Chronicle of Higher Education*, June 27, 1997.

David Heyd, ed. *Toleration: an Elusive Virtue*. Princeton University Press, 1996.

Rosalind Hursthouse, "Virtue Theory and Abortion." In *Virtue Ethics: A Critical Reader*. Ed. Daniel Statman. Edinburgh University Press, Ltd., 1997.

William J. Hutchins, "The Children's Morality Code." *Journal of the National Education Association*, XIII (1924), 292.

Immanuel Kant, *Grounding for the Metaphysics of Morals*, with *On a Supposed Right to Lie because of Philanthropic Concerns*. 3rd ed. Trans. James W. Ellington. Hackett Publishing Company, 1993. All rights reserved.

Catherine Lewis, *Educating Hearts and Minds: Reflections on Japanese Preschool and Elementary Education*. Cambridge University Press, 1997.

Thomas Lickona, *Educating for Character: How Our Schools Can Teach Respect and Responsibility*. Bantam Books, a division of Random House, Inc., 1991.

Mary Midgley, *Wickedness: A Philosophical Essay*. Routledge, 1984.

Michael Moore, "Torture and the Balance of Evils," *Israel Law Review*, 23: 280–344, 1989.

Nel Noddings, *The Challenge to Care in Schools: An Alternative Approach to Education*. Teachers College, Columbia University, 1992. All rights reserved. Excerpts from pp. 15–16, 21–22.

Martha Nussbaum, "Valuing Values: A Case for Reasoned Commitment." *The Yale Journal of Law and the Humanities*, vol. 6, pp. 197–217.

F. Clark Power, "School Climate and Character Development." In *Character Development in Schools and Beyond*. Eds. Kevin Ryan & George F. McLean. Praeger Publishers, 1987.

Theodore Sizer, *Horace's Compromise: The Dilemma of the American High School*. Houghton Mifflin, 1992.

Christina Hoff Sommers, *Ethics Without Virtue: Moral Education in America*. American Scholar, Volume 53, Number 3, Summer 1984. Copyright by the author.

Kenneth A. Strike and Jonas F. Soltis, *The Ethics of Teaching*. New York, Teachers College, Columbia University, 1992. All rights reserved. Excerpts from pp. 11–17.

Index

Made in the USA
Charleston, SC
22 September 2011